Complete Guide to

by **Carley Roney**
& the editors of The Knot

Complete Guide to

Weddings

in the Real World

The Ultimate Source of Ideas, Advice, and Relief

for the Bride and Groom and Those

Who Love Them

Broadway Books
New York

Broadway Books titles may be purchased for business or promotional use or for special sales. For information, please write to: Special Markets Department, Random House, Inc., 1540 Broadway, New York, NY 10036.

BROADWAY BOOKS and its logo, a letter B bisected on the diagonal, are trademarks of Broadway Books, a division of Random House, Inc.

Library of Congress Cataloging-in-Publication Data

Roney, Carley.
The Knot's complete guide to weddings in the real world : the ultimate source of ideas, advice, and relief for the bride and groom and those who love them / by Carley Roney. — 1st ed.
p.   cm.
Includes index.
ISBN 0-7679-0246-7 (pbk.)
1. Weddings—Planning.   2. Wedding etiquette.   I. Title.
HQ745.R66   1998
395.2′2—dc21   98-11805
                                                                         CIP

Design by Judith Stagnitto Abbate / Abbate Design
Illustrations by Kim DeMarco

01 02 10 9

Contents

Foreword

When we launched The Knot Web site in 1996, we just knew there were people out there like us—modern, smart, in-love couples looking for an up-to-date, stylish, and real-world approach to planning their weddings. Within a year we had a huge online following of hundreds of thousands of to-be-weds from all over the country. Word spread fast. It seems that couples simply can't find anything out there that matches The Knot's tell-it-like-it-is advice, fresh ideas, practical etiquette, and stress-relieving sanity. (Besides that, we are the only real resource out there for *both* the bride and groom.)

We're thrilled to be able to put in print the best of The Knot's opinions, exhaustive databases of information, and real people's experiences. You simply can't beat the completeness and portability of a book—never mind the fact you can snuggle down into bed with it (together).

Before you dig in, take a look at the table of contents. We've structured things in (sort of) chronological order. But don't think you have to sit down and read this book from start to finish. At the opening of each chapter you'll see what's covered. Scan and look for the headlines that address your current issues.

Since we know planning a wedding can be kind of intimidating, we've tried to make this book as user-friendly as possible. The sidebars offer easy nuggets of important info on saving money, resources, hot ideas, and more. If you're overwhelmed and don't have the vaguest idea where to begin, check out the "To Do" list in Appendix A. It tells you what to worry about when and tells you which chapters in this book will guide you through each to-do.

This is a working book, not a bible. Feel free to mark things, tear out pages, dog-ear to your heart's content. There's a fun and fact-filled resource section in the back of the book with phone numbers, resources, checklists, and worksheets. Make it your own.

Finally, as far as we're concerned, there's only one thing that really matters: that you have the wedding you want, not a nervous breakdown. Don't get too caught up in the details. Your wedding will be mesmerizing—no matter how big or small the budget, no matter how much or how little time you can devote to making it happen. So whether your wedding is an over-the-top 400-person formal religious affair or an intimate backyard barbeque after eloping, you're in the right place. Read up. Make decisions. Trust your judgment. Let go. Enjoy.

Acknowledgments

While I seem to be getting all the credit, this book is by no means my work alone. Many extra-ordinary individuals and organizations were critical in making *The Knot's Complete Guide to Weddings in the Real World* a reality. Here's my attempt to thank them all.

This book truly would not have been written without the expertise, incredible talent, and unfailing dedication of The Knot's managing editor, Tracy Guth. I am grateful to Cindy Hobson, who kept the site cruising despite my stealing her teammate. On behalf of editorial, I'd like to thank everyone else at The Knot for putting up with everything from our stress-induced moods to our constant taking over of the front table. Michael Wolfson, it was largely your hard work that gave us the opportunity to do this book in the first place. For this I am not sure whether to hit you or hug you. I guess we'll go with the latter. ;)

I cannot express enough my appreciation and respect for our team of incredibly skilled, smart, and hilarious writers, primarily Wendy Paris and Hagar Scher, but also the always game Robert Moritz. Wendy and Hagar, your terrific performance under such pressure will never be forgotten. Robin Sayers, who has been around from the beginning, is the ultimate source of The Knot's friendly, fun voice. And the many wonderful writers who have contributed to The Knot past and present also deserve credit for making this book as robust as it is.

We bow to Lauren Marino, our editor at Broadway, for believing in us. It was her under-standing of our vision and her careful ear and editing, along with that of Kati Steele, that made this book sound and feel as inviting as we wanted it to be. Thanks also to the rest of the great Broadway team who made it all happen.

To our agents, Chris Tomasino and Jonathan Diamond, all we can say is that we adore you and so appreciate your guidance and support in bringing the Knot brand into the print world. You are true experts, and we feel lucky to have you on our team.

Kim DeMarco, your illustrations have always gone far to define the spirit of The Knot, and this book would not have been the same without them. Andrew Eccles and Jean-Marc, thanks for making me look so fabulous.

Many talented photographers donated the use of their wedding photographs (see the photo credits page for their names!). Thank you—your stunning images make this book more beautiful. We also appreciate the time of all the couples who participated in putting together our True Tales. Your personal stories give this book an important added dimension.

Many friends and industry experts contributed their sage advice on subjects ranging from seating arrangements to wedding-night sex—as well as their support for this project and the work that went into it. We depend on your wisdom and experience to make our resources on and offline realistic and robust. So thanks, so much, to Marcy Blum, Maria McBride-Mellinger, Denis Reggie, Fred Cuellar, everyone at *Honeymoon* magazine, especially Adam Sandow and Cynthia Muchnick, Ilene Shack, Alan Dessy, John Dolan, Rob Fraser, Chaz Levy, Sari Botton, Bill Roberts of Lord West, Janet Peters of Jim Hjelm, Shu Shu Costa, Patrick Seymour, Mitchell Behr, Joan Hawxhurst, Gerard Monaghan, Helen Morley, Reem Acra, Melissa Sweet, JoAnn Gregoli, Tricia Thomas, Michael Sharkey, Polly Schoonmaker, Bruce Himmelblau, MaryBeth Shea, Mike Leonard, Wendy Pashman, Sari Locker, David Yeske, Les Newman of Botanica, Inc., Dr. Stephen Leatherman (a.k.a. Dr. Beach), David Rosario of Fifth Avenue Ballroom, Teddy Kern of Dance Manhattan, John Larson of Sound of Success Mobile DJs, Cecily Cole Jones of Papier Mache Wedding, Mark Luscombe, Simon Templer, Dr. Maria Mancusi, Martha Hopkins, Chef Amin Hossain of the Hard Rock Cafe, Chef Waldy Malouf of the Rainbow Room, Chef John Arminio of Tito Puente's Restaurant, Chef Michael Mina of Aqua, Carolyn Millard of the Dewes Mansion-Chicago, The Plaza-New York, Heather Duggan, Jessica Vitkus, Scott Cookson, Sitiva Peterson, Alan Lavine, Gail Liberman, Deborah Kwan, Judy Greenberger, Hilari Dobbs Graff, Dana Covey, Esther Perel, Joy King, David Buckner, Anat and Menachem Scher, Sue Lyon, Giles Lyon, Todd Spangler, and John and Barbara Roney.

Knot chat hosts and volunteers (especially my mom, Irene Howe), your dedication to The Knot and its members means so much to us. Thank you for your contributions to the research for this book and for making The Knot Online a lively and welcoming place 24/7.

We must thank our partner, America Online. Your continued belief and support of The Knot (AOL keyword: knot) have helped us grow into the number-one online wedding resource.

Last, but certainly not least, we have to acknowledge our amazing community on both America Online and the Web. It is from the brides and grooms who participate in The Knot every day and night that we learn the most. We admire your ideas, insights, and undying enthusiasm for your weddings.

Above all, my love to my sweet husband (and Knot CEO) David Liu, to my darling daughter, Havana, and to my partners—Michael and Rob—you are the best of companions on this crazy roller-coaster ride.

—CARLEY RONEY

Engagement Length

Spilling the Beans

Engagement Parties

Engagement Announcements

Engaged Ups and Downs

Buying the Ring

The Adventure Begins

There's nothing more fun than the week you get engaged. Having a secret, practically exploding with excitement and anticipation, blurting out the news to your best pals, letting your families in on it all. There are a few details to attend to, but your biggest task right now is to linger on cloud nine!

Engagement Length

When your feet finally hit the ground again, the first thing to consider is how long your engagement will be. It'll depend on a couple of factors, such as your ideal wedding date and how much time you'll realistically need to prepare the wedding of the millennium. A typical engagement lasts from six months to a year, but many couples stray outside those boundaries—if you want to get married next Tuesday or two years from today, do it!

In any case, no matter how long your engagement is, build in some break time from all things wedding-related—you don't want to be drowning in wedding planning every single minute from right now until the big day itself. Granted, your nuptials are about the most exciting thing coming or going, but they're not the be-all, end-all, and you need to remind yourselves periodically that normal life is happening simultaneously. You'll be a lot less stressed out if you take your mind off all things canapé, carnation, and calypso from time to time. Your single friends, and those long-married, too, also will appreciate a respite from licking envelopes and hearing about the woes of finding the perfect wedding venue. It will make your

Where the Words Come From

- Fiancé/e: Old French *fiancé*, a promise

- Betrothed: Be + the Old English *treowth*, truth

- Husband: Middle English *husbonde*, householder

- Wife: Old English *wif*, woman, or possibly based on Indo-European *weip*, "the hidden or veiled person"

Go to Chapter 2 for help figuring out when to do the deed.

life immensely more pleasurable and ensure that you remain healthily grounded in the real world—which is, after all, where you're going to be living once you descend gracefully from cloud nine.

Spilling the Beans

It's time to announce that you're taking the plunge. You could run buck naked together across the field during the live broadcast of the Superbowl, with the words "We're getting hitched!" tattooed across your chests. That way everyone you've ever met will get the news. On second thought, a little decorum can go a long way (and your families will probably appreciate finding out a bit more privately, too).

"You're probably getting bombarded with questions from all directions. If people keep pressuring you about details, don't get intimidated. Whatever you do, don't forget to enjoy those first few weeks."

—Myrna Ruskin,
New York therapist and
marriage-stress expert

Talking to Your Parents

Share the news with your immediate families first. Unless your folks are already great friends, your best bet is to tell each set of parents separately so that they (1) will be able to express their emotions freely and (2) won't have to deal with the surprise of the engagement and the possible discomfort of having to hug all their new in-laws simultaneously. Traditionally—if you must know—the bride's family gets first dibs on the news.

The greatest way to let Mom and Dad in on your big secret is together, especially if they know and like your sweetie. Invite them over for dinner, or wait until your next planned get-together, and blurt it out. In your perfect universe, they'll leap from their chairs to squeeze you both, crying for joy. (Of course, if you get engaged on a trip or live far apart and you just *can't,* by all means, call!)

If your parents don't know your intended, this is the perfect time to organize a visit home. However, we don't recommend introducing your one-and-only *and* announcing your engagement on the same occasion. If you can, wait at least until the second visit. Otherwise, whether you're pressed for time or simply feeling awkward, it's A-OK to go solo when telling your parents about the engagement; in fact, they may appreciate your discretion.

Likewise, you may want to break the news *without* your partner if your parents:

- Have a problem with your mate-to-be
- Are over-the-top protective
- Have concerns about your religious or cultural differences
- Have seen you go through one (or two or three) messy divorces
- Are otherwise opposed to the concept of you getting married

If need be, telling them on your own means you'll be able to have it out openly with your folks without dragging your love through any unnecessary and unpleasant stress and strain.

If your parents live on another planet—metaphorically speaking—and you don't quite connect, send them a thoughtful letter. If your parents are divorced, make the time to personally let both sides in on your plans. The bottom line: Do whatever feels right to you.

Kids Come First

If you have children from a previous marriage, *they* should be your first priority—even before your mom and pop. They're the ones who are getting a new stepparent (and maybe a stepsibling or two), and they'll need some time to get comfortable with the idea of becoming the Brady Bunch. Give your kids lots of undivided attention: The two of you should have a one-on-one-on-one with each child. Also organize a fun stepfamily outing (picnic, bike trip, movie and dinner)—you might find that "the more, the merrier" rule is right on the mark. If not, it's probably just a matter of time.

Don't let your ex-spouse hear about your engagement from the dry cleaner you still share or, worse, Junior himself. If you have children, letting him or her know is *not* optional. If you're not on speaking terms, drop a polite note with the news saying you're willing to discuss any worries or concerns, provided the skeletons in your relationship closet stay put.

Whom to Tell First

Don't share news of your engagement with your parents first if they've been negative about your relationship. Instead, turn to people you know will be thrilled. After they've showered you with love and approval, *then* tell your parents; you'll be fortified for the potential hostility.

BILL AND EMILY
Proposed January 7, New York City

WHEN BILL WAS READY to propose to Emily, he wanted to do something creative and romantic, something that spoke to her. The solution was obvious: a crossword puzzle. A puzzle devotee, Emily did the *New York Times* crossword every day without fail. So Bill called Will Shortz, the crossword editor at the *Times*, hoping he would agree to play cupid. Shortz liked the idea, and the plan was a go.

On the day the puzzle appeared in the paper, Bill played hooky from work and took Emily out for a leisurely day on the town. They went to a café, and Emily, unsuspecting, started the puzzle. Soon Emily said, "Look, my name's in the puzzle." A few minutes later she exclaimed, "Look! *Your* name's in the puzzle, too!"

Emily says she was skipping around the puzzle, and "it seemed very relevant to our relationship." The giveaway clue was "1729 Jonathan Swift pamplet"—"A Modest Proposal." When she finally looked up at Bill, she just said, "This puzzle!" At that point, Bill got down on his knee and asked, "Will you marry me?" After such a memorable proposal, how could the answer be anything but "Yes"?

Engagement Parties

The Brits of yore used to celebrate a couple's engagement with a party they called a "flouncing." These days this bash—usually scheduled sometime during the first two months you're engaged—comes in all shapes and sizes, but, basically, it's a chance to whoop it up with close friends and family. Sounds great, right? Here's the lowdown.

Gifts are optional at an engagement party, but chances are good that many guests will bring presents. You might want to register for at least some gifts by the time of the party. Go to Chapter 17 for registry info.

Parent Parties

Anyone can host these events, but tradition dictates that it's the bride's parents' prerogative to host the first soiree. Then the groom's parents can throw their own party, or, maybe both sets of parents will come together to host the fete jointly. They'll invite their dearest friends and a bunch of your relatives as well as friends of yours whom they know are important to you. These fiestas usually take the form of an informal meal or cocktail hour at someone's home, or perhaps a dinner in a restaurant's party room; you'll be toasted, fed, pampered, and ogled until you can't take it any more (for now!).

If your parents have never met your honey's before, you might think about organizing a *pre*-engagement party get-together. This may very well already be at the top of your mother's to-do list, but if not, take charge! Suggest a meeting at your favorite restaurant or whip up your world-famous lasagna and have your families over. If your parents live far away, suggest you all come together for a weekend retreat in a convenient-for-everyone locale.

The Where and How of Engagement Gifts

Not every engagement-party guest will bring a gift—don't embarrass anyone who didn't by opening presents you do get in front of everyone. Wait until later or open each gift alone with the guest in another part of the house/restaurant. And don't forget to send thank-you notes.

Host Your Own

Why not take charge and throw an engagement party for all your fab friends? More and more couples we know are jumping on this self-congratulatory bandwagon—and for good reason. Many of your crew may *not* be invited to your parent-hosted soiree, for lack of space or the fact that your mom and dad don't know them well, but you want to make them feel a part of your marriage not only from the start but *before* it. This is also a terrific opportunity to show your friends a great time before wedding planning kicks in full force

Go to Chapter 6 for the lowdown on prewedding bashes. (Hint: Get rest now!)

and they're called upon to help you in all ways great and small—including hearing you rattle off the entire potential song list.

Engagement Announcements

You may choose to broadcast the news of your engagement to the masses through a published announcement. Or you may decide to wait and publicize the actual wedding later on. If you're recently widowed or divorced, definitely wait to make the announcement; there's no need to place yourself smack dab in the middle of the gossip circle. You also should hold off on the announcement if you don't know when you're actually going to take the plunge, or if you're already having second thoughts about the marriage. (Some couples' therapists specialize in premarital counseling—go now.)

Get the Announcement Ball Rolling

Call your local newspaper, your parents' hometown rag, your alumni magazine, and anywhere else you want your engagement announcement to appear and find out the name of the appropriate editor or department. Ask for writer's guidelines or a standardized form, if available. Also ask if there's a fee for publication.

Typically, announcements mention career details about the two of you, your parents' names and places of residence, and your educational credentials (space permitting). Don't include your wedding date if you haven't quite decided, or if you have decided but want to keep people in suspense. (You could include something like "A June wedding is planned.") Do list the date if you'd rather publicize it now than answer a million "So when's the big day?" questions later. If you're interested, ask if the publication accepts pictures. Some publications only print actual wedding portraits, but if they will accept an engagement photo, get an eight-by-ten or five-by-seven glossy taken of your adorable mugs.

A Family Tradition

A treasured betrothal custom: the European hope chest. The bride's parents would stock a beautifully crafted wooden chest with linens, knickknacks, and other cozy items for her to take to her new home.

Word Up! Sample Announcements

Engagements usually are announced officially by someone other than the Happy Couple (unless they have no close relatives to give the honor to). When composing your announcement, select the textual variations that best reflect *your* reality, including who will be "sponsoring" (read: "hosting") the wedding and how (dys)functional your family is. Feel free to freestyle, especially if the publication you're announcing it in is hip or humorous. For those of you who need a helping hand, here are some typical engagement announcement wordings:

Standard, by the bride's parents. Mr. and Ms. John Doe of Little Rock announce the engagement of their daughter, Jane Annette, to Jack Smith, son of David and Beth Smith of Tishomingo, Oklahoma. Ms. Doe, a graduate of Vassar College, is a professor at Barnard College in New York City. Mr. Smith graduated magna cum laude from Princeton Law School and works at Smith, Golden, his mother's law firm, in Fort Lee, New Jersey. A June wedding is planned. (*Or:* No date has yet been set for the wedding.)

(The groom's family is also free to put an announcement in their hometown paper; it would follow the same format.)

Single parent sponsoring the wedding. Ms. Janet Jones announces the engagement of her daughter, Jane Doe, to Jack Smith . . . Ms. Doe is also the daughter of John Doe of Sioux City. *(This line is close to the end of the announcement.)*

(There's no need to mention the other biological parent if he or she wasn't involved in raising you.)

Remarried parent, sponsoring with new spouse. Ms. Janet Jones and Mr. Timothy Chapin announce the engagement of Ms. Jones' daughter, Jane Doe, to Jack Smith . . . Ms. Doe is also the daughter of John Doe of Sioux City.

If one parent is deceased. The engagement of Jane Annette Doe, daughter of Mrs. Janet Doe and the late Mr. John Doe, to Jack Smith, son of David and Beth Smith of Tishomingo, Oklahoma, is announced by the bride's mother. . . .

First Photo Op

Take a photo of yourselves on the day you get engaged. It's a great way to remember that great day—and may come in handy if you decide on a formal announcement or to use pictures on your engagement party invites.

If your parents don't support your choice of partner, or are deceased, another close relative—or even a dear friend—can announce your engagement. Ms. Julia Doe announces the engagement of her sister, Jane Doe, to Jack Smith, son of . . . The bride is the daughter of *(the late)* John Doe and Ms. Janet Jones of Little Rock.

You're announcing/sponsoring the wedding yourselves (in the case of remarriage or just because). Jane Doe, a professor at Barnard College, is to be married to Jack Smith, a partner at the law firm of Smith, Golden in Fort Lee, New Jersey. Ms. Doe is the daughter of Mr. John Doe of Sioux City, Iowa, and Ms. Janet Jones of Little Rock, Arkansas. Mr. Smith is the son of David and Beth Smith of Tishomingo, Oklahoma. A June wedding is planned.

Engaged Ups and Downs

Now that you've made your announcements, it's time for engagement quandary number one: How to use diplomacy with friends and relatives. You've only just shared the news about your impending nuptials and already everybody wants to know when the big date is (their calendars are filling up), who your attendants are going to be, and whether you're serving chicken or beef.

Stop. Take a deep breath. Try to answer all inquiries with maximum coolness and your trademark sense of humor (one of the best tools for rebutting sticky questions without bruising egos). Keep in mind that the people who are drilling you with endless, aggravating, even sometimes insulting questions—"Aren't you too young to get married? Won't this interfere with your promotion at work? What about your handball team? Did you go see the florist I recommended?"—aren't *trying* to drive you nuts. They probably just want to be part of the excitement and help you avoid pitfalls. Or perhaps they're so gaga giddy with excitement and nerves that they don't realize that *you* might be feeling some stress here, too, and don't need this extra pressure.

In any case, the dominant emotion you'll be dealing with during your engagement is sheer glee. Our bet is that all of your friends, family, and coworkers are basking in the light of your love. Well, *almost* all of them. There will always be a few black sheep in the flock who, for one reason or another, just can't digest your good news. Friends may be jealous or feel like you're abandoning them, that they won't see you as often now (and they're probably right). Try your best to be aware of their concerns and reassure them.

How do you handle evil-wishers like high-school enemies, your commitment-phobic squash partner, or that waiter with a crush from hell? Just ignore them, because:

1. Who cares what they think?
2. They'll get over it.
3. If all else fails, you can always slap 'em upside the head with your 3-carat diamond.

Go to Chapter 20 for more help with dealing with friends displaying bizarre behavior patterns.

Engage Your Imagination: Party Ideas

Creativity and informality are the buzzwords when it comes to today's engagement parties. If you or your parents don't want to make this a formal dinner affair, here are some alternatives:

- Bowling bash. Reserve lanes for your entire crew, order finger food, and play for great tunes on the jukebox.

- Cocktail soiree. Mix up some martinis, make trays of hors d'oeuvres, and have your favorite people over for a night of conversation.

- Picnic party. Take it to the park and pray for sun. Put out a delicious spread and play touch Frisbee, soccer, or volleyball.

- Chomp feast. Reserve a looooong table at your favorite restaurant.

- Where everybody knows your name. Have everyone meet at the friendly neighborhood watering hole.

Buying the Ring

The most universal of engagement traditions, by far, is the groom-to-be presenting his bride-to-be with a ring. Customarily, there's a luscious diamond involved, perched atop a band of pretty damn expensive metal. We love the ice, of course, but it's great that some people select a different precious gem, or group of gems—such as aquamarine, topaz, or tourmaline. Others opt for Victorian-inspired posy rings (bands engraved with inscriptions of love) or elaborate tattoos. It's also not unheard of for a woman to reciprocate and purchase an engagement ring for her man or to chip in for her own sparkly bauble. Other couples also give engagement gifts to each other.

Let's assume that you're a classic guy (or gal). You're ready to contribute to the $18-billion-a-year world of the diamond business. If you've got the guts, go traditional and surprise your honey with a beautiful ring. But we like the idea of asking for her (or his) input—clear, or slightly colored? Mounted low, or jutting out? Round, square, or heart-shaped?—before you go diamond hunting.

Name Your Price

Before you embark on your ring quest, figure out how much you have to spend (literally have in your budget, not "have to" as in must!). Generally, people set aside about two months' salary for the jewel, but you can spend as much or as little as you want (or, more realistically, can afford). A bigger diamond or swankier setting does *not* mean a better marriage.

Study Up

Once you've established a budget, ask friends and family to recommend a reputable jeweler. Make sure s/he's a member of the American Gem Corporation (212–762–0028) and offers stones that are in your price range. Be a savvy shopper; retailers will take you more seriously if you use professional lingo. Throw around a few of the buzzwords: clarity, carat, color, and cut (also known as the four Cs; we explain them next). However, don't act *overly* sophisticated if you aren't; your ignorance will betray you, and some jewelers who smell an easy kill won't hesitate to draw first blood.

Clarity: A stone's price tag is determined first and foremost by its clarity, or the degree to which it's free from internal flaws (professionally dubbed "inclusions"). The fewer the flaws, the more light reflected—and the more sparkle. Unless you're an oil tycoon, you'll probably have to settle for a diamond that falls between the VVS1 (very, very small inclusions) and the SI2 (small inclusions) categories. But don't worry about the inclusion rating too much. Slight inclusions may reduce a diamond's value, but they don't take anything away from its beauty.

Cut: The cut of a diamond also determines its brilliance. A skilled jew-

Sneaky Ways to Get Her Ring Size

- Sneak away to the jeweler's with a ring she wears on her ring finger.

- Ask one of her friends to play detective. She should try on a ring of your honey's and say, "Oh, this is too loose (too tight, just right)—what size are you?"

- Measure the circumference of her ring finger with a piece of string and use a pen to mark the right spot. (This method is recommended only if she's a deep sleeper!)

Don't Pay Retail

"When buying a diamond, keep in mind that the average jewelry store charges double the amount that they should, so don't even think about paying the sticker price! Generally, the price listed in the store can be cut in half. Be sure to negotiate."

—Fred Cuellar, author of *How to Buy a Diamond* (Sourcebook, 1996)

eler can make even an imperfect gem gleam like a cat's eye. The shape you select depends on your taste; the 58-facet round cut and the oval cut are today's most popular shapes, and the geometrical princess and emerald cuts are high up in the drama department. Ask your jeweler to show you the different stone shapes and explain how each cut will affect your diamond's shine.

Carat: The weight of a stone determines its size. One carat equals 100 points. A 0.5-carat diamond is the size of a very small pea; a 69-carat gem—like the one Richard Burton once gave to Liz Taylor—is the size of a golf ball. Don't get one this large—you'll snag it on *everything*. Of course, you'll pay more for a heavier diamond in the same clarity group. Size is a matter of preference when it comes to rings; by now you should know if your honey is the discreet or flashy type (or maybe she's made it crystal-clear to you how big a diamond she wants!).

Color: Most diamonds range from pure white to a faint yellow cast. Again, you'll have to exercise your aesthetic judgment here (or your judgment of your sweetie's aesthetic judgment). Most people prefer their rocks colorless. Your budget will come into play again; the more colorless a stone, the more expensive it is. (The exceptions to this rule are the extravagantly priced *fancies*, brightly colored diamonds in shades of blue, red, amber, and green.)

Close the Deal

When you've found a diamond she'd die for, make sure the gem is appraised by an independent expert before you buy. (Call the International Gemological Institute at 212–753–7100 for references.) When you're sure the ice is what the jeweler says it is, try to negotiate a better price if it seems appropriate (it's generally expected—think car-buying) before having it placed in a pretty little chic box.

Your Diamond

Examine stones in their loose state—not mounted in a ring—under a magnifying glass and in sunlight. Put several diamonds in a row to get a sense of each one's uniqueness. If you find one you like, have the jeweler "plot" (draw) its flaws on a piece of paper, so it can be identified later when you're ready to close the deal.

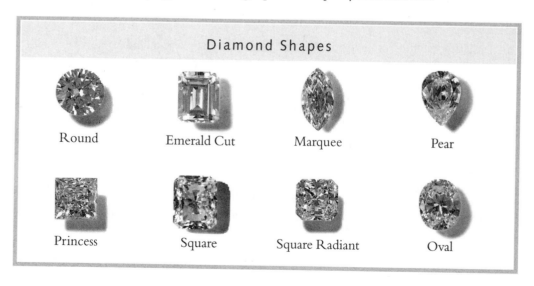

Diamond Shapes

Round   Emerald Cut   Marquee   Pear

Princess   Square   Square Radiant   Oval

You thought you were through with all the decision making, but there are a few more details to attend to:

- Choose the band you want the precious one mounted on. Generally, you're talking gold, silver, or platinum.

- Decide whether you want the diamond riding low or jutting out, or whether you want a more elaborate design option out. (This generally is referred to as the "setting.") These include the antiquelike *cluster* or *prong-solitaire*—jutting clusters—ring styles; the hill-and-valley geometric *bar;* the graduation ringlike *gypsy;* and the polka-dots-in-a-circle *channel* design. High-riding diamonds surrounded by several smallish gems and unique engravings in the metal band are also an increasingly popular option.

The Price of Ice

The heavier the ice, the larger the price. Average cost for a SI 1I diamond:

- 0.5 carat: $1,500
- 1 carat: $5,000
- 1.5 carat: $8,700
- 2 carat: $13,000
- 3 carat: $22,800

As we said, don't feel obligated to buy a diamond (unless you know you'll be in the doghouse if you don't). Gems like sapphires, rubies, and emeralds—long the preference of engaged European royalty—are now gracing the fingers of America's uncrowned princesses and dancing queens. Like diamonds (symbols of purity of heart and eternal love), these stones also bear messages of devotion. Sapphires connote sincerity; rubies suggest passion; and the emerald is the gem of Venus, goddess of l'amour. Another possibility is to choose a ring that sports your fiancée's birthstone as a way to say "I'm so glad you were born."

We told you getting engaged was fabulous—it's difficult not to get lost in the euphoria. Now, fresh from Cloud Nine time together and the shower of love from family and friends, you're ready to get down to the nitty-gritty of planning one of the best days of your life—your wedding.

Setting Your Priorities

Diving a Date and Time

Settling on Size

Finding a Site

Selecting a Wedding Style

Wedding Consultants

Envisioning the Event

So there you are, staring at a blank piece of paper with the words "Our Wedding" scrawled across the top. What now? The first step in planning your celebration is answering the big questions: the who, what, where, when, and how of the event. These are the primary colors of any wedding composition; they'll narrow down the variations that are right for you and make the planning process feel less abstract.

We're going to help you draw the picture of *your* ideal wedding—is it a candlelit evening ceremony in fall? A blue-sky spring garden luncheon? Do you want an intimate family gathering or an all-acquaintance extravaganza? It's time to think through the options and draw up a blueprint.

Setting Your Priorities

As in any other giant undertaking, you won't get anywhere with your wedding until you sit down and prioritize. What's important to you? Where should you start?

Talk About It

Close your eyes. When we say "fantasy wedding," what do you see? A $5,000 dress, shimmery and glam? Tons and tons of white roses? A floating reception on a yacht under a crayon-blue sky and yellow sun? Three hundred revelers waltzing in a regal ballroom? A spiritual ceremony and intimate dinner with only your MCI Calling Circle?

This kind of free-form fantasizing will help you identify your dream scenario so that you'll be able to figure out your exact wedding priorities. These details will be at the foreground of the party you plan; if need be, you can make adjustments and cutbacks to the other elements.

Chances are, your dream wedding "drawing" is *different* from your betrothed's. (We said different, not *better.*) Part of this initial visualizing process is putting your visions side by side to see how they can work together. Compromise is reality—and good practice for a blissfully long marriage.

Plan to Pull It Off

No matter what priorities you've isolated as list-toppers, we believe it's possible to pull off a close approximation of your fantasy regardless of your finances or outside pressures. Say you decide that your number-one priority is a formal, medieval-theme dinner reception in an authentic castle. That may prove *way* too expensive. But how about a semiformal, midday, medieval buffet banquet in an outdoor tent? Conversely, if you just want to elope at the Church of Hunka-Hunka Love in Las Vegas but your parents really want you to have a hometown reception, there's a way to make everyone happy. Go to city hall with select family and friends to shower you with confetti, and then invite a larger group to a local funky lounge bar for the party. The point is to take your vision and try to break it down into realistic pieces—so it'll actually *happen.*

Get Organized

Buy a binder, plastic file box, or accordion file where you'll put everything wedding—magazine articles, printouts from The Knot (www.theknot.com), notes, pictures, vendor information, fabric swatches, etc.

Divining a Date and Time

Does your man need a green card so he won't be kicked out of the country? Did your best friend Paulo just tell you he's moving far, far away in a few days, and since your heart is set on having him be your best man, he needs to make that toast ASAP? Have you decided that your honeymoon will be a once-a-decade, hyperdemanding polar expedition that leaves next week? Your ideal wedding date is pretty darn obvious—tomorrow!

Your Time Constraints

For the rest of us, choosing the precise wedding date can be an elaborate production. The exact date you select will depend on several variables, including:

Planning Time: How much time will you need to prepare your dream wedding?

Family and Friends' Commitments: Check for possible conflicts like graduations, birthdays, or pregnancy due dates so that you can select a day when your loved ones *can* attend.

Significant Dates: You may want your wedding date to have sentimental value, commemorating your first kiss, your grandparents' anniversary, or Valentine's Day.

Site and Vendor Availability: Is there a church or caterer you've had your hearts set on *for years?* If so, their schedule is going to influence—and may even dictate—yours.

Budget: Certain times of the year are generally more expensive than others. (See "The Monster Months" later in the chapter.) Depending on how cost-conscious you need to be, this *may* be a factor in your decision.

To create your own personalized to-do list, go to The Knot's Online Calendar at www.theknot.com.

Wedding Style: Certain kinds of weddings are more conducive to specific seasons and/or times. Formal clothing is much more fun when it's not 95 degrees outside; family affairs—with lots of wee ones—are best scheduled during the day.

Like everything in life, there will be pros and cons to virtually every date you consider. While a Valentine's Day wedding—complete with gorgeous rose centerpieces, red

MELANI AND HERB
May 17, Oracle, Arizona

FOR MELANI AND HERB, honoring the bride's grandparents became an integral part of planning their wedding. "My grandfather raised me as his own daughter; his life and death inspired our wedding and decision to have a family," Melani says. With this in mind, the couple chose to wed in Oracle, Arizona, in a house that had been built by the bride's great-grandfather—and where her grandfather, along with all of his brothers and sisters, had been born.

The date of their marriage was also significant—it was the fiftieth wedding anniversary of her grandparents. "We wanted to not only continue their love for each other but to also have our marriage certificate filed in the town where my grandfather's birth certificate is. It meant a lot that we were able to be married in the land that my grandfather loved and fought for—he was a major in World War II."

After the ceremony, Melani and Herb walked across the street to the cemetery where both her grandparents are buried. "We wanted them to share in our love and happiness as we shared in theirs."

velvet bridesmaids' dresses, and heart-shaped chocolate favors—sounds dreamy, getting a florist to give you great service at that time may be a nightmare better suited to Halloween. Scheduling your big day for a long weekend may seem like a great idea when it comes to accommodating your legions of long-distance guests, but your local pals may begrudge your interfering with three days of much-needed R&R. Once again, establish your priorities—and choose the date accordingly.

After you've settled on your ideal date, choose two or three back-ups just in case the temple or Sicilian caterer of your dreams is otherwise committed. Flexibility is vital during the planning process.

The Monster Months

These are the months when it seems like everybody and their cousin is getting hitched. The big three are June, August, and September, with May, July, October, and party-happy December hot on their heels. The more popular your wedding month, the less choice you'll have about the site, vendors, and exact timing. Competition for services may drive up your wedding expenses, too. By opting for an off-season month (November, January through April), you're bound to get more personalized service from your florist, baker, and officiant and have more control over the minutia of your minutia-packed event. The flip side, of course, is that a romantic garden wedding in February is about as appropriate as stiletto heels in a bowling alley.

Days in Demand

Saturday is the crowned Queen of Weddings, with Friday and Sunday the ladies in waiting. The attractions of a Saturday wedding are obvious; out-of-towners have ample time to get to your wedding without missing work and guests have roughly twenty-four hours to nurse any hangover before heading back to the office. With Fridays and Sundays, it's more of a scramble to get, respectively, to and from your wedding, and there's no chill-out day—but they're still far more convenient than a weekday. A midweek affair is not advisable if you're inviting a lot of out-of-towners or are planning an all-night bash, but it's a great way to cut costs and get a better pick of vendors.

Power Hours

When deciding on the time of day for your ceremony and reception, remember that the earlier the festivities, the lower the cost of the reception; a brunch or afternoon tea will set you back substantially less than an evening dinner reception, and there probably will be less demand for that time slot, too. Lunch and teas are exceptionally good choices if you're inviting lots of children (and their frazzled parents). However, evening and night weddings are far more appropriate if you're thinking black-tie or boogie-woogie.

**Beware
"Bummer" Dates**

Don't schedule your wedding for "bummer" days—any day during the week before Tax Day (April 15), an important work deadline, on the anniversary of your father's death. Also steer clear of the major tourist season in your wedding area, especially if you're inviting a lot of out-of-towners who need hotel rooms.

**Any Time Is
Reception Time!**

Arrival time indicated on your reception invite for:

- Breakfast: 10 a.m.–12 p.m.
- Brunch: 11 a.m.–1 p.m.
- Lunch: 1 p.m.–3 p.m.
- Tea: 3 p.m.–5 p.m.
- Cocktails: 4 p.m.–7 p.m.
- Dinner: 6 p.m.–8 p.m.
- Drinks and Dessert: 8 p.m.–10 p.m.
- Late-Night Fare: 8 p.m.–10 p.m.
- Midnight Madness: 9 p.m.–11 p.m.

Blackout Periods

One more thing to consider: religious restrictions. Often there are blackout periods when it is *not* acceptable to tie the knot. For example, conservative rabbis will not perform weddings between Passover and Shavuot, and many ministers are reluctant to officiate ceremonies during Lent. Consult a clergyperson about traditions that might affect you.

Go to Chapter 7 for more on incorporating religion into your ceremony.

Settling on Size

How many people to invite (not to mention who exactly) is one of the biggest decisions you need to make during this initial "sketching" period. This may sound like one of the most pleasurable aspects of your wedding preparation—the two of you, sitting down over a bottle of wine, taking stock of all the wonderful people you'll share this special day with. But the truth is, making the guest list is difficult, given all the forces (parental opinions, budgetary concerns, reception site considerations) pulling you in different directions.

The Guest List: What to Consider

There are five main considerations when figuring out how long you want your invite list to be.

Style: Is it more important for you to have one-on-one time with each beloved guest or to throw a bombastic, once-in-a-lifetime party for *all* your disparate friends and relatives? Is your fantasy wedding style more conducive to a small or large gathering?

Budget: There will be a per-head cost for food and liquor—more guests means more cash. There are many ways to cut expenses and still invite as many folks as you want, such as buying your own booze, opting for a buffet rather than seated meal, having relatives cater the affair as their wedding gift to you. But in general, you'll need to take monetary boundaries into account when deciding on a guest number.

Parents' Desires: If your mom and pop are adamant about inviting throngs of friends and extended family, you're going to have to hear them out—especially if they're footing a major part of the bill. Your mantra here: Compromise.

The Size of Your Extended Families: Obviously, the more relatives you simply *must* invite, the larger your guest list is going to be—unless you decide to make it a family-only affair and then throw a separate party for friends.

Logistical Constraints: If there's a dream ceremony or reception site in your vision, you're going to be limited by how many people it can accommodate. (You can't squeeze 500 people into a lighthouse.)

Who Gets to Invite How Many?

Once you've got your guest-list limit, it's time to decide who's in and who's out. Like limber limbo-ers, you and your wedding cosponsors have to slide everyone you love in under your quota. Traditionally, the bride and her family and the groom and his folks each invite half of the guests, with the parents on both sides—usually the major check-writers—calling most of the shots. But if you and your fiancé/e are underwriting the majority of the reception costs, it is definitely acceptable for you to determine the bulk of the guest list. Another

The Kid Question

Children can be the heart and soul of a wedding, but they also can be a royal pain on the big day. Deciding whether to make your guest list adults-only is tough. Which profile best reflects your feelings?

With Children:

You and/or your babycake has a kid or other special tiny someone—a godchild, one you've "adopted" through the Big Brother program, an irresistible nephew—who is an important part of your lives. You want them to share in your big day.

Children epitomize family, which is what many weddings are all about. Their presence can be spiritually meaningful.

Your nephews and nieces live far away; you've never met your best friend's four-year-old twins. Weddings are a great opportunity to enjoy overdue introductions and infrequent reunions.

You're shy of the limelight. Cute kids may capture your guests' attention and take some of the pressure off of you (if only in your minds).

You don't want to force your guests with kids to leave home without them. You know it makes them nervous.

You don't want to ruffle any parental feathers.

Without Children:

Children are the epitome of chaos, which is what you *don't* want your wedding to be.

You're planning an intellectually challenging ceremony or a Dirty Dancing reception—kids would spoil the desired effect.

You'll save money with no kids there. Cold? Maybe, but it translates into a few less mouths to feed.

You'll be giving your friends with children a night off-duty.

You can't invite every kid you know—and you don't want to ruffle any parental feathers through omissions.

arrangement that works especially well is to divide the invitee rations three ways: between the soon-to-be-weds, the bride's parents, and the groom's parents. If your parents are divorced, you're going to have to make even more divisions.

Leave Out
the Little Ones?

If you decide not to invite kids, don't write it on your invites. Simply address the invite to the parents, omitting the little ones. Let word spread by mouth.

Making the Dreaded Cuts

If you're having trouble keeping the numbers under control, consider limiting invitations for dates. If your best buddy has been through more flames than a Burger King patty, send him or her a solo invitation. (Your wedding will be good place for a friend like this to ignite new sparks.) It's also okay to invite a group of acquaintances, such as your office mates or rugby team, *sans* significant others. Heavily monogamous, engaged, or married guests should be invited along with their honey-pies.

If your guest list is *still* seriously bloated, implement some across-the-board limitations, such as no children under sixteen or no coworkers. Remember, the key to making these kinds of boundaries work is not to make

ASK CARLEY

Small-Wedding Blues

Q: My fiancé/e and I are having an intimate wedding and I'm afraid some people will be offended that they are not invited. What to do?

A: If it hasn't happened yet, it will. Everyone—from people you went to camp with to your nemesis from high school—will call with their congrats and fish around for that all-important invite. In the words of Nancy Reagan: "Just Say No." Be honest with people. Let them know that your wedding is going to be very, very, very small. (Honesty doesn't mean you can't exaggerate a little.) Explain that with two families to accommodate, it was simply impossible to invite everyone you wanted to. These might be difficult conversations to have, but most people will understand, and it's better than ducking into alleys to avoid non-invitees on the street.

any exceptions. Otherwise, you're likely to get a fair share of wedding curses along with your blessings.

On that semisour note: *Never* invite anyone to your blessed event out of guilt. They're the ones being rude by practically demanding an invitation. If you have to give a great deal of thought as to whether to invite someone, that person probably doesn't belong on your list; your wedding guests should be the people you adore.

After each party has retreated to compile his or her wish list, you need to hammer out a more manageable master list. Compare notes, eliminate repeat names, and help each other make additional necessary cuts. Now that you have your final guest list (okay, there may still be some changes along the way—but it's pretty darn near finalized), don't forget to raise a glass of the bubbly. Completing this task is well worth toasting.

Figure Out Your Guest List First

You will want to choose your wedding location after you determine your guest list. Answers to questions like "Where are the majority of our guests from?" and "How many people are coming?" can help determine the right place for your wedding.

Finding a Site

It used to be a given that couples would say their vows in the bride's hometown. For many that's still true, but today's couples are just as likely to wed in the groom's hometown, in their college town, in the city they live in now, even at their honeymoon destination. Some couples are even hosting two or more receptions to facilitate the attendance of loved ones scattered across the country or around the globe.

If you want to throw a raucous dance party reception for all of your current friends, the city you now call home is the logical choice. If you're planning a cozy, family wedding, choose one of your hometowns, or head to your parents' current home. If you're planning everything, have the wedding in your proverbial backyard; if Mom and Dad are footing the entire bill, it's gracious to say "I do" in theirs.

Go to Chapter 3 for more on destination and "progressive" weddings.

Long-Distance Planning

Obviously, the big drawback of having a wedding away from *your* home is that you'll be co-ordinating everything from afar. Unfortunately, the wedding industry has not yet joined forces with Silicon Valley to create a computer that coordinates all your preparations and shows vendors exactly what to do and how. (It's just a matter of time, we're sure.) That means that you have to take extra measures to get what you want when you're working long distance:

- Get a copy of the Yellow Pages from your wedding town so you know what's available, or go online for local listings of vendors.
- Hire an on-site bridal consultant to be your right-hand man or woman when it comes to finding available services, negotiating with vendors, and supervising preparation details. (For more on these professionals, see "Wedding Consultants," later in the chapter.) Or you may have a good, reliable friend (like Mom) who can serve as your point person instead. Just make sure they know what they're getting into.
- Get and use vendors' e-mail addresses or fax numbers to keep long-distance calls (and costs) to a minimum.
- Plan at least one visit to the wedding location. Have your in-town wedding rep schedule meetings for you with all potential or actual vendors. Visit the reception site, set up a test hair and makeup session at the salon of your choice, and so on.
- Get all business arrangements in writing. This is always important, but never more so than when you've got the distance disadvantage.

Inside or Out?

Go to Chapter 10 for lots more on ceremony and reception venues.

Once you've figured out what town or city is going to play host to your big bash, you'll need to answer another fundamental location, location, location question: inside, or out-of-doors? Obviously, this depends on your wedding date. A beach party in January is nutso (unless you're wedding south of the border). Likewise, if the banquet hall you want for your reception isn't air-conditioned, shy away from a July or August wedding.

While outdoor weddings would *appear* to be the cheaper option—after all, you're not paying for a fancy reception hall—hidden costs, such as a permit (necessary at a public space like Yosemite or a state beach), a tent, a generator, and transportation can really add up. The main reasons to wed under the sheltering sky are beauty and drama, not dollars and cents. Whether you decide to go *au natural* or not, start thinking now about how you'll spruce up your site to fit the dream-wedding picture you've been painting in your head.

Small Site? Separate

If you've selected a really intimate ceremony site, devise two lists: one for the select group who witness your vows, the other for those who will join in at your reception.

The Inside Scoop on Outdoor Sites

Reservations: Do you need one?

Weather: When is rain, hurricane, or extreme temperature season?

Insects: If there's a problem, can an exterminator take care of it?

Allergies: Do you or your wedding party have them?

Accessibility: Will transportation be a problem?

Vendors: Will they be able to work there? What extra expenses would this locale entail?

Comfort: You may want to rent a tent, a portable dance floor, and wooden chairs (not temperature-absorbing metal seats, no matter how chic they look).

Port-a-Potties: If there are no bathroom facilities, you'll need to rent some.

Parking: Consider hiring a valet service or running a shuttle bus.

Backup plan: Make one in case Hurricane Zachary strikes.

Lighting: String lights between trees, rent some spotlights, or scatter scores of lanterns.

Equipment: Make arrangements early to rent everything you'll need, including tables, linens, an electricity generator, a dressing trailer, etc.

Attitude: Assign several pals to attitude detail. If it rains, they'll remind you that rain on your wedding day is good luck.

Selecting a Wedding Style

There may be six degrees of separation between any two people, but there are only four degrees of formality when it comes to getting married: ultra-formal, formal, semiformal, and informal.

The formality of your wedding will be reflected first and foremost in the location of the wedding (ballroom vs. bar, for example) and second in the outfits you choose and the dress code you establish for your guests. If you decide to go all out, you'll probably be expected to appear in a classic, long gown with a train (her) and a white-tie tail coat (him), with guests opting for evening dresses and tuxes. With an informal wedding, almost anything goes.

The most important aspect of deciding which degree of formality best suits your wedding is your personal preference, although your time of day and season may also come to bear. If you've decided on a beach wedding, for example, go informal, or at least semiformal. Black tie doesn't always mix well with sunshine and hot sand. If you must wear a tux or a diamond tiara, wait until dusk. The formality also can affect the number of guests, the food, the decorations, the entertainment—and the debits to your bank account.

Whatever you decide, here's our advice: While you're in the throes of planning, incorporate your chosen formality into every wedding detail. You want the overall vision of your nuptials to be a perfect composition—and knowing how formal a look you're going for probably will make your decisions easier.

Budget-Friendly Black Tie

Want a formal wedding with tons of guests and chi-chi black tie but can't afford it? No problem. Make it a late-night champagne-and-cake (rather than a seated dinner), big-band affair at a formal location like a ballroom.

HOLLY AND DAVID
May 25, France

"MY HUSBAND IS ENGLISH, and I felt that if we had our wedding here [in the United States], it would be more my event than his," says Holly. "Having it in France, where his father lives, meant that he could have more people there, and it would really be a joint affair." The wedding was held at David's father's house, just south of the Loire Valley. For Holly and her mom, planning the event from far away was difficult, of course, but Holly says there was an added benefit: "Because it was their house, and their country, the groom's family had to get involved more than most."

Of the hundred guests at the wedding, about half came from the United States. The couple planned activities from Thursday to Sunday so that "it wasn't like flying to France for a five-hour event," explains Holly. With only a hundred guests and a three-day event, the bride and groom actually got to spend time with people. "It was so much fun," says Holly. "People really enjoyed themselves." The time, money, and effort friends and family put into coming to a wedding so far away made Holly and David feel very loved. "It was a fantasy," the bride says. "It wasn't just a wedding; it was an experience."

Wedding Consultants

Wedding consultants are professionals whose lives revolve around all things nuptial; they're part party planner, stage manager, financial adviser, vendor broker, shrink, and all-around wedding maniacs. Hire a full-time consultant to help you prepare your entire wedding, from announcement to Zurich honeymoon. Hire a part-time wedding consultant to devise a wedding blueprint—including budget, schedule, and lists of good vendor and site choices—before you launch solo into the preparations. Or you can hire one just to play ringleader on the actual day.

Consultant Pros and Cons

There are many good reasons to hire a wedding consultant, not the least of which is reducing your stress level. S/he will do all the dirty work, starting with researching your options—given your budget and ideal scenario— and ending with supervising vendors during cleanup, ensuring they hit the road in a timely fashion and leave minimal mess. An ideal wedding consultant plays bad cop to your good cop.

The catch is that you'll pay for it. To the consultant, time is money, and depending on how long s/he thinks s/he's going to have to toil to make your wedding a smashing success, s/he'll quote you a fee. As a general rule of thumb, make sure that price does not exceed 10

Looking for a Consultant?

Call for member referrals nationwide.

- Association of Bridal Consultants: 860–355–0464

What a Wedding Consultant Can Do for You

Set up a realistic wedding budget.

Devise a wedding master plan that maps out all the little details, from ceremony music to favors.

Show you the best and most original locations in the area, considering your wedding size, budget, and vision.

Find the best florists, photographers, caterers, bands, and DJs in your price range. Consultants' Rolodexes are full of the names of wedding professionals.

Cut you choice deals. Consultants bring volume to favored vendors; often they'll reciprocate by slashing prices or throwing in extras.

Read over all your vendor contracts.

Create a timeline that tells everyone involved in the planning process—vendors, members of the wedding party, you soon-to-be-weds and your families—when to do what. Plus the consultant will make sure you *stick* to that schedule.

Handle the invitations, from the wording and ordering to the addressing and mailing.

Counsel you on proper etiquette and what's hot on the wedding front.

Coordinate with the photographer, florist, musicians, and caterer/banquet manager to determine realistic setup times and when they should arrive on wedding day.

Manage the wedding day, supervising vendors, handling emergencies, and soothing nerves.

Serve as your spokesperson, conveying your every whim and desire to vendors or family members when you just can't deal with doing it yourself.

Help plan and book your honeymoon.

to 15 percent of your total budget if you're hiring a consultant for the whole wedding. (So if your budget is $15,000, for example, $1,500 is a fair price to pay.) Since fees for blueprint preparation or wedding-day coordination vary, we say you better shop around.

Before you say yes to a particular consultant, make sure you've got a great rapport and that you feel confident s/he won't try to force any wedding vision other than your own on you. You're hiring this person to help you make your dream wedding a reality—don't lose sight of that. If you think you'd feel better doing it on your own, or with the help of your mom, maybe a consultant is not for you.

Critical Consultant Tip

We can't emphasize it enough—do *not* hire a consultant who doesn't listen, is bossy, tries to convince you what's best for you, has no references, won't sign a written agreement, or wears acid-washed jeans. Period.

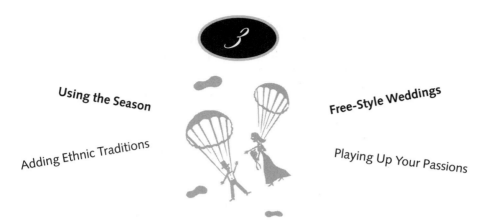

3

Using the Season

Free-Style Weddings

Adding Ethnic Traditions

Playing Up Your Passions

Taking It Personally

So you've made your decision. You want a laid-back afternoon affair on a summer Sunday. Or maybe it's going to be a dressed-to-the-nines occasion on a Saturday evening smack-dab in the middle of June. Now the key is making it *your* casual summer-day soiree, *your* black-tie ball-room affair. Create a wedding that's uniquely yours, a party that only you could have thrown, one people will remember long after they walk out the reception-hall door.

No matter what you do, just the fact that it's *your* wedding is going to make it personal. But if you're dying to be different, this chapter is for you—it's simply hundreds of ideas, some serious, some silly. Our aim is purely to inspire.

Using the Season

What's your ultimate romantic moment? A winter afternoon in the country. Pine trees and roaring hearth fires, crisp air against your skin, snowdrifts, and delicate flurries that transform the land into a misty netherworld. Or maybe summer is more your time of year—beach parties, bare legs, tropical drinks, romantic evening strolls. But then there's fall—the changing leaves, that smell in the air, delicious sweater weather. And spring's not too shabby, either—new beginnings, rose gardens, the most perfect temperatures. The season can help you decide on wedding food, music, flowers, favors, decorations, even your wardrobe. And the holiday wedding takes the idea one step further. It also lets you tap into the sentiment of the occasion—romance on Valentine's Day, eeriness (and fun!) on Halloween. Here are some of our favorite seasonal wedding ideas.

A New Year's bash. Ring in the new year with the ultimate resolution. Start late on New Year's Eve—the reception might not begin until around 8:00 or 9:00 P.M. Consider partying first and saying your vows at the stroke of midnight. (Imagine the anniversary celebrations!) Have your best man toast the two of you soon after the witching hour. Invite guests to wear their glitziest clothes. You, too, can dress in sparkly style; a bridal gown with silver or gold trim; bridesmaids' dresses shot through with silver thread; groom's and groomsmen's cummerbunds or vests in metallic shades.

A Valentine's party. For a February wedding, send invites that look like Valentine's Day cards. Or go with Victorian-style invitations embossed with hearts and flowers. The flowers should be roses, of course. Use a pink or red color scheme, with blush-hued bridesmaids' dresses and groomsman accents. For a cute, clever touch, attendants might all wear heart-shaped sunglasses down the aisle. (You could, too!) Have the flower girl drop heart-shaped confetti. Decorate with cupids, and scatter candy conversation hearts on all the tables. Choose songs for the playlist that always mention love.

Spring fling. For a springtime wedding, think growth and green. Spring is the season of renewal. (And *rain*—unless you're gamblers, you might not want to plan an outside wedding for this season—at least make sure you secure an indoor alternate.) Decorate with spring colors—watery blue, light purple, pale yellow, new-shoot green. Use a flower motif for the centerpieces and room decor. Give bulbs or pastel umbrellas as favors. Have classical music playing during the ceremony and reception. (How about Vivaldi's "Spring"?)

Easter affair. For the site, think garden, tearoom, or a greenhouse. Brides, wear a dress with pastel touches or simple lace details. Grooms, go for a light-colored linen suit and pastel tie. Serve a traditional Easter meal (ham, potatoes, *eggs,* pound cake for dessert) on tables topped with pretty pastel umbrellas; have your officiant do a traditional Easter blessing over the food before you eat. Decorate with plenty of lilies. Have an Easter egg hunt.

Summer lovin'. Make your June, July, or August wedding the essence of endless summer. Cover tables with red-and-white picnic tablecloths. Or go with limeade-green cloth and serve food on thick, matte-plastic plates in jewel tones. Serve upscale picnic food (grilled chicken, fish, and steak, along with tons of fresh fruit and vegetables). Use sand pails full of flowers as centerpieces. Dance together to Gershwin's "Summertime" (from *Porgy and Bess).* Or throw a pool party and give guests their own pool towels as favors, embroidered with your names and the wedding date. If you live near a beach, have a late-afternoon wedding on the shore. Start the ceremony around 6:00 P.M., with the crashing ocean and the sunset as your backdrop. Light a bonfire later and have the band kick in. The bride might wear a short white dress; bridesmaids, flirty sun dresses. The groom could appear in a linen suit or linen pants and shirt with no jacket.

Fourth of July. Want to express some national pride? Rent a Colonial-era mansion and hang a huge flag out front. Or plan your party at a site with a great view of your city or town's annual fireworks extravaganza. Make the meal an Independence Day picnic—grilled or barbecued chicken, potato salad, watermelon, Bomb Pops (those big red, white, and blue

Popsicles). Hand out sparklers wrapped with ribbon as favors, or use them to top off your wedding cake.

Fall fest. Fall offers great wedding weather. Choose a location with windows that look out on a valley of red, orange, and burnt umber trees. Or wed in a park, forest preserve, apple orchard, or vineyard (if it's not too chilly where you live). Include a pressed leaf with each invitation (available at craft stores), or go with a leafy border. Dress bridesmaids in velvet, jacquard, or brocade in rich colors such as magenta, hunter, bronze, and gold. Decorate with piles of leaves, bales of hay, pots of mums, and pumpkins. Hang gold netting with leaves woven into it over the cake table. Have hayrides available for guests, or set up a dunking-for-apples station. Serve turkey, stuffing, potatoes, cranberry sauce, pumpkin pie, caramel apples, and mulled cider. Decorate the cake with fresh leaves.

Monster mash. A Halloween wedding? Invite guests to come in costume. Or make it a black-tie (and orange accent) affair. Use jack o' lanterns as centerpieces, or opt for bouquets of dried or fresh flowers with sheaves of wheat and cattails surrounded by mini-pumpkins and gourds. Put bowls of candy corn on every table. Give Halloween masks, little pumpkins with your names and the date inscribed on them, or bags of Halloween candy for favors. Be sure to dance to the "Monster Mash."

Location Salvation

Fall weather can turn at the drop of a leaf—and so can spring weather, for that matter. If you're planning an outdoor wedding in October or November or during the rainy months of March or April, make sure to have a location backup.

Winter wonderland. Want to create that cozy, romantic feeling? Rent an estate or hall with a working fireplace. Decorate with huge silver, gold, and white pillar candles. Hang sparkly snowflakes from the ceiling, and put fresh pine or fir trees in the corners. Spray the windows with snow-in-a can, give snow globes as favors, and give snowflake pendants and faux-fur mufflers to your bridesmaids. Serve hot cocoa (spiked with Peppermint Schnapps for the big kids). Arrive at the wedding in a horse-drawn sleigh (or carriage). Or make it a decadent pre–Russian Revolution winter party. Choose a room with gorgeous chandeliers. Crown an overflowing buffet table with a swanky ice sculpture. Serve champagne, vodka, caviar, and smoked salmon. Hire strolling violinists to play during dinner. The bride can wear a white, fur-trimmed cape over velvet, taffeta, or silk. The groom might come in tails and a fur cap. Arrive and depart in a white limo.

White Christmas. If your ceremony's in a church, chances are quite good that it will already be decked out for the Christmas season. For your reception, decorate Christmas trees with white lights, silver balls, and red ribbons. Stack huge piles of oversized "presents"—boxes wrapped in holiday paper. Hang mistletoe *everywhere*. Serve eggnog, plum pudding, ham, and turkey. Have a cake decorated like a candy cane, and serve Christmas cookies along with it. Hire Christmas carolers or a barbershop quartet to lead guests in singing favorite holiday songs. Lots of young guests? Have Santa drop in!

Adding Ethnic Traditions

Show respect for your ancestors and your families—and get in touch with your cultures, too—by incorporating ethnic traditions. Blend rituals from both your backgrounds, making your wedding a mélange of customs. And keep in mind that there's no rule that says you have to stick to your own heritage. If you love the sentiment or meaning behind another culture's custom, add it to the brew.

African American broom jumping. This custom dates back to nineteenth-century slave weddings in the United States. Slaves' marriages weren't legally binding—even if a minister conducted the ceremony—so many couples jumped over a broom together to symbolize their entrance into married life. (A broom represents the home in certain parts of Africa.) Some believed that whoever jumped higher or cleared the handle first would rule the roost!

**More African American
Wedding Advice**

The best African American wedding-planning book is *Jumping the Broom: The African American Wedding Planner,* by Harriette Cole (Henry Holt, 1995).

Chinese red. In China, red is the color of luck and joy. Chinese and Chinese American couples often incorporate red into their wedding decor with red candles, favors, tablecloths, napkins. Guests present the couple with money or jewelry in red envelopes. Brides may change into several dresses throughout the ceremony and reception, the last one usually red. You might insert a sheet of red tissue paper into your invitations, choose red wedding flowers, walk down a red aisle runner, and/or tie red ribbons around your favors. Check out local Asian stores for Chinese party decorations or a red silk dress. Or wear white but have the bridesmaids wear red. The groom and groomsmen might wear red cummerbunds and ties.

You don't have to wear red to incorporate the Chinese tradition of changing gowns into your wedding. Some brides change from a white Western-style dress for the ceremony into a less-restrictive gown (such as a bone-colored slip dress) for the reception.

**More Asian
Wedding Advice**

An excellent book: *Wild Geese and Tea: An Asian-American Wedding Planner,* by Shu Shu Costa (Riverhead Books, 1997).

Chinese tea ceremony. Chinese couples traditionally honor their ancestors with a tea ceremony—the couple kneels before older relatives and family friends and offers a cup of tea as a gesture of respect. Each honoree hands the couple an envelope of money or gold jewelry, then gives the chair to the next relative in line. You can follow the tradition or honor your ancestors in your own way: Dance to your grandparents' first-dance wedding song, or give thanks to your parents or other relatives and toast them with tea.

English wedding walk. In English villages, the bride and her wedding party traditionally walk together from her home to the church, led by a young girl throwing flower blossoms in their path. The wedding walk is perfect if your celebration will be in your small, close-knit hometown where you can parade down Main Street, or if you're having your ceremony in the same site as your reception. Consider having the entire wedding party and all of your guests join the procession to the party area after you exchange your vows.

Indian henna. Having your hands and feet painted with henna—a popular prewedding ritual in India, Pakistan, and many Muslim countries (including some in Africa)—originated as a way to replace or augment the precious dynastic jewelry worn by fabulously rich Muslim brides. Typically, a hired henna professional visits the bride about a week before the wedding to draw elaborate, flowery scrolls on her hands and feet. Thicker than the henna used to dye hair auburn, hand and foot henna stains the skin for a couple of weeks. Henna has become a fashion accessory in the hipper enclaves of some large urban areas.

Hire a professional to decorate you, or ask one of your friends to do it. (Choose carefully; there's no washing off a wobbly henna job.) Look through a few photo books for design inspiration. Or call an Indian or Pakistani cultural center for a recommendation.

Irish toasts. Toasting is an art in Ireland. Here are some traditional toasts:

- "May your hearts be as warm as your hearthstone."
- "May God sleep on your pillow."
- "May you be poor in misfortune, rich in blessings."
- "May you know nothing but happiness from this day forward."
- "A generation of children on the children of your children."
- "If you're lucky enough to be Irish, you're lucky enough."

An Irish Ring Thing

Named after a fishing village in western Ireland, the Claddagh ring is worn with the crowns facing inward, toward the wrist, upon betrothal, and outward, toward the nails, to symbolize marriage.

At the end of the reception, the wedding party may gather around the bride and groom; everyone is poured a glass of mead. The newlyweds recite an Irish toast: "Friends and relatives, so fond and dear, 'tis our greatest pleasure to have you here. When many years this day has passed, fondest memories will always last. So we drink a cup of Irish mead and ask God's blessing in your hour of need." The guests respond: "On this special day, our wish to you, the goodness of the old, the best of the new. God bless you both who drink this mead, may it always fill your every need."

Japanese sake ritual. Japanese weddings include a sake-sharing tradition, popularly called *san-san-kudos* (*san* means "three," *ku* means "to deliver," and *do* means "nine.") Using three flat sake cups stacked on top of one another, the bride and groom take three sips each from the cups. Then their parents also take sips (for a total of nine), cementing the bond between the families. You can incorporate a sake-sharing ritual into your ceremony or do it at the reception. Ask your guests to join in after the last sip; you might give them sake cups as favors.

Latin American sponsors. In Latin American countries, a group of sponsors (usually married couples who are friends of the couple's parents) sometimes help host the wedding. Each couple (or person—there's no rule against a supportive single) hosts a different part of the celebration. If your parents have a tight group of close friends, include them in the wedding preparations. Let each sponsor choose which part to be involved in—the flowers, the food, the alcohol, the music, and so on. Thank them officially in your ceremony program.

If you're uncomfortable with financial help, include these special people in your wedding planning to create a sense of community *without* asking for money. Have sponsors to help organize or oversee various elements rather than foot the bills for them. Your aunt's a great cook? Ask her to help with the menu. Your uncle's a music buff? Ask him to listen to bands and narrow them down. Seat all the sponsors in places of honor at the ceremony and reception.

**Kids Will Go
Crazy For . . .**

In Mexico, a candy-filled piñata can be part of a wedding. Guests take turns whacking the papier-mâché creation until it bursts open and spills onto the floor. This is a great after-dinner tradition to incorporate if you'll have lots of child guests.

Native American corn. Navajos use that crop of all crops, maize (that's corn to you), to symbolize the marriage union. Families combine yellow corn (ground by the bride's family) and white corn (ground by the groom's side) in a pudding, which is brought to the reception. The couple tastes the pudding together, the first of many married meals.

You can tap into your Native American heritage by adapting the grind-and-taste ritual to suit your style. Serve a two-tone pudding (corn or otherwise) as a special dessert. Or offer marbled bread along with the wedding feast. If your mother makes a special dessert—such as pineapple pudding—and your honey's father is known for his chocolate cake, consider serving both. Let your guests in on the tradition by including a line about the special dish on a printed menu.

Norwegian night life. Nomadic Norwegian tribes traditionally held their weddings late at night. For your own midnight wedding, light the room with countless votives and candlesticks. Bridesmaids can carry candles instead of bouquets. Or set them on stands illuminating the aisle. Start your all-night wedding no earlier than 8:00 P.M. Have cocktails, dinner, dancing, and a breakfast buffet in the wee hours. Make sure to brew plenty of coffee! Serve Norwegian food—salmon, herring, vodka to drink. Use upturned Viking-style helmets full of flowers as centerpieces.

More Intriguing Cultural Traditions

More wedding traditions we're intrigued with:

For Polish village weddings, brides traditionally wore a crown or head wreath of rosemary woven by their friends. (Rosemary symbolizes remembrance.)

In Duth tradition, a pine tree is planted outside the newlyweds' home as a symbol of fertility and luck.

Czech newlyweds are showered with peas—not rice—after the ceremony.

A Japanese groom crushes a raw egg with his bare foot during the wedding ceremony. One meaning: to symbolize the delicacy of the marriage bond.

German brides carry salt and bread on their wedding day to symbolize wealth and good fortune.

Egyptian women pinch the bride for good luck.

Russian road trip. In Russia, newlyweds take a tour of their hometown's sites—snapping photos of themselves at various locations—before heading off on the honeymoon. You, too, can spend an afternoon of local appreciation before catching that flight to Bali. By taking stock of your hometown's own offerings, you're establishing a pattern of valuing what you already have.

Scottish fling. In Scotland, the reception includes a Highland Fling dance, a high-spirited performance with lots of kicking. Ask your Scottish uncle to give you a tutorial, or hire professional Scottish dancers—kilts and all—to perform during your reception.

Free-Style Weddings

You want a wedding that takes the ceremony/reception approach and puts it in the spin cycle? How about something that challenges your expectations? Confounds your assumptions? Takes you places you've never gone before (literally)? You can get married away (and/or alone), have multiple receptions, take your guests hiking up a mountainside, or let 'em in on the fact that there's a wedding going on only when it's about to start. Here's how to go free-style.

Get Married Away: The Destination Wedding

You've always dreamed of being married next to the ocean—unfortunately, you live in landlocked Iowa. If you can't bring the water to the wedding, bring the wedding to the water. Make it a destination wedding—a wedding and honeymoon in one that doubles as a vacation for everyone who attends. And it doesn't have to be in a tropical locale (although that tends to be the destination type of choice for couples who wed away); you can go for a Scottish or Spanish castle, a romantic city in Italy or France, the mountains of Tibet, wherever your hearts take you.

Educate Your Audience

Explain cultural traditions you include in your ceremony in the program; at the reception, announce the meanings of any rituals that are performed, or put little cards on the tables that note the symbolism.

International Info

To find info on the country you're interested in getting married in, check out the Tourism Offices Worldwide Directory at www.towd.com.

Destination Wedding Paperwork

You'll probably do less planning for a wedding away, but there might be a few more documents to deal with:

- **If you're marrying in the United States,** call the county marriage license department for the town in which you'll have the ceremony; ask for explicit guidelines regarding birth certificates, health tests, and proof of divorce (if applicable).
- **If marrying overseas,** ask the country's U.S. embassy or tourism bureau about residency requirements, documentation, medical tests, paperwork processing time, proof of divorce, witnesses, and the requirements for a religious ceremony vs. a civil ceremony.

Call potential honeymoon hotels for information about getting married there, too. Some resorts (and just about all Caribbean all-inclusives) have on-site coordinators who can do most of the wedding planning for you, including lining up an officiant, hiring a photographer, ordering a cake, and briefing you about the marriage requirements in the resort city or country. (Because destination weddings have become so popular, many countries have shortened residency stays before weddings and nixed at least *some* complicated rules.) Ask for pictures of previous weddings held at the resort to get an idea of what yours would be like. If you're considering a country and not a specific resort, call its tourism office and/or U.S. consulate or embassy for more details.

See "Destination Wedding Requirements" on The Knot (www.theknot.com) for the rules in some of the most popular wedding-away countries.

SOSSIE AND BILL
January 22, Rosarito Beach, Mexico

SOSSIE AND BILL FELT that the best way to celebrate what they felt for each other was to create a meaningful experience for their nearest and dearest. "We had fifteen of our closest friends, whom we called the Posse, arrive on a Thursday. For the next three days we all hung out. It was like camp," Sossie says. Well, camp in Rosarito Beach, Mexico, at a beautiful hotel built on fifty-foot cliffs at the edge of the ocean.

Because many of the couple's pals are artists and other creative types, Bill and Sossie planned a weekend of creativity: They watched films that friends had made and did a reading of a play one friend had written. On Saturday, the rest of the sixty guests arrived for the ceremony. As a prelude, two actor friends performed a scene from *Romeo and Juliet.* The ceremony was based in Judaism, which was important to Sossie, but the readings and vows were largely nondenominational. "In keeping with a Jewish tradition that any learned person can officiate at a marriage," Bill says, "a friend of ours married us, which was really special." Their filmmaker friend made them "the most amazing wedding video ever done," and a photographer friend took the photos.

"We were ambitious," says Bill. "When you're planning a wedding, families go crazy and everyone will try to talk you out of everything you want to do, but you have to do it for yourself. We ended up with the most wonderful wedding."

A destination wedding often is simpler to plan and manage than a wedding at home (less hands-on work). It also can be a lot cheaper—the two of you could fly to the Caribbean, get married, and have a weeklong honeymoon for $2,000 to $3,000 (including lodging, meals, and airfare). The downside of the destination route? Far fewer guests will be able to take the time (and spend the money) to fly to Jamaica to meet you. You may want to have a more casual party to celebrate with them when you return. And be sure to take plenty of pictures to show everyone back home.

Days and Days of Fun: The Wedding Weekend

Your mom lives in San Francisco, your dad in Boston. Your sweetie's parents are in Tulsa, you two live in Houston, and other friends and family are scattered all over the country. You're the perfect candidates for a weekend wedding—a three-day affair that'll make everyone glad they used their frequent-flier miles to come see you get hitched.

A weekend wedding requires a bit of "cruise directing" on your part; you'll want to have some preplanned activities set up. Definitely include a dinner for out-of-town guests the night before the wedding (or just invite everyone to the rehearsal dinner) as well as a pre- or postwedding brunch, as casual or formal as you like. You also might schedule a barbecue, picnic, or another organized activity, such as a round of golf or museum trip during the several days before the ceremony. For free-time activities, provide your guests with the information they'll need, whether it's a list of events from the hotel concierge, tourist brochures, or a "hot sheet" of fun activities you write yourselves. You don't have to stay at every event the entire time— ask close friends and family to oversee things, and be sure to make an appearance at everything.

Party On (and On): The Progressive Wedding

An alternative to the wedding weekend is the progressive wedding—several parties in various cities where far-flung friends and relatives reside. Hold your first ceremony and reception in your current hometown (or the town where one or both of you grew up). Then, for example, travel to Minneapolis—the groom's mother's home—and have a second reception for relatives and friends who live there. Bring along photos of the ceremony, favors from your current hometown, and a mini-version of the original wedding cake.

Then head to Milwaukee (where your honey went to college), and on to Dallas for a party hosted by your parents. Then it's off to San Francisco (where you went to college). You get the idea. Given the complexity of your family/social/career lives, this wedding might keep you busy for the next year. To smooth your path, work with a travel agent to create the best itinerary or try to work out a package deal. As with a one-stop wedding, plan ahead! Sure, you have less to do in each place, but there're more places to do it.

Why Do It Elsewhere?

"Destination weddings are ideal for couples who are adventurous, flexible, and want to have the majority of their wedding worries handled by a coordinator. You can still make many special requests for personal touches to your ceremony or reception."

—**Adam Sandow, president of _Honeymoon_ magazine**

Don't Be Demanding

Make weekend wedding activities optional—you don't want to force everyone to climb aboard a tour bus every day. Some guests may prefer to just hang out around the hotel pool and catch up.

Action! The Extreme Wedding

You need action; you crave excitement. Your lives are intense, and you want your wedding to measure up. For an active twist on the destination wedding, make it a high-adventure affair. Have your ceremony on a mountaintop and ask select guests to don hiking shoes to make the trip up with you. Say your vows in midair—while skydiving—with your most daring guests floating with you (and the rest waiting safely on the ground).

If you're set on a specific locale (a cliff, raging rapids, a bridge off which to bungee-jump), call the tourism office or chamber of commerce in that area to see how you can make your wedding dream come true. If you'd like an active wedding that's not *too* over the top, call companies that offer various degrees of adventure travel. Check with several to see where they can take you and how they'll get you all there, plus what arrangements they can make for the ceremony and accommodations. (Just how rustic are those rooms?) Some good places to start with include Backroads (camping or hike-and-bike trips; 800–462–2848) and Butterfield & Robinson (bike tours throughout Europe and Canada; 800–678–1147).

Just Do It: Elopement

You can just picture it—the two of you racing out of town in a borrowed Mustang convertible, the wind whipping through your hair. You're eloping! You can elope far away—make it a destination wedding you don't tell anyone about (how utterly romantic!)—or head over to city hall, then meet family and friends at a restaurant to celebrate (or simply take yourselves out and tell everyone else later).

Some couples even get parental consent to wed this way. Here's how it works: Offer to elope, saving your parents the $20,000 they'd spend on a big wedding. They see the brilliance of your thinking, slip you a check for $10,000 as a gift, and act shocked, surprised, and hurt about your decision (to save face before their friends). You wed at the courthouse and use the $10,000 as a down payment on your dream house.

Before you go, there are a few details to check on. Every state has its own rules for the waiting period between when you apply for your marriage license and when you actually can wed. Call the courthouse to find out the local law. If you want to elope abroad, call your dream country's tourist office, consulate, or embassy for rules and legal requirements.

More Info for Elopers

Caribbean Tourism:
212–682–0435
Fiji Visitors Bureau:
310–568–1616
Hawaii Visitors Bureau:
800–353–5846
Jamaica Tourism:
800–233–4582
Las Vegas Tourism:
800–NEVADA–8
Mexico Tourism:
800–44–MEXICO
Puerto Rico Tourism:
800–223–6530
U.S. Virgin Islands Tourism:
800–372–USVI

Playing Up Your Passions

What passions, interests, or (healthy) obsessions really say who you are? What do you two do on weekends, during the evenings, whenever else you have some spare time? What do you love about your work? Would any of these things make a great party theme? You don't have to go all out to the point of kitsch—you might just choose to personalize a detail, such as favors or decorations. No matter what your passion is, chances are there's something about it that you can use to uniquely accent your big day. Here are our picks for a personal wedding, passion-style.

Going Green

Whether you're fervent activists or just Earth-loving nature buffs, infuse your wedding with your passion for the planet. Print your invitations and programs on recycled paper. Wear a secondhand dress and tux. Use flowering plants as centerpieces and a variety of live plants and trees as decorations. (They'll be easy to replant later.) Recycle all disposable cups, bottles, and paper items (or better yet, use real plates, flatware, and linen napkins). Ask guests to donate money to an eco-organization instead of buying you presents. Give tree seedlings or flower seed packets as favors. Escape on a bicycle built for two or in-line skates. Take an eco-tourism honeymoon.

Do a Good Deed

A great green idea: Donate any leftover reception food to a food bank or shelter; give flowers to a shelter or retirement house.

Mad for Movies

If you two have seen every movie ever made (most of them twice) and have your own parking space at Blockbuster, incorporate your love of film into your wedding. Do up your reception room like a movie set—hang huge lights from the ceiling, put director's chairs everywhere, and stack old film-reel canisters on the tables as centerpieces. Or rent an elegant, landmark theater for the event—guests can sit in movie seats to watch the ceremony. Run silent films on the screen throughout the reception. Old theaters often have great lobbies (for the receiving line) and large areas or even a stage in front of the screen (for dancing and/or dining).

Wedding Colors

Favorite colors can be reception themes all by themselves. If you love purple, you can incorporate various shades of it into your invitations, flowers, decorations, and (of course) bridesmaids' dresses. Likewise, a cherished bloom such as a daisy or tulip can inspire an entire wedding plan.

A Bibliophile Bash

Do you spend romantic Friday evenings together each with a book in your lap and Sunday mornings fighting over the *Book Review?* You're perfect candidates for a literary wedding. Have the invitations read like a story ("Once upon a time, two fabulously interesting people fell in love. . . ."), or steal some lines from a treasured book or poem you both adore. Ask a loved one to read some of your favorite prose or verse during the ceremony. Have the wedding in a grand library hall or a used bookstore. Give favorite paperbacks or funky vintage bookmarks as favors. Take a literary honeymoon—head to the site of your favorite novel or visit the stomping grounds of your favorite author—Jane Austen's England, a Mississippi River cruise à la Mark Twain.

Old-Fashioned Romantics: Period Weddings

If you long for a bygone era, wrap your wedding around your favorite time. Research will be fun (and probably right up your alley). Rent your favorite period films from the era and hole yourselves up for a long weekend of armchair time travel. Pay attention to the clothes—cut, color, fabric, frills, gloves, hats, scarves, and jewelry—as well as to the music and decor. If you're mad for all things medieval, for example, hold your wedding in a Tudor-style mansion, English cottage, or period castle. Or rent the special-events pavilion at a Renaissance fair or medieval joust. Send invitations done in calligraphy on heavy parchment paper and tied with ribbon. Toast with pewter goblets. If you're more of a Gothic couple,

Going Victorian

Roses, lace, harpsichord music—few historical periods are as romantic as the Victorian era (1837–1901), or as popular for period weddings.

Invites: Go formal, the norm in the Victorian era. Use script-style engraved letters on pure white or ivory paper. Slip dried rose petals into your envelopes.

Where: Rent a Victorian-style inn, a ballroom done in Victorian colors (pinks, golds, and greens), an elegant room in a history museum, a botanical garden, or a nineteenth-century estate. Or have your wedding at your parents' home, a popular choice in the Victorian era.

Style: Decorate with roses, the quintessential Victorian (and wedding!) bloom. Make liberal use of candles, flowers, and old black-and-white family portraits in silver frames.

Food: The tea reception is classic Victorian.

Music: Hire a string quartet for the ceremony and/or cocktail hour. Go with harps, harpsichords, or chamber music for the reception. Learn (and then teach guests) a popular Victorian dance, such as a reel, waltz, or quadrille.

Favors: Give engraved lockets, ivory hair combs, or soft kid gloves to bridesmaids; chocolate truffles, ornate silver frames, romantic fans, or brocade-covered boxes to guests.

Resources:

- The Victorian Papers catalog is a great resource not only for invitations but for all things Victorian; call 800–800–6647.
- The Victorian Society in America, 219 South Sixth Street, Philadelphia, PA 19106; 215–627–4252.
- The Victorian Yellow Pages, full of more than 200 Victoriana sources; send $12 plus $3 shipping to: Teapot Press, P.O. Box 2048, Scotia, NY 12302.

take your cue from the *darkest* part of the Middle Ages and have a midnight gala in a castle illuminated with dozens of flickering candles. Have a fortune teller on hand.

Too dreary for you? Maybe you'd prefer an elegant Civil War–era lawn party. The bride can dress the part with a huge hoop skirt; the groom can don linen tails. Hold the wedding outside in the spring or summer, under a huge old magnolia tree. If you live in the South, take advantage of all those beautiful, historic antebellum mansions and rent one for your reception.

Period Wedding Wear

Wondering what to wear for your period wedding? Check out *What People Wore: 1800 Illustrations from Ancient Times to the Early Twentieth Century,* by Douglas Gorsline (Dover Publications, 1994). Your best bet for finding it: Check the library.

Travel Buffs

Perhaps it's not a time but a *place* that excites you. Whether you're frequent fliers or armchair enthusiasts, your wedding can reflect your love for a faraway locale. For example, if your heart is set on Spain, rent a Spanish-style hacienda or mission and hold the wedding in the central courtyard. Think wrought iron, balconies, stucco walls, and red-tile roofs. (If you live in the Southwest or California, you should have no problem finding the perfect locale.) Serve tapas (appetizer-size dishes) during cocktails and paella for the main meal. Hire Spanish classical guitar musicians for the ceremony and a flamenco performance for the reception. For favors, give Picasso-print notecards.

Career Couple

Maybe you live for the thrill of going to the office (or recording studio, or theater, or court-room, or trading floor). If work is your passion, enhance your wedding with it. You're stock-brokers? Name the reception tables after hot commodities. If you're journalists, have your videographer and a reporter friend "interview" guests during the reception, about how they

CATARINA AND PATRICK

October 15, New York City

PATRICK AND CATARINA ARE both designers—she an architect, he a graphic designer—so there was no question that there would be much attention to style and detail when it came to their wedding. "I'm an aesthetic control freak," Catarina laughs. "The idea of black-tie appealed to me, be-cause there was at least some control over how everything would look. Also, we de-cided that if we were doing the wedding in New York, we should do it in New York style." In keeping with that theory, all of the photographs were shot in black and white.

Catarina knew someone who was a member of the city's elegant Lotos Club who agreed to sponsor the couple so they could have their wedding at the landmark mansion. Every element of the event was in keeping with the simple elegance of the venue. Catarina's gown and her sisters' dresses were custom-made by a close friend from design school. The bridesmaids carried nosegays of cabbage roses; Catarina's bouquet was lilies of the valley, and Patrick wore one in his lapel. The cake was very simple, with just two unseparated tiers, and it was decorated with the same white cabbage roses that made up the cocktail-table centerpieces.

Catarina was a bit surprised that she didn't find it that difficult to plan her wedding. "I knew what I wanted, and I never had to hem and haw about anything," she says. "I just went in to everyone and told them what I envisioned."

met you, when they knew you were in love, any tips they have for marital bliss. Lawyers? Maybe your favorite judge would marry you two. If one of you is a teacher—or a doctor— be sure to put an apple at every place setting!

A Military Wedding

For a traditional military wedding, grooms wear the full ceremonial dress uniform, including gloves, hat, and bars and pins. Brides, you can go in uniform as well, *or* wear a wedding dress. You'll walk through an arc of swords or sabers (formed by an honor guard) on your way to the altar. You might have your reception on the grounds of the military academy you attended. At a seated dinner, military guests are shown to their seats in order of rank. Your unit head can give you more details.

Music Makes the Mood

One of the best ways to get a theme across is music. Use songs from your era of choice—be it 1970s, 1980s, Baroque, or Victorian—to set a reception mood.

Setting Your Budget

Budgeting Basics

Who's Paying and How?

Working with Wedding Professionals

Budget and Business

Enough fantasizing—on to the serious business of your wedding budget. We hate to admit it, but at the end of the day, dollars, not dreams, are the defining factor in what (and who) you'll have at your wedding. No budget, no matter how big, is ever big enough. Now that we've got that reality check out of the way, we can go on to tell you all you need to know to plan the perfect wedding—whatever the price tag.

Setting Your Budget

Before you buy anything—even that $5 garter—you've got to determine the dollar amount allotted for your big day. Where to begin? You have two options: (1) Figure out how much cash you (and/or your loving family) can spend, or (2) calculate how much the wedding you want will cost and then worry about where you'll get the bucks. For some perspective, the average American couple shells out $19,000 for their nuptials.

What Affects the Price Tag

Obviously, if you're planning on a formal candlelit dinner in the grand ballroom of that amazing hotel downtown, your budget is going to have to be much bigger than if you've sketched out a high-noon hoedown in your grandparents' backyard, catered by Dad. In general, several factors affect what you'll need to set aside:

Formality: The more formal the affair, the more expensive, because most ultra-formal weddings take place in the evening, and because you'll have to match the site, food, and musical entertainment to the overall upscale tone.

Go to Chapter 2
for help mapping
out scheduling
considerations.

To create your
own personalized
wedding budget,
go to The Knot's
Big-Day Budgeter
at
www.theknot.com.

Date and Time: Certain months and times of day tend to be pricier.

Guest List: The more people you invite, the more money you'll spend—there's a per-head cost for food and liquor.

Food: The financial burden for a full meal is greater than for hors d'oeuvres; dinner is usually more expensive than breakfast or lunch; seated service is pricier than a buffet.

Reception Site: The use of some locales will set you back more than others. Some—such as your aunt's verandah or a city park—can be had at no (or low) cost.

Location: Some cities and towns are just more expensive than others. New York, Chicago, and Los Angeles are the obvious culprits, but small towns also can be pricey if things like flowers, produce, and a DJ have to come from afar. Tourist towns can also up your wedding price tag, because of high demand.

How to Prioritize

If many of the wedding elements you're considering veer toward the amazingly expensive side of the scale, *don't* panic. It may require compromises, scheduling changes, or groveling for help from family and friends, but even with a limited budget you can probably approximate your ideal wedding.

Prioritizing is paramount. Throughout the budgeting process you will need to coolly and calmly chip away at extraneous details that you can do without in order to have what's of tantamount importance to you. If there's no question in your mind that your florist bill is going to be huge, given your penchant for dramatic and lush arrangements (and lots of 'em), maybe it's not that important to wear a designer dress—your mother's gown will be a beauty once those rhinestone butterflies come off. You say your hearts are set on a nighttime party, when costs tend to be higher? Perhaps you can scale back your expenses by opting for a DJ instead of a live band, food stations as opposed to tableside service, and a basic photography package instead of a paparazzi extravaganza. We'll get into more specific cost-cutting strategies later in the chapter.

Organization Is Key!

Keep all your budget and business paperwork in one place. Get yourself a large folder or binder where you can keep track of all contracts, estimates, phone notes, and receipts.

Who's Paying and How?

In the days of yore (okay, as recently as the 1980s), it was the bride's family who paid for the wedding. Today, reflecting our ever-more-egalitarian society and ever-rising wedding costs, the division of financial duties is incredibly fluid. Our favorite? The communal model of wedding financing: Each family gives to the best of its ability and all come together for their collective happiness. Before you nail down your budget and begin allocating dollar amounts for different wedding elements, you need to know who will be doling out the dough. Why does it matter? you ask. Because those who pay have the say. Here are the options and our advice.

Three's Company: You Two and All Your Parents Pay

Our favorite wedding budget model is the one-third approach, in which the bride's family, the groom's family, and the couple—yeah, *you*—each contribute. You're getting the best of both worlds. You're not flying solo (and thus possibly dipping into your nest egg or saying bye-bye to your Christmas vacation), but you're also not completely relinquishing financial control, which often means that you're ceding creative authority, too. The three-way split is also a surefire way to make both families feel like significant partners in your wedding preparations, paving the way for a love-filled bash and years of extended-family happiness.

There are two ways to work out this arrangement. You can approximate the total dollar amount you're going to need and then split it three ways, or you can designate specific things that each party will pay for, based on how much they can contribute: your parents, rehearsal dinner, flowers, and music; your honey's parents, food, drink, and site fees; you guys, attire and photography.

However you decide to swing it, splitting things three ways is going to require lots of communication and teamwork. Asking your parents for cash and making sure everyone is happy with the budgetary decisions you make requires the grace of a ballerina, the communication skills of a preacher, and the diplomacy of, well, a diplomat. In all your interactions with your loved ones, remember these cardinal rules:

Be Informed: Your folks will feel a lot more comfortable about ponying up the cash if they know you're taking the budget seriously. Before you approach them about making a contribution, consult friends and relatives whose wedding styles were similar to the affair you're planning about *their* total budget. If you have time, get some definite price quotes from key vendors such as caterers, florists, and musicians. That way everyone involved will have a more realistic idea of the financial requirements—and you won't have to deal with the stress of dropping last-minute bombshells. ("Mom, Dad, the caterer's bill was $4,000 more than we thought it would be—sorry!")

Be Direct: Your parents will respect you more and feel less manipulated if you just tell them straight up how much money you think you're going to need from them as opposed to taking the "Well, I guess we'll never have the wedding of our dreams (sigh)" approach. Together, hammer out how close to your ideal budget you can get and then powwow on ways to cut your costs.

Be Sensitive: If your mother and stepfather have recently emptied their savings account to pay for an emergency heart operation, it's not such a good idea to ask them to make a major contribution. Likewise if your honey's parents are struggling financially right now. Instead, make them feel like an integral part of your wedding plans by asking if they're interested in helping with organizational tasks (picking up out-of-town guests, reading over vendor contracts), advice (coming along to the baker's, hosting an appetizer-tasting party), or contributing special skills (doing the floral arrangements themselves, sewing a veil, or baking the cake). Remember, time is money—and their contributions probably will cut your costs nicely.

Be Good Listeners: You can't just hit your parents up for money and run. Since they

Different Strokes?

If you foresee serious conflicts because of differing tastes, ask your folks to cover specific costs—flowers and transportation, say—as opposed to having them contribute to a general wedding pot. This way you'll be able to gracefully define what details they deserve input on.

How to Ask for $$$

Q: We're several months into planning our wedding and my future in-laws have not yet offered to make any contribution financially (or otherwise). I asked my fiancé to speak with them, but he seems very reluctant to do so. What can I do? They're nice people—I don't want to offend them. But we could use their help.

A: The way you interact with your brand-new family members while planning your wedding can really set the tone for how you'll get along once you're married, so it makes sense to be savvy and sensitive. First off, it's essential that you two talk honestly about the situation. Find out why your soon-to-be is hesitant about approaching his parents. If he knows they're broke, figure out some nonmonetary aid they can give you (calling vendors for prices, reserving hotel rooms, addressing and mailing invitations). If he's plain old nervous about their reaction, come up with a good strategy together. (If it's the bride's family who hasn't offered financial help, this same advice applies—we're not trying to make it family-specific. These days, any combination of financial contributions is possible, and there's no "right" way for it to work.)

Usually, it's best for your honey to approach his parents alone so they feel comfortable discussing a touchy issue. "Rehearse" the conversation with him to boost his confidence level, finding a light-but-direct opening line, such as "You know, Mom and Dad, Eva and I were talking about how great it would be if you could help us pay for the wedding so we can invite everyone on both our lists and not have to cut people that are important to you and us." If your honey is more comfortable approaching his folks hand in hand with you, as a team—oblige him. However you handle this anxiety-laden situation, make sure your expectations aren't *too* high; there are many good reasons why his parents may not be able to help out (college bills, approaching retirement, etc.). Then again, you might be pleasantly surprised with the results of your directness and initiative.

Who Pays for What?

In the old days, the bride's family paid for: invitations; announcements; wedding consultant; gown and accoutrements; the reception, including site, food, flowers, photographs, videographer, and music; transportation for the wedding party.

The groom's family paid for: marriage license; officiant; bride's bouquet; boutonnieres; the rehearsal dinner; the honeymoon.

are making a financial sacrifice for this event, it's important that you make them feel appreciated. Solicit their advice on major decisions, such as where to have your ceremony and which caterer to use. Hear out any concerns they may have (the florist's bill is too high, the venue you've chosen is unrealistic cost-wise). You don't always have to go with their recommendations, but we guarantee they will be a lot happier—and thus more helpful—if you make them feel like business partners and not faceless investors.

Flying Solo: Paying for It Yourselves

Legions of modern couples are opting to pay for their weddings themselves. Their motivations are diverse. Some simply don't have families able (or around) to help out; others are making lots more money than their parents; still others are control freaks who simply don't want anyone else's input.

The upside of this option is that you're going to be totally free to focus on those wedding elements that are most important to you and to do things *exactly* the way you want 'em. Who can argue with that?

You're probably wondering how you're going to be able to get the money you need before the curtain goes up. Good question. Of course, there is no pat answer, but we can offer you several pearls of wisdom.

Start Saving Early: The sooner you begin putting money away, the more you'll have come wedding day. As soon as your feet hit the ground after your engagement, set up a realistic savings plan. It's a good idea to set aside between 10 and 20 percent of every paycheck you get from now until the big day for wedding expenses, although your individual circumstances may make this difficult. Whatever your monthly savings target, remember that little cost-cutting tactics like brown-bagging lunch, snuggling in front of the VCR, entertaining friends at home, and postponing major purchases until after the big day go a long way.

Open a Wedding Account: It's a good idea to establish a separate bank account for your wedding fund. By putting whatever money you can save in one place, you'll have a clearer idea of how much you have to spend. It also will spare you the added stress of having to transfer funds from your personal accounts whenever you need to write a major check.

Maximize Your Savings: Putting some of the money you already have in a bank certificate-of-deposit (CD) or short-term mutual fund is a great way to make the most of your money. You'll earn a lot more interest than you would if you left everything you had in a regular savings account.

Take the Do-It-Yourself Approach: Whenever possible, do wedding-related tasks yourselves to cut down on vendor costs. For example, be your own calligraphers, or buy the liquor yourselves. Ask (but don't expect) friends to help you accomplish certain tasks; have an invitation-preparing party or a favor-making fiesta.

Consider Hiring a Wedding Consultant: At first glance, this may seem like an *added* expense, but often a professional party planner can help you make the most of your budget—whatever it is.

Communicate and Compromise: Before you decide exactly how much money you'll be putting toward your bash, know what you are—and are not—willing to splurge on and ask your partner to speak her (or his) heart and mind. Find a middle road. For example, if your honey is willing to withdraw $10,000 from her mutual fund account to finance a gigantic rave with cage dancers, an all-night buffet, and an elaborate laser show, while you're adamant that the two of you purchase a house in less than five years, decide that each of you will contribute $2,000 of your savings toward a smaller (but just as wild) dance party at your favorite club. You don't want resentment to spoil this excellent adventure; make sure both of you are satisfied with the wedding budget you work out.

Be Realistic: You may be more in debt than your beloved is, which means the sum you can contribute is smaller; you can even things out by doing more of the time-consuming preparation tasks. Or perhaps you can't contribute *any* money, because you're in grad school or you've just quit your job. In this case, you'll probably have to scale back your wedding expenses considerably and do most of the wedding work on your own.

Your Savings Potential

My monthly income
x .20 = _____ (A1)

A1 x months of engagement
= _____ (B1)

My honey's monthly income
x .20 = _____ (A2)

A2 x months of engagement
= _____ (B2)

B1 + B2 = Total potential wedding budget

Go to Chapter 2 to see how a consultant can save you money and time.

When Your Parents Pay Your Way

If you are among the lucky few whose parents are footing the entire bill, you may have to deal with one potentially sleep-disturbing problem—those who pay for the wedding have a major say in the plans. Even if you trust your parents not to become wedding control freaks, it's important to set some ground rules early. Be frank with them about things you are absolutely not willing to budge on and areas where you're totally open to their input. Our bet is that they'll respect your deepest wishes. However, if your dad is adamant about his beer-and-bingo wedding vision, you're going to have to bring him around. Talk to your other parent and get him or her on your side; chances are he or she knows which strings to pull better than you do.

Even if they say they'll write you one big check, it's still a good idea to sit down with your parents and bang out the total budget number together. Come up with a realistic spending cap now, so you won't be put in the uncomfortable situation of having to ask for another check later.

Be Thankful

Never, ever, ever *expect* your parents to pay for your wedding. Accept their financial help graciously. Contrary to popular belief, it's not a birthright.

Budgeting Basics

Now that you know how much money you have to work with and where it's all coming from, it's time to figure out how you're going to spend it. You've got to break the big number down, allocating each part of your wedding budget for items such as food, flowers, and clothes. This means considering things like whether you want imported orchids in your bouquet, color photographs or black and white, and how much each option will set you back. Yep, this is the tough part. Don't panic. Start by mapping out all the possible elements you may wish to include in your nuptials. Some—like the officiant's fee and refreshments—are mandatory; others—like a wedding video, limo, or string quartet for the ceremony—are optional.

Go to Appendix A and use our handy worksheet, "Your Big-Day Budget."

Breaking It Down

Your actual wedding ceremony will be a very small part of your total cost. Assume that about 50 percent of your total will go toward your reception, including the cost of your venue, food and drink, and service. Even if you're having a home-cooked backyard brunch, chances are that the cost of the ingredients, renting chairs and place settings, and hiring servers still will eat up half your budget. You're also likely to spend more on your reception flowers, decorations, and music than on those for your ceremony.

Before you spend a dime on anything, create a budget breakdown that you can stick to. (We will spend 40 percent of our budget—or $2,000—on food; 7 percent of our total on flowers.) These are general guidelines; every couple's priorities are different.

Food: About 40 percent of your budget will go toward food (hors d'oeuvres and meal), beverages, the cake, and service.

Reception Venue: About 10 percent will go toward the reception-site rental plus any other rentals (chairs, tables, dinnerware, tent).

HEATHER AND GREG
January 3, North Caldwell, New Jersey

THE BRIDE'S FAMILY spared no expense for Heather and Greg's exquisite wedding. The ceremony was held in Notre Dame Church in North Caldwell, New Jersey; the reception site was the Pleasantdale Chateau. The wedding was elaborate, as were the extras. For example, all out-of-town guests who did not attend the rehearsal dinner were given Broadway show tickets, plus transportation into New York City for the evening.

Number of guests: 200

Total Budget: $80,000+

Reception (food only): $33,000 (41%)

Fashion (bride's dress): $5,000 (6%)

Photography: $5,000 (6%)

Flowers: $4,000 (5%)

Music (reception only): $7,500 (9%)

Invitations: $3,500 (4%)

Transportation: $2,000 (2%)

Attire: About 11 percent will go toward the bride's dress, head-piece/veil, hair/makeup, shoes, and lingerie, groom's attire, and going-away garb for two.

Flowers: About 8 percent will be needed to cover the bride's bouquet, bridesmaids' bouquets, boutonnieres, corsages, ceremony and reception arrangements. (If you're doing a floral headpiece, you can steal from your attire budget.)

Photography/Videography: About 7 percent will go toward the labor costs for photographer and/or videographer, plus the cost of the photography/videography package(s).

Music: About 7 percent will go toward ceremony music (vocalists, string quartet, organist, etc.) and reception music (band or DJ).

Stationery: About 3 percent will go toward invitations, announcements, and thank-you notes.

Gifts: About 3 percent will go toward attendants' gifts, favors.

Let Us Manage Your Money

The Knot's Big-Day Budgeter (www.theknot.com) is an amazing resource for to-be-weds, if we may say so ourselves. Plug in how much money you can spend and it suggests how much to allocate to each wedding feature, with specific advice on how to get the most for your money.

Wedding Rings: About 2 percent will go toward bands for both bride and groom.

Ceremony Costs: About 2 percent will go toward ceremony-location fee, officiant fee, and programs.

Transportation/Parking: About 1 percent will go toward bride and escort's ride to the ceremony, couple's ride to the reception, wedding-party transport and guest shuttle (both optional), and parking.

Miscellaneous: Try to set 6 to 10 percent aside for extra and unforeseen costs like marriage license, overtime costs, tips, taxes, and last minute purchases.

Note: If you choose to use a wedding consultant, his or her fee will cost you up to 10 percent of your total budget.

Asking for Help

While you're working on your budget, think of any shortcuts you might be able to take to get things done. Maybe Grandma would bake you a wedding cake or let you wear her heirloom veil. Perhaps your best friend is a DJ who would do your wedding at a discount. Be careful, though. Be polite and ask; don't declare or expect anything.

Protect Your Investment

Look into wedding insurance, offered by the Fireman's Fund Insurance Company (800–ENGAGED). You're sinking a lot of money into your wedding—protect your investment. Depending on the policy you opt for, you'll be covered for vendor screw-ups, a natural disaster–inspired cancellation, stolen gifts, guest injuries, even the bride or groom's absence due to last-minute military duty.

Working with Wedding Professionals

If you haven't figured it out yet, you'll soon discover that weddings are a big business, generating $32 billion a year. Those profits are the combined efforts of the wedding professionals whom you'll soon work with and be billed by. They're vendors: bakers, caterers, florists, photographers, banquet-hall managers, bridal retailers. You need them to make your wedding a reality. To get the most out of your relationships with the pros, follow the advice below.

The Ten Vendor Commandments

First Commandment: Vendors come good, bad, and ugly. Find good vendors through word-of-mouth (recently married friends are your best resource), an initial consultation with an in-the-know wedding consultant, and/or the advice of other (trusted) vendors.

Second Commandment: Shop around. Put aside ample time to call and visit a variety of vendors to get a sense of their price range, style, and expertise.

Third Commandment: Get *written* estimates from several vendors in each category (chosen because they suit your budget, your taste, and your timetable). Use these documents in future negotiations as a benchmark, adding or deleting elements to get the price you can afford.

Fourth Commandment: Ask for references of other couples who've used the vendor. But since no one's going to refer you to a couple who was unhappy with their service, also be sure to call your local better business bureau to see if any consumer complaints have been filed against any vendors you're considering.

Fifth Commandment: Schedule meetings with vendors you're interested in. Ask lots of little questions—hidden fees, size of staff available to you on the big day, how they'll make the site work for them—so you know exactly what you're going to get. (Each vendor chapter includes the specific questions you'll want to ask.)

Sixth Commandment: Haggle. Vendors want your business, especially during down months and on weekdays. Talk them down or get them to throw in extra perks. Vendors have needs, too—they'd rather make it work than see you walk away.

Seventh Commandment: Get a contract or written agreement—composed in easy-to-understand language—that spells out everything you've discussed. Have an expert eye (a lawyer friend, your detail-oriented aunt) look over the contract to make sure it's kosher and clear, and that nothing has been forgotten. (Each vendor chapter includes critical contract points.)

Tipping Tips

To tip or not to tip—that's another big question on your wedding day. You certainly don't want to stiff the people who are working to make your wedding dreams come true, but how do you know who to slip a few extra bucks for their hard work? Here are some guidelines.

Designate someone to be in charge of tipping—the host of the event or the wedding consultant usually handles this job.

Talk to the hotel or club manager directly if you are unsure of the tipping policy. S/he can let you know how tips have been handled in the past and make suggestions.

The gratuity is often included in the bill, so read it carefully to avoid double-tipping.

Remember, no one should *expect* tips; they're a bonus for a job well done.

Plan ahead. Have tips ready in sealed envelopes. Most likely you will want to go ahead and tip everyone who did a great job for you, but you won't want to have to think too hard when the time comes. (You'll be too busy kissing guests good-bye.)

At the same time, keep in mind that tips aren't doled out *automatically*. Most of these pros are providing a service for a previously determined fee. They've got to do their job first before you give 'em a penny extra. If you got what you paid for, offer a tip.

Here are guidelines for what to tip the people who make the reception run smoothly:

Maitre d'hotel: 15–20 percent of the reception bill.
Club manager/hotel banquet manager: 15–20 percent of the reception bill (less if there is a maitre d').
Wait staff: At least $20 each (maitre d' will distribute the tips for you).
Bartenders: 10 percent of the total liquor bill.
Powder room and coatroom attendants: At least 50¢–$1 per guest.
Parking attendants: At least 50¢–$1 per car, or arrange a gratuity with the hotel or club management.
Limousine: 15–20 percent of the limo bill.
Delivery-truck drivers for florist, baker, etc.: At least $5–$10 each.
DJ, musicians: $20–$25 each.

Eighth Commandment: Sign the contract only when you're completely comfortable with it. Keep two copies signed and dated by you and the vendor so it will be legally binding.

Ninth Commandment: Pay necessary deposits; always get a receipt.

Tenth Commandment: Your vendor is there to serve you. Call him/her periodically during the preparation period to make sure things are on schedule and that no details slip through the cracks. Never hesitate to speak your mind (as long as you're not simply being a paranoid maniac).

Crucial Contract Points

Each and every contract you draw up with a vendor should include these items. Don't sign until they are all in there.

**Credit Cards
to the Rescue**

Pay all deposits with your credit cards. That way you'll have the law on your side if the vendor doesn't deliver on his/her promises; credit card companies are legally required to investigate any claim that a consumer has been wrongfully charged, and *they'll* get the vendor to cough up the dough if they find in your favor.

- The date of the wedding.
- The length of service: exact start and finish time, including setup and breakdown periods.
- An hourly overtime rate. (Make sure the vendor will be available for overtime; you don't want wrap-up work interrupting the party if it's still in full swing.)
- Details, details: a list of *everything* the vendor will be supplying, down to the minutest of minutiae.
- Exact prices, including tax. (A detailed list of gratuities is optional.)
- A staff dress code that's appropriate for your wedding's formality.
- Cancellation/refund policy.
- Contact numbers where you and the vendor can reach each other easily.
- Rental returns, if applicable. (Make sure it's clear when the vendor will deliver equipment and when you need to give it back.)

Some Smart Cost-Cutting Ideas

We've been to a million-and-one weddings, and we know all the tricks to trim your wedding bill. If you can afford everything you want, just the way you want it, congratulations! But if you need to lower your numbers, check these suggestions out.

- Start shopping for everything as early as possible, so you can hunt for bargains and avoid feeling pressured into buying the first things you see.
- Pay for everything on a credit card that gets mileage. You may earn your way around the world (or at least, depending on your budget, to your honeymoon destination).
- Avoid Saturday Night Fever. You'll be able to slash spending if you have a Friday, Sunday, or daytime wedding.

- Fewer people get married in the winter (December is an exception), so you'll generally get better deals during those months.
- Wear your mom's (or grandma's) dress. Even with the cost of alterations, you'll save a bundle.
- Or find a sample dress that fits, dry clean it—and voilà!
- Hire the regular musicians at your church or synagogue to play during the ceremony instead of bringing in outsiders.

LISA AND SCOTT
April 8, West Hills, California

LISA AND SCOTT'S spring garden wedding was a study in ingenuity. The ceremony and reception were at Orcutt Ranch, a publicly owned park outside of Los Angeles with a Spanish mission-style house on the premises. Everybody pitched in money, expertise, or time to assure that Lisa and Scott pulled off their dream wedding.

Lisa wore her mother's dress (made by her grandmother), and her great-aunt made her veil. A luncheon buffet was served—*sans* alcohol. A friend of the bride who owns a floral-arranging company did the flowers as a wedding gift. There was no dancing during the reception, and so no band or DJ expense. Photography was the couple's priority; they chose a photographer recommended by newlywed friends and were so happy with the results that they sprang for a very expensive package. The wedding was videotaped with the best man's father's camcorder.

The most ingenious money-saver was the groom's doing: Scott, a graphic designer, designed the invitations. The paper and envelopes were company overflow, which otherwise would have been thrown out. A printer who frequently did work for Scott's company printed them along with another job. The only expense was postage!

Number of guests: 120

Total budget: $7,252

Reception: venue/food/cake: $3,530 (49%)

Fashion: shoes/accessories/groom's attire: $196 (2.5%)

Photography: $2,900 (40%)

Flowers: $200 (3%)

Music: $300 (4%)

Invitations: $126 (1.5%)

- Buffets and pasta bars are generally less expensive than seated meals; cocktails or dessert are even cheaper.
- Mexican, Indian, or Chinese food is often cheaper per head than more traditional wedding fare.
- A good cake is dessert enough—you don't need pastries and ice cream, too. (Maybe just some fresh fruit for the hard-core health buffs.)
- Serve wine, beer, and soda—no hard liquor.
- For all of your refreshment purchases (food *and* liquor), use house brands.
- Home-grown flowers and produce invariably will be cheaper than exotica.
- Use greenery like vines to fill out bouquets and pew decorations; use stunning potted plants with itty-bitty lights as centerpieces.
- Hire a young photographer, videographer, vocalist, or graphic designer recommended by a good local academy or university.
- Do you really need a video *and* pictures? Photos probably are going to be more memorable in the long run. Have a techno-guest videotape the festivities.
- If you do get a video, say no to "extras" such as sound effects and artsy editing.
- DJs are low budget (way less than a band). CDs are no budget. Or ask friends to make mix tapes with their favorite dance tunes.
- Rather than renting a limo, ask a friend or neighbor to donate a ride in her snazzy car (as a wedding present).

Using the ancient arts of smart planning, compromise, resourcefulness, and taking good advice from those in the know (us), you *will* come up with a wedding budget. We promise. Then you'll be ready to really get down to wedding business.

Attendants and Guests

From honor attendant to flower child, you have plenty of wedding roles to fill. This is good news: There's a place for all your favorite folks—best friends, childhood buddies, siblings, other relatives, a mentor, coach, even your dog. The one guideline? Ask the people you love the most to be part of your wedding. Not everyone has to stand at the altar; there are tons of ways to include everyone you want to. And don't forget that your guests are a big part of your big day, too—make sure they feel that way.

Attendants and Their Roles

While it's an honor for your attendants to be asked, it's also an honor for you that they accept! Keep in mind that your wedding party is agreeing to spend their hard-earned money and donate their hard-pressed time. Give them the consideration and kindness they're due. Keep them informed about all your plans and their roles in them, show them a good time, and make sure they know how much you appreciate them. Before you to pop the attendant question, check out our rundown of attendant duties so you'll be able to let everyone know what to expect.

The Honor Attendant

The maid or matron (a married woman) of honor is the bride's center—the person she feels closest to and wants by her side throughout the wedding preparations and at the altar. Traditionally your sister or best friend (though

**Be Clear and
Be Kind**

Don't assume the maid of honor knows what to do. Fill her in on exactly what tasks you'd like her to handle. And don't forget to thank her—early and often. This is voluntary service, not a full-time job.

you can choose your mom, daughter, or even your closest guy pal—a man of honor), the honor attendant is responsible for overseeing a variety of essential minutiae as well as providing unflagging moral support. Even if she can't perform all the physical tasks (because she lives in a faraway city or is doing med-school rotations), make sure you choose someone who will be available to help you ride the emotional roller coaster of getting married. Specifically, she should:

- Offer to help with aspects of wedding planning.
- Help shop for dresses (yours and the bridesmaids'); pay for her own dress.
- Spread the news of where you two are registered.
    - Host a bridal shower, tea, or luncheon (with help from maids or family).
    - Work with the best man to organize a couple's shower (if you're having one).
    - Assign someone to keep track of all those great gifts (enabling you to write personal thank-you notes).
    - Organize a bachelorette party (if you're having one).
    - Keep the bridesmaids abreast of all parties to attend and help host.
    - Make sure all bridesmaids get their dresses, go to fittings, and find the right jewelry.
    - Make sure all bridesmaids get to the rehearsal; coordinate transportation (and lodging, if necessary).
    - Attend the rehearsal dinner.
    - Make sure all maids get their hair and makeup done, get to the ceremony on time, and have correct flowers.
- Be with you before you walk down the aisle, assuring you that you look stunning; remind you to *breathe.*
- Walk down the aisle before you.
- Arrange your veil and train once you're at the altar; hold your bouquet during your vows.
- Hold the groom's ring until you're ready for it.
- Sign the marriage certificate as a witness.

Double Duty

Two best friends? Have twice the fun with two maids (or matrons) of honor. If you're going with multiple honor attendants, just make sure to distribute the duties clearly among them. Don't leave it to them to figure it out—someone's sure to get stressed.

Go to Chapter 6 for the skinny on showers and bachelorette bashes.

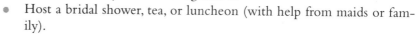

ASK CARLEY
Uneven Attendants

Q: Help! I have four best friends and a sister, and I want them all to be in my wedding party. But my honey only has two friends on the whole planet. What should I do?

A: Easy—include them all. Scrap that old one-bridesmaid-for-one-groomsman "rule" and adapt your down-the-aisle approach to suit your reality. Have your maid of honor walk alone, while each groomsman escorts two bridesmaids, for example.

- Stand in the receiving line, if you choose.
- Help you remove your headpiece and bustle your train so you can start partying.
- Sit at the head table, (if you're having one).
- Pile the food on a plate for you (if it's a buffet) so you don't have to wait in line; make sure you sit down and eat something.
- Give a toast after the best man, or lead the toasting (if you want her to).
- Dance with the best man and the groom during a formal first-dance sequence (if you're having one).
- Serve as an auxiliary hostess during the reception, helping to introduce people and make everyone feel comfortable.
- Collect any gift envelopes guests bring to the reception and keep them for you. (She may deposit them in your bank account, along with the best man, or hang onto them until you return from Bora Bora.)
- Listen to your fears, complaints, and concerns; help smooth over any disputes (with family or bridesmaids); and keep her (and your) sense of humor intact.

The Best Man

Ahh, for the days when every man had a valet—a trusted servant always at his side to polish his shoes, pour his whiskey, and make wry, witty comments. Enter the best man. Usually your best male friend, dad, or bro (although you can choose a female friend or sister—a best maid), the best man serves as your personal aide and adviser throughout the planning and the wedding. You want someone reliable, who's not too busy to help you handle the details of doin' the deed, who's pro-marriage (or at least pro *your* marriage), and who's prepared to help keep your spirits up if you hit any emotional landmines. As leader of the groom's crew, he will:

- Work with maid of honor to organize a couple's shower (if you're having one).
- Organize the bachelor party (with help from the groomsmen).
- Help you choose and rent (or buy) your tux.
- Coordinate the groomsmen's rentals; pay for his own tux.
- Pay extra attention to groomsmen roles during the rehearsal (in case they're snoozing).
- Attend the rehearsal dinner.
- Coordinate groomsman wedding transportation (and lodging if necessary).
- Stand next to you at the altar.
- Hold the bride's ring until you need it.
- Sign the marriage certificate as a witness after the ceremony.
- Hand the officiant his or her fee after the ceremony.
- May stand in the receiving line at the reception.

**Not Up
to the Task?**

While asking someone to lead the toasting is an honor, giving him a nervous breakdown isn't. If your main man is a mouse in front of a mike, ask your bride's honor attendant, mom, or dad to lead the toasting. A joint toast with the maid of honor is also an option.

- Sit at the head table, (if you're having one).
- Kick off the reception-time toasting, traditionally.
- Dance with the maid of honor and the bride during a formal first-dance sequence (if you're having one).
- Collect any gift envelopes guests bring to the reception and keep them for you.
- Have cash in hand for anyone who needs tipping, paying, or bribing.
- May drive you to your wedding-night hotel or to the airport after the reception.
- Listen to your concerns, reassure you, and make you laugh throughout the planning and the wedding.

Go to Chapter 8 for more tips for great toasts.

Tips for Toasting

Traditionally, the best man's toast is an homage to you and your new bride. It should be sincere, *kind,* and sprinkled with lines that make the crowd laugh. If he's tongue-tied, give him a copy of our very own Best Man Toast Writer. He'll have the crowd weeping (and laughing) in no time.

Standard opening: Hello there. I'd like to take this opportunity to thank you from the bottom of my [body part] for joining us here tonight as we celebrate the union of [bride's name] and [embarrassing male nickname]. It would be difficult to imagine two more [adjective] people meeting one another, falling in love, and deciding to spend their lives together. I'm honored that they've asked me to say a few words tonight.

If he's known you since childhood, he can add: As you may know, [groom's first name] and I first met each other [number] years ago when we were [adjective] boys who liked nothing better than a day spent climbing [plural noun], playing with [animals] and shouting "[exclamation]!" as we [adverb] dove into his [relative]'s freezing swimming pool. Back then, girls were [adjective] and [sports figure] was God. Since then, we've shared a lot of good times together. . . .

If you've met more recently: I still remember the day [groom's name] and I first met. We were [fraternity brothers/coworkers/cell mates] with a mutual devotion to [television show] and [snack food]. Since [graduation/the downsizing/parole] we've remained close and have shared a lot of good times together. . . .

If he knows the bride well, he may add: And during these last few years, we've been lucky enough to have [bride's name] along to share more than a few of them.

If he barely knows her: And I look forward to sharing even more of them with both [groom's name] and [bride's name] in the days to come.

Time to pull the heartstrings: [Groom's name] has been more than just a [adjective] friend to me, he's been a inspiration. I can't say that I'd want to marry him (pause for laughter), but I envy the woman who did. So please raise your glass and join me in a toast to a very [adjective] couple and their many, many years of happiness to come.
Salut!/Cheers/L'chaim!

The Bridesmaids

This is your chance to surround yourself with a court of adoring attendants. In the distant past, bridesmaids escorted the bride as she traveled to the groom's village for the wedding, protecting her (and her dowry) from attack by highway robbers or scorned suitors. Today your maids probably won't have to do double duty as a defensive line, but they do have a variety of other challenging tasks. Choose considerate friends who work well with others. (Traditionally women, bridesmaids can be guys, too—bridesmen.) When you ask your friends to be maids, make sure they're clear on their responsibilities—and be realistic and understanding about how much time and money it will take. Here's what bridesmaids do:

- Help plan the bridal or couple's shower and bachelorette party (if you're having one).
- Offer to help with general wedding planning tasks—addressing invites, making favors, decorating the reception site, etc.
- Help scout out bridesmaids' dresses; pay for their own dresses, shoes, lingerie, and jewelry.
- Attend the rehearsal dinner.
- March on down that aisle before you and stand at the front during the ceremony.
- May dance with the groomsmen during a formal first-dance sequence.
- Serve as auxiliary hostesses at the reception, introducing people and making sure everyone's comfortable.
- Serve as dance starters, hitting the floor when the band kicks in and scanning the ranks for any toe-tapping guests eager to join them.
- Offer you emotional support during planning and on the wedding day.

You Can't Be Too Clear

Go over the list of everything you want your best man (and other attendants) to do before the big day—and one last time the night before. Better to be redundant than ringless.

Go to Chapter 12 for help outfitting all your attendants.

The Groomsmen

Your groomsmen are the loyal, responsible friends who've been there when you needed them and will make you feel like the star you are on your wedding day. Back in the days

---

ASK CARLEY

Breaking the Bad News

Q: Help! I've chosen five bridesmaids and there just isn't room at the altar for more. But I don't know how to face the unchosen ones—I know they'll hate me for excluding them. What do I do?

A: You have an understandable reason for limiting your bridesmaids—the size of your ceremony space. Call each friend you didn't ask (or make a dinner date), tell her how excited you are about your wedding and how much you want her there. Let her know, straight up, that you were only able to choose a certain number of attendants and would love her to take another special role. Make her job a positive rather than a negative. "You're such a great singer (writer/speaker/baker), I would be honored if you'd sing at the wedding." While you don't want to lie, there's no harm in making up a good reason to help someone feel less slighted. ("I'm not having any out-of-town attendants; it's just such a pain for them. But I hope you will come and be an honored guest!")

when a groom would capture his bride—literally—and carry her away to be wed, the groomsmen were his trusty warrior buddies who helped fight off opposing forces (families, suitors) trying to get her back. Today your groomsmen probably won't engage in hand-to-hand combat. But they do more than just show up in a tux:

Give 'Em a Break

If your wedding is costing your bridesmaids a bundle (the shower, the dress, etc.), let them know that their participation is the only wedding present you want.

- Help plan bachelor party and/or couple's shower (if you're having one).
- Rent their own tuxes and shoes.
- Attend the rehearsal dinner.
- May serve as ushers, helping seat guests before the ceremony. (See "Roles for Other Important People: Ushers," later in the chapter.)
- Serve as information central during the wedding, directing wayward guests to the restroom, chapel, and/or reception site.
- Stand at the altar during the ceremony (may escort bridesmaids up the aisle first).
- May dance with the bridesmaids during a formal first-dance sequence.
- May serve as dance starters, surveying the room for any guests who are dying to disco.
- Decorate the getaway car, if there is one.
- Offer support and their unfailing sense of humor throughout the preparations and during the wedding.

Introduce Your Crew

Get all your (local) attendants partying together early on in the planning process. By instigating some group-bonding activities, you'll help make it easier for them to work together—and ensure that they'll have more fun at the wedding.

Lining Up the Little Ones

So you have twenty-seven little cousins who are so cute, you have to include them? Great—there are plenty of roles for little folks. But keep in mind that part of kids' charm is the fact that you never know what they'll do—this sort of unpredictability tends to be more charming the less im-

How to say "thanks" to your supporting cast? Buy 'em something super. For presents with pizzazz, go to Chapter 17.

ASK CARLEY

Who Pays for What?

Q: I'm having twelve bridesmaids, about half from out of town. Do I have to pay for their dresses *and* hotel rooms?

A: Generally, your attendants pay their own way for what they wear and their travel and lodging expenses. But you can help make it *a lot* easier by reserving a block of hotel rooms at a reduced group rate, or putting out-of-town attendants up with local bridesmaids or your nicest friends. If someone you really adore won't be able to make it/participate because of costs, it's your prerogative to offer financial help. (Just keep it low key so other maids don't get jealous or angry.)

ASK CARLEY

Sibling Rivalry?

Q: My fiancée wants me to ask her brother to be a groomsman. I don't hate him, *exactly.* But we've never been close, and I don't think he'll feel comfortable with my friends. Do I *have* to ask him?

A: No way, José. Your groomsmen are just that—*your* guys. Your sweetie can ask her bro to stand up for her. Or the two of you can create a special role for him. Of course, ultimately you might decide to ask him out of consideration for her and a personal desire to get in good with your soon-to-be in-laws (and pursue a better relationship with your brother-in-law). But it's your call completely.

portant the occasion! Generally, save the action parts for kids older than four, and make sure all tasks are age-appropriate.

Junior Groomsmen/Bridesmaids/Ushers

Include young friends and relatives (ages nine to sixteen) as junior ushers, bridesmaids, or groomsmen. Young guys can wear tuxes and do basically the same things as your older pals—seat guests, precede you down the aisle, snicker when you drop the ring. Young gals can wear less sexy versions of your bridesmaids' dress and walk down the aisle before you as junior members of the bride's squad. Girls can always seat guests, as well.

Flower Children

Typically, these wee folks (ages four to eight) walk (skip, crawl) down the aisle before the bride, scattering flower petals. While flower *girls* are standard, there's no rule that says your adorable male cousins can't do flower duty, too. If you're having more than one flower child, have them hold hands, two by two, to give them courage. If you're afraid you'll slip on those slick blossoms and topple into your guests, skip the scattering part and have your flower child carry a basket or ball of flowers (a pomander), a single stem, or a bottle and wand to blow bubbles instead. Seat your flower children's parents up front to wave them in and seat them at the end of their march.

Don't Count On It

Don't expect too much of young attendants. Even your very mature thirteen-year-old cousin might eat too many Sweet-tarts for breakfast and spin off into a sugar-induced mania during the ceremony. Kids will be kids—give any critical duties to adults.

Ring Bearers

Traditionally a small boy (age four to eight), the ring bearer walks down the aisle either before or along with the flower child, holding a small, fancy pillow with your two rings tied to it. Afraid your rambunctious cousin Randy will run off with your new platinum bands? The ring bearer usually touts fake rings while the real ones wait safely with your honor attendants. If you don't like the artifice, have someone hand over the pillow with the real rings *just before* he starts his walk. Or skip the ring pillow and have your ring bearer carry something real, and less valuable, instead, such as a flower to hand to his mother when he meets her at the end of the aisle. The purpose of the ring bearer is to make your guests melt with affection—he can carry a Tonka Truck and still succeed.

Page/Train Bearer(s)

A pair of pages (ages six to nine) follow the bride down the aisle, carrying her long train. This English tradition usually is performed by two little boys, but girl pages are fine, too.

Candle Kids

Steady-handed preteens (ages nine to twelve) can light candles at the altar directly before the mother of the bride is seated (in a Christian ceremony). They can either dress like the junior attendants (to further highlight their roles) or come as they are. Your candle kids might stick around after the ceremony to snuff the flames.

Bored of Blossoms?

Your littlest attendant can carry:

- A little lantern
- Photo of special relative to remember
- Bible
- Basket of candy
- Arrangements for the altar
- Favorite toy

Fitting In the Folks

You can't choose your parents, but you can decide what role they play in your wedding. While the bride's mother was the official hostess traditionally—meaning her hubby paid and she did all the work—parental involvement today is more a question of comfort and closeness than cash (especially since you two may be putting the whole wedding on your Gold Card, or the groom's parents may be paying more than the bride's). You can have your folks fill the traditional roles if it's appropriate and will make your wedding run more smoothly, but it's your call. No matter what you decide, keep in mind that the more they pay, the more they may want to play. If the idea of planning a wedding with Pop sounds about as fun as being stuck in an elevator with an unleashed crocodile, think seriously before accepting his generous offer of financial aid.

Mother of the Bride

If you get along great with your mom (and she has plenty of time), feel free to ask her to help with just about everything, easing your burden and giving you some serious mother-daughter bonding opportunities. (If your mom is also your matron of honor, she'll be taking an even bigger part in your wedding planning; make sure she knows what she's getting into before she agrees.) You decide (or decide together) which of the following tasks you want Mom to tackle:

- Help scout out wedding and reception sites and ask friends for recommendations for caterers, florists, and so on.
- May serve as the main contact for wedding professionals.
- Help choose your wedding dress (and honeymoon bikini!).
- Compile her (and Dad's) guest list of family and friends.

- Talk to the groom's family about how many people they want to invite and deal with the difficult task of limiting the number of guests, if necessary.
- Help choose family or ethnic traditions to incorporate into your ceremony or reception.
- Coordinate with the groom's mom on clothing; they'll feel more comfortable if they're dressed equally elegantly.
- Attend most showers and the rehearsal dinner.
- May walk you down the aisle if Dad doesn't. (Both Mom and Dad accompany the bride in a Jewish wedding.)
- In a Christian wedding, be seated in the first pew directly before the ceremony and leave the chapel first afterward.
- Stand in the receiving line to greet guests—traditionally, as reception hostess, she heads up the line.
- Sit at the parents' table (if you're having one).
- Dance with your dad and your honey during a formal first-dance sequence.
- Remind you often how special you are and that you'll be the most beautiful bride in the history of the universe.
- Let you cry on her shoulder anytime, day or night (you know, be a mom).

Token Tasks

If you need a stiff drink to get up the nerve to call your mom (or dad)—or if she's too busy working on her Ph.D/latest novel/next divorce to pick up the phone—you're better off asking for help with small, specific tasks (if any at all).

Mother of the Groom

The groom's mom traditionally had only a shadow role—greeting guests in the receiving line and sitting at the parents' table. The unspoken assumption: This was the bride's family's party. But it's time for the groom's mom to step off the bench and get into the wedding action! By giving her a big role in the wedding planning, you not only make her feel important to both of you, but you also garner one more pair of capable hands. And believe us, there's plenty of work to go around. Your mom isn't losing a son, she's gaining a second career—wedding planner. She can:

Go to Chapter 20 for help dealing with meddling mothers and infuriating fathers.

ASK CARLEY
Managing Two Moms?

Q: I'm close to my mom and my stepmom. Whom should I include in my wedding and how?

A: Include them both, but make sure you divide the duties. For example, if you ask Mom to walk you down the aisle, maybe your stepmother should be the last person seated before the procession begins. Try to keep their feelings in mind—your mother might feel her "Mom-ness" threatened by your stepmother; Stepmom might feel uncomfortable being involved because she's not your "real" mother. Wishy-washiness about who does what can create unnecessary friction. Have a heart-to-heart with each mom well before the wedding to let them know you're planning to include both of them and to see what they are comfortable (and uncomfortable) with. Decide together what roles they'll take on your wedding day.

- Host a dinner to introduce your bride to your side of the family.
- Help scout out wedding and reception sites and ask friends for recommendations for caterers, florists, etc.
- May serve as the main contact for wedding professionals.
- Draw up the guest list for your family.
- Attend showers.
- Help you choose family or ethnic traditions to incorporate into your ceremony or reception.
- Consult with the bride's mom on her wedding-day outfit, making sure that gold lamé jumpsuit will match the formality and style of the bride's mother's attire.
- Traditionally, plan and host the rehearsal dinner along with your dad.
- In a Jewish ceremony, escort you down the aisle along with your dad.
- Stand in the receiving line after you two (along with your dad).
- Sit at the parents' table (if you're having one).
- Dance with your dad during a formal first dance.
- Bring down the house with you during the mother/son dance.
- Grow weepy periodically about how her baby has grown up.

Father of the Bride

The sterotypical father of the bride signs the checks and shows up in a tux. But there's no reason he can't participate as much as your mom. Don't assume your dad doesn't want to help just because he doesn't offer. Even if he's a tough guy at the office, he may be shy around all things wedding-related. Ask him for help on specific items. For example, Dad can:

- Help you come up with a budget.
- Pay for the wedding. (Be grateful if this is the case—it's not a given anymore.)
- Help with everything from scouting out reception sites to recommending dance tunes.
- Help your mom create their guest list.
- Find the perfect wardrobe for himself (tux? Scottish kilt?) and let the groom's dad know he should do the same.
- May attend the bachelor party and/or a couple's shower.
- Attend the rehearsal dinner and be prepared to toast the groom into the family (may also pay for/help plan this party).
- May ride with you to the ceremony.
- Walk you down the aisle and "give you away" or "support" you in marriage. (Both parents march in a Jewish ceremony.)
- May stand in the receiving line, next to your mother.
- At a Jewish wedding, may offer a blessing over the wine and bread.
- Sit at the parents' table (if you're having one).
- Dance with your mom during an official first-dance sequence.

- Kick up his heels for a special father/daughter dance with you.
- May make a toast after the best man.
- May help organize (and oversee) the bar.
- Stay until the bitter end of the party, possibly settling final bills.

Father of the Groom

No more sitting back and watching the bride's father squirm. The groom's father also plays a far bigger role these days, very likely shouldering some of the cost of the wedding. What your dad does depends a lot on his time and interest, and your relationship with him. The groom's father can:

- Contribute to wedding expenses (traditionally, the marriage license, officiant's fee, corsages, boutonnieres, the bride's bouquet, groomsman's gifts, liquor, and/or music).
- Help with planning.
- Help create the groom's family guest list.
- May attend the bachelor party and/or a couple's shower.
- Host (read: pay for) the rehearsal dinner (with your mom).
- Buy or rent a new tux or other wedding attire.
- In a Jewish wedding, escort you down the aisle, along with your mom.
- May stand in the receiving line after your mom.
- At a Jewish wedding, may offer a blessing over the wine and bread.
- Sit at the parents' table (if you're having one).
- May give a toast (after bride's parents).
- Dance with your mom and the bride during a formal first-dance sequence.
- May help organize (and oversee) the bar.
- Stay until the bitter end of the party, possibly settling final bills.

Roles for Other Important People

Maybe you were voted "Most Popular" by your high-school class, college dorm mates, and bowling league. Or perhaps you come from one of those families that considers everyone in the area code a cousin. Don't inflate your wedding party to a Rockettes-size line—make those VIPs into VIEs (Very Important Extras). You can acknowledge special people in a relatively passive way, by giving them corsages, seats of honor, or a place in the family pictures. Or you can make them part of the party by inventing entirely new roles for them. Your creativity is your only limit. Just make sure your honor roles are actually honorable—there's nothing particularly appealing about punch bowl duty or bathroom detail! Thank everyone with a small gift and/or a mention in the ceremony program. Below are some great ways to include VIEs.

Ushers

Ask special friends or relatives (male or female) to serve as ushers, walking your guests to their seats, rolling out the aisle runner (if you're having one), tying pew ribbons across the rows (if you're using them), and acting as general guest guides. Groomsmen often double as ushers, but if it's a huge wedding (you need one usher per fifty guests) or there are lots of people you want to include, go with the designated usher approach.

Huppah Holders

Ask four strong-armed friends to hold up your huppah (if you're having a Jewish wedding). They carry it down the aisle on four tall stakes before the wedding party enters and hold it steady throughout the ceremony. They might even help make it, if they have the time and creativity. Ask your rabbi for specs.

Attendants Wearing Tails

He's the love of your life (just after your honey). So what if he walks on all fours and drools? He's the person (all right, dog) second closest to your heart. Have him walk down the aisle in a flowered collar (led by a two-footed friend, of course).

Candle Lighters

If you're having a dramatic nighttime ceremony with candles along the aisle (or any other area), appoint a special friend to candle duty, asking her to light up directly before the ceremony begins. Or have her distribute candles to all the guests to be lit as a part of the ceremony. At a Jewish wedding, you can honor someone by asking her to light a candle during the reception.

Readers and Class Acts

Have a well-spoken, special friend do a reading during your ceremony. You can choose the text, or ask him to select something he loves. Alternately, you could ask a literary type to write something to read, or to be printed in your program. Or ask a talented friend to be a featured performer during your ceremony or reception, singing a special song or playing an instrument.

Tradition Bearers

Celebrate your family's uniqueness by having a tradition bearer walk down the aisle with an item of familial significance—a coat of arms, the state or country flag, a sprig of a magnolia from the family plantation. Or show your family's heritage by having someone march down the aisle in the costume of your country (a kilt, a kimono, traditional African garb). Alternately, you might have someone carry a photo of an honored family friend or relative, or read a letter from an important relative who couldn't attend. Seat your tradition bearer in the front row.

Etiquette Guru

If your Aunt Esther is the type who keeps a copy of *Miss Manners' Guide to Excruciatingly Correct Behavior* by her bedside (or if she just always seems to know *exactly* the right thing to do), ask her to be the official arbiter of etiquette, on call to answer questions of conduct or attire posed by members of the families and wedding party (even guests, if she's up for it). Discuss your personal etiquette preferences so she'll know what to tell guests. If the thought of anyone else wearing white turns you green while black seems perfectly peachy, let her know.

Transportation Captain

If your Uncle Albert (or anyone else) is mad for all things mobile, has wallpapered his den with road maps, and considers clocking distances on the odometer a leisure-time activity, appoint him transportation captain and let him take charge of your guests' vehicular needs. He can check on the parking possibilities at your sites, chart the best course from the ceremony to the reception, keep abreast of any serious traffic problems on your wedding day, and—most important—create, copy, and distribute maps. He also may research the best place to rent a limo or a bus if you'll be routing guests to a remote or hard-to-find reception location.

Toast of the Table

Seat a special guest at each table—someone who had a major impact on your life or traveled from Siberia just for your wedding. Designate her place with a flower or card. Ask all special guests to stand up during the toasting and briefly explain their significance to you. Then toast them, along with all your guests, together.

Greeting Those Guests

If you've got scores of out-of-town guests, you have extra issues to think about—namely where they'll sleep, how they'll get around, and what they'll do with their spare time. This isn't just the biggest day of your life; it's also a party for your friends and family (who just doled out a lot of dough for a tux and that cappuccino maker you had to have). Take steps to ensure they have an awesome time.

Keep Them Informed

This is a party, not a game of Clue. Don't make your guests use super-sleuth skills to get to your wedding. Let them know early what the dress code is, when to R.S.V.P. by, where you're registered, how to get to the ceremony and reception, and the dates of any extra parties or activities they're invited to. You can include this info along with your invitation (except where you're registered—that's word of mouth). Appoint someone as Guest Services Coordinator, on hand to answer any questions. You might include this person's phone number in your invite. And think about setting up a Web page with all the pertinent info.

Get Them There

Provide maps and directions for out-of-towners. In addition to including a small map in the invite, you may want to leave a packet of info in each hotel room for them. Your Transportation Captain (see "Roles for Other Important People," earlier) can handle the details.

Advice on Volunteers

Beware of giving critical tasks to nonprofessionals. If your Aunt Esmeralda offers to make the bridesmaids' dresses, and she's a professional seamstress—bring on the pinking shears! But is she just happens to enjoy sewing, she may not have the facilities or experience to do the deed right. And, believe it or not, even the best people can flake out if they're not being paid. Assess the seriousness of your volunteer's skill and commitment *before* accepting a gift of catering, photography, flowers, clothing, or music.

HEIDI AND AARON
October 19, Miami Beach, Florida

HEIDI AND AARON worked hard not only to make their reception gorgeous, but, more important, to have their guests feel welcome and comfortable. The only lights in the room were pinpoint spotlights in the ceiling illuminating the centerpieces, which hung *above* the tables. Candles were placed on each table, giving the room an ethereal glow, and there was no wedding video—Aaron didn't want one, and Heidi didn't mind because the lighting involved would ruin the effect of her carefully chosen lighting scheme.

For the wedding cake, Heidi says, "Aaron and I have more books than anyone we know, so we thought, why not do one shaped like books?" Titles were written on the spine in frosting, including a joke title—*The Case of the Missing Ushers*—because Aaron had no ushers, only grooms*women*. The groom's cake was made in the form of a chessboard with sugar chess pieces—in honor of Aaron, who plays chess.

Having no ushers clinched Heidi's decision not to do the garter thing, and that led to another twist on wedding tradition: "We had both boys and girls come out on the dance floor for the bouquet throw." And rather than letting the dancing peter out, Heidi and Aaron stayed until the end of the reception and planned a last dance—to the Beatles' "In My Life." Everyone formed a circle around them. "Everyone we loved was around us," Heidi says. "It was so emotional—the perfect ending."

While out-of-town guests often rent their own cars, you can welcome them in style (or ask your parents, friends, or relatives to do so) by greeting them at the airport and chauffeuring them to the hotel if they need you to. You also might arrange for a hotel shuttle to take a group of guests to and from the wedding. Talk to the hotel manager about options.

Reserve Rooms

To keep your guests up-to-date on the wedding, go to www.theknot.com and create a free personal wedding Web page.

Contact a local hotel convenient to your wedding sites about six months before the big day to ask about a discounted group rate if you send all 50 to 200 of your guests their way. Reserve a block of rooms, then include the hotel info (address, phone number, directions, and special rate) on an invitation insert. Be considerate of your crowd's budget constraints; if appropriate, reserve rooms at two hotels—a super-luxe one for your flush friends and a less-expensive option for your budgeting buddies. (If you have close local friends or relatives with empty guest rooms, they may offer to house a guest or two for free.)

Keep Them Entertained

Appoint an outgoing, *very* loving friend or relative to play "cruise director" and arrange activities for your guests. Of course you'll have a rehearsal dinner and probably a brunch for out-of-towners. But your cruise director (or your attendants) might set up other activities, such as a golf game, a trip to the zoo, or a tour of the city. She should make sure that a local guidebook, a list of hot spots (with phone numbers, addresses, and hours), and a list of pertinent phone numbers (hers, the other guests staying in the hotel, the bride's and groom's families) make their way to each hotel room. You pay for the supplies; she donates her time.

Show Your Love

Make out-of-towners feel extra-wanted (and let them know that you appreciate the fact that they've used all their frequent-flier miles to see you wed). Welcome them with a basket of fresh fruit, local candy, or luxurious bath foam in their room. Attach a personal note, thanking them for coming, or make an announcement during the reception. Or get everyone coupons for dinner for two at your favorite local seafood shack, free skate rental at the area rink, or a manicure at the hotel salon.

The Buddy System

Out-of-town guests who are traveling alone? Create a buddy system. Appoint a kind, *willing* family member to welcome the guest to town and offer his phone number for questions. Your buddy probably won't get woken up at 4:00 A.M., but the knowledge that he's there should help nervous travelers relax.

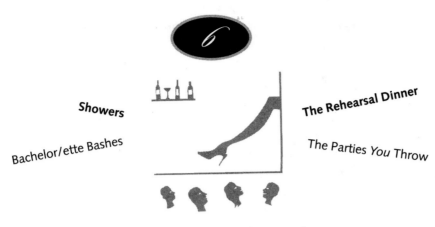

Showers

Bachelor/ette Bashes

The Rehearsal Dinner

The Parties You Throw

Prewedding Parties

The period between your engagement and your wedding is busy, hectic, and stressful, but it's also a time for some serious partying. Some soirees are in your honor (showers, bachelor/bachelorette bashes), some are practice runs (the rehearsal dinner), but all provide important (and fun!) opportunities for your respective friends and families to get to know each other before the big day.

We thought we'd serve up some tips for organizing prewedding fiestas so you can pass them along to your fantastic hosts and hostesses. Do keep in mind that these parties cost your pals time and money—keep others' feelings and pocketbooks in mind before you go overboard with your suggestions, okay?

Showers

The prewedding shower's very purpose is to shower the bride (and more and more often, the groom) with gifts that will help her make the transition to married life. Here's the lowdown.

The Women-Only Affair

At a bridal shower, the bridesmaids and close female friends and family members come together to toast your soon-to-be-wed good fortune, bombard you with great gifts, make goo-goo eyes at your fabulous ring and glowing complexion (ahhhh, love), and take all the pressure of harried wedding preparations away for a few hours. Heaven! Historically, the shower was a way of decking out the bride-to-be with a decent dowry of all the things it was crucial for a woman to bring to her new home (and her man). Today it's simply a beautiful gesture on the part of your (female) loved ones. It's also a win-win situation—while the bride is feeling like a queen, her girl guests get in some good female bonding before the wedding.

Who Hosts? Usually the honor attendant, with help from the other bridesmaids, female friends of the bride, and family members. In some cases, a female member of the bride's family—sister, mother, daughter—will coordinate the festivities. Although etiquette says relatives should not throw this bash, claiming it looks like they're fishing for presents for the bride, we say go for it. In some regions (the Midwest, for example), it's standard. And if the honor attendant lives far away, is superbusy, or is clueless when it comes to party planning, it makes sense for the bride's mom or sis to pitch in.

Who's Invited? The guest list includes the bridesmaids, the bride's other close girlfriends and relatives, as well as her honey's tight women friends and family members. Important tip: *Only* women who will be invited to the wedding should be part of the shower. It's common sense, really. If Cousin Gina brings a comforter as a shower gift, Cousin Gina should receive full access to that fantastic all-you-can-eat buffet you're planning. Otherwise, she'll feel like she's only as good as her gift—and that's hurtful.

In order to make sure that no mistakes are made, the bride may be consulted about the guest list; if it's a surprise party, your honor attendant or mother will probably spearhead the invitation committee. In terms of the actual size of the guest list, there are no hard-and-fast rules. While most showers are intimate affairs, we've been to a few that gave the actual wedding reception a run for its money.

When? Scheduling the shower depends on when all the core guests are free, when the hostess has ample preparation time, when the chosen venue is available (even if it's at the hostess's house, there may be conflicts), and, perhaps, when the bride-to-be is in town. A shower can take place six months before wedding day or at two weeks and counting. The only fixed rule is that the shower should come sometime *after* the engagement parties but *before* the big day. (We don't recommend having the shower the same week as the wedding—there's going to be way too much going on.)

If a lot of shower guests will be traveling from afar, they should be consulted about days that are good for them—and given the final date at least two months ahead of time. If it's a surprise shower, a well-placed spy (the groom-to-be, perhaps?) should snoop through the bride's day planner so there will *be* a guest of honor.

Where? Many a valiant shower hostess has chosen to throw the fiesta in the comfort of her own home, but more and more women are getting far-out funky with the party site, getting together at a bar, hotel tearoom, restaurant, beach, or park. If it'll be a surprise party, consider the bride's fave pizza joint, her parents' or sister's living room, or even her own place.

Keep Track

As the bride (or couple) opens shower gifts, the maid of honor or another willing attendant should record who gave them what, so it'll be easy to write thank-you notes.

Shower Love

The first bridal shower took place in the Netherlands, where a young lass had made up her mind to marry a poor-but-hunky miller. Her father disapproved and refused to provide her with a dowry (necessary for the marriage to be legit). So the girl's friends came to her rescue by *showering* her with gifts.

Decorations are advisable, if just a few floral bouquets and balloons; background music is a must.

How? The shower hostess delegates jobs (to bridesmaids and any willing friends)—inviting guests, preparing eats, making punch, hanging decorations. Written invitations are not obligatory for small parties, although it's always nice to send people a written reminder of the date. R.S.V.P.'s are crucial either way, however, so the hostess knows how big a refreshment spread to prepare.

What Happens? Noshing snacks, sipping drinks, and opening presents are the only mandatory ingredients for a shower. Then again, flour, eggs, milk, and sugar are the only necessary ingredients for a cake. If the bride will be into it, we say go wild with party protocol, incorporating games or a theme (see below), or anything else that will up the fun quotient.

What Else? A shower is not necessarily an isolated event. There probably will be one big bash hosted by the bride's closest pals, but she also may be "showered" by her coworkers, belly-dancing class, or volunteer group.

The Couple's Shower

This increasingly popular variation on the classic bridal shower includes both male and female guests (friends, attendants, and possibly family members) in a coed gab-and-gift fest. Some refer to this prewedding bash as a Jack and Jill. No matter what you choose to call it, the who, what, where, and how of a couple's shower are similar to the bridal shower, except that both sexes help with planning and enjoy the festivities.

We love his 'n' her showers. For starters, they shatter the outdated notion that only women get excited about weddings. And they're an opportunity for *all* your favorite people to get friendly before the wedding, ensuring a smashing reception. Yes, a couple's shower is much more like a flat-out *party* than a traditional shower.

If you're really gung-ho about the idea, take aside your attendants soon after your engagement and tell them you two would *love* a coed shower. Chances are they, too, will relish the idea of mixing it up. If you think a bridal *and* a couple's shower sound cool, it's fine to have one of each—and who knows, maybe your wish will come true. Your pals might decide to throw you both. Or maybe your mom will take care of the bridal shower and your attendants will put together a coed party.

Registry FYI

Information about where the couple is registered can be included in the shower invitations. If you're not doing written invitations, spread the registry lowdown by word of mouth to simplify the present-buying process for guests.

Just Theme It! Great Shower Ideas

Whatever kind of shower it is, a sure-fire way to host a hit party is to theme it. Guests automatically will feel like integral parts of the festivities because they've bought a gift or dressed up accordingly. It's also a natural icebreaker when bringing together people who don't know each other well, because you'll all feel complicit in the outrageousness/goofiness/fabulousness.

An added bonus of a theme is that it makes the shower host(ess)'s life easier. He or she can delegate with less fear of screw-ups, since once friends hear the theme, they'll have a firm grasp on the party vision. Guests also benefit; gift-shopping is easier when there's a guiding principle.

If you're sold on the theme approach (and of course there are tons of fantastic *un*-themed showers, so no pressure!), go hunting for a suitable one. Good starting points are the bride or couple's nationalities, honeymoon destination, occupation, or favorite leisure-time activities. Eras and styles also can be conducive to partying—for example, Disco Nights, Toga Trysts, Flapper Follies, Diner Days . . . whatever the theme, make it run it through all the party elements—from the invitations, food, and decor, to the gifts, music, and activities. More ideas:

Country-Western: Invites attached to a little lasso; ribs and fried chicken; cold Buds; a country juke box; line-dancing or horseshoe-tossing; give cowboy boots or a group gift of a dude ranch getaway.

Art: Invites on famous-painting postcards; art opening–like hors d'oeuvres (shrimp skewers, pâté on crackers, olives); jazz music; play Pictionary; give an easel or a subscription to a local museum as gifts.

Games People Play

Games are great for bringing people together and upping the laugh quotient. Here are our top four picks:

Charades: Give each guest three slips of paper to write down three things that are characteristic of the bride-to-be or couple, like "Sailing," "Tandoori chicken," or "Fuzzy car dice," and let the good times roll by taking turns acting them out. (The correct guesser is the next one up.)

The To-Be-Wed Game: This riff on the popular TV game show will make the guests-of-honor blush, giggle, and laugh out loud. Split the soon-to-bes up and have them answer questions about each other—tap into close friends' and families' knowledge of the twosome when writing questions—and see if their respective answers mesh. Be prepared: It's only fair for the happy couple to put *other* couples on the spot after they've been through the ringer. For a bridal shower, get the groom's answers to the questions before the party and then put the bride on the spot.

Wedding Scattergories: Make up game cards using about eight wedding-related categories, such as Flower, Party Song, Site, and Honeymoon Destination. Put all the letters of the alphabet into a hat, draw one letter each round, and take a minute to fill in the categories with words that begin with that letter. (An hourglass would be perfect here.) For the letter D, for example, guests could write: Daisies; Disco Inferno (Burn, Baby, Burn); Dance Hall; and Disney World. Players get 1 point for every category filled appropriately (no newlyweds in history have honeymooned in Detroit) and 3 for an answer so original that no one else wrote it down.

Roast 'em: A couple's shower is a good opportunity to host a raunchy-but-friendly roast of the soon-to-be-weds in the company of their closest friends. Prepare strips of paper with situations in the couple's life together as well as those that *might* arise, such as "Jane tells John she can't go to the play with him because she made plans to play darts with the girls," or "Jane and John argue about baby names." Put John and Jane in front-row seats (with a nice bottle of wine to dull the pain) and have guests come up in twos, draw a slip, read it out loud, and then act out the scene. John and Jane get score cards—from 0 to 10—with which they will rate the accuracy of each skit after the curtain comes down.

High-School Sleepover: Girls only; boys are icky! Teddy-bear invites; junk food; '70s or '80s pop rock; Truth or Dare; give a certificate for a facial, rollerskates, or a party "outfit" as gifts.

This Is Your Life: Make a photo-montage invite; serve the guest(s) of honor's favorite foods; play their fave tunes; invite "mystery" guests from their pasts (*no* exes); show home videos and have people reminisce; gifts include a Polaroid camera, plane tickets to their first vacation spot, and compilation CDs.

Futuristic: UFO-shaped invites; silver-wrapped truffles, funky power drinks, star-shaped pasta; techno or ambient music; sci-fi movies playing; twenty-first-century stuff as gifts (how about a digital TV as a group gift?).

Around the World: Globe invites; a spread of different "ethnic" foods; a mix of world music; Trivial Pursuit—just history and geography categories; gifts from around the world *or* a group gift of a getaway to a foreign country.

Twelve Months: Calendar invites; one dish from each season; Vivaldi's "Four Seasons"; the board game Life; assign each guest a month and ask them to get a related gift.

Bachelor/ette Bashes

In a way, the notorious bachelor party is the guys' version of the bridal shower. It's men only—the best man hosts, with the rest of the groomsmen, close male friends and sometimes relatives on the guest list. (The bride's bros and buddies may come along, too.) It happens before the wedding (used to be the night before, but then some genius figured out hangovers and wedding days don't mix that well).

However, these two proud prewedding traditions differ on one essential point—and therein lies the problem. Whereas the girls' event usually is geared toward celebrating the bride's entrance into the wonderful world of marriage, the guys' party often focuses on giving the groom one last taste of "freedom" (read: $20 lap dances, tequila shots, and drunken antics), as if marriage were a punishment.

We don't need to tell you that the historical bachelor party—and the underlying ball-and-chain message—has been the source of friction in many a to-be-wed relationship. But we are here to offer two great solutions to the bachelor-party blues that should prove more effective than the usual: "Honey, I'm just not comfortable envisioning you with some scantily clad stranger gyrating on your lap." "But honey, I just wanna chill with the boys. Don't you trust me?"

Shower Gifts

Nontraditional:

- A sexy satin slip
- Certificate for a day at the spa
- Velvet bra-and-panties set
- Monthly wine or fresh-fruit club membership for a year
- Silk sheets and pillowcases
- Funky pair of heels
- Coffee-table book
- Great workout wear
- Cappuccino machine

Traditional:

- Toaster
- Cutlery
- Linen
- Candles/candlesticks
- Picture frames
- Crystal
- China

The Bachelor Party: Good-bye Sleaze, Hello Creativity

Let's face it: Getting drunk at a strip club is not, how shall we say, the most *original* form of entertainment. Our favorite bachelor parties do not resemble the movies *Showgirls* or *Animal House*. They're studies in alternative thinking, outdoorsiness, and old-fashioned guyness, instead. Come to think of it, these are all great bachelorette options, too. Consider these more creative (and more fun) options:

Surf and Turf: A day at an upscale gym or spa—relaxing in the pool and hot tub and on the massage table—followed by a visit to an A-list steakhouse.

Go Wild: White-water rafting, cross-country skiing, mountain biking, fishing, or camping with the boys for a long weekend.

Show Him the Money: Forty-eight hours in Atlantic City or your favorite neighborhood casino.

Beach Bums: Volleyball, cold brews, sun, surfing, and harmless bikini-watching. Need we say more?

Extreme Pleasure: A group skydive or bungee-jumping session followed by a feast and lots o' cocktails.

ESPN Fun: Choice seats at a major sports event—or a grueling trip to the racetrack, bowling alley, or pool hall—and a hearty barbecue dinner.

Swingers: Eighteen holes or, preferably, a three-round weekend retreat. Get a Keg Caddie.

Puffers: A night at your favorite cigar bar—martinis, single-malt whiskey, and beef sold separately.

The Bachelorette Party: Evening the Score

If your honey and his crew just *gotta* go out for one last look at some T&A, we say two can play at this game—and should. If it's really that important for the groom to have that one last free-falling sleaze-fest, the bride should get one, too—but hers will be a "night out with the girls." Bridesmaids and/or girlfriends should plan the bachelorette party for the exact same night. Let the ladies don their skimpiest skirts and tightest tops (or coolest clubbing

---

ASK CARLEY

Who Plans the Bash?

Q: My best man and brother-in-law are putting together a bachelor party for me. Can I add my two cents? Am I supposed to be helping?

A: Yes—and no. While there aren't many etiquette rules about planning a bachelor party (after all, we're talking about an event that could take you anywhere from Hooters to a Hootie and the Blowfish concert), we suggest you take this opportunity to chill. (You won't have that many opportunities to just hang in the days before your knock-out nuptials.) Let your buddy and brother-in-law do most of the dirty work, but do get involved in the guest list. Clue the host(s) in to who would kill your mellow mood (testy relatives, overly obnoxious frat brothers, pompous coworkers). Your special night/weekend/week with the boys is too important to leave the human element to chance.

ensembles) and head for the all-nude male revue (or the bride's favorite place to dance the night away). Not only will dual parties help diffuse any feeling of one-sidedness, but they'll also greatly reduce morning-after friction. (It's pretty hard for the bride to chide the groom about staying out till dawn and smelling like a vodka refinery if they're both in exactly the same boat.)

Rules of the Game

Before you set out in a rented limo stocked with Riunite, take a look at our Rules of the Bachelor/ette Party Game:

The groom should . . .

- Talk to the best man in advance about how you'd like to limit the evening's raunch factor, giving specific examples of where to draw the line (nudie bars? strip-o-grams? mud wrestling? Swedish videos? *Baywatch* reruns?).
- Shield your honey from guy friends' attacks. If they think she's the reason your bachelor bash is PG-13, set the record straight. Your future will be rosier if your pals treat your beloved with R-E-S-P-E-C-T.
- Ask the party host to let your honey in on his plans. Being in the know will put her mind at ease. Who knows? Maybe she can even contribute something to the bash—a raunchy audiotape saying what she's going to do to you come wedding night, perhaps?
- On the night of your bash, refuse to take part in anything that will make you uncomfortable (or will leave you with a grand secret to keep from your fiancée). But don't throw a public temper tantrum. Just graciously bow out.
- Reassure your honey when she expresses her fears; this isn't a good time to practice your eye-rolling skills.

Alternative Bachelorette Ideas

- Day-spa getaway
- Sailing jaunt
- All-night disco-hopping
- Comedy club
- Ski weekend
- Group scuba-diving lessons at a beach resort
- Salsa bar
- Helicopter ride
- Night of karaoke
- Concert
- Day hike

The bride should . . .

- Chat with the hostess(es) about what craziness is thumbs-up and what's a no-go. Maybe you're just not into Chippendale's—maybe you'd rather go catch Brad Pitt's latest flick and go to your favorite tapas bar.
- Ask the party planners not to invite anyone who has serious problems with your honey. You only want to party with people who think he's hot stuff!
- Excuse yourself elegantly from any debauchery that makes you uneasy. They're yelling for all the boys in the bar to French-kiss you; tell them you'd rather have some innocent pecks on the cheek.
- If he's getting queasy at the thought of turning you loose, ask your maid of honor to call your honey up and assure him there will be no wet-boxer contests involved. (It's nice to know he's worried, though, isn't it?)

The Rehearsal Dinner

The rehearsal dinner is a time to focus on the people nearest and dearest to you. It's a stellar opportunity to thank individuals who have put in outstanding supporting performances during your wedding planning, including the attendants who will help make your big day a success. It's a time for both sets of parents to get to know each other better (if they haven't already), for relatives and family friends from both sides to mingle, and for everyone actually involved in the big production—including the officiant—to wine and dine away their jitters.

Who Hosts? Traditionally, the groom's family throws this prewedding bash (it's a point of pride for many mothers of the groom), but these days, it's up for grabs. You two might take matters into your own hands, or both sets of parents may choose to do the honors together.

Who's Invited? Your entire wedding party (and their spouses/significant others), both of your immediate family members, any child attendants (and their parents), and your officiant (and the officiant's spouse, too) are the only mandatory guests. If you're having a lot of out-of-town guests and many will already be in town, they also can be invited, or you can keep things more intimate.

When Is It? Traditionally, this prewedding bash immediately follows the ceremony rehearsal (usually held on the night before the wedding).

Where Is It? The sky's the limit. You can have a formal meal at the ritzy revolving restaurant atop a downtown skyscraper, or you can have a backyard cookout. Other options include a classy picnic in a lush park, a looooong table at your fave Indian eatery, or an informal cocktail affair in your living room. A rehearsal *dinner* also can be a brunch or lunch affair, a good option if you're having an early-morning wedding the next day.

What Happens? Although there are no strict rules about what a rehearsal dinner should be, a few elements generally are incorporated into the festivities.

Toasting: This is a great opportunity to really spend time thanking all your loved ones—there probably won't be time to publicly toast everyone at the reception itself. As host of the party, the groom's dad often goes to bat first, toasting his soon-to-be daughter-in-law and her family; the groom also says a few words. We say the couple should thank everyone present together, as well—this includes your parents!—and then open the floor to anyone else who'd like to say a few words.

Relaxing: This is an ideal opportunity for you, your families, add the wedding party to relax a while before the big day begins. Although it's the host's call, we think a rehearsal party should be fairly informal. You're bringing together a disparate group of people in an intimate setting—you want everyone to feel comfortable. Besides, you don't want to upstage the main event.

Giving Gifts: You may choose to give your attendants their thank-you gifts at this juncture (or see "The Parties You Throw," below, for an alternative time). Make sure to also

Out-of-Towner Time

Schedule a welcome cocktail party or brunch if out-of-town guests are not invited to the rehearsal dinner. They're investing time and money to attend your wedding; the least you can do is make them feel included in the surrounding festivities. You'll also be giving them a chance to unwind from their trip and make it possible for them to get acquainted with some of the people they'll whoop it up with at the wedding. Ask a close friend or family member to host this soiree.

JENNIFER AND ANDREW
September 6, Lenox, Massachusetts

JENNIFER AND ANDREW wanted to enjoy their friends and family for more than one day, so they made their wedding a whole weekend affair. "We wanted our wedding to be an opportunity to really spend time with all our closest friends and family," says Jennifer, "and we wanted to force our friends and family to get to know each other!" Jennifer and Andrew knew that if they had the wedding in New York City, where they live and where both grew up, it would be so big and unwieldy that they would never have the experience they wanted. The wedding they did have, with only a hundred guests at the beautiful Wheatleigh Hotel in bucolic Massachusetts, was exactly what they'd dreamed of.

During the two-day event, the couple planned several activities that their guests could take part in. With only seventeen guest rooms, the former mansion was taken over by the bride and groom and their friends, while "the 'grown-ups' stayed at nearby bed-and-breakfasts." The great thing about having the hotel to themselves, Jennifer says, "was that everyone you ran into all weekend was a friend or family member."

present your parents and anyone else who was an integral part of the wedding-planning team with a token of your appreciation—flowers, a nice bottle of wine, or even a huge hug will do.

The Parties *You* Throw

You may end up throwing a few bashes yourselves—attendants' get-togethers, working parties, a night-before chill-out, a morning-after breakfast. These informal get-togethers are optional, so don't feel obligated. But they're fun—and helpful, too.

Attendants' Parties

It's just plain-old good manners to celebrate your closest friends' and relatives' willingness to don those dresses and tuxes, keep the peace at the punch bowl, and dance with your single cousins at the reception. All you have to do is gather your wedding party in a hotel suite or your living room a few nights before the wedding (depending on when people are getting into town), drink a little bubbly, listen to some good music, and chat. You may opt to give your happy helpers their personalized presents in this intimate setting rather than at the rehearsal dinner.

Working Parties

A great way to tackle wedding-related tasks (like licking envelopes and preparing favors) without making your pals feel put-upon is to create a party out of the work. Don't get stuck in the gender trap; men are just as capable of test-tasting cheese puffs or preparing place cards as women are!

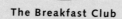

The Breakfast Club

Prewedding breakfasts/ brunches are becoming a trend now that so many guests are coming from so many different places and making a two- or three-day deal out of weddings. A close relative or friend may offer to host this morning fiesta, or you, your honor attendant, or your parents can organize it. If you're feeling too stressed/overwhelmed/ crazed/to attend, just make a quick appearance.

The Morning-After Breakfast

You and your honey may be in the clouds (literally) soon after your reception wraps up. But if you're not flying (or driving or sailing) away to your honeymoon right away, we think it's a great idea to gather your closest friends and family members—as well as out-of-town guests who made a colossal effort to come party with you—for one last wedding-related bash the morning after your big to-do.

Anyone can host this get-together (be it an adoring neighbor, an eager uncle, or a gracious friend), so definitely accept any offers—you'll have one less thing to worry about while you're trying to close that suitcase and dashing to the drugstore to buy sunscreen. You may, however, decide to do the honors yourselves, with or without the help of your ace parents, as one last thank-you to your excellent guests. It's also a chance to reminisce about last night's follies, talk about your plans for the future, divulge your honeymoon itinerary, and be up close-and-personal.

Keep this party decidedly low key; it's an opportunity to talk and snack with your loved ones in an intimate, completely relaxed (finally!) setting. A buffet breakfast or brunch laid out in a living room is a perfect idea (have a nearby deli cater it), or invite everyone to the best little pancake house in town, where you've arranged for a mega-long table and pitchers and pitchers of maple syrup. You also could take the party outside, gathering in a public park for a cheese, crackers, and fruit picnic or even a noontime franks-and-burgers barbecue.

Religious vs. Civil Ceremonies

Finding Your Officiant

Ceremony Basics

Ceremonies with Personal Style

Religious Ceremony Specifics

Interfaith Ceremonies

Second Weddings

Commitment Ceremonies

Standing on Ceremony

The ceremony *is* the wedding. It's the big event, that thrilling moment when the two of you stand face to face and share your most intimate, profound feelings for each other while your closest friends and family members look on. If anything from your wedding day is going to be permanently imprinted on your brains, it's bound to be the moment you look into each other's eyes and exchange your vows. Your ceremony is about who the two of you are, together. If you have to make small compromises on the reception, okay. But don't compromise on your ceremony (except with your sweetie, of course).

Religious vs. Civil Ceremonies

Religious or civil? That is the question. And it's one of the most important questions you'll ask yourselves during the ceremony-planning process. The answer will help determine who officiates, where you'll have it, and what elements you'll include. It may already be clear to you (a given, really) which way you two will go, but if not, read on.

Using Your Religion

While a civil ceremony is all that you *need* to be legally married, many people want their church (or congregation) to recognize their marriage, too.

What It Involves: A religious ceremony is officiated by a religious official and incorporates the wedding customs, traditions, and rules of that faith, along with the state's legal requirements. The wedding can be short and sweet or long and lavish, although it generally follows a specific format prescribed by the religion. The precise elements may depend on the branch and (sometimes) congregation.

A religious service can be held in a church, temple, mosque, or meeting room. Some clergy will officiate at nonreligious sites. You usually can wear whatever you like, although certain houses of worship may have restrictions against anything too revealing. (You'd simply wear a stole or shawl over your sleeveless dress.) You'll have several sessions of prewedding counseling with your officiant—a great time to talk about any wedding or relationship concerns. For more info on your religion's requirements, see "Religious Ceremony Specifics," later in the chapter.

Who Does It: If you're part of a religious congregation and your honey is of the same faith or a compatible one, you'll likely want to go religious. Even if you're not a member of a specific church or temple, you still may feel a strong spiritual or cultural connection to your faith. If your honey shares your feelings (or isn't opposed to them), you may decide on a religious ceremony. If your parents are very religious, you may go this route to show respect for them. Similarly, if you've been meaning to get back to religion, hope to raise your children with it, or want religion to be an important part of your married life, you may choose to make your ceremony the first step. If one of you plans to convert to the other's religion, the ceremony can be a great time to begin involvement with the new faith. If you plan to keep your separate faiths, you may want to create an interfaith ceremony as the first of a lifetime of blending rituals.

If you believe in God or some other spiritual force but not in organized religion, you may want to find an alternative, nondenominational clergy member (a Unitarian minister, for example). Look for someone who understands your religious sentiments, or a faith that is open to your beliefs.

Let's Be Civil

A civil ceremony isn't necessarily a drive-through Vegas-style affair. It can be a full production with attendants, rituals, and plenty of parental weeping. "Civil" merely means in accordance with the state's laws rather than in the eyes of the church or temple.

What It Involves: A civil ceremony is officiated by a legal official—a judge, magistrate, justice of the peace, county or court clerk, mayor, or notary public (not the *Love Boat's* Captain Steubing, or any other boat captain, unless he also holds one of the above civil titles). The exact requirements vary state to state (and even county to county) but generally include a charge to the couple ("Do you, Tracy, take Todd to be your lawfully wedded husband. . . ."), a ring exchange, and the pronouncement of marriage by the officiant.

After that, it's pretty much free-style. You can hold your service anywhere (providing your officiant agrees to come). And you can dress as you please—whether it's in white taffeta or blue jeans (unless your officiant requires something more formal). Call your county's marriage license bureau for the lowdown on the civil process in your area.

Who Does It: If neither of you is religious, or you're uncomfortable with the idea of a religious ceremony (and you're getting no profound opposition from your parents), you'll likely want to take the civil route. If your ideal ceremony is too creative for your clergy, you may go civil style, too. If you've both got religion, but not the same one, you may take the civil route to sidestep the interfaith headache. While some religious officials will tailor a service to include beliefs of both partners, others may refuse to do so, making that judge friend of yours an increasingly attractive option. (See "Interfaith Ceremonies," later in the chapter, for more.) Similarly, if this is a second wedding for one or both of you, you may take the civil path to avoid the obstacles your religion may present.

Other reasons you might choose a civil ceremony: Your dream wedding is a slip-out-and-do-it-during-lunch affair; you want to get married at an alternative venue (Jamaica, the top of the Empire State Building) and your religious official won't make the trip; you want to get married next Tuesday.

Finding Your Officiant

Once you decide what kind of ceremony to have, it's time to figure out who's going to officiate. This person will be more than just the ceremony director; he or she is the conductor of your wedding, spiritual or otherwise. All of the following guidelines apply for a civil or religious officiant.

Reworking the Wording

The basic civil ceremony in the United States generally follows the wording from the Episcopalian *Book of Common Prayer* ("Dearly beloved, we are gathered here today. . . ."). Many officiants use their own adaptation. Ask to see what your civil officiant plans to use and then see if you can adapt it to reflect your unique styles.

What to Look For

Look for an officiant who understands you, your relationship, and your ceremony priorities. The officiant plays a *huge* part in shaping the ceremony; make sure he or she is open to any plans you have for writing your own vows or incorporating unique elements and ethnic traditions. If your potential officiant is inflexible, dismisses all your great ideas, or simply seems uninterested, keep looking.

If you know who you'd like to officiate, call and ask if s/he's available on your planned date (or on one of your alternate dates), then set up an initial meeting to discuss details.

Where to Look

If your ideal officiant is booked, or if you don't have one in mind, where do you find a fabulous officiant?

- Ask friends and family for recommendations.
- Call your city hall or the marriage license bureau for civil referrals.
- Look in the phone book under "Churches," "Weddings," or specific religions.
- Ask consultants and other wedding professionals.
- Consider reconnecting with a childhood or college church, synagogue, or clergy member.
- Get married in the church or synagogue your parents belong to.
- Call that beautiful church or temple you love to drive by, and ask to make an appointment with a clergy member. Some churches may require you to join before hosting your wedding, while others will marry nonmembers or rent their spaces.

Talking to Potential Officiants

When you meet with an officiant, you'll discuss your wedding plans, find out if the officiant is open to your ideas, ask about the requirements, and decide if the three of you want to work on this wedding together. If s/he's clergy, don't say you just *love* the site and could take or leave the religion. You should be intrigued by more than just the architecture.

First Conversation

- Is the officiant available on your date?
- What documents should you bring to the first meeting?
- Are there any special rules or restrictions?
- Is the officiant open to personalized vows, readings, poems, or music?
- Will the officiant give a sermon or speech?
- What kind of prewedding counseling is required, if any?
- What is the ceremony fee?

When You Meet

- Can you tour the sanctuary/ceremony room? (Check seating capacity, number of aisles, general layout; wheelchair accessibility, if that's a concern.)
- What does the church/temple/site provide and what would you provide yourselves (pew ribbons, runner, flowers, candles)?
- Are there any specific restrictions on the type of music you can play, or the readings?
- Will the officiant give you input on your vows and proposed readings?
- Will you have input on the sermon and/or hear it beforehand?
- Is there a dress code?
- Can the officiant help you deal with family conflicts connected to the ceremony?
- Do you bring your marriage license to the ceremony, or will you all sign it together before the wedding?
- Can you have a videographer/photographer in the sanctuary/ceremony room?
- When would the rehearsal be?
- Would the officiant (and his/her spouse) like to come to the reception/rehearsal dinner?
- Would s/he play a role there (giving a blessing, etc.)?

The Do-It-Yourself Officiant

Convinced the therapist who saved your (spiritual) life should officiate at your wedding? Or maybe the friend who fixed you up? Ask that special person to be a legal officiant; he or she can apply for a minister's license by writing to the Universal Life Church, 601 Third Street, Modesto, CA 95351; 209–527–8111. Include his or her name, address, and the state where the wedding will be, and request the church's list of marriage laws for each state. The church will process the request and get the license in the mail in about twenty-four hours.

Prewedding Counseling: What's Involved?

Generally, if you choose a religious officiant, you'll have about three sessions of counseling before the wedding. We asked two officiants to describe what happens.

"Couples should come prepared to discuss themselves, their feelings about their religion, and what marriage means to them. I might ask how they met, how the subject of marriage came up, whether or not their families support them in their decision to marry, even why they want to get married at all. I want to find out how the couple communicates. I want to see if they're talking about a marriage or a wedding day."

—Reverend Richard G. Francesco, a Catholic priest
and administrator of St. Benedict's Church, Newark, New Jersey

"The first meeting is usually all the logistics—date, time, and so forth. During the second meeting, I want to get to know the couple better. I ask how they deal with money issues, and sex, and how well they know each other. I ask what Judaism means to them, and what kind of Jewish home they want to create. I want them to open up to each other and be aware of issues they need to work on as a couple. During those first two meetings, I'll also discuss the details—for example, I'll ask if they're writing their vows and what kind of Ketubah they will have."

—Rabbi Judy Schindler,
Westchester Reform Temple, Scarsdale, New York

Ceremony Basics

Before you begin cooking up the ceremony of the century, take a look at the ingredients. Whether your service is civil or religious, it will follow this general outline—a civil officiant will simply omit the religious rituals. Each state, religion, and sometimes congregation has its own approach. You'll probably start with your officiant's basic structure and then add custom details.

- Procession
- Officiant's opening remarks
- Charge to couple: ("Do you, James, take Ashley to be your lawfully wedded . . . ?")
- Vows
- Ring exchange and any other unity gestures
- Pronouncement (The "I now pronounce you . . ." part)
- The kiss (finally!)
- The officiant's closing remarks and final blessing
- Recession

Now let's take a more detailed look at each part to help you get familiar with what a ceremony entails.

Officiant Finances

The officiant fee probably won't make much of a dent in your wedding budget, but it's still something to factor in. Fees range from free to $500, depending on the congregation and/or individual officiant.

Also, make sure to thank your officiant, pay him or her (even if s/he accepts donation only; add a little extra to show your gratitude), and invite him/or her to your reception. (S/he may not come, but s/he'll appreciate the gesture.)

The Procession

The procession is like a flowchart of what's about to happen. You and your beloved each make your way to the altar separately, symbolizing the fact that you're coming from different backgrounds and families. You meet at the altar or stage and move closer to each other throughout the ceremony (holding hands, exchanging rings, planting the kiss), representing the merging of your lives into one new unit.

The doors of the church, synagogue, or Hyatt Grand Ballroom are thrown open, and your wedding party marches down the aisle. In a traditional Christian procession, the bride is escorted by her father; the groom waits for her up front. In a traditional Jewish procession, both parents escort both the bride and the groom. Or you can choose your escort based on your situation. If you're close to both your parents, it's fine to make the march a *pas-de-trois* (both parents) regardless of your religion. If your mother and stepfather raised you, you could acknowledge their support (emotional and otherwise) by walking with them. If your aunt raised you and is your closest confidante, ask her to be at your side. If you feel you've arrived at this moment on your own, you may want to go it alone.

Who heads down the aisle when? If you're having a civil ceremony, you can improvise, or you might choose to follow the order of religious processions. Here are the basic plans:

Aisle Runner Reasoning

The aisle runner, traditionally red or white, was believed to protect the couple from evil spirits lurking in the floorboards. A red runner also connotes a sense of honor (like rolling out the red carpet), while a white runner represents a pure pathway.

Christian Procession

The officiant, groom, and best man wait up at the altar for the:

- Groomsmen (who walk in from the side or accompanying bridesmaids; also may wait at the altar with the other men)
- Bridesmaids (starting with the attendant who will stand farthest from the bride at the altar)
- Ring bearer and/or flower girl (child attendants can be seated with their parents once they reach the front)
- Honor attendant(s)
- The bride, walking to the left of her escort

Jewish Procession

- Rabbi and/or cantor
- Grandparents of the groom
- Grandparents of the bride (the grandparents are seated in the first rows; groom's on the left, bride's on the right)
- Groomsmen (in pairs)
- Best man
- The groom and his parents (dad on his left, mom on right)

- The bridesmaids (starting with the one who will stand farthest from the bride under the huppah)
- Honor attendant(s)
- Ring bearer and/or flower girl
- The bride and her parents (dad on left, mom on right)

CHRISTIAN PROCESSIONAL

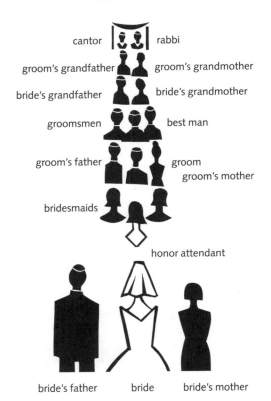

JEWISH PROCESSIONAL

ASK CARLEY

Whom Should I Walk With?

Q. Whom should I have walk me down the aisle? I'm close to my mom, dad, and my stepdad.
A: If everyone gets along and they all agree to it, why not walk with all three (your dad on one side, your mom and stepdad on the other)? Or start out with Dad and do a parental hand-off halfway down the aisle, finishing with Mom and Stepdad. Just make sure you and your folks are comfortable with the format—and that the aisle is wide enough!

The Officiant's Opening Remarks

Once you're up at the altar, the officiant calls things to order—welcoming the guests (and acknowledging God, if it's a religious ceremony). You've heard it a hundred times in the movies: "Dearly beloved, we are gathered here today . . ." By including your guests, the introduction reminds them that they are sharing this important event with you, acting as witnesses to it, and agreeing to support your marriage. The call to God is there to remind you and every-one else of the seriousness and solemnity of marriage, and to make this ceremony, and your marriage, holy. It gives you a minute to recognize that you're getting married not only in front of your friends and family but also before the Almighty One.

You need a license to wed. Go to Chapter 21 for marriage license how-tos.

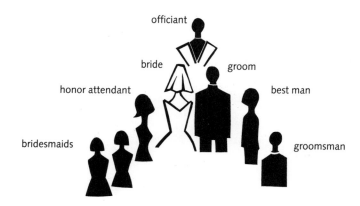

CHRISTIAN CEREMONY POSITIONS

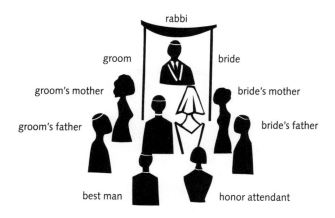

JEWISH CEREMONY POSITIONS

Take a Seat: Who Sits Where?

As a rule, the closer the person is to you emotionally, the nearer he or she sits to the action, and the later he or she takes a seat:

First and second rows: Immediate family, parents, siblings, grandparents
Third through fifth rows: Aunts, uncles, cousins, and godparents; stepfamily; other special guests

In Christian ceremonies, the bride's mother is *always* the last person to be seated (right after the groom's mother), signifying that the ceremony is about to begin.

Generally, in Christian ceremonies, the bride's family and guests sit on the left (when entering from the back) and the groom's side takes over the right. For Jewish services, it's reversed. A mixed marriage? Either choose a system that works for you, or make it a free-for-all. If you've invited 120 people, and your honey has, well . . . Mom and Dad, *don't* divide by family. Have your ushers direct people to the best seats available to create a balance.

Traditionally, an usher offers his right arm to a female guest, while her male escort follows them down the aisle. If that seems too formal for your crowd, the ushers can merely greet guests at the door and say, "Please follow me," or "Hello. Right this way." Plan to have one usher for every fifty guests to keep things flowing. Who's an usher? A groomsman on double duty, your teenage cousins, or good friends.

Altar Arrangements: Who Stands Where?

There isn't *one* correct altar arrangement, but several options from which to choose. Or design your own with your officiant. Here are the details on the traditional line-up.

Bride and groom: Traditionally, the bride stands on the left (with her back to the congregation), with her groom to the right (in a Jewish ceremony, this is reversed).

Attendants: Attendants generally divide by the sexes (ushers to the groom's side, bridesmaids to the bride's), or walk and stand in pairs (one usher/bridesmaid pair to the right, the next to the left, etc.). They either line up diagonally behind the spot where you'll stand or form a big semicircle around you. If you take the couple's approach, each usher/bridesmaid pair remains together in the line, or the bridesmaids stand on a step behind their escorts. In a Jewish wedding, your attendants stand under the huppah with you, honor attendants one diagonal step behind you, other attendants behind them.

Parents: Your parents' places depend on how much you want to include them in your ceremony. If both your parents walk both of you down the aisle, all four might remain standing with you for the entire service (as in a Jewish ceremony, where the parents remain under the huppah, on either side of the rabbi). Traditionally, if the bride's father walks her down the aisle, he either leaves her at the altar with her groom or remains standing between them until the officiant asks "Who supports this woman in marriage?" at which time he gives his blessing and takes his seat in the front pew with the bride's mother (as in a Protestant or Catholic service). The groom's parents traditionally sit in the front pew throughout a Christian ceremony. But again, if you prefer family closeness over tradition, they can stand with you.

Kids: Include pint-size attendants in the altar line-up only if they're old enough to stand still comfortably for the duration of your ceremony. Otherwise, stand them behind you, in front of your older attendants, or have them sit with their parents.

Readers/performers: They rise to do their bit, then retake their seat.

Charge to the Couple: Saying "I Do"

The "Do you, Mary, take John to be your lawfully wedded husband?" part, to which you each respond "I do" or "I will," verifies that you're marrying of your own free will. (This isn't an official part of a Jewish ceremony, though some rabbis will include it.)

The Exchange of Vows

Your vows are your promises to each other—a statement of your intentions and expectations for your marriage. You may choose to use the familiar "To have and to hold, for better or for worse" vows; repeating words that have been worn smooth through years of use gives some couples a sense of permanence, a bigger-than-both-of-us feeling. Or you might decide to write your own vows. Make sure they express what's unique about your relationship and what you want your future together to be like. Some couples read prose or poetry passages that are meaningful to them. If you take the personalized approach, you'll probably need to run your plans by your officiant. S/he may check to make sure your vows clearly define your views on marriage and address the commitment seriously. (See "Vows That Wow," later in the chapter, for more.)

Face each other when saying your vows, not the officiant. And hold hands. You're marrying each other, after all, not the guy or gal in the robe.

About Face

Consider facing your guests, with your officiant's back to the congregation instead of yours, while you say your vows. This will allow everyone a good view of the exchange and make them feel more a part of the moment.

The Ring Ceremony

As you exchange rings, you generally say "With this ring, I thee wed." You may add something a bit more personal about what the ring (and your sweetie) means to you.

Ring in the Wedding

You'll be sporting a shiny "occupied" sign on your ring finger for the rest of your lives. So choose wedding bands you like. Any kind of ring can be a wedding band, but consider your choice carefully—this is the ultimate symbol of your union. If you're both getting bands, they don't have to match (unless you want them to). You can get them engraved on the inside (with your initials, wedding date, mushy sentiment, private joke) at the same store where you buy them. Here's our guide to all things shiny:

24k: 100 percent gold
18k: 74 percent gold
14k: 58.5 percent gold
Yellow gold: The higher the gold percentage, the richer the color and the softer the band. If you're active, go with 14k rather than 24k—its alloys (those nongold additives) help make it stronger than the pure stuff.
White gold: Karat for karat, white gold is stronger than yellow gold, although it's more brittle. It looks like silver and is a good choice if you like the look better or if you're allergic to yellow gold.
Platinum: Stronger than gold and more expensive.

The Pronouncement of Marriage

The officiant makes it official ("I now pronounce you husband and wife").

The Kiss

It doesn't have to be a quick peck on the cheek—go ahead and show some emotion! Give each other a good, tight hug. Make it last as long as you like. Try to fix that moment in your mind to remember it.

Closing Remarks

Your officiant wraps up the wedding with a few words to you and a blessing, if it's a religious ceremony. If it's a Jewish wedding, the groom—and sometimes the bride, too—will step on a glass wrapped in a napkin. When the glass shatters, the crowd shouts "Mazel Tov!" meaning "Good Luck!"

The Recession

You're done—it's time to party! Here's how to leave the ceremony and get to the reception on time.

Kissing Comes From . . .

The final ceremony kiss is an ancient Roman tradition. Contracts were sealed with a kiss. It was also believed that when you kissed, you exchanged a bit of your soul with your breath.

The Christian Recession

After the ceremony, the wedding party retraces its steps, the men escorting the women back down the aisle in this order:

- Bride and groom
- Flower girl and ring bearer (optional)

Places, Please: The Rehearsal

How are you supposed to remember all this stuff? Practice, practice, practice—at the ceremony rehearsal.

Who: Everyone who has a part in the ceremony—you two, your parents, your attendants, ushers, readers, singers.

When: Generally, the night before the wedding, though you can do it two or three days in advance. No earlier, or everyone will forget their lines!

Where: At the ceremony site, so everyone can see where they're supposed to stand, etc. It's followed by a celebratory dinner.

Why: Not everyone has your stage presence and nerves of steel! The rehearsal helps all the participants calm down and study up.

What: Attendants find out their entry and exit order and practice walking. Your special performers learn where and when to do their thing. You two practice your aisle style, along with your folks and/or escorts. You'll all do a ceremony run-through; you won't say your full vows, but you will go over the exact order of elements and any cues that inspire actions such as rising, sitting, kissing, or exiting.

- Honor attendants (maid/matron of honor and best man)
- Bridesmaids and groomsmen, in pairs

(Parents leave the pews directly after the wedding party recesses, followed by the congregation.)

Ring Lore

Brides in ancient Rome wore wedding rings on their thumbs; Puritan couples didn't wear any because they were considered frivolous jewelry or "relics of popery." In Colonial times, people started giving "marriage thimbles" (useful, and therefore accepted). After the marriage, the bottom of the thimble would be cut off to create a ring.

The Jewish Recession

Again, the procession is essentially reversed:

- Bride and groom
- Bride's parents
- Groom's parents
- Ring bearer and flower girl (optional)
- Honor attendants (maid/matron of honor and best man)
- Bridesmaids and groomsmen
- Cantor and/or rabbi

Ceremonies with Personal Style

Most ceremonies have a similar structure, but you can personalize yours with vows, readings, songs, speeches, unity symbols, free-verse beat poetry, or a surprise performance of spiritual Yanni music—whatever elements help express your thoughts and feelings about your marriage. Discuss your ideas with your officiant to make sure they don't conflict with the requirements of your religion, church, synagogue, or hall.

Vows That Wow

Personalized vows are one of the best ways to say what your marriage means to you. Here are guidelines on how to write your own:

- Your vows can follow the traditional format: "I vow to love, honor, support. . . ." (Use your officiant's standard version as a template.) Or you can write them in your own style: "I promise to remember every day how much I love you and how lucky I am to have you. . . ." Think about what you want to give and receive from your marriage.
- Sit down and talk about what it all means to you. This will not only give you a good starting point for writing, but it also will ensure that you're both aware how your partner views marriage and, more specifically, *your* marriage.
- Write down the typical wedding words and emotions (love, support, cherish, devotion, respect, honor), and think about personal ways to express them. Flip through your thesaurus. Take inspiration from biblical, poetic, or great prose passages.

- If your favorite poet or essayist said it more succinctly than you ever could, quote her.
- Make your vows reflect *your* situation. Are you from different religious backgrounds and committed to making them mesh? Do you want to affirm your belief in marriage, despite the fact that both of your parents are divorced, twice? Address your background in terms of how it will help shape your future positively—be discreet and upbeat.
- If your marriage is a union of two different cultures or religions, consider incorporating lines by great poets or scholars from each.
- If your family speaks English and your honey's communicates in Portuguese, have someone translate the vows for you. Or each of you can recite them in both languages.
- Try to keep them under three minutes—vows are your marriage vision highlights, not the daily play-by-play.
- Once you've written your vows, read them out loud. What looks good on paper doesn't always sound so smooth once you hear it. Whenever you're writing something to be heard by others (not read by them), use short, simple sentences—they're easier for people to follow (and for you to memorize).

The Wedding Program

Like a theater playbill, a wedding program outlines the acts to come and gives interesting background info about the players and the show. You can use yours to highlight special rituals included in your ceremony (a great idea for an interfaith wedding, or one that includes ethnic customs) and to thank the supporting cast. You can get programs printed along with the invitations, or take the make-at-home computer approach. Have someone pass them out before the ceremony begins, place them on the seats, or leave them on an entrance table.

What should you include? Consider:

Names of the wedding party and why they're special to you (or how they're related)
The order of your ceremony
Names of songs (and, perhaps why you chose them)
Names of readings (and explanations, where appropriate)
Words of poems or free-verse recitation
Thank-yous
Photos
Tributes (to deceased relatives)

ANDI AND KEN
June 2, New York City

ANDI AND KEN met when she took out a personal ad and he responded. The rest was history! Before the wedding, their rabbi (a woman) asked to see Andi's ad and Ken's written response—they thought she was going to use it to get to know them better. But at the ceremony, she surprised them by saying "Do you, sensual, petite, blonde, take this optimistic confident banker. . . ." Andi and Ken loved how personal it was. "We both love surprises," says the bride. "We chose our rabbi because we felt comfortable around her. We had no idea how funny she was!"

Readings to Remember

A reading can be traditional, biblical, poetic, humorous, or serious—anything that elaborates on your ideas of marriage and your relationship. Just make sure you clear what you want read with your officiant first; some churches and temples may have restrictions.

The Bible is, of course, a great source for tried-and-true wedding readings, but there are many other places to look for ideas. Listen to your favorite CDs (or read the lyrics); peruse your best-loved poems, stories, essays, fables, Hallmark cards, romance novels, plays, op-eras, and self-help books. Ask recently married friends for suggestions; they've already done all this research and may have a pile of prescreened books you can borrow. See if your family or clergy member has any folktales or religious wedding texts you might be interested in, too.

Ask friends, relatives, stepparents, or mentors to read at your wedding. Or read yourselves, alternating verses of a poem or different paragraphs of the same story. A reading doesn't have to be formal; you might choose to talk (tactfully) about your relationship history, what specific challenges you face, and how you think this relationship will help you grow and flourish.

Include your guests by distributing copies of that great wedding poem, or print it in your program.

Say It with Song

You can march to music during the procession and recession, have musical accompaniment during a silent meditation, feature a special song (or songs), or use music to break up elements of the ceremony. Music is one of the most intense emotion conveyers—a perky tune will create an entirely different mood than a somber one. Pay attention to how your desired tunes make you feel. And check with your officiant *before* booking the band; there may be restrictions on the types of music you can use.

> **Where to Find Great Readings**
>
> The Bible
>
> *Library of World Poetry*, edited by William Cullen Bryant (Grammercy, 1995)
>
> *The American Poetry Anthology*, edited by Daniel Halpern (out of print, check your library)
>
> *Into the Garden: A Wedding Anthology*, edited by Robert Hass and Stephen Mitchell (Harper Perennial, 1994)
>
> Poetry by Ranier Maria Rilke, e.e. cummings, John Donne, or Walt Whitman

Procession, Recession, and Ambient Music: Ask the cantor (if you're Jewish), the church choir, or a talented friend to sing throughout the procession. Or go with a Gregorian chant group, a brass section, a classical trio, a harpist, pianist, flutist, Flamenco guitarist, or great harmonica player. If you have the interest but not the financial assets for marching music, choose great recorded tunes and assign someone to CD or tape-deck duty.

Featured Songs: If your best friend was an opera major in college, invite her to sing an aria as a featured act during your ceremony. Or ask someone to perform "your" song. If you're the one with the great voice, sing something yourself. (Do a romantic serenade.) Or ask a friend with a great voice to lead the entire congregation in song. (Distribute copies of the words, if necessary.)

Singer/Songwriter: Write your own song to sing to your sweetie, or to the crowd in general. If your dad is a basement composer, bring his best song to light at your wedding, or ask him to compose something new for the occasion. You could even hire a professional composer (or your favorite local band) to write you a wedding song.

Go to Chapter 16 for more on making your ceremony sing.

Ethnic and Regional Options: Spice up your ceremony by including music from your families' countries of origin. Hire a twelve-piece mariachi band to play Mexican music for the procession. Go with the smooth sounds of steel drum band if you're from the Caribbean. Or have racy guitar music from Spain. You also can use regional sound stylings—a zydeco band from Louisiana, soulful blues from Chicago, bluegrass or Dixie from the Deep South.

Unity Symbols

Incorporate visual representations of the marriage bond—two people becoming one while each retaining their own identities. You can include your families in the ritual to symbolize a broader blending of two clans.

Unity Candle: The bride and groom, each holding a candle, light a third, centrally located candle together. You may blow out the individual flames, or all three candles may remain lit throughout the rest of the ceremony. You could initiate the process by having your mothers each light a candle first; your mom uses hers to start up yours, and your sweetie's mom does the same on her side. Sometimes the entire congregation holds candles, which get lit from the final, unified flame.

Unity Cup: Each family fills its own cup with wine. The bride and groom each pour half of their "family" cup into one, shared cup. Then they each take a sip. The half-filled family cups represent their individuality, the shared cup their new union.

Other Options: For the vessel and rose rite—a recently created unity symbol—the groom gives the bride a rose during the ceremony. She gives him an earthen vase, and then puts the rose in the vase while the officiant comments on their union. You, too, can create your own unity symbol, drawing on an ethnic custom or just using your own vision. Your symbol might be a tree you plant together. It might be a food- or wine-sharing ritual. It could be religious—such as the figure-eight–style rosary that's draped over both partners' shoulders in a traditional Mexican ceremony. Ask your parents, grandparents, or a local cultural center about ethnic ceremony customs you could incorporate or adapt. Blend customs from both your heritages, or borrow those from other countries that you like. Then run your ideas by your officiant.

Honoring the Deceased

How can you pay a tribute to a special someone who's passed away?

- Write something about him and read it aloud.
- Read his favorite poem or a selection for his favorite author.
- Have everyone sing her favorite song.
- Have your musicians play his favorite song.
- Wear something belonging to her.
- Display a memory photo album.
- Leave your bouquet on his grave.

Religious Ceremony Specifics

If you're having a religious ceremony, that ceremony will be shaped, in large part, by the rituals and requirements of your faith. If you have different religions (or have been habitually non-observant), this is a good time to choose a faith (or to decide how you'll handle religion once you're married). Below is a look at what major U.S. religions require for weddings. But rules may vary; check with your officiant for details.

Buddhist Ceremony

Buddhist customs differ depending on the sect, or "school," and there are very few hard-and-fast wedding "rules." Sometimes the wedding date is set by an astrologer, according to your birth dates. The ceremony might take place in a temple or at a special altar erected for your marriage somewhere else.

Here's how the Japanese-based "Jodo" Shin or "Pure Land" Shin Buddhist temple handles weddings in the United States: The ceremony opens with chanting by the priest and meditation by everyone else. The priest then reads some of the Buddha's words on marriage, followed by a charge to the couple ("Do you take this man . . ."), and a standard American-style ring exchange. Then bride and groom each take a pinch of incense and place it on the altar in front of the statue of Buddha (to show respect and gratitude to the Buddha and to each other). The officiant pronounces the couple husband and wife, gives the go-ahead for the kiss, and delivers a short closing message. He also may hand the newlyweds a set of meditation beads and a book on Buddhist teachings.

Islamic Ceremony

An American Islamic wedding tends to blend Muslim and American culture.

Before the Wedding: The bride and groom agree on a "meher," a specific sum of money he'll give her. The meher is considered the bride's security and guarantee of freedom within the marriage. The meher has two parts: The "prompt" is due before the groom has "conjugal rights"; the "deferred" is an amount he'll give his bride during the course of his life. The meher can be $1 or $20,000 (or as much as you two want). Before the ceremony, the groom proposes to the bride in front of at least two witnesses, giving the details of the meher agreement. The amount is officially recorded. Today a lot of couples make the ring the "prompt." (The groom hands it over during the ceremony.) The "deferred" can be anything you two decide on.

During the Ceremony: Both bride and groom must bring at least one witness. The ceremony generally follows the basic American style, but when the officiant says the "Do you take . . ." part, he mentions the names of the witnesses and the meher amount. And the sermon might be in Arabic rather than English. There isn't a class of clergy in Islam; any Muslim person can officiate your wedding. The marriage is considered a contract between the couple and Allah.

Jewish Ceremony

Minhag is the term used to describe the Jewish wedding customs. Jewish traditions may vary depending on the affiliation, the synagogue, and the individual rabbi. But here's a look at some of the minhag musts.

The Huppah: This canopy, held aloft over the bride and groom, dates to the tent of Abraham and those nomadic desert days when all Jewish wedding ceremonies were held outdoors. Back then the huppah was used to create an intimate, sanctified space. Today it represents your new home (with open sides, inviting friends and family in). While you don't technically *need* a huppah to have a wedding, many people feel it's mandatory (and it is nice!).

Wine: A Jewish wedding has two wine rituals, one at the beginning of the ceremony and one near the end. Each time you and your beloved drink from a shared cup.

Tangible Goods: To be valid, a Jewish wedding must contain an exchange of something of value. Today this generally means the ring ceremony.

Jewish Wedding Wisdom

Check out *The New Jewish Wedding*, by Anita Diamant (Summit Books, 1986; reprinted by Fireside).

Ketubah: After the ring exchange, the rabbi reads the Ketubah, or marriage contract. It's usually ornately decorated. The Ketubah belongs to the bride and lists her rights in the marriage. It's signed in the presence of a rabbi and two witnesses, usually directly before or during the ceremony. In Orthodox weddings, only the groom signs it; in Conservative or Reform ceremonies, the bride gets to, too.

Seven Blessings: This is the heart of the Jewish ceremony. The rabbi and other significant people in your lives recite the seven marriage blessings.

The Breaking of the Glass: Nothing says "Jewish wedding" more than the sound of a breaking glass. Depending on whom you ask, the breaking of the glass is, among other things, (1) a symbol of the destruction of the Temple in Jerusalem; (2) a representation of the fragility of human relationships; and/or (3), a reminder that marriage changes the lives of individuals forever. (Contrary to popular belief, the glass breaking has nothing to do with virginity!) It's also the official signal to shout "Mazel tov!" The glass is wrapped in a napkin and special pouch for safety. The groom smashes it with his foot, or bride and groom can stomp on it together.

The Yichud: The word means "seclusion," and it's a totally private affair. Immediately after the ceremony, the couple retreats to a private room for fifteen minutes of staring into each other's eyes. In the past, bride and groom would head to a nearby tent to consummate the marriage! This isn't done much these days, but it is customary for newlyweds to seize a Yichud moment and feed each other a bite of something.

Church of Latter-Day Saints (Mormon) Ceremony

There are two types of Church of Latter-Day Saints (Mormon) services: an official "temple wedding" or a standard church service. A temple wedding is always held within one of the world's fifty-three holy temples and is considered a marriage for life *and* afterlife. The wording is "for time and all eternity," *not* "until death do you part." The devout strive for a temple wedding, which requires advance permission.

Before the Ceremony: To get permission for a temple wedding (also called a "sealing ordinance"), you each set up a private interview with your own local bishop, during which you'll answer questions about your religious diligence. Basically, you attest that you believe in the church's teachings and that you're following the specific precepts. These include following the "Code of Health" (abstaining from alcohol, tobacco, coffee, and tea), being "Morally Clean" (abstaining from sex, or even heavy petting, according to some bishops), and following the law of tithing (paying 10 percent of your income to the church). If your bishop finds you diligent, he'll sign a "temple recommend," which gives you permission to enter a holy temple.

Then you take your temple recommend to the "stake president," a leader overseeing several bishops in a large region. He'll ask you the same basic questions, and, if he's satisfied with your answers, sign your temple recommend, too. After that, you're ready to tie that eternal knot. Once you set up the interviews, you can complete the whole process within a week.

The Temple Ceremony: The ceremony itself is similar to a standard Protestant wedding, except that your guests must have a temple recommend to attend, as well, meaning it may be a *lot* smaller than a nontemple wedding. (Usually it's just family and close friends.) The temple president or a "temple sealer" (a clergy member with authority to officiate a wedding) will oversee. You need at least two witnesses.

A Nontemple Wedding: This is open to any member of the Church of Latter-Day Saints. You don't need a temple recommend, and your wedding can be overseen by your local bishop at any church. If you take this route or have a civil ceremony, you may be able to have a second ceremony later (after you've begun following the church's precepts), to "seal" the marriage for eternity.

Protestant Ceremony

The standard American wedding is basically Protestant in nature. Almost all Protestant weddings share the same procession, recession, and altar positions. The traditional call to worship, "We are gathered here today in the presence of God . . ." comes from the Episcopalian *Book of Common Prayer* (and it's almost identical to the Presbyterian opening, "We are gathered here today to witness the marriage of . . ."). Most Protestant services also include the giving away (or more modern "blessing") of the bride, your vows, the blessing and exchange of rings, prayers, and closing words.

Beyond those basics, each church will have a specific take on music, sermons, a unity candle, and audience participation. If you're Methodist, Lutheran, or Presbyterian, you'll probably follow the guidelines of your church's ceremony service book. If you're Unitarian, you'll work with your minister to create your ceremony. There's no set liturgy, meaning plenty of creative input for you. If you're Baptist, your church will set the rules regarding marriage specifics within it. Talk to your officiant about details.

Quaker Ceremony

If you want a Quaker wedding, you mail a "letter of intent to marry under the care of the monthly meeting" to the clerk of your meeting house. Though Quaker Sunday services are basically silent, each congregation has a monthly business meeting to discuss important issues such as marriages. The clerk will bring up your letter at the next business meeting, and the community will appoint a two- to three-member "marriage committee." Your marriage committee meets with you to decide if they think you're ready to tie the knot, based on their assessment of things such as your maturity, education, finances, plans for children, and the like.

If your marriage committee gives you the go-ahead, you'll then have a "wedding committee" assigned to you. The wedding committee is like an official honor attendant/helpful mom/supporting sponsor all rolled into one (actually, three to ten people). Your committee members will help you with wedding details, from reserving the meeting house to dealing with reception logistics.

The Ceremony: The most noticeable variation from the Protestant

Ethnic Ceremony Ideas

At Egyptian weddings, a range of musicians plays the processional music on not-so-subtle instruments like drums, bagpipes, and horns. Belly dancers slink down the aisle, along with men carrying flaming swords—a far different effect from a string quartet!

The Apache mix colored sands in a crystal bowl as a symbol of unity.

For Hindus, red, not white, is the color of marriage. The bride might wear a red sari (or veil) and sport orange-red henna designs on her hands, feet, and along the part of her hair.

The sake-sharing ritual is the main bonding rite of a Shinto ceremony (an ancient religion, practiced primarily in Japan). The couple also honors ancestors with a food offering before family shrines.

In an Eastern Orthodox wedding (Russian and Greek), the bride and groom exchange their rings three times to represent marriage under the Holy Trinity. Then they slip them on the fourth finger of their *right* hands.

norm is the lack of an officiant. You two will be marrying each other before God, without any intermediary. During the wedding (usually held on a Saturday), you and your committee sit on "facing benches" before the rest of the congregation (your guests). Everyone worships silently until you two feel that it's time to say your vows. You stand up, face each other, hold hands, and deliver your promises (which you've written). Then you sit back down for more silent worship. Congregants and guests will stand, if they want to, to say a few words or voice their support for you. The meeting usually ends with a nod from one of your committee members. Then it's on to the reception!

Roman Catholic Ceremony

Considered one of the Seven Sacraments, or channels to God's grace, the wedding ceremony is a serious affair in the Catholic church. Often the wedding includes a full mass (called a nuptial mass), including readings and communion. Your priest probably will help you choose prayers, hymns, and readings from the Scriptures to customize the service. After you exchange your vows, he blesses your rings before you slip them on each other's fingers. The procession, recession, and altar positions are identical to those of a standard Protestant wedding ceremony (although your attendants may sit for most of the mass and stand with you during the vows).

To marry in the Catholic church, one of you (or both, depending on the officiant) must be Catholic. If you want to marry in a church other than your home parish, you must get permission from your pastor. You'll have to show your baptism certificate and proof that any previous marriages were officially annulled.

Some churches still do a modified posting of the banns. In the past, banns (basically, a notice of your intention to wed) were physically tacked outside the church doors. Anyone in the community who knew of any reason why you *shouldn't* get married (another spouse already in the picture, for example) would see the notice and stop the wedding. Today your banns might be printed in the church bulletin or announced from the pulpit during a Sunday service.

Interfaith Ceremonies

"Religion in a wedding is great," you say, "but, sadly, we don't share the same one." Rather than let this become a source of stress, rejoice in the fact that you have two great traditions from which to draw. We know many interfaith couples who had great weddings. (Some of our parents, for example!) In fact, more than 40,000 Jewish/Christian couples get engaged in the United States each year. Sure, arranging an interfaith ceremony can lead to disagreements and family pressure aplenty, but their increasing presence and acceptance means it should be easier than it's ever been for you to plan one.

Finding an Interfaith Officiant (or Two)

Each religion has its own view on interfaith unions, from "Go for it!" to "No way." Some religions and sects leave the decision up to individual clergy members. If both of your religions are somewhat flexible, you may look for an officiant from each to preside over a joint ceremony. This is the most complicated plan but also the most popular because it guarantees that each side's beliefs are included. It also reflects the meaning of marriage; you're joining your lives here. Think of your ceremony as the first of many blended rituals.

In some cities (including Chicago, San Francisco, and Washington, D.C.), you'll find Christian/Jewish "clergy teams." These ministers and rabbis have performed many interfaith ceremonies and will work together to help you plan yours.

If your religion is in the "no-way" camp (such as Orthodox Jewish), forget the dual-officiant approach—it's not gonna happen. You could hold two separate ceremonies instead—only one is legally binding; the other serves as a blessing over your union. A clergy member who won't officially oversee your wedding may be willing to bless it in a smaller, more private setting. Your other options include going with one of your religions, finding a third, neutral religion, or taking the civil route. To find interfaith officiants:

- Ask other interfaith couples you know for referrals. (It pays to get references!)
- Look in the society wedding pages of your local newspaper for names of clergy who have conducted interfaith ceremonies.
- Ask any clergy members who turn you down for names of officiants they know who are willing.

Planning an Interfaith Ceremony

You and your fiancé/e should sit down together to discuss your values and identify what is meaningful to you about the wedding ceremony in general. Then talk to your officiant(s) about which religious traditions you can use that won't conflict with the tenets of the other. Your officiant(s) should be able to help you choose appropriate customs that will enhance the ceremony without stepping on any religious toes.

For readings, consult texts from both religions. Consider each reading passages from the other's faith, or asking family members to do so. Create as many opportunities for family to participate as possible; it will make everyone feel included in this joining of two different backgrounds.

It's impossible to list what *exactly* you can incorporate in an interfaith wedding—the details depend entirely on the two of you, your officiant(s), and your house(s) of worship. But here are two samples of *possible* mixed ceremonies.

Catholic/Jewish Ceremony: Hold it under a huppah in a nonreligious location; include the blessings over the wine, the reading of the Ketubah, the seven blessings (be sure to ask non-Jewish family members to recite a few), and the breaking of the glass. From the Catholic tradition, include prayers, hymns, a priest's sermon, and a closing peace-be-with-you handshake. And don't forget your personal vows, the rings, and readings, of course.

Interfaith Weddings

Interfaith-accepting religions:

- Baha'i
- Buddhist
- Hindu
- Protestant
- Quaker
- Shinto

Somewhat interfaith-accepting religions:

- Catholic (more than ever these days)
- Eastern Orthodox (as long as the non-EO partner is Christian)
- Church of Latter-Day Saints (but not in one of the fifty-three holy temples)
- Muslim (man can marry a Christian or Jewish woman and still have an Islamic wedding; a woman can only marry a Muslim man)
- Reform Jewish

Go to Chapter 19 for more help with interfaith angst and other relationship stumbling blocks.

Buddhist/Christian Ceremony: Hold it in a neutral location and set up a Buddhist altar. After a standard Christian procession and officiant welcome, have a moment of silent meditation (during which time your Buddhist officiant might chant; Eastern music could be playing). After the pastor's sermon, your Buddhist officiant can share the Buddha's words on marriage. Make your readings a combination of biblical passages and Eastern thoughts. In your vows, promise to respect both religions and religious traditions. After the ring ceremony, give an offering to the Buddha at the altar.

Finding an Officiant

Check out local college campuses for chaplains and other clergy likely to be comfortable with an interfaith wedding. Or call the American Ethical Union (212-873-6500) for info on finding an officiant to perform an interfaith ceremony in your area.

Second Weddings

This is your chance to do it all over again, exactly the way you want to. Planning the wedding this time around just may be more fun—there's bound to be less pressure from parents or other well-meaning opinion-meisters. Since second-timers often foot the bill themselves, they have far more freedom to call the shots. And, having done it before, they know exactly what shots to call.

A second wedding can be a huge soiree with all the trimmings or an intimate, family-only affair. Brides, you can walk down the aisle with your parents again (or anyone else you choose) or go it alone. You both can wear anything you want—white, off-white, red-velvet jumpsuit. (But brides, you might want to skip the veil this time—you're going into it with your eyes open, and the veil is a first-time bride tradition, anyway.) Basically, a second wedding is just like a first wedding, except one (or both of) you has a bit more experience. And you'll probably feel less tied to tradition.

Major Religions on Second Marriages

Here's a brief look at religions' views of remarriage:

Buddhist: Divorce and remarriage are allowed, provided the priest has no reservations about the couple's commitment.

Church of Latter-Day Saints: You can remarry in a temple, providing you're both living according to the church's precepts (including reabstaining from sex until after your wedding).

Islam: Divorce and remarriage are permitted, according to the Koran. You'll need legal documents proving your divorce is final, and there's a waiting period of about three months.

Jewish: You can remarry after a civil divorce if you're Reform. If you're Conservative or Orthodox, you need a *get*—a Jewish divorce decree from a rabbinical court.

Protestant: Views about divorce vary, but Lutheran, Methodist, and Presbyterian churches, in general, allow divorce. Baptist churches each have their own authority; some ministers permit second marriages, others don't. Episcopalian rectors review each case individually and make recommendations to the bishop about whether to grant a remarriage or not. The process takes about two months.

Roman Catholic: You must get an annulment to remarry within the Catholic church. Because marriage is considered a sacrament, you must get it officially declared null and void.

Unitarian Universalist: Each minister sets his/her own criteria.

If you have kids, include them in the ceremony. Even if they're thrilled about your honey and your wedding (cake, presents, party!), they'll probably need reassurance about their continued importance in your life (particularly if they live with you). Your new status gives them new status, too—and it wasn't of their choosing. Don't expect them to do more at your wedding than they usually can—if your five-year-old refuses to stand still for ten minutes on an ordinary Saturday afternoon, he won't suddenly do it at your wedding. And if your kids don't want to participate, try to respect their feelings.

If you're still friendly with your ex-spouse and your ex–family-in-law, go ahead and invite them, if you want to. If your ex is the father of your children, including him shows your kids that they don't have to "take sides"; your new spouse doesn't mean they get a replacement parent. But consider the feelings of your partner, too. If he or she will be uncomfortable with your ex at the wedding, you might want to withhold that invite.

Be considerate of each other during the planning process, and respect the fact that your differing experiences may lead to different desires and expectations. If this is your second wedding and your fiancé/e's first, don't make too many comments like "Last time we used this caterer," or "I know because I've done it before." You want the first-timer to know that *this* is the most important wedding in the history of the universe.

If you're the first-time partner, don't dwell on your to-be's past. Focus on *your* wedding. Don't ask about the first wedding or dig out old photo albums from your honey's basement. If s/he keeps bringing up last time, keep explaining that this is new to you and that you want to start from scratch.

Commitment Ceremonies

If you're planning a same-sex wedding, the good news is you're probably not going to get a lot of pressure to have traditional ceremony. And since same-sex weddings are not legal (as of this printing), there are fewer details to worry about. But just because it isn't legal doesn't mean you shouldn't do it! Having a commitment ceremony, "Holy Union," or whatever you want to call it serves the same purposes as a traditional wedding. It:

- Makes a public proclamation of your love and intent to remain together.
- Brings your family and friends together to support your union.
- Gives you a sense of permanence, stability, and security.
- Helps you secure domestic partner status (in some states).

A wedding ceremony can have added significance for a gay or lesbian couple—since you're not getting a legal paper, the ceremony itself is *the* binding ritual (as it should be). A wedding ceremony—gay or straight—is about the two of you, your commitment to and belief in each other.

Roles for Little Folks

How can your kids participate?

- Take vows accepting their new siblings or family.

- Be a flower girl, ring bearer, or usher.

- Be a junior bridesmaid or groomsman (teens).

- Escort you down the aisle and "give you away."

- Read a poem, biblical verse, or prose piece.

- Sing a song; play the guitar; accompany a singer on the banjo, guitar, violin, tap shoes.

- Create the program.

- Decorate the getaway car.

- Pass out candles, flower petals, birdseed.

Finding an Officiant

A civil servant is somewhat gratuitous, since his/her primary role is to legalize the event—and that's not what's happening here. But you *can* ask a favorite judge or justice of the peace to symbolically sanction your ceremony. If you want your union to be blessed before God, you have a few choices. You can go with an officiant from a gay-friendly religion (Metropolitan Community Churches, Unitarian Universalists, or the Universal Life Church). You could find an officiant from a religion that leaves the same-sex decision to the clergy (Buddhist, some Protestant, Reform Jewish). Or, you could ask a sympathetic but congregationally restricted minister or rabbi to conduct an off-duty ceremony, lending his/her presence to the event without actually representing the church or synagogue.

Or ask someone you admire or no one at all. Since it isn't legal, you can ask a layperson whom you respect to conduct your ceremony. Or don't ask anyone—run the show yourselves. To find an officiant:

- Ask friends within the gay community for referrals.
- Call gay-friendly churches or other religious organizations.
- Look through gay newspapers and magazines.
- Check out the *Gay Yellow Pages* (Box 533 Village Station, New York, NY 10014; 212–674–0120).

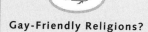

Gay-Friendly Religions?

Friendly:
- Metropolitan Community Church
- Unitarian Universalist Church
- The Universal Life Church

Sometimes Friendly:
- Buddhist
- Judaism
- Protestant

Unfriendly:
- Church of Latter-Day Saints
- Islam
- Roman Catholic

Gay Wedding Guide

Check out *The Essential Guide to Lesbian and Gay Weddings*, by Tess Ayers and Paul Brown (HarperCollins, 1994).

Creating Your Commitment Ceremony

Your ceremony can incorporate any or all of the traditional wedding customs, but you may want to create some new traditions of your own. You're breaking ground for all the same-sex weddings that come after yours; you can help determine what elements will go into the developing "canon" of gay wedding rituals.

Focus on the vows, readings, and unity symbols; these are the areas most open to creative input. You could have a standard unity candle. Or create a new unity symbol, perhaps a unity bouquet. Each member of both your families (or close friends) holds a single rose (your family red, your partner's white, or go with rainbow hues). Participants in the unity bouquet ceremony approach the altar one at a time to give you the flowers and a blessing. Then the two of you combine your roses into one bouquet. The rose petals represent the tenderness of love; the thorns, the obstacles you may face; the fragrance, your joy in life and love.

For readings, you don't have to address gay issues; you could read something about love, friendship, companionship, trust, growth, or whatever you want to. By choosing something *not* specifically gay-related, you're focusing on your personal commitment, not on politics.

Now that you've got the basics, it's time to start planning the ceremony of the century. This is the most meaningful part of your wedding; don't get so wrapped up in reception details that you forget the reason that you're here in the first place. Do the deed right. Then party down!

A Rousing Reception

Your wedding reception may well be the biggest and best party you ever get to throw, so really think about what kind of event you want it to be. How do you want to mingle—quietly over canapés and caviar, a quartet in the background, or bumping and grinding on the dance floor after a five-course filet mignon dinner? The reception is the hardest part of your wedding to plan—there are so many details involved in setting the mood you want (and the next section of this book will take you through all of them). There are also a ton of reception rituals, like the bouquet toss and cake cutting, which you may choose to do or not. Don't feel obligated to include anything you're not comfortable with or that you feel doesn't work with tone of your party.

What follows is a framework for the "classic" wedding reception—just so you know what to expect (and what's expected of *you),* plus some great twists.

What Happens When

What you do at your reception depends largely on the kind of party you're throwing. The more elaborate and traditional the reception, the more classic elements you may want to include.

If it's a simple champagne-and-cake reception or cocktail reception, the order of events goes something like this:

- The receiving line forms.
- Cocktails are served; guests mix and mingle.

- Champagne is served. If it's a Jewish wedding, the bride's father (and maybe grandfather) offers blessings over the bread and wine.
- Toasts are made.
- The bride and groom cut the cake.
  - Guests enjoy a slice.
  - The bride may toss her bouquet; the groom may toss her garter.
  - The bride and groom make for the getaway car (or stay until the end of the party with guests).

If you're serving hors d'oeuvres and cocktails followed by a dinner accompanied by a fourteen-piece orchestra—or otherwise having a reception that includes a meal and dancing—the party will go more like this:

- Cocktail hour begins.
- You arrive and the receiving line forms.
- The cocktail party continues.
- It's meal time. The catering manager and waiters begin letting guests know they should take their seats and/or head to the buffet. You may decide to have dinner announced, by the DJ or bandleader if s/he will emcee, or by someone else you've designated—a friend, the banquet manager, whomever. You take your seats, or wait to be announced (along with your attendants and perhaps your parents). You may do your first dance before you sit to eat; father/daughter and mother/son dances also may happen now.
- Your officiant may offer a blessing. Your parents also might give a blessing over the about-to-be-served food and wine (a tradition at Jewish weddings). Waiters serve the first course, or guests make for the buffet. The band continues playing background music.
- Time for the toasts. The best man kicks them off, followed by the groom, the bride, and any other guests who want to say something.
- Dinner continues; you may do special dances after the salad course or after everyone's finished with the entree.
- Serious dancing begins, including any ethnic dances.
- Things get thrown (bouquet and garter toss).
- You cut the cake.
- Everyone does dessert.
- More dancing; the party starts winding down.
- You two head out to your car under a shower of flower petals, or stay until the bitter end to bid guests thank-you and adieu.

Don't Be Your Own Emcee

Don't even think about running your own reception. If you don't have a wedding consultant to handle the details, appoint someone as Reception Master. (This person can be a friend, relative, even the banquet manager or caterer.) Let your RM monitor the party and make sure everything happens on schedule.

Jewish Reception Blessing

At a Jewish reception, the rabbi, the couple's parents or grandparents, or another honored guest gives a formal blessing, called the *hamotzi*, over a loaf of shiny egg bread called challah. Hunks then are passed around to all the guests.

The Receiving Line

Say it's not your wedding. It's just an ordinary party—a summer backyard picnic, for example. As all your guests arrive, do you: (1) rudely ignore them and hope they find the potato salad, or (2) hurry over as soon as you can and say "Oh, Sylvan! I'm so happy to see you! Would you like a drink?" Survey says: Option B. These are your friends and relatives. You've got to welcome them to your wedding celebration, and let them know you're glad they came.

Why You Should Have a Receiving Line

That's basically what the receiving line does. It's a formalized greeting period that lets you welcome everyone in an organized manner and *guarantees* your guests a minute of face-to-face time with you on your wedding day. With the greet-them-as-you-see-them, casual approach, you may spend the whole party ducking out in the middle of conversations to say hello to people you haven't greeted yet. As you can tell, we are receiving-line fans, especially if you're inviting more than fifty guests.

How to Receive

Here's everything you must know about your receiving line.

When: Directly after the ceremony or at the beginning of the reception.

Where: Outside the ceremony site's doors—in the vestibule, hallway, or on the front porch—or somewhere near the reception party room—by the doors, in the cocktail lounge, or in the lobby.

Reception Timetable

For a formal, seated meal reception, hours break down pretty much like this:

- Beginning: Receiving line, cocktails.
- First hour: Cocktails and hors d'oeuvres continue. (You may do photos.)
- Second hour: Everyone is seated for the meal, blessings, and toasts; first dance and other special dances.
- Third hour: Bouquet and garter toss; more dancing.
- Fourth hour: Cake cutting, other desserts and coffee; party winds down.

ASK CARLEY
Stepparents in Line

Q: My stepdaughter is getting married next year and I would like to know if I should be in the receiving line—and how do I introduce myself? Her father and I have been married for thirteen years. Her brother was married four years ago and I was in the receiving line but felt as if I didn't belong there.

A: Comfort is key for all the family members at the wedding. First, talk to your stepdaughter—she and her groom are really the ones who should make the decision about which parents are in the receiving line. Let her know that it felt awkward for you to be in her brother's, but if she wants you there, you would love to be there (assuming you would). There's no clear-cut answer about whether stepparents *should* be in the line—it really does all depend on the family and how comfortable everyone is with it. But rest assured that it's completely appropriate for you to be there, especially since you've played such a significant role in the bride's life. You didn't say whether the bride's mother is planning on standing in the line—that may also be a factor in your discomfort. If you both are in the line, you should be standing next to your husband, and the bride's mother should not be standing next to either of you, so guests will understand what the relationships are. If you are in the line, simply introduce yourself as the bride's stepmother. If you're not in the line, start to circulate with the guests, greet and thank people—and introduce yourself as the bride's proud stepmom.

Who Stands in It: Traditionally, the bride's parents head the receiving line and are the first to greet guests. You and your honey stand next to them, with the groom's parents filing in after you. If you choose to include them, the honor attendant and the bridesmaids line up after the groom's parents. If most of the guests are your friends (not your parents'), you can head the line yourselves and be the first greeters.

What You Do: Introduce your sweetie and your parents to all guests they haven't met. ("Honey, this is Rob, whom I used to work with at the ad agency," or, "Dad, I'd like you to meet Sally, my next-door neighbor.") Your new husband or wife will introduce you to guests you don't know as well. Accept their congrats, hugs, and kisses, and thank everyone for coming. It's that easy!

New Ways to Greet: If there are less than fifty guests, you could make the entire cocktail hour a meet-and-greet instead of doing a formal receiving line. You and your receiving team form a big, amorphous shape in the center of the room; guests get their drinks and then head over to say hello. The amoeba approach creates a more casual atmosphere and lets you introduce your guests more easily to more people. (You're not limited to the two on either side of you.)

Seating Your Guests

You remember the seating chart from grade school. Having a personalized place to sit each day gave every student a feeling of stability and security, and it also helped the teacher organize the class; she could position problem kids near the front, scatter strong students throughout. The re-

---

Great Guest Books

Put a guest book for people to sign somewhere very visible, such as on a table in the entranceway or on a stand near the receiving line. You don't have to use a traditional, leather-bound keepsake book. Here are some other ideas:

A silver platter with your names and the wedding date engraved on it; have an engraving pen on hand for guests to sign their names.

A book with blank pages in which guests attach a Polaroid of themselves arriving at your wedding (snapped by a photographer). Guests write their greetings next to their photos.

A handmade book with photos from your childhood to give guests creative inspiration.

A wedding "yearbook," which the bridesmaids or you make and get professionally bound, with photos of the two of you during your dating years, head shots of your wedding party, "guest appearance" shots of your caterer, officiant, dressmaker, ceremony site, and anything else you want to include.

A memory book in which guests paste pictures of themselves with one (or both) of you. Don't forget to ask them ahead of time to bring a photo. (You could include the request on an invitation insert.) Guests write comments next to their photos.

Blank sheets of colored paper on which guests write or draw whatever they want to. You bind them together after the wedding.

Have them say their wishes to your videographer for an electronic memory "book."

ception seating chart does essentially the same thing. You decide who sits at which table, taking the confusion, hassle, and fear of choosing the wrong spot out of your guests' hands. And you can shape how much fun everyone has, too, since you can choose wise positions for volatile divorced parents or guests who hate each other and sprinkle good conversationalists and great wits throughout the room.

Why Seating Is Important

Your goals, of course, are different from the teacher's in a critical way—you *want* people to talk to each other. Unlike the grade-school plan, your seating chart should designate only the tables where guests sit, not the specific chairs they'll take (unless you're having an ultra-formal affair). Have *some* faith in your guests' social skills.

JENNIFER AND OMAR
August 28, New York City

JENNIFER AND OMAR wanted to incorporate some of Omar's Middle Eastern background—he's originally from Saudi Arabia—into their wedding reception. What the couple chose to do dazzled and amazed their guests—they hired a belly dancer to greet everyone and perform. "As our guests arrived at the reception, the dancer lured them in and made them feel welcome," Jennifer says. "It was certainly very different from the traditional receiving line—no one expected to be led in by a belly dancer!"

The dancer, who was recommended by the Middle Eastern band that played at their reception, performed during dinner and then again after dessert. "It really got everyone in a great mood," Jennifer says. "For Omar's family, it was very festive. For my side, it was exotic and exciting."

After performing her routine, the dancer invited the guests to dance along with her. "Most of our guests had no experience belly dancing, but a lot of them gave it a try," the bride recalls. "Everyone talks about how much they loved it—I was glad to introduce people to something they had never seen before."

You don't need a seating chart for a cocktail- or dessert-only reception. If it's a very casual or very small party, it's fine to skip it, too. But we highly recommend it for a seated meal, whether buffet or waiter-served.

Seating Smart

Heed these tips and your seating chart will be flawless.

When: Start planning your seating *early,* and think about creative ways to let people know what table to take. You'll finalize who sits where about two weeks before the big day, once you have your final head count.

Where: Table cards (or your interesting equivalents) are arranged alphabetically on a front table where guests can find them as they arrive. Each card has the guest's name (or names, if you're assigning by couple) and the number (or other identifying icon) of the table where they'll sit. Each table is marked in some noticeable way—traditionally by a number sticking out of the centerpiece or otherwise standing on the table. Place cards sit on or above each plate or napkin (if you decide to assign seats).

How: Think of a fun way to identify tables. Name them after something personal—important dates in your shared lives, countries you've visited together. The personal approach provides an instant conversation starter for your guests as they try to figure out why, for example, their table is called July 14, 1995. ("Is that when he proposed?" "No, that's the night he first said he loved her." Everyone will say, "Awww, that's so *sweet!*" and they'll all instantly be friends. You also could place a written description of the date's importance to you on the table to take the guesswork out of things!) Or make your table distinctions correspond with your overall reception vision. For a garden wedding, name tables after flowers. If you're having an arty party, name each table after a favorite artist, and reproduce a masterpiece for the table cards.

Get Set with Seating

Don't wait until the night before to decide who should sit at which table. It takes a lot longer than you might think to make a chart for 200 guests.

Tips for Talkative Tables

Put people with similar interests together.

Put people of similar ages together.

Put family who live in opposite corners of the country together (if they like each other) so they can squeeze in some quality time during your wedding.

Seat your officiant at a table with family members (usually your parents).

Generally, let divorced parents host their own tables, or seat one with your honey's parents and the other with the officiant, family members, or other special guests.

If you're using place cards, we recommend the boy-girl-boy-girl approach; it's more exciting for your guests. (And for you—few things beat the thrill of playing matchmaker for your single friends.)

Put an even number of guests at each table; people tend to pair off in conversation, and if you have five, seven, or nine people at each table, someone is *always* the fifth (or seventh, or ninth) wheel.

Try to make sure every guest will have at least one person at the table s/he'll be thrilled to talk to.

Put dance lovers near the dance floor—they'll get the party rocking.

Reception Rituals

So you've greeted your guests and everyone's found their seat. Now what? The majority of reception time (that is, time when people aren't eating) is spent dancing and carrying out reception customs. Here's the lowdown on each.

Here Comes the Couple: Being Announced

Many couples choose to be "announced," along with their wedding party and sometimes their parents, once guests are seated. You all assemble outside the reception room. The banquet manager, DJ, or someone else you've designated then takes the mike and announces everyone by name—"Please welcome the bride's parents, Jane and John Smith"—and everyone walks in as couples. After the bride's and groom's parents comes the wedding party, walking with the partners they had at the ceremony. You two, "for the first time as husband and wife," come in last.

Waltzing into Marriage: The First Dance

The first dance physically reiterates what the ceremony just stated: You and your honey are a unit now. The first dance is a way of bonding to the beat. (Of course, if you rate dancing in public up there with standing naked on a table at an office party, it's fine to skip the spotlight first dance and open up the floor to everyone instead.) You'll probably also want to plan a father/daughter dance (bride and dad) and/or a mother/son dance (groom and mom), which will come later in the reception.

When: Your first dance as newlyweds can happen right when the band starts playing, after the toasting, after the first course has been served, even after everyone finishes eating. The point is, it's not necessarily the first dance of the evening, just the first time you and your sweetie hit the dance floor as newlyweds.

Who Does What: You could dance the entire song together while everyone watches, or do a formal first-dance sequence; after you've made a few laps around the floor, you switch partners—the bride dances with her father while the groom dances with his mother-in-law. After another few turns, it's switch time again—the bride dances with her father-in-law and the groom kicks it up with his mom. Then switch once more—the bride spins about with the best man and the groom twirls the maid of honor. You'll probably want to ask your emcee to act as a guide so no one gets confused.

A Twist on Tradition: Rather than dancing to a traditional first-dance song, consider using something more unusual—a swing, tango, salsa, lambada, or flamenco song, perhaps!

Go Ethnic: Make the first dance a traditional ethnic one that represents your backgrounds. Do the Jewish horah and invite everyone to join in. (You two can dance in the center of the circle.) Or do an Italian tarantella. Take lessons ahead of time, or ask your

Control Your Emcee

If you want your bandleader or DJ to serve as announcer during your reception, give the person specific instructions about how much talking you actually want him or her to do. If you *don't* want this person announcing things, make that very clear.

Get into the Groove

Afraid people won't dance? Appoint a few friends as "dance starters"—the delegated first group on the floor whenever the band (or DJ or boom box) kicks in. Or resort to group dances that everyone will do—the limbo, hokey pokey, electric slide, a conga line.

grandparents or parents to lead the dance. It's a great way to tap into your heritage, and to pay respect to your family.

Go Period: If you're doing a twenties-style party, make it a Charleston. If it's a '50s malt-shop party, do the jitterbug. If it's a '70s night, do the hustle.

Go Family-Style: You can personalize the father/daughter and mother/son dance, too. Brides, if you and your dad are known for your fabulous Lindy hop, do it! Grooms, if your mom taught you to hand-jive back in fifth grade (to impress the ten-year-old girls), hand-jive with mom.

Here's to You Two: Getting Toasted

Toasting is a way of stopping in the middle of some fabulous event to acknowledge your good fortune and say, "Hey! This is a truly fabulous event!" It lets everyone take stock *now* of just how good things really are, rather than waiting twenty years from now to say "Boy, those were the good old days!" Toasting also lets you thank those around you for sharing in your happiness (and in the work it took to celebrate it). Toasting is *not* meant to be another painful rite of passage. If you'd rather ski the North Pole in a bikini than speak in public, just say a quick word. ("Thanks for coming, everyone!")

When: Toasting usually begins after everyone has found a seat and gone through the buffet line (or been served the first course). You also can toast during cocktails, after everyone has been served champagne.

Who Does What: Traditionally, the best man leads the toasting, offering one up to the bride and groom. Then the groom takes the floor, followed by the bride. (This doesn't happen nearly enough. Brides, take that mike!) Thank your guests, your parents, each other. Then parents, other relatives, and other members of the wedding party may speak. After that, it's a free-for-all. The toasters stand up and speak from their places, or head to the dance floor and take the microphone. Everyone else remains seated (even the toastees—you don't have to stand when you're being toasted.)

Toasting Hints: Ask friends and family to talk about when they first knew you were in love or when they knew you'd be getting married. Or invite them to share some funny

---

Classic First-Dance Order

- Bride and groom
- Bride and her father; groom and his mother-in-law
- Bride and father-in law; groom and mother
- Bride and best man; groom and honor attendant
- Everyone else!

ASK CARLEY
Which Dad to Dance With?

Q: I don't know if I should do the father/daughter dance with my dad or stepdad. I grew up with my stepdad and feel closer to him. But I don't want to offend my real dad. Help!

A: You could handle it in a few ways. Start the dance with your dad and then switch halfway to your stepdad, or vice-versa. (Let them know your plans so they won't be surprised.) Or do a complete dance with each one. You don't have to do an emotional "Daddy's Little Girl"–type song if it feels fake. Dance with Dad to something fun, like the Twist. Or choose an instrumental piece. Or skip the entire father/daughter dance sequence and show respect by including them in the receiving line instead.

memory from your mutual past. But they should make it a story *everyone* will enjoy hearing. If you suspect your old single-days gal pal intends to give a detailed list of all the guys you dated before finding your honey, ask her to share that story at your bachelorette party instead.

For your part, say something you mean. You may want to thank your parents for their support and your honey for—everything. You may thank members of your wedding party for their help, and tell everyone how much their presence at the wedding means to you. Or share some hilarious story about how you two met.

SALLIE AND JASON
November 30
Cliffside Park, New Jersey

JUST ABOUT ANY COUPLE can tell you about the swingin' music or scrumptious seven-layer cake they had at their wedding. But how many people can say they also ate kimchi or wore the matrimonial robes of Korean royalty?

By choosing to serve Korean cuisine, wear traditional costumes, and incorporate Korean customs into her otherwise all-American wedding, Sallie was able to share something that is important to her—her heritage—with some of the people who are most important to her. "That includes my new husband, Jason, who is not Korean—although now we like to joke that he is, at least by marriage," Sallie says.

For the reception, held at a fancy Korean restaurant, the couple served traditional Korean foods like kimchi (a spicy pickle made of Napa cabbage, red pepper, and garlic that's practically Korea's national dish) alongside the American fare. But perhaps one of the highlights of the wedding was the Korean p'yebaek ceremony that Jason and Sallie did for their parents as all of their guests looked on. "Back in the old days, p'yebaek marked the first time a bride greeted her husband's family as his wife," Sallie explains. "Dressed in bright silk clothes, the newlyweds would perform a series of elaborate bows to the husband's family, to whom the bride now belonged. In turn, the groom's parents tossed handfuls of dates and chestnuts into the bride's skirt—the more she caught, the more children she was supposed to bear." Jason and Sallie recreated this ritual at their unforgettable wedding.

It's a Toss-Up: The Bouquet and Garter

The bouquet and garter toss traditions are modern takes on old superstitions. These days they're designed to help hurry single friends to the altar—the woman who catches the bouquet and the man who snags the garter will be the next to get married (though not necessarily to each other!) Some couples wouldn't dream of omitting these entertaining traditions, but others are known for retreating to the bathroom when they came up at past weddings. If the mere thought of these traditions makes you cringe, it's okay to skip them. Or skip the one you don't like and do the other.

When: Toward the end of the party; usually before the cake cutting, but they could happen right before the couple make their getaway (if they're doing so).

The Bouquet Toss: The single female guests gather on the dance floor. The bride either faces them or turns her back and lobs her bouquet over her head. According to tradition, whoever catches it will be next to marry.

The Garter Toss: The single men gather in the same area. The bride sits on a chair while the groom lifts her skirt up to remove her garter, slipping it off her leg with his hands (or teeth!), and then whips it at the crowd of single men. Whoever catches the garter poses for a photo, dances with the winner of the bouquet toss, or slips the garter on her leg.

Tossing Alternatives: If you'd rather present your bouquet to a close friend or female relative, you can do so privately. Or make an announcement about the meaning of your hand-off. Another idea: Have both women and men try to catch the bouquet.

Breakaway Bouquet

If you want to save your bouquet but still do the flower toss, ask your florist to create a smaller piece that can be separated and tossed. Or just have a separate smaller bouquet made.

So Sweet: Cutting the Cake

Go to Chapter 13 for more on cake.

Wedding cake serves two purposes—it taps into the ancient ritual of sharing a bite of food to seal the marriage bond, and it's *cake,* for God's sake! Cutting the cake is one of the tastiest wedding traditions.

When: Near the end of the reception—the cake cutting is often guests' signal that it's okay to leave now. Or after the receiving line or ceremony at a champagne-and-cake-only affair.

Who Does What: The groom puts his hand over the bride's and they slice through the bottom layer of their cake together, feeding each other from the slice—whether or not to smash each other in the face with it is up to you. Often they use some special silver cake cutting knife that they've registered for or that has been bequeathed by their parents. Cameras flash. Then the couple may each serve slices to their in-laws.

Great Cake Tip: You can include others in the bonding tradition by asking your married and as-good-as-married guests to do the feed-each-other's-face routine along with you. Wait until everyone has a slice of cake and then lead a group first-taste. You also could add a dessert-time version of an ethnic food-bonding ritual: Sip dessert wine from a two-handled cup, like the traditional *coupe de marriage* used at French receptions. Or do an after-dinner take on the Japanese sake–sharing ritual.

Do Them a Favor: Take-Home Gifts

Favors are a way of spreading the joy, literally. They're not a required element—it's likely that people won't miss them, they can get expensive, and in some parts of the country they're not even expected. But they are a fun way to give something back and to say "Thank you for coming and sharing the day with us."

When and Where: Guests usually find favors waiting at each place setting when they take their seats. But favors also might be in fun party bags on the chairs, piled in baskets by the door, or distributed at the end of the party. You might even use take-away centerpieces—piles of fruit and candy, plastic sand buckets filled with flowers, or a heap of mind-teaser games guests can keep.

Go Edible: Give a regional specialty such as jalapeño jelly from Texas, hot sauce or Cajun spice rubs from Louisiana, or Vermont cheddar, maple syrup, or Yankee cider from the Northeast. You also could incorporate favors into the reception flow—serve coffee in great imprinted cappuccino cups guests can keep. You may be able to personalize your food favors—wrap microbrewed ale in specially printed labels for your wedding, or stamp jars of local honey with your names and wedding date.

Go Living: Symbolize the idea of marriage as a living, growing entity by giving seed packets, flowering plants, or individual flowering bulbs. Or use a dozen individual, potted herbs as centerpieces, and let guests choose their own. If you're really ambitious, you could even grow your own favors.

Go Personal: Find favors that really relate to the two of you—lava lamp key chains if you're '70s buffs, cool bookmarks if you're writers (or readers).

Go Seasonal: Find something seasonal that you know they'll use now—striped toe socks you bought in bulk for a winter party, or bright flip-flops for a summer bash. Look for things that match your wedding style—vintage Christmas tree ornaments for a Christmas Wedding Spectacular, funky masks for a Halloween wedding.

The Getaway

Traditionally, people tied cans and other loud objects to the back bumper of the newlyweds' car because they believed that the cacophony would drive away any evil spirits chasing after the couple. Today members of the wedding party, family, or friends might decorate your car as a way to salute (or embarrass) you. Usually someone with a cheerleading background and concurrent spirit-raising experience will volunteer to head up the decorating squad. If no one thought of it ahead of time, members of a self-appointed decorating team may sneak out near the end of the reception and hit the nearest Walgreens in search of supplies. After the reception, you go out to the car under a stream of who-knows-what-this-time (guests are tossing it) and discover that your new Jeep Cherokee has been gussied up with hearts, "Just Married" slogans, and streamers.

Where Do These Traditions Come From?

- The term "toast" stems from the sixteenth-century custom of placing a piece of toast at the bottom of a wine cup.

- The garter toss comes from two different Old English traditions. After the wedding, friends crowded into the honeymoon suite, the women to throw the groom's stockings backward over their heads at him, the men to do the same with the bride's. Whoever hit the mark was believed to be the next to marry. Guests also used to rip pieces from the bride's gown for luck; women began offering up their garters to keep the rest of their outfits intact!

- The bouquet toss comes from an ancient belief that certain herbs are lucky. A bride would give her bouquet to a friend for luck.

If you don't have a car (or don't want it decorated), your friends might sneak into your honeymoon suite and loose their creativity there instead. They could scatter rose petals on the bed, pile sex toys on the nightstand, and write encouraging words on the mirror. Or maybe they'll just call your honeymoon love nest in Niagara Falls and request a bottle of champagne or welcoming sign to greet you there.

Not all couples make an official getaway from their reception these days—many stay and visit with guests until the end of the party. Especially because couples increasingly wait until the next day to leave for their honeymoon, they figure they'll spend more time with loved ones. Very nice, we think!

It's a Toss-Up

Historically, different cultures have thrown different things at couples as they left their wedding. In Italy, guests threw coins, dried fruit, and little pieces of candy (the original *confetti*). Today your guests may throw birdseed or flower petals, blow bubbles, ring miniature bells, or even release birds, to symbolize a life of plenty.

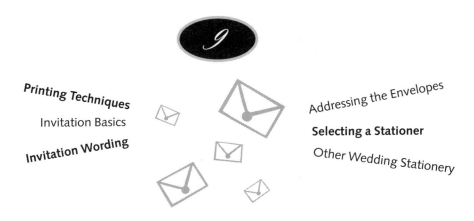

Printing Techniques

Invitation Basics

Invitation Wording

Addressing the Envelopes

Selecting a Stationer

Other Wedding Stationery

The Paper Trail

Invitations are the first tangible evidence your guests have of your wedding—they can go a long way toward setting the tone. Think of them as a grand direct-marketing opportunity. Besides just letting guests know when and where the festivities will take place, invites provide clues as to the formality of the affair (which will tip them off to the dress code) and a sneak peek at your wedding vision. Ideally, you should get busy with invite investigating at least six months before the wedding.

Printing Techniques

Probably the most important factor in an invitation's character (and certainly price tag) is not the paper but the print. There are four main printing techniques, each with its own distinct charm and price range, and one fancy extra called embossing. Depending on the formality of your wedding style and, of course, your budget, here are the options.

Engraving

This is the most expensive of print methods, used for all ultra-formal wedding invites (and hoity-toity party invitations in general). The printer uses a metal plate engraved with the text you've provided to stamp the words onto the paper from behind. The final product is textured, with raised letters in the front and "cavities" in the back.

Choose this if: you have a generous invitation budget; can find a retailer that does this (mass-market shops sometimes don't); can wait up to eight weeks for the job to be completed (high style hurries for no one); are having an ultra-formal affair with a *huge* guest list (the engraving will tip guests off that you mean formal business; also, the larger the order, the more cost-effective engraving is).

Thermography

This is the most popular method, used by most large stationery printers and mail-order companies. A heat-based process fuses ink and resinous powder to create raised lettering; it's virtually indistinguishable from engraving work unless you feel the back of the invitation, which remains smooth.

　　Choose this if: you have a less-than-gigantic budget but still want formal invitations; you're not concerned with having the absolute crème de la crème when it comes to the invites; you want an off-the-wall ink color (often not available with engraving); you don't have the two months you'd need to wait for an engraved order.

Offset Printing

This is the flat printing that's used on most every flier, letterhead, or birthday card the world 'round. A rubber cylinder is used to press ink onto the paper. Many ready-made invitations, thank-you notes, and R.S.V.P. cards are made using this technique, but not all retailers offer this option for wedding stationery (thermography being all the rage these days).

　　Choose this if: you need all the cost-busting you can get; you want to play with different colors of ink (with both thermography and engraving you are pretty much limited to one color); you want to use highly textured paper (pressed with flowers, say) that won't work with raised lettering; you want to put a photograph on your mail-outs; you're having a theme wedding and want invitation art that will reflect it (with this method, specially crafted stamps can be used to create, for example, a rose garden for an English tea wedding, lovey-dovey giraffes for a safari wedding, or a heart-shaped baseball diamond for a sports-related weekend wedding).

Calligraphy

The ancient art of gorgeous, curvy, curly handwriting. You should be able to locate calligraphers through your local phone book. (Be sure to get references and check out samples before you hire.) You'll spend a *very* pretty penny for this hand-crafted look, but—thanks to technology—you can get a similar effect for less by using calligraphy software, available at many stationery shops.

　　Choose this if: you're having a small wedding and want handwritten, intimate invites to match; you're planning a Victorian or other suitably themed wedding; price is no object, or calligraphy is important enough to you that you're willing to pay for it.

A Grave Decision

Don't stress over choosing thermography over engraving. Most people won't know the difference, and you'll shave up to 50 percent off your invitation costs.

Paper Prices

What a hundred invitations with standard text at Kate's Paperie in New York City cost:

With Printed Envelopes
　Engraving: $375
　Thermography: $244

Without Printed Envelopes
　Engraving: $284
　Thermography: $204

Paper Types

The type of paper you use is as important as your actual design in terms of establishing a "mood" with your invite. The lingo to know:

100% Cotton: Elegant, understated, and pure.
Vellum: A cotton blend (thus, somewhat less expensive) with a smooth finish.
Laid: Like Vellum except with a rougher, "bumpy" finish.
Linen: Another classic choice. Linen papers are grainier than pure cotton stocks.
Moiré: Named after the fabric, this stock bears subtle watermarks.
Jacquard: Screen-printed paper that creates an illusion of layering; for example, paper that looks like it's overlaid with a swatch of lace.
Parchment: Cloudy, translucent paper that creates an airy, dreamy effect.
Mylar: Shiny, mirrorlike paper that's highly modern.
Corrugated: Thick, folded stock that says "urban chic."

Embossing

A raised printing method usually used for large initials or borders; because of its high price tag, hardly anyone has an entire invitation embossed. Upscale stationers usually will be able to oblige, however.

Choose this if: you want spectacular-looking initials on your thank-you notes or formal couple's stationery; your wedding is formal and you want a border or other raised detail on your posh invites; you're a sucker when it comes to "extra" touches.

Invitation Basics

You can have the most gorgeous invitations on Earth (and we're sure you will!), but when it comes right down to it, this handy-dandy piece of paper is a functional item, spelling out the essential wedding info—it tells guests who's getting married, who's hosting the wedding, and where, when, and what time the festivities will take place. So it's important that they are not only attractive but easy to read and understand. Just about every wedding invite includes the names of the wedding hosts/sponsors (that usually means your parents), your names, the day of the week, the date, time, and address of the ceremony and/or reception, and R.S.V.P. information (unless you're sending separate response cards). See "Invitation Wording," below, for specific examples.

Ordering Your Invites

Order invitations as soon as you have your guest list nailed down—shoot for five months before your wedding day. You'll have time to choose the exact invitations you want, have them printed, fix any printing mistakes—and still get them out six to eight weeks before the big day.

How Many?

Order enough invitations for your entire guest list (that includes the wedding party), plus twenty-five extra for the inevitable boo-boos and last-minute changes (such as replacement guests for nonacceptances). We also think giving your parents a few invitations as keepsakes to place in their wedding albums is a nice idea—and you'll want to keep a few for yourselves, too.

Prepare for Postage

Go to the post office and weigh a complete invitation so you know *exactly* how much postage to put on each one; your mailing costs might be relatively high if you have lots of inserts. Having your invites returned for insufficient postage can throw your wedding-planning schedule for quite a loop!

Send 'Em Early If . . .

If you're having a destination wedding (in Maui, say) or marrying over the holidays, send out invites early (ten to twelve weeks before the wedding instead of six to eight) to give guests ample time to plan to travel or clear time in their busy holiday schedules.

What Style?

There are thousands of invitation designs—and millions of custom-made possibilities. When selecting yours, consider:

The Formality of Your Wedding: From engraved block or script print on ecru, ivory, or white paper (for a super-formal affair) to a beach ball imprinted with text (for an informal seaside bash), your invitation should clue guests in to what to expect—and wear.

Your Personal Style: If you're not buttoned-down types, people aren't going to expect a hoity-toity invite, so go nuts! Conversely, if Class is your middle name, go the whole nine yards—with tissue paper, lined envelopes, embossed seals, and all.

A Theme: If you have one, kick it off with your invites: petal-strewn, hand-crafted paper for a country inn wedding; a design with a knight and damsel-in-distress smooching for a medieval wedding; black lettering on a silver or gold background for a midnight reception. You get the idea.

Your Wedding Colors: Opt for coordinated paper or ink.

How Many Invitation Inserts You'll Have: If you need to include a map, separate response cards for five different weekend events, and hotel information, keep the design simple so that your invitations don't weigh a ton (and thus cost a bundle to mail).

The Size of Your Wedding: If you're inviting fewer than fifty guests, it's fine to handwrite your invites on pretty paper—a great money-saver (and time-saver if you're marrying quickly). If your handwriting is less than wonderful, get someone else (Mom? a bridesmaid?) to do the dirty work. Bribe them with your undying devotion.

The Envelope, Please

Don't forget to order your envelopes. Get fifty to one hundred more than the number of people on your guest list. (Wedding invite envelopes have to be handwritten, and that means mistakes—if you know you'll make many, get yourself lots of extras.) If you'll have inner envelopes (most invitations, and definitely formal ones, are assembled with an inner and outer envelope; see "Assembling the Invites," below), get fifty to one hundred more than double your guest list.

Invitation Wording

As far as what to actually print on your invitations, the must-haves are who is getting married, who is hosting the party, when the ceremony will begin, and where. Beyond that, it's up to you, although most people go with the formal, polite wordings we're about to spell out. You can add your own personal flair, but in general, it's a good idea to keep the text simple.

The wording of the invitation should reflect who's hosting the party. Typically, the phrase "request the honor of your presence" is used formally; "request the pleasure of your company" is a bit more familiar.

Below are sample wordings for typical family/hosting situations. Ask your stationer for help and advice, as well, and don't be afraid to adapt these based on your families' circumstances.

When the Bride's Parents Are Hosting the Wedding

(Adapt for groom's parents if they're sponsoring.)

Mr. and Mrs. Peter Johnson
(or *Peter and Miranda Johnson*)
request the honor of your presence
at the marriage of their daughter
Heather Amanda
and
Jeffrey Michael Harris
son of
Mr. and Mrs. Bradley Harris
(or *Bradley and Wendy Harris*)
Thursday, the thirteenth of May
at six o'clock (*"in the evening"* is optional)
Chip of Heaven Church
111 Yuma Avenue
Kirkwood, Missouri

More Intimate Invites

Add a personal touch to your wording. Suggestions:

- "Sara Amanda Ferrari and Todd Alan Springer invite you to join them in a celebration of their union."

- "We ask those closest to our hearts to help us celebrate our marriage . . . (where, when info goes here) . . . Sara Ferrari and Todd Springer."

- "Sara Ferrari and Todd Springer are getting married! Come dance till dawn and raise a glass (or two or three). . . ."

- "Love is in the air—and you're cordially invited to come smell the roses at the wedding of Sara Amanda Ferrari and Todd Alan Springer. . . ."

- "Sara Amanda Ferrari and Todd Alan Springer request the pleasure of your company at their wedding reception" (if you're using separate ceremony cards).

If the bride's parents are primarily paying for the wedding, the names of the groom's parents traditionally are left off the invite, but we like adding the "son of" line and acknowledging the groom's parents, too. Be forewarned, though—if one set of parents is putting out lots of money for the wedding, they may object to this "equal" treatment.

When Both Sets of Parents Are Hosting

Mr. and Mrs. Peter Johnson
and
Mr. and Mrs. Bradley Harris
request the pleasure of your company
at the marriage of their children
Heather Amanda
and
Jeffrey Michael
Thursday, the thirteenth of May
etc.

When the Couple Is Hosting Their Own Wedding

Ms. Heather Amanda Johnson
and
Mr. Jeffrey Michael Harris
request the honor of your presence
at their marriage
Thursday, the thirteenth of May
etc.

Reception afterward at
The Roseland Ballroom
222 Grove Street
St. Louis, Missouri

The reception info can go in the lower right- or left-hand corner of the ceremony invite, or you can have separate reception enclosure cards printed. If the reception is in the same location, put "Reception immediately afterward" on the ceremony invite.

Mr. Peter Johnson
requests the honor of your presence
at the marriage of his daughter
Heather Amanda

to

Jeffrey Michael Harris
Thursday, the thirteenth of May

etc.

Kindly respond
Mr. Peter Johnson
44 Leaf Way
Kirkwood, Missouri

R.S.V.P. information can be included on the invite in lieu of separate response cards—this is the formal way to request a handwritten response.

When a Divorced or Widowed Parent Is Hosting with Spouse/Bride's or Groom's Stepparent

John and Miranda Peck
request the pleasure of your company
at the marriage of Mrs. Peck's daughter
Heather Amanda Johnson

to

Jeffrey Michael Harris
son of
Mr. and Mrs. Bradley Harris
Thursday, the thirteenth of May

etc.

When Divorced Parents Are Hosting Jointly

(Stepparents can be included on the same line as their spouses if everyone agrees to it.)

Mr. Peter Johnson

and

Mrs. Miranda Peck

request the pleasure of your company

at the marriage of their daughter

Heather Amanda Johnson

to

Jeffrey Michael Harris

son of

Mr. and Mrs. Bradley Harris

Thursday, the thirteenth of May

etc.

Never put divorced parents on the same line on an invite; it may confuse guests as to their relationship. Only the names of couples who are married should go on the same line.

Assembling the Invites

1. Depending on the style of your invite, it will be left flat or folded in half or in fourths, with the text on the front of the "booklet," the fold on the left, and all other "pages" blank.
2. Tuck any enclosures inside, or set them on top of the card.
3. Place all the paperwork in an unsealed (inner) envelope with the print facing the back so that it's immediately visible upon opening. (Note: A high-end printer probably will place a piece of tissue paper on your invites to prevent smudging. It's your call if it stays in or not.) Leave the inner envelope unsealed.
4. You can forfeit the inner envelope—and thus steps 3, 5, and 6—if you've chosen a low-key invite and wedding style or are very environmentally conscious (and so don't want to use the extra paper).
5. Handwrite the guests' names on the inner envelopes. The formal way is with titles only: "Mr. and Mrs. Smith" (or "Ms. Jones and Mr. Smith," alphabetically, if a couple has different last names). If your wedding is more casual and intimate, you can use just first names or familiar titles ("Aunt Zoe"). Check out "Addressing the Envelopes" for more.
6. Place the inner envelope inside the outer envelope, with the guest's name facing the back.
7. Handwrite guests' full names and mailing address on the outer envelope, or have a calligrapher do it. See "Addressing the Envelopes" for guidelines. Your stationer probably will have a booklet all about titles that will help you with other specific questions you have.
8. Go to the post office and have the finished products weighed. Opt for some of those "Love" stamps—they're a nice touch. Presto! Let the U.S. Postal Service do its magic.

Addressing the Envelopes

You've got a stack of invites on your kitchen table, and you're staring at a bunch of blank envelopes. Here's what to do next.

The Outer Envelope

The outer envelope is where you write the recipients' full names, official titles, first names, and all. It's where tradition is upheld, decorum celebrated; that means no cutting corners with abbreviations such as Dr., NY, or St. (Mrs., Mr., Ms., and Jr. are the only okey-dokey shorthands). Some examples:

Single Recipient

> *Ms. Abigail Ansch*
> *44 Acorn Drive*
> *Houston, Texas 77380* (Zip is very, very important)

If the single guy or girl is bringing a date, get the individual's address and send a separate invitation. "& Guest" on an outer envelope is too impersonal. Roommates who aren't honeys also should each receive their own invite.

Married Couple, Traditional

> *Mr. and Mrs. Harold Paris*
> *92 Pacific Avenue*
> *etc.*

Married Couple, Modern

> *Harold and Emma Paris*
> *92 Pacific Avenue*
> *etc.*

Common Titles

Here are how titles should appear on the outer and inner envelopes, respectively:

- **Lawyer:** Ms. Ingrid Innsbruck, Esq.; Ms. Innsbruck
- **Physician:** Jill Jamal, M.D. or Doctor Jill Jamal; Dr. Jamal
- **Professor:** Professor Kirk Kant or Kirk Kant, Ph.D.; Prof. Kant
- **Judge:** The Honorable Lucy Lindqvist; Judge Lindqvist
- **Mayor:** The Honorable Marion Myrtle Missioni, Mayor of Grand Forks; Mayor Missioni
- **Captain:** Captain Neville North, U.S. Army; Captain North
- **Minister:** The Reverend Olivia Orton; The Reverend Orton (Roman Catholics use Father)
- **Rabbi:** Rabbi Pinkus Pressman; Rabbi Pressman

Married Couple, Different Names, or Unmarried Couple, Living Together

Professor Connie Chideya
Doctor Darren Duncan (list the names in alphabetical order)
18 Blueberry Road
etc.

With Kids

Names of children under eighteen need not appear on the outer envelope (phew—you were afraid you'd run out of space), but over eighteen-ers who live at home should either appear on their parents' envelope or, preferably, be sent their own invitation. Examples:

Mr. and Mrs. Ebert Estonia
Farrah Estonia
195 Oak Street
Chicago, Illinois 60010
or
Farrah Fisher Estonia
Mailbox 13301
Harvard University
etc.

The Inner Envelope

Formal invitations always are slipped into an unsealed inner envelope that is placed inside the outer envelope. They are addressed in a more informal fashion—typically only title abbreviations and last name—and include the names of all invitees at the address, including children.

Single Recipient, Traditional

Ms. Ansch

Single Recipient, Casual/Intimate Wedding

Abigail
or
Aunt Carol

Mr. and Mrs. Bailey

or

Ben and Tamika

Married Couple with Different Names, or Unmarried Couple, Living Together

Prof. Chideya and Dr. Duncan

or

Darren and Connie

A Family

*Mr. and Mrs. Estonia
Farrah, Gilbert, and Harriet*

Order in Bulk

Think about your wedding-related stationery needs (invites, thank-you notes, etc.) *before* you find a stationer. You'll have more leverage in terms of getting a price break (bulk customers rule the retail world), and you'll save yourselves time and energy by placing all your orders at once. Always order extras to save yourself time and money having to print more later.

Selecting a Stationer

Now you're ready to find yourself a stationer—there are almost as many options as invitation styles.

A Large Stationery Store

This is the most popular option. You browse through scores of stationery catalogs, pick out the style you like best, submit the wording you want, indicate special requests (like extra artwork), and wait anywhere from a few days to a couple of months to pick up your order, depending on the complexity.

Pros: Mainstream stationers work with major-league printers (who deal with gazillions of customers), so prices most likely will be lower than those of mom-and-pop printers or upscale retailers.

Cons: You're confined to the catalogs they carry, in most cases. Some shops may be willing to special order, but the above-mentioned cost advantage might thus be offset. If you're thinking Picasso-esque creativity, you may want to look elsewhere.

Early Addressing

When you order your invitations, see if you can take the envelopes home immediately—or at least request that they be delivered ASAP if you're having a return address printed on them—so that you can start addressing while your invitations are being printed.

An Independent Printer/Stationer

In our big business–dominated world, small print shops are following the fate of the dodo bird, but you should be able to find a great independent stationer through friends' referrals or your local Yellow Pages. Instead of looking for your perfect invitation (and other stationery) in a thick catalog, you sit down with the owner or a salesperson and design your own, or peruse an original book of designs.

Pros: You have more stylistic leeway. That means multicolored invitations, several ink colors, or weird shapes are all avaiable. (Plus, you're supporting the small-business economy that makes this country great.)

Cons: Customized work is always more expensive. Also, it usually takes longer for a small operation to fill your order, so don't go this route if you're pressed for time.

A Department Store

Many upscale stores have wedding-stationery services to augment their registry programs. The idea is the same as with a large stationer; you choose from ready-made designs.

Pros: One-stop shopping; order your stationery and register for gifts on the same day. Often you can get a good deal if you're registering at the store; after all, you're bringing in lot of business. In addition, upscale department stores tend to be choosy about the stationery they carry (with a penchant for classic designs), so if you know you want mainstream-highbrow, they've already made the first cut for you.

Cons: As impersonal as the large stationer, but with less selection.

Mail-Order Catalogs

Bypass the retailer and go directly to the printing company from the comfort of your own home. Catalogs come in all shapes and sizes, so there are thousands of styles to choose from.

Pros: Unbeatable prices, convenience, and quick turnover (sometimes within a week of placing your order). If you're having a theme wedding, often you'll find quirky (or kitschy) invitation designs to match, which will be much cheaper than custom-ordering.

Go to Appendix B for a list of our favorite mail-order invitation catalogs.

Cons: High screw-up potential; spelling mistakes are not uncommon when dealing with a printer over the phone. Even though many reputable catalogs will fix their errors at no extra charge, the time advantage may be eaten up. Also, excellent designs are fewer and farther between, and paper quality may not be great—you're going to have to do a lot of browsing and checking of samples.

A Graphic Designer

Find a talented pro by word of mouth, or ask a designer friend to create your stationery in lieu of a wedding present; he or she will design super-duper, one-of-a-kind stationery for you and probably hook you up with a trustworthy print shop.

Pros: Artistic flair; originality; the good deed of feeding a freelancer.

Cons: Unless the design work is, in fact, a present, you'll have to pay two people—the graphic artist and the printer—which could wind up being more expensive than the other options. This process can also take a while, so get started early.

Doing It Yourselves

If you have good desktop publishing software (like Quark Xpress or PageMaker) and a creative streak (maybe one of *you* is an artist or graphics guru), design your own invites, notes, cards, even stationery. After you've perfected your creations, get the job done on a laser printer on high-quality paper; this may mean taking a trip to your local copy shop or output service.

Pros: Total creative freedom; one-of-a-kind specimens; quality time together (albeit in front of the computer).

Cons: This method is the most time-consuming for you two.

MARGARET AND RICHARD
October 19, New York City

THE 120 GUESTS invited to Margaret and Richard's wedding each received a handmade, one-of-a-kind invitation that could only have come from Margaret. Why? They were made from sugar. A cake designer, Margaret also sculpts with sugar. For the invitations she decorated the paper with sugar designs. "They were so great." Margaret laughs. "When they went through the mail, some of the sugar would fall off, so the envelope made this nice sound when you shook it."

Margaret's creations were featured at the event, as well. Instead of flowers, her table centerpieces were sugar chalices, goblets, and bowls. She also designed her cake, of course—but then enlisted the help of various smaller folk: "I wanted to take some of the focus off my own work, so instead of decorating the cake myself, I got my friend's kids and my new nieces and nephews to come over and make the decorations. They loved it, and it let them be a real part of the celebration."

Other Wedding Stationery

Reception or Ceremony Cards

If your ceremony and reception will be at two different places, *or* if you have separate guest lists for each event, you'll need a small card to add to your invitation. *(Don't* invite to the ceremony but not the reception; if you want a very intimate ceremony, however, vice versa is fine.) Wedding invitations generally give the ceremony lowdown; however, if you're inviting *many* more people to the reception than to the ceremony, you may want to simplify your life by printing up smaller ceremony cards instead and giving the reception information on your main invites.

What Should They Say?

Formal Reception Invitation

Mr. and Mrs. Peter Johnson
request the pleasure of your company
at a reception to celebrate the marriage
of their daughter
Heather Amanda
to
Jeffrey Michael Harris
Thursday, the thirteenth of May
at six o'clock
The Roseland Ballroom
222 Grove Street
St. Louis

Ceremony Enclosure Card to Go with a Reception Invitation

Ceremony
at four o'clock
Chip of Heaven Church
111 Yuma Avenue
Kirkland, Missouri

Reception
at six o'clock
The Roseland Ballroom
222 Grove Street
St. Louis

How Many? The number of guests at the event plus twenty-five extra.

Choices? If you are inviting only a handful of people to the ceremony, use reception invitations, and handwrite personal notes to the select vow-observing crew instead of printing up ceremony cards.

What Else? Save paper—and money—by printing a map on the back.

Response Cards

We are big believers in spontaneity, but *not* when it comes to how many people are going to show up at your wedding. That's where the response card comes in. Unless you're including telephone or e-mail R.S.V.P. info on your invites, this is an *essential* bit of wedding stationery. By returning the card, guests are letting you know that they understand all the details of your wedding, and they'll be there (or not).

What Should They Say? There are a few possibilities:

- Blank Cards. All that *you* write is the response deadline; the guest composes her own message. Example: "Kindly respond by March 1" *or* "The favor of your reply

---

The Write Stuff: Talking to Your Vendor

No matter whom you choose to rock your stationery world, roll out the usual consumer caution. If possible, find your vendor through recommendations from people whose own party invitations or personal stationery have caught your eye. Then ask to see examples of the stationer's work and, when possible, contact other references. It's also always a good idea to visit at least three stationery retailers, so that you get a general sense of available styles and price ranges. In addition, never forget to:

1. Get in writing the vendor's liability for printing mistakes.
2. Predetermine a reasonable price for extra orders if the need arises.
3. Carefully proofread all master texts *before* placing the order and again when you pick it up.

is requested by the first of March." This is our favorite option because guests can get creative and wacky on you, turning the response cards into keepsakes.

- Fill-in-the-Blanks. Easy to use, for you and your guests; all they need to do is write a few words and draw a few circles.
- Checklist. This is a great option for long weekend or extended activity weddings. Have a check-off box for each nuptial-related fiesta (prewedding picnic, late-night beach party, post-wedding brunch, etc.) so you'll know how many people the hosts should prepare for at each event.

How Many? Print enough for all your guests plus twenty-some extras for replacment guests.

Choices? Ask for responses on your invite. (This may mean more work for you, however, because people are less likely to sit down and compose and mail their own note than check off a box on a ready-made card; they may forget, meaning you'll have to make follow-up calls.)

What Else? Include a stamped response-card envelope addressed to the person in charge of the guest list (you, Mom and Dad). You also can use a small stamped postcard.

Map-Hotel Info Cards

If you're inviting a lot of out-of-town guests to your wedding or are getting hitched in an out-of-the-way place, order map cards to insert in your initial invitation mailing. If you've also reserved a block of rooms at local hotels for far-out guests, include that info on the same or a separate card.

What Should They Say?

Map Information: Sometimes you can get a map from the venue itself (ask the site manager), which you can have printed onto your cards (or just fold the pieces of paper into fourths). Or you can do a hand-drawn map; get someone who knows what they're doing to help you out. It should clearly spell out road names and major orientation points.

Hotel Information: Some hotels will provide printed materials; otherwise, call up the hotel manager and get the reservation line number and the going rate for your rooms. Those are the essential tidbits you'll need to include for each of the hotels you've made arrangements with, as well as maps of how to get there from major ports (airport, train station, bus terminal).

How Many? Number of guests plus twenty.

Choices? Instead of getting this info printed up on hefty cards, photocopy it onto regular pieces of paper that match your invitation colors.

What Else? You may want to put this information in a letter that you mail out long before the invites (four to six months before the wedding, say) so that guests can get a head start on making travel plans and reserving rooms. This is especially important if the wedding is in a popular tourist destination or is scheduled for the same weekend as another big event in town.

**When Do You
Need R.S.V.P.s?**

Set your R.S.V.P. deadline for no later than two weeks before wedding day (after that point, you need to call nonresponders so you can get a final head count), leaving you ample time to make last-minute arrangements for seating and catering orders.

Ceremony Programs

Programs are a wonderful way to make your guests feel a part of your ceremony, especially if you're incorporating original readings or special ethnic traditions. Instead of having your guests whisper among themselves to try to figure out what's going on, why not spell it out?

What Should They Say? Include the names of everyone in your wedding party—and perhaps their relationship to you. There should also be a ceremony itinerary so guests know what's coming next. Include any original texts or literary passages you'll be reading so people can follow along more easily, and explain any special rituals.

How Many? Guests plus thirty. You'll want to keep a few as keepsakes and so will your guests of honor.

Choices? Have some historical pictures of the religious practices you're incorporating printed in your programs to heighten the sense of tradition.

What Else? The program is the place to include any special tributes or thank-yous you want to make to close friends, relatives (especially deceased ones), even each other.

Secure Honored Guests' Seats

If you're having a very large ceremony, consider printing up pew cards to include in the invites of your closest relatives and friends. Pew cards tell the usher that these guests of honor are to be seated in specially reserved pews close to the altar. Or just have a trusted friend or relative brief ushers on who should get white-glove treatment.

Earth-Friendly Stationery Suggestions

All this talk about paper, paper, and more paper has got you bummed out about your complicity in this ecological fiasco? Cheer up. These environmentally sound tips will have you, your guests, *and* Mother Nature smiling:

Use recycled paper. There are many great options for your invitations, thank-you notes, and envelopes (napkins, too!), including handmade sheets with flowers and ribbons mixed into the pulp or corrugated heavy stock—perfect for a rustic wedding.

Concentrate information. Instead of a separate R.S.V.P. card for each wedding-related event, mail out a one-stop checklist.

Reuse materials. Wrap attendants' gifts in recycled brown packing paper.

Think small. The smaller your invites and thank-you cards, the fewer trees suffer—and the more you cut down on waste.

Double-side it. Put that map on the back of the actual invitation. Put hotel information on the same sheet as the itinerary.

Find a stationer who uses nontoxic inks and dyes.

Skip the frills. Don't use inner envelopes; ask the printer to skip the tissue paper; don't get layered invites.

Instead of having people send you their R.S.V.P.'s, have them phone or e-mail.

Wedding Announcements

There are going to be people you're fond of whom you simply couldn't invite to the wedding. It's a common practice to share your happiness with these individuals—and to let them know that they're on your mind—by sending a wedding announcement, typically mailed immediately after your ceremony. (Some say on the way to the reception, but we'll allow you the next day; you're only human, after all.)

What Should They Say?

Traditional

> *Mr. and Mrs. Peter Johnson*
> *and*
> *Mr. and Mrs. Bradley Harris*
> *have the honor to announce*
> *the marriage of their children*
> *Heather Amanda*
> *and*
> *Jeffrey Michael*
> *on Thursday, the thirteenth of May*
> *One thousand, nine hundred and ninety nine*
> *Kirkwood, Missouri*

From the Couple

> *Heather Amanda Johnson*
> *and*
> *Jeffrey Michael Harris*
> (or *Jeffrey and Heather Harris*)
> *announce their marriage*
>
> etc.

How Many? This will vary depending on the size of your wedding and, thus, how many people are not receiving invitations.

Choices? Personalize the announcement by sending the same favor your reception guests received. If you feel uncomfortable telling people about your wedding via mail, pick up the phone and spread the good news verbally.

What Else? Don't expect gifts! If you receive them, though, be sure to send a thank-you note.

Rain Cards

If you're having an outdoor wedding, we *strongly* urge you to order some cards that will inform guests where to go in case of bad weather.

What Should They Say? Give the location of the wedding and reception "In case of rain/sleet/hail."

How Many? Guest list plus twenty-five.

Choices? Instead of having a printer do a formal job, handwrite the info on little raindrop- or umbrella-shaped cards.

What Else? Send these to your vendors, too, as a reminder of Plan B.

A Perfect Match

While you're taking care of (paper) business, order table cards (for a seated reception meal) that are coordinated with your overall wedding stationery look.

ASK CARLEY

Recalling Invitations

Q: What is the proper way to inform guests that a wedding has been canceled when your invitations have already gone out?

A: When a wedding is canceled or rescheduled, you can let guests know with printed cards, personal notes, or even by phone if you don't have much time. If possible, a written mailer is preferable; that way you don't have to explain the sad circumstances over and over and over, which can be painful whether the wedding was called off because of a sick parent or because of cold feet.

An official card is generally worded like an invite:

Mr. and Mrs. Ray Ronco
announce that the marriage of
their daughter
Talula Justina Ronco
to
Javier Terzo
will not take place/has been postponed
or
Mr. Ray Ronco
regrets that the death of his wife
obliges him to recall the invitations
to the wedding of his daughter

A personal note generally should give the same information, just not as formally. In any case, specific reasons for the cancellation need not be included. Typically, only a death or illness is mentioned.

Thank-You Notes

Rules of etiquette dictate that every gift deserves a thank-you note. This means that between the gifts you'll receive before, on the day of, and after your wedding, you two will be doing a lot of writing. A thank-you note is traditionally a simple ecru sheet or folded card. You might add a monogram, choose ready-made cards, or design something original with your stationer.

Go to Chapter 17
for more on
thank-you notes.

What Should They Say? How grateful you are for the gift. Whatever you do, personalize each note to reflect your relationship to the addressee and the specific gift s/he gave. It doesn't have to be a work of genius; a dash of humor and a sprinkle of loving sentiment are the essential ingredients.

How Many? Lots and lots. Many people will be giving you more than one gift (for your engagement, your shower, etc.). You're going to get a lot of stuff, and thank-you notes never go bad. Stock up.

Choices? The sky's the limit. For an elegant look, match your thank-you cards to your invitations.

The paper trail has come to an end. You've dealt with one of the biggest items on your planning schedule—getting invites, which should be ordered six months before the big day, ideally—and taken care of countless other details, such as place cards, ceremony programs, and thank-you notes. One more page of your wedding book has been written. Let's bandage up those paper cuts and move on.

Hello, My Name Is . . .

Couples have long sent out at-home cards with word of their new address. In recent years, with all the new name-changing scenarios, name-change cards have become the new thing, a way of letting others know what to call you besides "the couple formerly known as Sunil and Anne." Or order new letterhead to do the talking; it'll show people where you live *and* what your (new) names are.

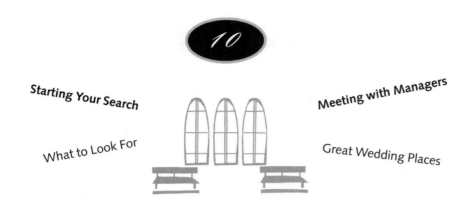

Location, Location

Your first big planning task to tackle is deciding where to do the deed—where to have your reception and, if it won't be in a church or temple, your ceremony, too. Your location is the backdrop for your wedding—a grand ballroom plays host to an affair far different from an intimate, bucolic garden.

If you're set on a wedding style, you'll be able to focus your location search. If you're not sure yet, surveying sites can help. That crumbling castle may finally get you in touch with your long-lost dreams of a medieval marriage. Unfortunately, you don't have too much time for dreaming here—the hottest spots go quickly. So get going!

Starting Your Search

Whether you have an exact, general, or just a vague and sketchy sense of where you want to wed (okay, you have no idea), your next question is "Where the heck do we start looking?" This is where all those research skills you learned in school will come in handy.

Big Yellow. Uncurl yourself from the couch and let your legs do the walking—over to the Yellow Pages. The phone book is an easy place to find out what kinds of sites are available in your town. Headings to check include: "Banquet Facilities," "Clubs" (private clubs often rent out their facilities), "Halls and Auditoriums," "Hotels," "Museums," "Parks," "Party Planners" (they often have lists of locations they represent), "Restaurants," "Special Event Coordinators," and "Wedding Supplies and Services." Start a list of potentially useful phone numbers.

Local 'zines and papers. City magazines and bridal guides published by local newspapers can be good places to find out about party rooms and/or bona fide wedding-reception places. Call your newspaper and ask when (and if) they're planning a special wedding issue, or track down a past one at the library (maybe the paper even has some extras).

Historical societies. If you're thinking about a historic mansion, castle, or estate, get in touch with the historical society in your wedding area. They'll be able to give you a list of all the local historic landmarks, plus let you in on which ones allow special events on their grounds.

Tourism bureaus. Even if you've lived in the same city or town all your life, chances are there are great places nearby that you don't even know about. Call the tourism bureau for location ideas close to home—you may discover something fabulous, such as the fact that you can have your wedding party at certain museums, civic buildings, bed and breakfasts, state or national parks, historic areas, farms, or orchards. State and local bureaus of parks and recreation are also good places to contact.

Chambers of commerce. Local business organizations are great resources for hotels, banquet and catering halls, country clubs, and other party locations. Call the chamber of commerce, an entrepreneurs' association, the Realtors association, and any similar groups you can find.

Web sites. A great place for leads (and so conveniently located!), the Internet offers endless travel sites that may give you good ideas as well as the home pages of historical societies and special-interest associations. You'll find the Yellow Pages on the Net, and you also can search for the home pages of local facilities.

Wedding professionals. Wedding consultants, caterers, photographers, DJs, and other people who make a living on weddings likely have been to more receptions than Liz Taylor's closest pals. Consequently,

Spectacular Sites A to Z

- Aquarium, Aboretum, Airplane Hangar
- Boardwalk, Bed & Breakfast, Bowling Alley
- Castle, Cave, Covered Bridge, Casino
- Disco, Disneyland, Dock on a Bay, Dunes
- Empire State Building, Historic Estate
- Farmhouse, Football Field
- Gallery, Greenhouse, Golf Course
- Harley-Davidson Convention, Hot Tub
- Ice Skating Rink, Inn
- Jazz Club, Japanese Gardens
- K-Mart (Blue Light Special?)   *(continued)*

Booking It

Take a trip to the library and head to the reference desk. We know what you're thinking: "The library? I haven't been there since I got Netscape!" But the library has resources that the Net doesn't—including physical copies of phone books, association directories, tourism brochures, location catalogs, the National Register of Historic Places, and—perhaps most important—the librarian.

Visit bookstores, too. Local stores should stock books or guides listing locations in your area. For example, bookstores in New York, New Jersey, and Connecticut display *The Down the Aisle Directory* (MRS Publications, 1991; 212–337–3770) and *The Locations, Etc. Directory for Corporate, Bridal, and Social Events* (Lyle Green Benjamin, 1996; 212–463–7499). Also swing by the travel section for regional guides with creative sites like B&Bs, ranches, zoos, and so on.

they've probably seen and worked at every location within a fifty-mile radius. Call them up and pick their brains. Make it part of your vendor-selection process. When you ask a photographer about his style, for example, also ask him where he's shot local weddings and which venues he liked best. Not only might you get some good location ideas, you'll also find out how experienced he is—a factor you'll want to consider when hiring a shutterbug.

Other couples. No one's more willing to talk weddings than freshly married couples (the fresher the better). Ask newlywed friends about great sites they saw. Inquire about other weddings they attended. Ask coworkers for ideas. Ask the guy who repairs your shoes, people at the gym, the salesperson at your favorite clothing store. Okay, ask anyone who'll listen. You never know whose brother owns a really cool downtown gallery where he'd love to start hosting special events. Firsthand accounts of the success (and failure) of various venues can give you invaluable tips.

What to Look For

Okay, now that you know where to look for the greatest locations, you need to know what you should be looking for (aside from that sense of rightness you know you'll have the moment you see the perfect spot). Shopping for a site is a lot like finding a mate, a test you've obviously aced. You should be looking for the same sorts of things—charm, personality, depth, more than just a pretty face (although looks do count!). Take this list of what to look for with you—in your head or on paper—when you're ready to go scouting.

Wide open spaces. First, make sure the room is large enough. It may look like Yankee Stadium when it's empty, but wedding essentials—tables, chairs, a buffet, a bar, the band or DJ setup, the dance floor—can take up a lot of space. Not to mention your guests, who'll need some elbow room. Even if you choose an outdoor site, you'll need ample room on the lawn, in the arboretum, or poolside. The best way to assess size? Ask to check the place out when another wedding is being set up. Space is one of the biggest reasons to have an idea of how many guests you're thinking about inviting before you start your site scouting. Of course, if you decide you *must* have your wedding at your favorite bar (the one with one bathroom, two booths, and three feet of floor space), you always can work backward and tailor your guest list to match.

A place to park. Make sure the site is near a good parking lot, garage, or big, empty (safe) street that's okay to park on. If parking is a problem, look for other ways to get everyone there. Can a shuttle bus or vans take guests from the ceremony to the reception? Inadequate parking isn't necessarily a deal killer, but it may mean spending more time and money figuring out a viable vehicular alternative.

- Lighthouse, Library (shhhhhh!)
- Museum, Mountain Top, Mission
- Nature Reserve, National Park
- Oceanside, Orange Grove
- Poolside, Parade
- Quarry, Quebec
- Rodeo, Roller Coaster
- Ski Slope, Stables, South of the Border
- Train Station, Toy Store, Theatre
- Under the Stars, Underwater (scuba vows?)
- Vineyard, Vintage Car
- Waterfall, Windmill, in the Woods
- X . . . um, ahhhh . . . ?
- Yacht, Backyard
- Zoo

Privacy, please!. Privacy varies widely from place to place, as does the importance couples place on it. If you're having a daytime bash in a public spot, such as a park or botanical garden, be prepared for strangers to trek past your party. They may even smile and wave and come by to offer their good wishes. If this is okay with you (the more the merrier!), go for the park. If not, opt for a lovely lawn on a private estate. Or hold the reception at a restaurant or gallery that will post a "closed for private party" sign.

But don't think you're safe just because you're indoors. Banquet halls and hotels often hold more than one affair at a time. If there'll be other events going on simultaneously in rooms close to yours, you may hear karaoke-loving guests singing their hearts out to Madonna through the walls, or meet them over the hot-air dryers in the bathroom. If this bothers you, try to schedule your wedding when there won't be another one next door. If this is impossible, visit the site on a dual-party night and see how the sound carries, and whether there really are any major people problems, before you make a decision.

Seeing the light. Light can make—or break—the mood. If you're marrying during the day, make sure your hall has plenty of windows. Who wants to spend six hours in a dark room when the sun is shining? If it's an evening affair, make sure the room's not *too* dim—or that the lighting can be controlled for the big entrance, dinner, and dancing. If you're marrying outside, say at dusk, will you be able to set up candles if necessary?

Try to see the site at the same time of day as your wedding is planned for. Even if the space looks swell by candlelight, you may be surprised by the sight of that twenty-year-old carpet during the day. You'll also miss a chance to see how sunlight streaming from floor-to-ceiling windows completely transforms the room if you check it out only in the evening.

The right color. If you're having a party that necessitates a certain color palette—say a Victorian tea done in pink, green, and gold—that brown shag carpet is really going to wreck the effect. The place doesn't have to be done in the *exact* colors as your planned decorations, but the walls, carpets, chairs, and curtains shouldn't clash or conflict with your party's mood or theme. If you want a spring wedding brunch, look for a space that's done in light (perhaps pastel) colors or florals; black walls and red leather booths just don't say "spring." But they'll look great if you're going medieval (or 1980s, for that matter). For classic elegance, consider a room done in neutrals or black and white.

A great view. What will your guests look at (when they're not gazing at you or smiling for the videographer)? Whether it's a stunning vista of rolling mountains beyond the windows, the crashing sea on the sand behind you, Picasso prints on the walls, fine Persian rugs on the floors, period furniture in the corners, or an amazing crystal chandelier as the room's centerpiece, exceptional locations always have something fantastic to see.

Eating, drinking, and partying areas. There should be logical places within the space where guests can eat, drink, talk, and dance. See if you can envision where each activity would happen (especially if your ceremony will be there, too). If a room is too small to separate into sections accordingly, you may feel cramped. If it's shaped like an S or other oddball figure, that could compromise your party's flow, as well. Also note the locations of columns or other obstructions in the room—will they block people's views?

Ample outlets. Make sure your room has lots of places to plug things in—especially if you're partying in a place that's not used to hosting weddings. Your main outlet user will be the entertainment crew. Take note of where the outlets are; if their location will force your DJ to spin records in the bathroom, make sure s/he has plenty of extension cords.

Good vibrations. If the place is too echo-ey, it could give some weird reverb to the band, not to mention making it difficult for guests to hear each other talking. A tile or wood floor, for example, will amplify sounds, while a thick carpet will tend to muffle them. Try to take a listen to the room during an event. And tailor your music to the acoustic conditions. A jazz combo will sound better at an intimate art gallery than a fourteen-piece orchestra would (not to mention taking up less floor space).

KELLEY AND STEVEN
May 14, New Marborough, Massachusetts

CHOOSING THE PERFECT SITE for their wedding was crucial to both Kelley and Steven. They lived in New York City, and they wanted a spot outside the metropolitan area yet not too far away.

"The Berkshire Mountains were the perfect solution," Kelley says. "We both spent a lot of time there while growing up and we had many good memories of the area." The wedding took place on a hillside, giving it a very casual and intimate feel. The reception site was a renovated barn.

Although at first they were concerned that their friends would think it was too far to go for a wedding, in the end the bride and groom were convinced everyone was glad they came. "We tried to make it a relaxed country weekend," Kelley says, "One that happened to include a wedding on Saturday night."

Meeting with Managers

Okay, you've narrowed down your list and you're armed with the knowledge of what you need in a location. You're ready to go out there and meet the owners and managers. Call the places that interest you, ask to speak to the person in charge of weddings or special events, find out if the date you have in mind is available, and make an appointment.

Your Contact

Don't just head to the site and look around. Make sure to meet the person you'd work with if you had your wedding there. Is s/he enthusiastic about the space and about working with you? When you ask questions or make comments about wanting something specific or different, does s/he say, "That sounds great. Let me see what I can do." Or do you get "No. We don't do that here. No. No, no, no"? You're going to be dealing with this person for a while and you want to feel comfortable with him or her. And you want him or her to *understand* you and what you're trying to do with your wedding.

Keep in mind that this person is working for you—not vice versa. Don't let yourself be talked into (or out of) anything. If the place seems like a possibility, ask your contact for references and then actually call them and see what they have to say about the place.

Check the Place Out

Even if you fall in love with a site and the references are glowing, keep in mind that most establishments aren't about to give you the names of people who hated the service they got. The best way to make sure a place is reputable is to call the local better business bureau. Ask how the place is rated and whether any complaints have been filed against it.

How Much It'll Cost

The location fee is likely to be one of your largest wedding expenses, especially when you combine it with catering costs. Of course, this isn't always true—if you have a beach bonfire wedding, you may have to pay only for a permit. But generally your location will run you from $500 to $3,000 (more in larger cities, less if it's an unconventional site or someone's doing you a favor). Usually you will pay a flat fee; some places may charge by the hour. And you're going to be asked to put down a deposit of 10 to 25 percent.

Say you think you want to move forward on a specific place. You've checked off all the

Ways to Save Location $$$

If you're getting married in the off-season—say January, instead of June or September—you're likely to finagle a much better rate. Plus you'll probably have your pick of rooms or dates.

The day of the week can make a difference, too. Saturday nights are the hottest. You may pay less for a Friday night or Sunday afternoon.

If you're celebrating in a hotel or club with guest rooms, have your out-of-town guests check in there. Not only will they avoid annoying transportation issues, but they'll also save money, because you'll be able to get a discounted group rate for them. And you may even get your wedding-night room free.

When to Walk Away

They want more than 50 percent of the rental cost up front.

The place is downright dirty.

You just *don't like* the person you'd have to deal with.

The place refuses to draw up and sign a written contract—or refuses to add your specific requests onto the standard contract it uses.

Your celebration is being squeezed in between two others in the same space and it seems too tight time-wise.

The references you call tell you the place treated them horribly. (Pretty amazing, because if the establishment gave you the reference's name, *they* must have thought things went pretty well!)

You feel like you're "settling."

great location factors, and all of your questions have been answered to your satisfaction. Can you negotiate on the price? Of course you can, and you should. But first, find out what's being offered at competing establishments nearby. If you can get a better deal at another place but you like this place better, see if it can match or beat the price.

A big, expensive reception may help you negotiate for lower costs on small things. If you're having a huge party, for example, with a lot of overnight guests, you may be able to get some of the smaller fees waived— like charges for napkins, microphone stands, or cake cutting. Similarly, a less-popular date may lead to some super savings. If you're getting married smack dab in the middle of June, your chances of getting a deal are much slimmer than if you're marrying on the first of February. (In June, there'll be a line of couples behind you waiting to take your place and pay full price.) Make sure you know what you've agreed to pay for and that you get everything in writing—in a detailed contract.

Protect Yourselves

If the site's not insured, it's in your best interest to get your own wedding insurance. Call 800–ENGAGED.

Questions to Ask

There are a lot of points to talk through before you make your final decision to reserve a reception site. Here's what you need to find out before you sign anything on the dotted line.

- How much will it cost to use this site? What's the payment plan?
- Is there a reception "package"? Exactly what is included?
- Does the place have liability insurance? (In case someone gets injured during the party, you don't want to be held responsible—or if you are going to be, you want to know about it.)
- How many hours will you have the site? Is there an overtime fee if you stay longer? Is there a *minimum* amount of time you have to rent it for?
- Will there be another party right before or right after yours (or both)? Will there be enough time to decorate and take stuff down before the next wedding begins? Is there any chance of an awkward overlap?

- Will you be required to leave everything "as is," or can you move things around and/or decorate to suit your purposes?

- Are tables, chairs, plates, glasses, and so on available, or will you have to provide (rent) those yourselves? (This can jack your costs way up.)

- Is there an in-house caterer, or can you bring in your own? Can you use an outside caterer instead of the in-house person?

- Are there kitchen/cooking facilities? (Caterers will charge you extra if they have to haul in things like refrigerators and stoves.)

- If there's parking, is it free? If not, what are the rates and/or gratuities for valets? (You can and should pay this up front so your guests don't have to tip.)

- Will there be, or can you set up, a coat room? Are there bathrooms nearby? (Look at them to make sure they're nice!)

- If there's no bar—can you set one up? More important, does the place have a liquor license?

- Is there a private room off the main room where you two can change or just be alone for a few minutes? This is a nice perk.

- Is there a dress code that you'll need to inform guests of—coat and tie after 6 P.M., for example?

  - Does the site have any restrictions or regulations about what kind of music you can play and/or a time by which it must be turned off? Are there guidelines about what kinds of decorations you can use?

  - Will someone who works at the location be there to supervise during your wedding? This really should be the person you make all your plans with, *not* someone you've never met until that day.

  - What about security? Will you have to hire your own security guards, or does the place hire them or have them on staff? (The point is to find out just how safe the place is and to decide whether you're comfortable with its level of security.)

  - What's the cancellation policy? (This is important to know, because some places will give you most of your deposit back if you cancel far enough in advance since there's still a chance they can rent the space for another party. But after a certain date you may *not* be able to get your deposit back, or at least not all of it.)

Cancellation Happens

Don't assume there's no chance you'll cancel—you never know. You may *have* to change the date or postpone things due to unforeseen circumstances (a bad illness, a death in your family, a great new job in Europe, etc.). Protect your investment.

Great Wedding Places

It used to seem like every wedding ceremony was held in a church or temple, every reception in a hotel ballroom. Of course, many people still take this route—it's quintessential wedding! But since the first hippies tied the knot barefoot on the beach in the 1960s, the idea of the alternative wedding location has become so popular, it's downright mainstream.

Don't just look for the trendiest or prettiest place. The best weddings are the ones

Location Contract Points

Here's what should be in your *written* contract.

☐ Total cost and a line-item breakdown of what's included.
☐ Amount of deposit and when it was paid.
☐ Balance and when it's due/payment schedule.
☐ Exact date and time of your wedding.
☐ Exactly where it will be (e.g., "In Main Gallery," "In Presidential Ballroom").
☐ A detailed list of everything the place is providing (tables, chairs, linens, amplifiers, whatever).
☐ The name of the site representative who will be on hand on your wedding day, as well as the name of an acceptable substitute.
☐ Cancellation/refund policy.
☐ Anything else you agree about orally that you want to ensure happens.

guests walk away from saying "That was so *them.*" Maybe your first date was in a funky Mexican restaurant—that might be a perfect reception venue. If you're both animal lovers, consider the zoo. That little hotel on the bluff overlooking the beach—come on, the one where you got engaged!—has that beautiful party room, remember? If you studied together and then fell in love at the college library, wed on the university's gorgeous grounds. If you're into feng shui (the Chinese art of harmony in placement), choose your wedding spot based on the size, shape, location, and spirituality of an area—a perfectly circular clearing in the woods, a hilltop cliff overlooking a leafy valley. Unless you're having a Catholic ceremony (the majority of Catholic priests will not officiate at a wedding ceremony outside of a church), chances are you can exchange vows in most of these places too.

The Old Standbys: Hotels, Banquet Halls, Country Clubs, and Restaurants

If these traditional reception locations have one thing, it's experience. Weddings are their business. They know what's supposed to happen at a reception; they know how long one typically lasts. They've set up dessert buffets and band lighting a million times. They can offer suggestions on things you're unsure about. Conveniently, they'll often have an in-house caterer (in a restaurant, obviously, the chef will do your food) and maybe even a florist. This can make everything incredibly easy for you—but it also can be a hassle if you want to bring in vendors from the outside or decide that you don't jibe with the style or philosophy of one of the in-house professionals.

At a hotel or banquet/catering hall (or anyplace else that has a special events staff), you'll probably deal with (surprise) a banquet or catering manager. The most important thing to find out from him/her is exactly what the establishment will take care of. Will food, drinks, and the cake be handled in-house? If you want to bring your own cake, say, are they going to charge you extra to slice it? Be very specific when you first sit down to talk about what the place will (or can) provide. For example, many catering halls will give you

JULIE AND DAVID

*August 16, Oceanside,
California*

JULIE AND DAVID weren't always sure where their transcontinental lives would take them—she's from a Lebanese family and lived abroad for much of her childhood, while he spent several years in the Peace Corps in Tunisia. It was while he was there, and Julie was interning at the American Embassy in Paris, that the romance started at University of San Diego blossomed. Tunis is only a two-hour flight from Paris, and they traveled back and forth for visits for a year. "It was an easy time and place to fall in love," Julie says.

So when they were considering a site for their ceremony, the cou-

ple decided on the exotic, ornate Mission San Luis Rey, a Spanish mission and National Landmark founded in 1798. "We chose it because it has such spiritual and historical importance," Julie says. "The mission has a very rustic feel that brings you back to its original days as the 'King of All Missions,' as the Spanish Franciscans called it. It was also a great place for our guests because it's a destination; not only were they attending a wedding, but they were visiting a National Landmark and enjoying a piece of California's history." The site had such presence that no flowers were needed for decorating: "They would have paled in comparison to the colors and painting on the walls," Julie says.

The southern-California–style reception was at Julie's parents' home in Vista, California. "My parents' home was built with Mediterranean 'villa' architecture in mind—lots of arches, red-tile roof, on a hill overlooking the town below," Julie says. Cocktails and hors d'oeuvres were around the pool, and there was a tent on the tennis court for dinner and dancing. The area is surrounded by lush trees and tropical flowers; in order to avoid competing with the natural beauty, the linens and decor were all white with some silver accents.

The reception lasted from 4:30 p.m. to 2:00 a.m. "Most everyone left by midnight when the music died down," Julie says, "But there we were, the wedding party plus our friends sitting on the top of the poolhouse with my dad, drinking champagne and not wanting this incredible night to end."

arches, votive candles, or potted trees to use free of charge, while most hotels won't—you'll have to go through your florist or rent stuff. Knowing up front what you need to get yourselves will make it clear what you're in for—and how much extra money you'll spend (or save) if you settle on this locale.

Home-Grown Weddings

Marrying at home sounds perfect, especially if you or your parents have a gorgeous, big house with a beautiful backyard. Think about a ceremony under the old oak tree you climbed as a kid, dinner in a tent in the yard, or even an intimate family meal in the living room. This is about the most personal wedding place there is. Instead of spending money *buying* things to make some hotel banquet room feel like home, all that personality is already in place, and—bonus—there's no fee!

Raring to Rent?

Call the American Rental Association at 800–334–2177 for referrals to local rental stores and companies.

But don't think it's just that easy—home weddings come with a set of considerations all their own. Where will you put everyone? Where will they sit and what will they eat off of? We're talking rentals. Tables, chairs, dinnerware (you may be able to find a caterer who will bring this stuff along), a tent—it can add up fast, and you may end up spending just as much as you would to rent a hotel banquet room. Of course, once you've got all the stuff, you'll be marrying on very familiar turf, instead of being wedding number 4,623 of the day at Your City Hotel. And most of your guests already will know how to get there. But there may be that parking issue again. And you really should tell the neighbors what's going on. (Easier yet, invite them!) Oh—and one more thing—the weather. If you rent a tent, make sure it's equipped to keep everyone dry if it rains. Also have an inside game plan—will everyone fit inside the house if they have to? Home is an amazing wedding place, but there's lots to think about.

The Great Outdoors

Getting married outside is the ultimate for many couples. From the quintessential outdoor celebration on the beach to a pretty garden (botanic or grandma's), poolside at a ritzy resort or smack dab in the middle of a National Park, outdoor weddings are fantastic.

**In Case of
Rain . . .**

Be sure to have an alternative *indoor* site in mind. You can't control the weather—the possibility of a torrential downpour is the riskiest part of choosing an outdoor wedding site.

Of course, utter perfection comes with a price—even though it usually costs less to rent the great outdoors than to rent a room with a roof over it. The most critical step: Find out if you need a permit to party in a public area. If you're thinking beach, public park, or forest preserve, you can't just congregate—you'll need to reserve the area with the local parks and recreation department. Find out when you apply whether you'll also need permission to have cooking fires on the grounds, and if it's okay to have a band or DJ. Like home weddings, outdoor weddings may require you to rent tables, chairs, a tent, maybe even portable toilets. Also think about lighting—if it's an evening reception, do you need lights? Then there's bug control—light citronella candles and tie ribbons around mini-bottles of insect repellent as favors.

Mansions, Castles, and Other Great Old Buildings

The biggest advantage to renting a landmark location? Major photo ops. The place is going to be gorgeous! Many historic mansions and estates also come complete with beautiful grounds—perfect for romantic walks. You might even employ a strolling chamber orchestra for the cocktail hour. Castles may come with cool period relics and/or instruments, though they'll probably be off-limits for use. Find out if you're renting a look-but-don't-touch museum (not necessarily a bad thing)—will you have to pay a security deposit to ensure that no period furniture, priceless artwork, or Persian rugs get damaged during the party? Make sure to find out exactly what the restrictions are: Which rooms of the house you can use, what parts of the grounds are off-limits, which precious porcelain vases can't you touch? Otherwise, just enjoy—often these sites are so picturesque, not much extra decoration is necessary!

Boats, Trains, and Trolleys: Weddings on the Move

Cruising through New York Harbor on your wedding night, riding around Chicago in a double-decker bus with all your guests, or saying your vows on a New Orleans trolley are pretty dang romantic options. What is it about modes of transportation that we love so much? Maybe it's the moving forward aspect—a perfect marriage metaphor. You may have to do some digging to find train, bus, or trolley lines in your city. A wedding on water floats your boat? Any town with a decent-size body of water nearby will have boat lines, from yachts to riverboats. But keep in mind that when it comes to water transport, you can't exactly get off until it docks—you and your guests are stuck until the reception's officially over. Have some Dramamine on hand (just make sure it doesn't get mixed with champagne), serve light foods (good with waves) and, perhaps most important, make sure that boat's big enough to keep people who don't get along on opposite ends.

Ten Great Cities, Ten Great Locations

Boston: The grounds of Harvard
Chicago: The Shedd Aquarium
Honolulu: Foster Gardens
Los Angeles: L.A. County Museum
Miami: On the beach
New Orleans: Franklin Square
New York: Central Park Zoo
San Diego: Hotel Del Coronado
San Francisco: Golden Gate Park
Washington, D.C.: Union Station

Great Party Rooms in Not-So-Typical Places

If you're not into hotels or banquet halls but you like the idea of celebrating in a party room, think about other places, public or private, that host special events—museums, aquariums, train stations, nightclubs, university buildings. Some will have special-events staff ready and willing to help you plan the event. Others won't, so you'll be bringing in your own caterer and other wedding professionals. Price will vary. If you want to use the private party room at New York's Metropolitan Museum of Art, it's going to cost you a pretty penny, while your favorite nightclub may give you a great deal. And if one (or both) of you is an alum of the college whose space you're looking at, you may get a break on the price.

Rental Rules

You already know the number-one rule of reception-throwing: Thou shalt not mortgage thy parents' house for the perfect party. So how can you have a Beverly Hills–style affair on a Beverly Hillbillies budget? Rent it!

You can rent everything from a yellow-and-white tent for your circus reception to the tables, chairs, plates, parquet dance floor, disco ball, and smoke machine for your all-night dance party. Begin the search for your perfect rental company early—you'll want three to six months' lead time. Ask around for catalogs and prices. And assign someone to return duty—getting that elephant back to EZ Rent will be the last thing on your mind as you head off on your honeymoon!

Know Your Needs

Visit potential rental companies with the following info in hand:

- Date, time, location, and approximate number of people
- Reception budget
- Event style (Medieval? Flapper '20s?)
- Event type (Lawn party with kids? Formal dinner?)
- Site specifics (Underground sprinklers, wires, cables, or sewer easements that would interfere with an outdoor tent? Enough electric outlets for five cotton-candy machines?)

Choose Your Crew

Whether you go to Paul's Party Shop or the local branch of a huge chain, make sure you're working with pros. Your ideal rent-a-center will:

- Be a member of a business or trade group like the American Rental Association. (Call 800–334–2177 for members in your area.)
- Show you the inventory. If the china is cracked and caked with mashed potatoes from the last party, keep looking.
- Send staff to help with setup.
- Accommodate last-minute changes (additional tables for unexpected guests or extra tents if it rains).
- Offer names of past customers as references.

Check the Contract

After you've chosen your source and tagged your goods, get the details in writing. Your rental agreement should specify that all goods will be in great condition, plus:

- When and where your products will be delivered (or picked up).
- The exact length of your rental agreement.
- The store's rental rates, hours, and return policy.
- The fact that the store will replace equipment that breaks down.

Bridalwear 101

Where to Get the Gown

Going Shopping

The Search Is Over

Dressing It Up: Accessories

Preserving Your Dress

The Gown

As what-to-wear occasions go, your wedding tops the list. In fact, the bride's dress is so incredibly important that we're giving it its very own chapter. Maybe you've wanted to wear a big, poofy ball gown since the first time you saw *Cinderella*. Or maybe your tastes have changed, and these days you're into more modern styles and shapes. Maybe you'd never be caught dead in one of those confections they call bridal gowns, and you've got a smashing suit in mind. Well, you're in luck: bridal fashion in the '90s includes all of the above. Whatever your dream or preference, what you wear on your wedding day is completely up to you. That goes for first-time, second-time, even third-time brides (and up!). The only requirement is that you feel great in whatever you choose to wear—because if you feel great, you'll look great.

Buying your wedding dress is going to be an unforgettable—and quite possibly, harrowing—experience. This dress has a special significance, and besides that, it's got an entire industry attached to it. Your goal—to purchase the dress of your dreams and remain a savvy consumer. Since buying a wedding gown is not something most of us do very often, there's a lot you probably don't know at this point. But never fear. As usual, our job is to fill you in.

Bridalwear 101

Before you even step out the door to the store, read up on the lingo that'll get thrown your way when you set foot in a bridal salon. Wedding-dress shopping comes with its own language, and the more you know about what types of silhouettes, necklines, and shades of white might flatter you, the easier shopping for your dress will be.

The Shape's the Thing: Silhouettes

As with suits, skirts, and other dresses, the silhouette of a wedding dress can make or break how it looks on you. Here's our guide to who looks especially great in which wedding-dress shape. No, we don't mean Christy Turlington vs. Cindy Crawford. We're talking body shape here. As with everything else in life, it's all about proportion.

A-Line/Princess: This shape flatters just about everyone. It elongates your torso with seams running from the shoulders or bust straight down to the skirt, with no seams at the waist, so it's great if you're short-waisted. The skirt falls in a slightly flared triangular shape, hence the "A line." Even while A-line dresses follow the natural curve of the torso, they're not quite as fitted as sheaths (see below), so more kinds of women are apt to feel comfy in them.

Ball Gown: The classic ball gown has a fitted bodice, a natural waist, and a full skirt. It's truly feminine (that "Cinderella" connection), and looks particularly good on women with boyish figures (narrow hips), because it'll make you look more curvy.

Basque Waist: Are you full-figured or hourglass-shaped? Think about a dress with a basque waist, which comes to a V in the front at your stomach. It has a slimming effect on your waist and deemphasizes hips. Like ball gowns, basque-waist dresses usually have full skirts and fitted bodices.

Empire: This is that tiny-bodice dress with a high waist and a skirt that falls in a slight A-line from right below the bustline. (Did you see the movie *Emma*?) This silhouette lets you minimize your waist, because it really *has* no waistline. If you have a large chest or full hips, you probably want to stay away from this one—but it depends on the dress. Some come with fabric overlays that flatter.

Sheath: If you're petite or just have a fabulously sleek figure, consider this form-fitting style, which follows the body's natural line. A slim silhouette adds length, and it won't overwhelm a small woman like a big, elaborate gown could (anything too poofy might look as if it's wearing you)!

If you're short, keep it simple. Stay away from anything with tons of beading or lace—look for something with detail around the shoulders (this also holds true if you have a small chest) to bring the focus up to your face.

A Question of Formality

Brides are lucky—they've got more flexibility when it comes to what's appropriate for a "formal" vs. "semiformal" vs. "informal" wedding than grooms do. (See the next chapter for groom guidelines.) Basically you should just use common sense. A sequined, long-sleeved gown wouldn't be appropriate for a daytime garden wedding, right? Velvet isn't really a summer fabric, and a floaty chiffon number with spaghetti straps might not work in a blizzard. (That isn't to say you can't wear a sleeveless gown from November to April—you most certainly can.) As a rule of thumb, consider the typical temperature on your wedding day when selecting a fabric, and save the shiny stuff for evening. Otherwise, the bride gets to wear what she wants, when she wants.

Neck and Neck: Bodices

Although the neckline's main duty is to frame your neck and face, the best one for you also depends on body shape—arms and especially bust. You'll see most necklines on all different dress shapes, so they are in large part independent from silhouettes, but the combination of a specific dress shape and neckline probably will hit a home run on you. Think about the length of your neck when you're considering necklines. The lower the neckline, the longer your neck will look; the higher the neckline, the shorter it will seem.

Jewel: Also known as the "T-shirt neckline," this is a round neckline that sits at the base of the throat. If you're full-chested you already know the effect a T-shirt has on your bust—this may not be the best choice for you. But for petite or flat-chested women, this neck can enhance you on top.

Off-the-Shoulder: This one is self-explanatory—the neckline sits below the shoulders, with sleeves that cover part of the upper arm, and just about everyone can wear it. Especially when combined with a sweetheart shape in front (see below), this neckline is super-flattering to medium or full-chested women. (If you've got fuller arms and are a bit

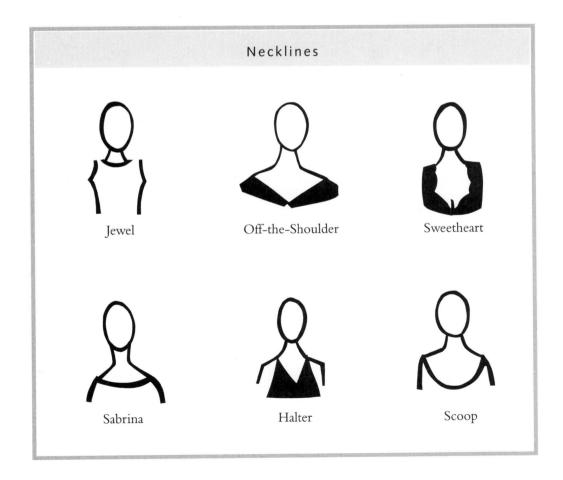

Necklines

Jewel

Off-the-Shoulder

Sweetheart

Sabrina

Halter

Scoop

uncomfortable with baring your shoulders, think about a portrait neckline, which is similar, but with extra fabric framing the neck and/or a bit of on-the-shoulder material.) The prettiest thing about the off-the-shoulder neckline? It exposes your collarbone, which looks beautiful *and* a bit sexy.

Sweetheart: This neckline is shaped like the top half of the heart, and full-chested women look great in it, because it really accentuates the décolletage. (Don't be shy—if you've got it, flaunt it!) If you don't dare to bare, the sweetheart often is done with an overlay of lace or sheer material that rises higher than the heart shape.

Sabrina: This shape gently follows the curve of the collarbone, almost to the tip of the shoulders—it's cut straight across, so less of the décolletage is showing. It's a very modern look and a good neckline for women who are less endowed on top.

Halter/High Neck: The cut-out halter shape (often with an open back) and the high-neck gown, often sleeveless, both necessitate broad shoulders and a fairly athletic build. The size of your bust is inconsequential, but these shapes look best on taller women—5' 7" and taller.

Scoop: The scoop, a square neckline with rounded edges (or a variation on that shape) is practically retro now—it's associated with Jackie O. It can be low cut, but not uncomfortably low. Often the scoop continues on the back of the dress. Just about everyone can wear this one, too.

Go to Appendix B for dress designer phone numbers.

The Long and the Short of It: Sleeves

Are you comfortable with baring your arms? Kind of baring them? Or not at all? Remember, too, that you also can wear a shawl or little jacket over your dress. Sleeves in a nutshell:

Spaghetti Straps: Thin straps that come straight up from the bodice and go over your shoulders.

Off-the-Shoulder: With this type of neckline, the sleeves may simply be bands of fabric that cover part of your upper arms. This coverage may be all you need to feel comfortable.

Cap Sleeve: Little sleeves that pretty much just cover your shoulders, but at least make you feel like you're not going sleeveless.

T-shirt Sleeve: Longer than cap; about as long as your average T-shirt, strangely enough.

Three-quarter: Straight sleeves that end midway between your elbow and wrist. A very elegant look.

Long: Sleeves that come all the way to your wrist, often with cuffs banded in lace, satin, even velvet. Also in this category is the unfortunately named leg-of-mutton sleeve, which tapers to the wrist to further deemphasize full upper arms.

Fabulous Fabrics

Most wedding dresses are made from one or a combination of the following fabrics. Why is it important to know this? Because different fabrics will hang differently off your body; the same style of dress may look (and feel) quite different on you in a different fabric. They're different weights and thus may be appropriate for different kinds of weather. And, of course, there are price differences, too—silk is the most expensive material.

Brocade: Jacquard-woven fabric with raised designs. A popular fall and winter fabric that has started to sneak its way into warmer-season dresses, as well.

Charmeuse: Lightweight, semilustrous satinlike fabric.

Chiffon: Delicate, sheer, and transparent—made from silk or rayon, with a soft finish. Popular for overskirts, sheer sleeves, and wraps.

Silk: The most sought-after and cherished wedding-dress fabric (and fabric in general!). There are different types, with different textures and weights. Raw silk and silk mikado are two examples.

Organza: Crisp and sheer like chiffon, but with a stiffer texture. It's popular in skirts these days—it has an effect similar to tulle, but it's more flowing. It's also popular on sleeves and bodice or back overlays.

Satin: A heavy, smooth fabric with a lustrous face and dull back. There's some satin on just about every wedding dress.

Silk Gazar: A four-ply silk organza.

Silk-faced Satin: Smooth silk with a glossy front and a matte back.

Shantung: Similar to a raw silk, with a rough, slubbed texture.

Taffeta: Crisp and smooth, with a slight rib. You probably remember it best from high-school prom dresses; it's not used as frequently on wedding dresses as it once was.

Tulle: Netting of silk, nylon, or rayon, it's used primarily for skirts and veils (think ballerina tutus).

Velvet: This fabric is being used more and more, for details at sleeve cuffs, on bodices, even for the dress itself.

Made in the Shade: Color

These days, white is simply a color of celebration—it no longer symbolizes purity or virginity. No need to worry about guests gasping in horror if you choose a wedding dress in ivory or eggshell—or one in pink, for that matter! What's important is choosing the shade of white that looks best on you.

Many wedding dresses are available in multiple shades, so color is not necessarily tied to style. But it *is* tied to fabric. For example, organza, because it is a lighter, sheerer fabric than most others, is a softer white, and it reflects the color of the lining. A stark white dress can be lined in an off-white fabric to create a softer white. A wearable option for many skin tones: lining a white organza gown in soft pink or coral.

Stark White: The brightest, crispest white you can get. This whitest white is best achieved with synthetic fabrics (satins, taffetas, polyester blends). Looks stunning against dark skin. Fair-skinned beauties should stay far away—it'll wash you out.

Silk, Diamond, or Natural White: The whitest white for natural fibers, like silk (hence the name)—a shade off of stark white. It looks pretty much the same in photos but is

Hot vs. Cold-Weather Fabrics

Hot Weather fabrics:
  Chiffon
  Linen
  Organza
Cold Weather fabrics:
  Brocade
  Faux fur
  Velvet
All-Weather fabrics:
  Satin
  Shantung
  Silk
  Tulle

Why White?

Queen Victoria turned the wedding-fashion world on its ear when she wore white to marry Prince Albert in 1840. Before that brides simply wore their "best dress" to marry, no matter what the color.

much more flattering to most skin tones (especially skin with yellow undertones). Just about anyone can get away with this shade.

Ivory: Also referred to as "eggshell" or "candlelight." Some ivory dresses have yellow undertones, making them look creamy; some are just a "quiet" white. Fairer skin tones look best in a yellow-ivories and warmer natural colors. Women with pink undertones in their skin also should stick to these creamier colors. If you're not sure of your skin tone, avoid yellow-whites; they can make you look sickly if they don't complement you.

Rum or Champagne: Has pink undertones but looks nearly white in photos. Great for dark complexions or yellow/olive undertones.

Other Colors: There's no rule that says you *must* wear white! In recent seasons designers have created dresses in soft shades of lavender, rose, even blue. Also more and more dresses are being designed with color in the details: embroidery, lace, bands of satin. If your complexion gets totally washed out by white—no matter what shade—send up the white flag and try a color.

Do the Locomotion: Trains

The train is that extension of your wedding dress that starts at the waist, trails out behind you, and demands your maid of honor to readjust it constantly so it fans out perfectly at the altar. Generally, the more formal your wedding is, the longer of a train you'd wear; some dresses don't have a train at all. If your dress doesn't have a detachable train, you'll want to "bustle" it after the ceremony so you can move around freely at the reception. This entails pulling the train up and attaching it to your dress by tiny hooks, buttons, or snaps sewn onto the back of your gown and the train.

Sweep: This is the shortest train, extending back a foot or less after the fabric hits the floor.

Chapel: Extends three and one-half to four and a one-half feet from the waist.

Semicathedral: Four and one-half to five and one-half feet from the waist.

Cathedral: Six and one-half to seven and a one-half feet from the waist.

Extended Cathedral/Monarch: Flows to twelve feet (or more) from the waist.

Not Quite White

The samples in bridal salons may be less than spotless—all those brides trying 'em on—so while the fabric is "white," it may appear a shade off from its actual color and more flattering than it really is against your skin. Be sure to look at a clean fabric swatch—put it up to your face—before making your final decision.

Do the Bustle

You can't bustle your dress by yourself! Make sure your maid of honor and/or another attendant learns how to do it and that they practice a few times before the wedding.

Where to Get the Gown

Okay, now that you're so well versed in bridal-speak that you'll amaze and impress every salesperson you ever meet (as well as your mother, sister, bridesmaids, and even your fiancé, who's a little scared at this point), you're ready to go out and use it. But where? The following are your options for acquiring the dress of all dresses.

Bridal Salons

These stores sell custom-made, designer wedding dresses and are the most traditional places to shop. You'll find boutiquey salons in upscale urban shopping districts, suburban downtown areas, strip malls, real malls, and also in some larger department stores. Check the Yellow Pages under "Bridal Shops" or "Wedding Services" to see what's near you. Then call stores you're interested in—you may need an appointment—and check out "Going Shopping," later in the chapter, for in-depth advice before you go. You also can buy bridal accessories such as veils, lingerie, shoes, and gloves at most salons. Besides the day-to-day business of selling dresses, salons also hold special wedding-dress events:

Trunk shows are shows to which a specific designer (or a representative of a bridal manufacturer) brings his or her entire latest line of dresses for brides to try on. The advantage—you get to see *every* dress in the line of a designer you really like, not just the styles that store chose to sell. And you also may get the small thrill of chatting with the designer herself and even having her check out what her dress looks like on you.

Sample sales are sales at which dresses usually used only for brides to try on are sold. Some stores have sample dresses in an array of sizes, but the general sample sizes are 6, 8, and 10. Wedding dresses run small—see "Just Your (Wedding Dress) Size," below—so if your regular dress size is a 2, 4, 6, or 8, you may be in luck. The dresses may not be super-clean, but you may get a great price, and you can put some of the savings toward a good dry-cleaning. (Designers also hold sample sales—so if you live in or near New York, where most are based, call around to see when these are happening!)

Shopping in a bridal salon is not cheap. These are dresses made by top bridal designers in the finest fabrics, you're getting full service (a salesperson well versed in the world of wedding gowns helping you, fittings), and your dress is going to be custom-ordered and altered for you. Expect to pay at least $1,000 and up to $6,000 or $7,000 for a really amazing designer or dress. But even if you don't end up buying your dress at one, a salon is a good place to try on a lot of dresses and get some expert feedback on what looks best on you.

Warehouses/Outlets

Inside these sometimes huge, more often cramped, stores is row upon row of racks of wedding gowns. Some are top designers' past designs that have had their run in the salons; others are designed by lesser-known (or not-known) companies whose names you may not recog-

Ethnic Options

Want to celebrate your heritage with what you're wearing?

African: Kente cloth details, gold thread, headdress/ crown

Chinese: Red silk details or a red *cheung sam* (a form-fitting dress with intricate designs)

Japanese: A traditional kimono

Indian: A colorful sari, a bindi on your forehead

Scottish: Tartan details or sash, lace

Spanish: A mantilla veil, black lace, colorful silk flower details

nize. But shopping here can save you some money. It's kind of like shopping at TJ Maxx or Marshall's—if you look through enough racks, who knows? You just may find something you love for a to-die-for price. (We must warn you, though, diamonds in the rough are sometimes few, and prices aren't always that low—you'll find dresses that cost $1,000 or more at warehouses, too.)

Some warehouse stores have salespeople that are assigned to you when you walk in the door; this person may or may not be as knowledgeable about wedding dresses as someone in a bridal salon. In others, you get to just wander (which isn't such a bad thing). Alterations usually can be done by the store. As in a bridal salon, often you can also buy veils, headpieces, shoes, gloves, and other accessories here, as well. Our take on warehouses and outlets? If there's one near you, it's worth taking a look. You never can tell. And if you're not very caught up in name-brand wedding dresses but you *are* into getting a good price on a traditional style, this may be for you.

Looking for the perfect dress—in your price range? Go to The Knot's Bridal Search at www.the knot.com to view thousands of choices. Go to Appendix B for dress designer phone numbers.

Rent the Dress

If you're not the type to get particularly attached to a piece of clothing (even a special one), the logic of buying a multithousand-dollar dress to wear for one day may be lost on you. Some clothing-rental stores have wedding dresses in stock—you might even find a store near you that just rents wedding dresses. In a good one, you should be able to find a dress in wedding-picture-perfect condition. You won't have to worry about dry-cleaning or storing the dress after the wedding—you just take it back to the store. Some shops may be willing to order a brand-new dress like the used one you find in the store—you still rent it, but it's

---

Period Costumes

Having an antebellum, Renaissance, medieval, or Victorian wedding? Here's where to look for clothes:

The Society for Creative Anachronism is a medieval recreation group that holds medieval and renaissance fairs around the county; they'll send you tons of information as well as put you in touch with a local chapter of the organization, which will help you find not only the right clothes, but local sites appropriate to your theme; 800–789–7486.

Designs by Jane Wilson-Marquis are decidedly (and beautifully) medieval; 212–477–4408.

Designer Pat Kerr is known for her Victorian designs; 901–525–LACE.

The Vintage Bride Catalog features over 100 pages of historic gowns. Call 619–291–8709 for a catalog, or find them on the Web at www.victoriana.com/c/bridal.html.

Reflections of the Past is a mail-order company with European antique and vintage costumes and accessories, including Victorian corsets, hats, purses, parasols, shoes, shawls, and fans. Call 216–835–6924 for more information, or look on the Web at www.victoriana.com/antiques/index.html.

Amazon Dry Goods catalogs, from a company known as a "purveyor of items for the nineteenth-century impression." Merchandise includes lace fans, high-laced shoes, dainty parasols, corsets, ready-made vintage dresses, and dress patterns. Call 800–798–7979 or 319–322–6800 for more information.

A Medieval Journey (705–645–2522) and Museum Replicas Ltd. (800–883–8838) are other period-based retailers.

never been worn before. On the downside, you probably won't find the selection you'd find at a bridal salon or even a warehouse or outlet; you'll be able to choose among only the dresses that the rental shop has, which may not be in the latest styles. If you do find the *perfect* style, just hope you don't get too attached to it on your big day! To find a bridal dress rental shop in your area, look in the Yellow Pages under "Bridal Shops" or "Wedding Services."

Direct from Designers

Each spring and fall, wedding-dress designers come together in New York, Chicago, Las Vegas, and Dallas for bridal markets, biannual fashion shows during which they present their new lines to the media and to bridal-shop owners—so they'll buy them and sell them to you. A majority of the designers and manufacturers are based in New York City, many in the Bridal Building (1385 Broadway, in the Garment District) and in the building next door (1375 Broadway). If you're planning to visit New York, you might want to check out the Saturday sales, when sample and new dresses are offered direct to the public. You can save 50 percent on sample dresses and 20 to 25 percent on orders. You'll probably find the largest selection of sample dresses in the months directly after the markets.

Not everyone is in the Bridal Building, though—be sure to check some of the many individual New York design studios (Cynthia C., Reem Bridals, Amsale, and Vera Wang, to name just a few). You may want to get on the mailing lists of designers you really like so you'll be among the first to hear about sample sales.

Getting a Dress Made

You loved several of the gowns you tried on in salons, but you have such amazing taste that they all cost more than $5,000. Or maybe you can't seem to find the dream dress you can see in your head in any store, anywhere. Find yourself a good seamstress and have her create your vision. Show her pictures of dresses with features you like (sleeves, waistline, etc.). She'll probably be able to create a "test" dress in muslin first, so you'll be able to see what it will look like.

You pay for the material, which you can pick out yourself and bring to the seamstress. Or you can talk to her about what you want or bring her a swatch and have her buy the fabric for you, if that makes you more comfortable. Fabric can be expensive—for example, good silk may run you $40 to $50 a yard, and you'll need eight to ten yards for the full dress—but it's still less than you'd pay in the salon. The other expense, of course, it paying the seamstress to design and create your dress. Cost can vary; for example, a simpler design will cost you less than a complicated one. Still, you probably won't pay much more than $1,000—if anywhere near that. Extra bonus— since the seamstress is making the dress for you, she'll probably alter as she goes along. At any rate, you won't have to take the dress elsewhere if it needs to be taken in or let out when it's finished.

Just One of the Girls

Want to really save a bundle on your wedding dress? If you're looking for something straight and simple, consider a stylish bridesmaid dress in white or cream.

Test Your Seamstress

Think you've found someone to create your wedding gown? Have her make you another dress—a shift for work, maybe—so you can see her work and how you work together before you entrust your wedding dress to her.

TIMBERLY AND ROBERT
August 16, New York City

TIMBERLY KNEW exactly what she wanted her wedding dress to look like but didn't want to spend a fortune to get it. Her vision of the perfect dress was simple and elegant, which she found out translated to outrageously expensive. But as Timberly soon discovered, who needs a fashion designer when you have friends like hers?

"My sister-in-law and roommate are both excellent seamstresses. They both offered to help make my dress," Timberly says. The bride picked out an ecru material and a Ralph Lauren pattern, and the two seamstresses got to work. The two didn't know each other well before the project, but they turned out to be an exceptional team: after three fittings, the dress was perfect. "It turned out exactly the way I pictured it, and it only cost me $400," says the grateful bride.

Wearing Mom's (or a Vintage Gown)

You love the sentiment behind wearing the same dress your mom wore when she married dear old dad, and you know it would mean a lot to her if you chose to wear it. And just your luck—you *love* the style, and it just about fits! Not only will this save you money, it's a great way to personalize your wedding wear (and make your mom cry). Or maybe Mom's gown doesn't quite fit or look right on you, but you're into the idea of a vintage dress, and you've found a gorgeous one in the bowels of a thrift store.

Wearing an old dress often means restoration is in order. Maybe the dress needs updating, or a little brightening and mending. Take it to someone who specializes in restoring old wedding gowns. Check the Yellow Pages under "Dry Cleaning"—if wedding gowns are someone's forte, it will usually say so. Or call around and ask. If your Mom preserved her dress properly (see "Preserving Your Dress," later in the chapter), it's a plus—if the fabric is torn or weakened from moisture or mildew, the chances of successful restoration are not as good, unless the affected areas are small. If the dress is made of polyester, you're in luck—it's the easiest material to restore. (Silk is one of the most difficult.)

If restoring the dress is a go—or if it's in great shape as is—you can update it by getting it altered to fit differently, adding different sleeves, cutting it short, or putting on beading or other appliqués. Seek out a seamstress (see above) to get it wedding-day perfect.

Going Shopping

Okay, this is definitely not like going to the mall for a pair of jeans. Shopping for a wedding dress is overwhelming. Salespeople know this. They also know you've never done this before. The key is to do your homework before you go so you're not a clueless customer. You wouldn't buy a car without researching what you need and want first, right? Don't buy your wedding dress that way, either. Read our shopping tips and you'll be in the know.

Simplicity Is In

"I try to be sophisticated and elegant at the same time. I like simplicity—clean lines, touches of embroidery or lace. Not a lot of details. Definitely not ruffles and flowers everywhere."

—Dress designer
Carolina Herrera

When to Begin

Be prepared to shop early—as in nine to twelve months before the wedding. That's right. Unless you buy a ready-to-wear dress or a sample gown right off the floor, wedding dresses are custom-made, which means they need to be ordered well before the wedding day so the manufacturer or designer has time to create the dress and you have time for multiple fittings. (See "The Perfect Fit," which follows.) If all goes well, the right dress will arrive on time—but the earlier you start, the better (and the less stress)! We're not saying you won't be able to do it in less time—just make sure your salesperson is aware of your schedule.

Before You Go

Before browsing in a salon, do a little research. Read "Bridalwear 101," earlier, so you'll know what's out there and how to talk about what you like. Look at pictures of different designers' dresses online and in magazines to get an idea of the latest styles and shapes, colors, necklines, and so on. At least you'll have a shopping starting point. Then call and make appointments at salon(s) where you want to start.

Who to Take with You

Mom, your sister(s), your honor attendant, your bridesmaids, and close friends or relatives whose advice you trust top the who-gets-to-go list. But try to maintain crowd control: Limit your shopping entourage to no more than three friends or family members at once. Otherwise, you'll feel overwhelmed (and so will your salesperson). There will be more than one shopping trip—trust us—so everyone will get a turn.

Also shop on your own at least once. It sounds like the exact opposite of what you'd expect wedding-dress shopping to be like, right? But chances are that after you've gone a few times and you get into the swing of how the process works and what you like, you'll be the most focused on what dresses feel right on you when you're alone in the dressing room. Maybe you'll narrow down the choices on your own and then invite Mom and sis to help pick the winner.

What to Take with You

When you're trying on dresses, you want to get an idea of how the entire package will look on you. This means bringing along some accessories.

- A strapless bra or bustier, for trying on strapless gowns or those with corset-style bodices.
- Control-top panty hose (sometimes a dress goes on more smoothly with them on, and you'll be wearing them on wedding day).
- A slip.
- Shoes with the same heel height as what you want to wear on wedding day (obviously you don't need the exact pair yet).

Many salons have bras, petticoats, and shoes available for your use while trying on dresses, so you may not have to bring your own. Ask when you call to make your appointment.

Dealing with Salespeople

At a bridal salon, a specific salesperson (sometimes called a "bridal consultant," not to be confused with those wedding professionals you can hire to plan your entire wedding) will be assigned to help you. You will work with this person every time you come into the store and after you buy the dress (for alterations, etc.). A good salesperson will ask you what kind of wedding you're having (i.e., style and formality), how you envision yourself looking on your wedding day, and what kinds of dresses you're drawn to. She also will probably check you out and decide for herself what kinds of dresses will look good on you (based on your body type, height, weight). Then she'll bring you dresses to try on.

At some salons and shops, you'll be able to look through the sample dresses and choose what you like. (This is definitely true at a warehouse or outlet.) At others, it's "closed stock"—you don't get to see *all* the dresses, only the ones the salesperson finds it in her heart to bring you. If you're uncomfortable with this, try to find a store where you're free to look through everything.

If you find a dress you love in a magazine ad, bring it with you. Make sure you have all the information the store will need—don't rip out a picture without the designer's name and other information. If the store doesn't carry the particular style you liked, ask whether it's willing to order a sample for you to try on. (If so, make sure you're not obligated to buy it!)

Notice how you're treated and how the salespeople make you feel. Are they treating you respectfully, as every good retailer knows you should treat a customer? Or are you feeling like a little girl who couldn't possibly know the first thing about buying a wedding dress? This is where all the knowledge you've armed yourself with comes in—if you can talk expertly about silhouettes, laces, and shades of white, the salesperson will know she's dealing with an informed consumer.

Take advantage of a salesperson's expertise. She works with brides every day—if anyone knows anything about dresses, she does. Bounce ideas off of her and consider her advice if you think it's given in good faith. But if anyone tries to talk you out of or into something, or makes you feel uncomfortable about your decisions, remember: A good salesperson will never pressure you to buy something you're unsure about.

Important Shopping Tips

Read our crucial shopping advice and you'll be ready for some stress-free dress shopping.

Avoid Shopping on Weekends. And evenings, if you can swing it. Bridal salons can get insanely busy. Especially if you're marrying in a popular wedding month, there are going to be a lot of other brides shopping along with you.

Take Along an Open Mind. You may think you already know exactly what kind of dress you want—or at least what shape and color are best, which neckline will suit you, and so on. But even if you think you want a scoop neckline, for example, try on an off-the-

What to Wear?

"The bride needs to identify the personality she wants to project on her wedding day. Some brides go into the shopping process thinking they want to be a glamour queen, and then they backpedal and say, well, I actually want to be pretty and romantic—a very different look."

—**Dress designer
Helen Morley**

Authorized Dealers

Some stores cut the tags out of their sample dresses, so that on first glance you won't know who the designer is. If you ask the salesperson who designed the dress and she won't tell you, ask why. If you don't get a satisfactory answer (and you won't, because there isn't one), don't shop there. Why? Well, first of all, you have a right to know whose merchandise you're spending money on. And it's important to know which designer's dresses a salon is *authorized* to sell. You know how sometimes store names are listed on a dress ad? Those stores are authorized to sell that dress. (They're not the only ones, but if their names are there, they are among the authorized stores.) If you buy your dress at a salon that's not authorized to carry that designer, there is *no guarantee* that you're going to get the dress you ordered in a timely fashion—or at all. If you're unsure, use the 800–number list in Appendix B to call the manufacturer and find an authorized dealer near you.

shoulder and halter, too. Something that looked great in a picture might not look so great on you—and something you thought you didn't like might be perfect.

Don't Eliminate Anything on First Glance. If the salesperson brings you something she says you *must* try—hell, try it, even if you detest the way it looks on the hanger. We know lots of brides who ended up walking down the aisle in a dress the salesperson persuaded them to try on.

Try a Range of Styles. One of the hardest things about wedding-dress shopping is that you're probably a virgin when it comes to long, white dresses. (Sorry, we couldn't resist!) Even though certain styles are best on certain body types, don't let those "rules" narrow your search too much. It helps to try on all different kinds of dresses—full skirt, A-line, sheath, long-sleeved, off-the-shoulder—and then decide what shape and style you look and feel best in.

Keep Your Dress Budget Flexible. (If you can, of course.) Don't tell anyone your price range unless it's so strict that you absolutely *have* to restrict it—otherwise you may inadvertently limit the types of dresses you're shown. On the other hand, you may want to look at dresses only in your specific range, so there's no chance you'll fall in love with a dress out of your financial league. Remember, though: If you realize that to afford the wedding dress you want you'll have to cut back in other wedding line items, cutting back is an option.

Look in Various Kinds of Stores. You may find you prefer shopping in a small boutique or designer's studio to navigating a large, bustling bridal salon or warehouse. Or vice versa.

Trust Yourself. If you have to be reassured that the dress looks great on you, ask yourself how much—or even if—you really like it. Even the most well-intentioned people may project their own dress fantasies onto you.

Don't Buy on the First Day Out. You didn't get engaged on your first date, right? Of course, it's happened that brides go back later and buy the first dress they tried on. But no matter how much you love it, give yourself all the options and the time to think by shopping more—and elsewhere—before you buy.

Sleep on It. Even after you think you've found it. Since dresses are custom-made, most salons put a no-return policy into their contracts; if you can get any money back, it probably won't be more than 50 percent of the total cost. So you should be absolutely sure that this is the one for you.

The Search Is Over

It's happened! ("Hallelujah Chorus" starts playing in the background.) You've found the perfect dress, and now that it's been on your body (maybe it still is because you won't allow the saleswoman or your mother to even come near you—she might try to unzip it), you're never letting it go. Okay. So it's a go. What now?

Before You Buy: Ordering Tips

Don't be shy—ask questions. This is an important investment you're making. If you don't get the "right" answers (or don't feel comfortable for any other reason), you may want to take your business elsewhere.

- If you don't know already, find out who designed the dress and make sure the store is authorized to sell it.
- If you love the dress but are thinking you'd adore it with slightly different sleeves or another neckline, find out if it's possible to make those changes and how much extra it will cost. If you think you might decide you want something like that done *after* the dress is in, will they do it then? Will it cost more?
- Ask how long the dress will take to come in and whether it can be rushed if you're shopping late (or you didn't find The One until the last minute).
- Ask to see fabric samples, so you'll know the exact color you're ordering the dress in; sample dresses can get worn and dirty. (See "Color" in "Bridalwear 101.")

Staying Spotless

Ask the salon for quick cleaning advice for the fabric your gown is made of. A wedding-day spill will be less of an emergency, more of a momentary hassle.

Dress Contract Points

Make sure all of the following are listed on your dress receipt:

☐ Manufacturer/designer name and style number
☐ Color ordered (white, candlelight, champagne, etc.)
☐ Full price quoted
☐ Size ordered
☐ Date the dress will be in
☐ Deposit amount required and paid
☐ Special-order requests and costs (taper sleeves, change bodice, etc.)
☐ Other costs (pressing, etc.)
☐ Alterations estimate, specifying exactly what type of alterations it covers
☐ Future payments schedule/when balance is due
☐ Cancellation/refund policies (most stores will refund 50 percent tops if you change your mind)

- If you're planning to sit for a bridal portrait (see "Picture This," Chapter 15), will the store let you borrow the dress for pictures and return it to the store to be pressed so it looks fresh for the wedding?
- Ask how much alterations will cost and get a written estimate before you buy the dress. This usually is not included in the price of the dress; some stores will charge a flat fee and others bill according to the work needed. (See "The Perfect Fit," below, for more fittings info.)
- Make sure the store accepts credit cards—and use one. For such a big and important purchase, you want to be able to dispute a payment (which you can with the credit-card company) if something goes wrong.

Just Your (Wedding-Dress) Size

Wedding dresses run small—which means you probably will need to order a size or two larger than your regular dress size. Don't let this bum you out! Even though you'd think if *any* kind of dress would run large, just for the buyer's mental health (don't you love when you get to buy a dress in a *smaller* size than usual?), it'd be wedding dresses, the fact is they don't.

You're So Vain

Do not, we repeat, do *not*, insist on ordering a smaller size than fits you because you're planning to lose a lot of weight before the wedding. It costs less to take a dress in than to let it out.

When you're ready to order your dress, the store will take your measurements—the typical bust, waist, and hips. Each manufacturer has its own measurements chart, and that's what the store will use to determine which size to order for you. Ask to see this chart so you'll have a better understanding of how it works—and to make sure the correct size gets ordered.

The Perfect Fit: Alterations

So you ordered the dress and it reached the store intact. It's the right dress, the right size. Yay! But wait, there's more. Every wedding dress needs alterations. That's because the size generally is ordered based on your largest measurement. For example, if you've got a large bust and fairly narrow waist, it makes more sense (and costs less) to order the size large enough to comfortably fit your bust and then take the waist in. Get it?

You'll probably have at least two fittings, which you'll schedule with the store when you buy the dress; more may be necessary, so leave ample time before the wedding. Alterations can be as simple as just taking in the waist a bit and hemming the dress to shortening sleeves, taking in the bodice, or even adding beading or lace if that's what you request. (If the store doesn't do its own alterations, chances are the salesperson you've been working with can recommend a tailor or seamstress that the salon does a lot of business with. But most bridal salons do it in-house.)

Dressing It Up: Accessories

A wedding dress by its very nature is gorgeous, but that doesn't mean you shouldn't accessorize. From the top of your head to the tips of your toes, there are plenty of enhancing extras that really do the job of transforming you into The Bride: your veil and headpiece, the right lingerie, the perfect shoes, and—optional—glamorous gloves and a wedding-day purse.

Go to Appendix B for contact information for accessory manufacturers.

Topping It Off: Headpieces

The bride originally wore veiling because the groom wasn't supposed to see her before the wedding—not just in the hours before the wedding, but *ever* before the wedding. These days veils and headpieces are about celebrating rather than cloaking your identity.

Some dresses are made with matching headpieces, which can make it easy for you—you may even be able to get your bridal salon to alter a headpiece if it doesn't sit quite right with you. You'll probably choose your headpiece at your first dress fitting (if your salon sells headpieces; if not, bring your chosen headpiece and veil with you to the fitting), although you may try some on while you're shopping for your dress. The options and combinations are many. Here's a glossary to ease your way:

Veils: Veils usually are made of tulle or organza, either plain or embellished with lace, sprinkled with crystals, or bordered with satin.

> **Bare That Back**
>
> If your dress has beautiful back details, don't choose a veil so long that they're hidden!

- Blusher: A short veil worn over the face down the aisle and turned back over the headpiece when the groom kisses the bride. Often it's attached to a longer veil or a hat.
- Fly-away: Multiple layers of veiling that brush the shoulders.
- Fingertip: Several layers of veiling that extend to the fingertips. This is probably the most popular veil length.
- Waterfall: This one, all the rage in the '60s, has made a 1990s comeback. It sits on the top of the head with tulle cascading down, usually held in place by a satin headband. Look for one with more than one tier of tulle, which gives the veil its shape and fullness.
- Mantilla: A Spanish-inspired lace veil that is worn without a headpiece, draped right over the head with a pretty lace border framing the face.
- Ballet/Waltz: Falls to the ankles, often in simple, multiple layers. A luxurious look that's once again making an impression; it can practically double as a train.

Headpieces: Some headpieces look better with either long or short hair—read on to decide what will look best on you.

- Headbands: These look great with any hairstyle and are perfect for prettily pulling hair away from your face, so everyone can see that bridal glow in your eyes and cheeks. For short hair, choose something narrow, maybe jeweled; longer-haired brides can opt for a wider band of satin or silk, or something decorated with beads or stones.

- Tiaras: Tiaras are a wedding mainstay—and they made their way into high fashion in general during the '90s, as well. These days they are not as tall and more delicately made—more like 3-D headbands than queenly crowns. Rhinestones are always popular—they catch the light so beautifully—but metal fashioned into different shapes, beads, or jewel-toned stones, are popular, too. Long- or short-haired brides can wear tiaras; they look equally as gorgeous in long hair worn down or in a simple updo.

- Headpieces: Some headpieces are made out of plastic or another sturdy material and decorated with rhinestones, lace, embroidered appliqués, pearls, crystals, silk flowers, even sequins. Often they're built onto a comb or series of small combs so you can attach them to your hair, or they're attached to a band. Depending on the style of the headpiece, these can work on either long or short hair. Backpieces, which sit at the back or crown of the head where they can be attached to a veil, can add a lot to your look without having to be an integral part of your hairstyle. Backpieces work best for those with shoulder-length hair or longer.

  - Barrettes: Who says you *have* to wear a headpiece? Pull long hair back with one pretty barrette—in white satin, with beading, or decorated with lace, maybe—and attach veiling with Velcro (so you can take the veil off at the reception); a comb can serve the same purpose. If you have a short cut, think about holding bangs to the side with a pretty little jeweled or plain barrette or two.

  - Hats: They look best on short-haired brides—but hey, try a few on and see! Choose from a pillbox to a dramatic, wide-brimmed hat—you even can tie veiling around it. Are you a second-time bride who's not comfortable in a veil again? A hat may be for you.

Keep a Cool Head

"There's a trend toward simplicity in headpieces—they're smaller, with cleaner lines, with veils that aren't quite so full. There's a narrower cut to them; they're less 'poofy.' If a veil has ribbon or some other trim, it's narrow."

—Headpiece
designer Tia Mazza

Your Lingerie

What you wear under the dress is just as important to looking good and feeling great as the gown itself. Here're some quick tips on the various bridal undergarments.

The Bra: Many of the bras and bustiers sold at bridal boutiques, while sometimes pricey, have wedding-dress-specific proportions that are quite useful with the right dress. But you should make comfort your priority—you don't want insufficient support or annoying wires cutting into your sides on wedding day, so take note of these things when you're trying pieces on.

If your dress has a low- or wide-cut neckline or skinny little straps, you'll want a strapless bra. The most versatile style is one with removable straps, which also will let you create a criss-cross or halter back. For a completely backless dress, get a backless bra that hooks at the waist. Or consider an "Unbra"—flesh-colored, tape-on support that you actually stick right to your skin. While an Unbra doesn't offer the same support as a full bra (it's probably not a good choice if you're full-chested, either), you can dance assured you've no straps to show. Want to pump up the volume on your cleavage? It's Wonderbra time.

It's smart to begin by looking for the correct style and type of support from your usual brand's offerings—you're already used to how that brand fits you. Take home a handful of styles and try them on with the dress. Move around a bit, do some dance moves—test the bra for comfort and to make sure it stays hidden.

Slimmers: While old-fashioned girdles went out of style after your mother's wedding, a number of contemporary slimming undergarments that use Lycra or Spandex rather than stiff stays or ancient whalebone are available. If you plan to use a slimmer, make sure to take it with you to your fittings; a body-support garment will give a slightly different shape than just sucking in your gut. And consider wearing it before your wedding day for practice. You want to make sure this is a type of support garment that you can wear for the duration.

Underwear: As with the bra and slimmer, choose panties that offer comfort over sex appeal. (There's just no way to discreetly rearrange a pair of creeping underwear through a wedding dress!) If your dress has an unusually slinky cut, you may want to go with a pantyhose/underwear combo; your guests don't need to know what style panty you chose.

Hose: If you want to wear a fancy garter belt with hooks to hold up thigh-high hose, make sure you choose one that fits snugly around your waist (and that won't be seen through your dress!). The pressure of the hose can pull an inexpensive elastic garter belt right over your hips, leading to wrinkly knees and an endless evening of trying to hitch up your hose (a task nearly as hard to hide as tugging at underwear). If you think you'll kick off your heels as the evening progresses, you might want to choose tights rather than sheer hose to avoid holes in your toes. Or go with knee highs that you can slide off along with your shoes.

There's the Run

Be sure to buy a few extra pairs of hose so that when you accidentally shred one leg on wedding morning, you can continue dressing without missing a beat.

Give 'Em a Hand: Gloves

Gloves are a Victorian artifact that had a resurgence in the 1930s and '40s, when they were worn for just about every formal occasion. Not only that, they're totally glamorous. They come in all kinds of fabrics—silk, satin, lace, cotton eyelet, knit, even kid leather. Some have trims that you can match to the details on your dress. Some handling tips:

- Wear wrist length gloves with short-sleeved gowns, elbow length with cap-sleeve gowns, and over-the-elbow gloves with strapless gowns.
- If you're wearing a long-sleeved dress, skip them altogether (or wear wrist gloves, if you absolutely must).
- If you have full upper arms, avoid over-the-elbow gloves; wear a pair that stops at the elbow.
- Over-the-elbow gloves don't do much for short brides, either, who have shorter arms. Keep the glove length to a minimum if you're of less than average height.
- Take gloves off in the receiving line and while eating and drinking during the reception (you'll end up wearing them mostly during the ceremony and for formal photographs).

Glove Etiquette

Q: I want to wear gloves during the ceremony but I'm not sure what I'm supposed to do when we exchange rings. Should I take the left glove off and put it back on after, or take both of them off at that point and leave them off?

A: Here's what you do: Carefully unstitch the seam of the ring finger on the left glove so you have a small opening. During the ring swap, slip your finger out, and once the wedding band is in place, slip it back in—no taking on and off of gloves! You could take the glove off and hand it to your honor attendant during the exchange, but if the gloves are long, you may be left struggling and fumbling at the altar, so practice beforehand. (And since it would probably be too much trouble to put it back on again at that point, prepare to be asymmetrical for the rest of the ceremony.)

Walking on Air: Shoes

Of course you want a gorgeous pair of wedding-day shoes, but you also want them to feel good on your feet. Let's face it, this is not a day on which you're going to be spending a lot of time sitting. If you opt for heels, don't go too high (or too stiletto-like): Two inches is enough. Many styles are available in different shades of white or are dyable, so you can match them to the hue of your dress. (You don't have to buy "bridal" shoes, but do if you want them to match your dress exactly.) The options:

It's a Shoe-In

Wear your wedding shoes before the big day to get used to them and to scuff the soles so you don't slip.

- Silk or satin pumps with square or round toes—plain or decorated with appliqués
- Mary Janes
- Strappy sandals (We love gold or silver ones for the wedding day!)
- Slingbacks with closed or open toes
- Satin ballet slippers
- Bridal boots with ribbons for laces—very Victorian
- Decorative, pearl-studded, sequined, or beaded sneakers, or Keds with lace laces
- White Doc Martens

Preserving Your Dress

Don't just throw it back on the hanger any old way after that band o' gold is around your finger and the party's died down. Okay, you can do that at first, but you're going to want to take steps to protect your treasured dress against age. Hey, maybe your daughter will want to wear it some day!

- Get your dress (and veil) to a professional dry cleaner who specializes in wedding dresses as soon as possible after the wedding. Call the International Fabricare Institute (301–622–1900) for a referral.

- If you're leaving for your honeymoon directly from the reception or first thing next morning from a hotel, ask a bridesmaid, relative, or friend to drop your dress off at the cleaners for you.
- Point out any stains you're aware of—champagne spills, lipstick, makeup.
- Have the dress packed in acid-free tissue paper and placed in a box that protects it from light, insects, and acid. Avoid boxes with cellophane windows, which can discolor fabric.
- If you don't want to pack your dress away, wrap it in a white muslin sheet and hang it on a padded hanger once you get it cleaned.
- Don't store the dress in a room where temperature is extreme (too hot, too cold, damp) or where there's direct sunlight, which can cause fabric to decompose.
- Check the gown in a year and take it back to the dry cleaner if any stains that weren't caught the first time appear or something else looks wrong.

Men's Formalwear 101

Dressing the Bridesmaids

Clothing Your Wedding Kids

Fashion Tips for Mom and Pop

Tuxes and Dresses

To-be-weds spend so much time stressing over what everyone should wear—the cummerbunds have to match the bridesmaid dresses; the maids' ensembles (and hairstyles) must be identical; it's mandatory for the moms to plan their coordinating wedding-day wardrobes carefully. We say—lighten up! The goal here is to get everyone looking good and feeling great. Let go of your ideas of how you think everyone *should* look and concentrate on making every individual look fabulous. Here's all you need to know to do just that.

Men's Formalwear 101

The land of formalwear is confusing territory for pretty much anyone who's never been a maitre d' for a living, so to help you make sense of all your wedding fashion choices—and the cryptic jargon tux salesman love to ramble on about—here's our handy groom's formalwear glossary:

Jackets and Coats

Tuxedo Jacket: The basic tux coat can be single- or double-breasted with your choice of three lapels: peaked (a cut in the lapel points upward, giving a broad, V-line look), notched (a triangular piece in the lapel is cut at the collar line and points outward), or shawl (there is no cut in the lapel, creating a retro rounded look). It's worn with black satin-striped trousers.

Tail Coat: Short in front and long in the back, it tapers from the waist into one or two tails down the back. Usually black, but sometimes you see it in white.

Cutaway/Morning Coat: Also short in front and long in the back, it tapers from the waistline button to one broad tail in the back, with a vent. Usually in pinstriped charcoal gray.

Stroller Coat: A semiformal jacket cut like a tuxedo, it's usually gray and often has pinstripes.

Dinner Jacket: Tuxedo-cut jacket in white or ivory (think James Bond). You also can get it in other colors or funky fabrics. It's worn with black satin-striped trousers.

Spencer Coat: An open coat without buttons, cut right at the waistline. Worn in the evening or daytime, depending on color (black for evening).

Shirt Collars

Wing Collar: A stand-up collar with downward points. The most formal style.

Turndown or Point Collar: Similar to a business-shirt collar, but in a more formal fabric.

Spread: Similar to a turndown collar but less pointy.

Mandarin Collar: Narrow banded stand-up collar without points. Can be worn with a button cover but not a tie.

Accessories

Ascot: A wide, usually patterned, scarf looped under the chin and fastened with a tie tack or a stick pin (very British) and worn with a wing collar, usually with a cutaway/morning coat.

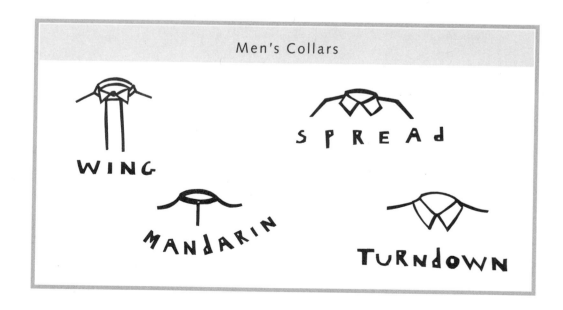

Men's Collars

WING

SPREAD

MANDARIN

TURNDOWN

Bow Tie: It's, uh, you know, a bow tie. Comes in multiple colors. Wear it with any collar.

Cummerbund: A pleated sash made of brocade, silk, or satin worn to cover the trouser waistline with pleats facing up. The color may or may not match your jacket, but it usually matches your tie.

Vest: Worn instead of a cummerbund or suspenders under the coat, vests have become hugely popular in the '90s. In black, white, or any other color or pattern, they're great under tuxedo or dinner jackets; they come in full or backless versions.

Waistcoat: Like a vest except usually cut lower in front, it's a more formal look, especially appropriate with a cutaway/morning coat or tailcoat.

Finishing Touches: Cuff links, studs, tie tacks, stick pins, pocket squares, suspenders. Feel free to drop some extra cash for a special pair of links—dice, rainbow trout, ball and chain—that will always remind you of your big day.

What to Wear When?

Rumor has it that at a wedding, the only person people pay attention to is the babe in the white dress. Not true! Grooms get noticed, too—especially if they're dressed wrong. But what could be so "wrong" about a tux—aren't they all the same? Think about it. James Bond wears a tuxedo—and so does the maitre d' at your favorite restaurant. So . . . no. There are a few guidelines.

Most of the rules about what kind of tux to wear have to do with whether you're getting hitched before or after the sun goes down and how formal or casual the festivities are going to be. The best resource for picking the right style of tux to match your occasion? The salesperson who helps you at the formalwear store. Let him in on the time of day you're getting married and how formal the wedding will be (describing where it is and what's in store will tell him all he needs to know), and then try on as many different outfits as he's willing to show you. Here's a quick lesson in some of the standard wedding dress requirements.

Semiformal Daytime: The groom and groomsmen wear suits (navy or charcoal are great year-round; reserve khaki or white linen for the warmer seasons) with nice shirts and four-in-hand ties (like the kind worn with business suits).

Semiformal Evening: The groom and groomsmen can wear black tuxedos with bow ties and cummerbunds or vests (or simply nice dark suits if they prefer). Their shirts may have wing-tipped or turned-down collars and are either white or ivory to match the bride's gown. Not required (unless your bride insists): cummerbunds that match the bridesmaids' dresses.

Formal Daytime: Choose gray strollers with ties and vests, cummerbunds, or waistcoats, or formal suits (again, in white or light colors for the summer—darker shades in the winter).

What Renting Costs You

Approximate cost of renting specific formalwear styles, according to Lord West:

- Classic tuxedo: $75
- Evening tails: $100
- Designer tux: $110

Time for Tuxes

The old rule: No tuxedos before 6:00 P.M. The new school: If your *reception* starts at 6:00 or later, it's okay to wear a tux for a late-afternoon ceremony. Tuxes for morning or early afternoon are still a no-no—so go for a morning coat, stroller, or great daytime suit instead.

Formal Evening: In the evening, formal usually means black tie: The groom and groomsmen wear black tuxedos with white or ivory shirts and black ties, cummerbunds or vests. (It's totally legit to inject some color into things, however.) Another option for formal evening: white or ivory dinner jackets (the 007 look).

Ultraformal Daytime: The groom and groomsmen traditionally wear cutaway coats with charcoal-colored striped trousers, gray waistcoats (sometimes available with a print), wing-collared shirts, and ascots or striped ties. It's a very dapper look that you're not going to get away with at any other occasion—and your bride will love it, trust us.

Ultraformal Evening: White tie (also known as "tails full dress") is reserved for the most elaborate evening weddings. The groom and groomsmen wear black tail coats with white waistcoats or vests, wing-collared shirts, and white bow ties. They also may wear fancy studs and cuff links, and their shoes are black patent leather. (You can skip the top hats and canes.)

Get the Guide

For a copy of the American Formalwear Association's free pamphlet, "Your Formalwear Guide." Send a self-addressed, stamped envelope to: The American Formalwear Association, 401 North Michigan Avenue, Suite 2400, Chicago, IL 60611–4267.

Going Shopping

For most grooms, renting a tuxedo probably will suffice. But if you think you'll have reason to wear a tux in the future, it may be worth buying one. Look at it this way: Renting costs about 25 to 30 percent of the price of a new tuxedo. The average cost for a good one is between $300 and $500. So if you attend three or four formal events a year, it's worth it to buy. And as long as it's a classic style, you'll be able to wear it for quite a few years.

But even the most expensive tux on the rack will look and feel awful if it doesn't fit you right. Since you're pretty much at the mercy of your salesperson, it's nice to know your way around the tux shop. Here's what to keep in mind when you formalwear-shop—share these tips with your groomsmen, too.

Comfort Is Key: Sure, looks mean a lot. But comfort, especially in a wedding tux, is a really close second—you'll be wearing it for four to eight emotional, fun-filled hours, after

---

Formalwear Contract Points

☐ Designer, style, and style number(s)
☐ Color of each
☐ Number of suits rented
☐ Accessories covered in rental fee (ties, shoes, vests, etc.)
☐ Date everything can be picked up
☐ Total cost
☐ Deposit paid and date balance is due
☐ Additional fees (fitting, cleaning, late return)
☐ How store will fix last-minute problems like poor fit, wrong style, etc.
☐ Refund and cancellation policy
☐ Date everything must be returned to store

Stand-Out Grooms

There are lots of fresh ways for the groom to contrast yet complement his groomsmen. You want people to know which one of you is the lucky guy, right?

Wear a white dinner jacket; best man and groomsmen wear black jackets. Or vice versa.
Wear a solid or patterned vest instead of a cummerbund.
Wear a long silk tie instead of a bow tie.
Wear different ties (e.g., groom in gold, groomsmen in silver).
Wear a different style or color shirt than the other men.
Wear different flowers in your boutonniere or be the only man to wear one.

all. You should be able to move around easily—do lots of twists, turns, and arm raises when you're trying one on.

Try 'em on for Size: It's a good idea for everyone to pick up and try on their formal-wear at least two days before the wedding. Sounds like a no-brainer, right? You'd be surprised. Many mismatched bridal parties or ill-fitting jackets are the result of guys skipping this simple step. Procrastinate at your own risk.

The Fit

When you're sizing up a tux, here's what to look for:

The Jacket: Should fit comfortably at the neck and shoulders and fasten easily. Try standing and sitting with it buttoned.

The Shirt: Should fit comfortably at the neck, shoulders, and waist. About one-quarter to one-half inch of cuff should show below the jacket sleeve.

The Vest: Should fit comfortably across your chest with the buttons lining up to the front of your jacket. The bottom should fall slightly over your trouser waistband. Usually you can adjust the waist with a slide strap for a good fit. Or consider a vest with a full back, so when you take your jacket off during the evening you're not flashing a strap and the back of your shirt.

The Trousers: Should button comfortably and feel good when you sit down. Many styles have adjustable waistbands, or you can opt for suspenders. The hem should break just over shoe tops.

More Rental Tips

Choose a formalwear store that has updated their inventory regularly since 1976. (If you see powder blue and ruffles, run.)

A good formalwear dealer will know how to measure you properly (inseam, waist, jacket size) and give you a fitting in advance of the wedding.

The store also can supply you with all the accessories you'll need: bow tie, cummerbund, cuff links, suspenders, even shoes.

Finally, all the groomsmen should get their clothing at the same shop, to ensure color

ODINE AND DAVID
March 6, New York City

HOW DID THE BRIDE, from New York, feel about her English groom wearing a kilt to their wedding? "That's how I met him," Odine says, "that's how I was going to marry him." Odine and David met in New York—David had come from Australia, where he was living, to attend the wedding of a friend, who happened also to be a friend of Odine's. The wedding was formal, and David was thus in his standard formal-wear—a kilt.

That gave Odine an easy way to introduce herself. "I asked him to dance by saying 'I've never danced with a man in a skirt before.'" She laughs. The couple carried on a "9,948-mile-apart" romance until David, once again in a kilt, proposed.

David's kilt has been in his family for generations—it's a McCleod tartan, meaning the pattern represents the McCleod clan, which is his Scottish ancestry on his mother's side. For the wedding, David wanted his father, brothers, and male cousins in their clans' kilts, as well. Almost none of them owned a family kilt, but, luckily, kilt shops in Scotland rent them, and David managed to locate the appropriate tartan for each man, which his dad then brought across the ocean.

Odine's mother is French, and Odine and David's friends are scattered around the globe, so the couple wanted to hold the wedding somewhere that would be a treat for guests coming from several continents. They found the perfect spot—a restaurant directly across the East River from Manhattan, so that the event's backdrop was the famous twinkling skyline of the Big Apple.

and style coordination. If you've got faraway groomsmen, get them to go for a fitting at a store near them (they can try on the tux you've chosen to check out how it fits them) and then send their measurements to you.

Dressing the Bridesmaids

First of all, we've got to tell you—bridesmaid dresses these days are nothing like the teal taffeta confections of weddings past. In fact, we think you'll be hard-pressed to find a dress your bridesmaids truly hate. That doesn't mean, however, that we're going to tell you to choose "something they can wear again." Why? Because, unless you pick a black velvet or satin sheath dress that hits at the knee, they probably won't. Even if they adore the dress you choose (or let them choose), it's still a bridesmaid dress. They'll associate it with your wedding. This is not a bad thing. It's a souvenir. The point is, don't get obsessed with the wear-again concept of every bridesmaid dress you see. Okay?

The Many Options

The choices for bridesmaid dresses these days are practically endless—and that's a good thing! And no longer do your maids all have to wear the same exact thing if you (and/or they) don't want to. Here's what to think about before you even start shopping.

Styles and Colors: You may be shocked at just how many styles of bridesmaid dresses you find out there. Just about all of them are floor-length, but you'll see fitted sheaths, A-line styles, empire looks (with high waists), two-piece skirt-and-top sets, overskirts, stoles and chiffon scarves, and matching jackets with jeweled buttons. Most bridesmaid dresses are fairly simple—they won't have too much detail (lace, beading, jewels). Most are in solid colors, but you'll also see two-tone dresses and floral prints (especially in spring).

Identical Maids: Traditionally, all the bride's attendants have worn the same dress. This works best when all the women have similar body

They Gotta Be Them

Your maids don't have to be identical. Even if they all wear the same dress, let them each choose how to wear their hair or select their own jewelry. They're not going to upstage you—they're just going to be more comfortable, which will make you look even better (and the pictures, too.)

Bridesmaid Lore

Did you know that the bridesmaids' dresses all used to be *identical* to the bride's? They dressed just like her to confuse and stave off evil spirits on her wedding day.

ASK CARLEY

Pregnant Bridesmaid?

Q: My best friend, who's also my maid of honor, just told me she's pregnant—her due date is about a month after my wedding! Can she still be in the wedding party?

A: Just because your friend will be pregnant at the time of the wedding doesn't mean she can't be in the wedding! Let her wear an empire-style dress (the "waistline" is just below the bust), leaving lots of room for her tummy. You can have extra material added to the dress if need be. And make sure there's a chair for her to sit down in during the ceremony so she won't be on her feet the whole time.

types—which doesn't happen all that often! Most of your attendants are tall and thin, and one is shorter and rounder? Keep in mind that she may need a lot of alterations done to her gown to make it fit her well and comfortably; you might want to let her wear a slightly different, more flattering style.

Stand-Out Honor Attendants: Some brides choose to put their best friend or sister (whoever serves as honor attendant) in a dress that's slightly different from the rest of the bridesmaids', to emphasize her place of honor in the wedding party.

Same Style, Different Colors: You might decide to ask your maids to all wear the same style dress, but each in a different color—of your choosing or the shade each woman feels she looks best in. You can create a rainbow of jewel tones or pastels this way, or put the attendants in different shades of the same color (purple, lavender, lilac, etc.).

Go to Chapter 11 for info on dress silhouettes and necklines.

Same Color, Different Style: One designer may have several dresses you like that flatter different body types, all available in the same color. If you go this route, your maids will match in shade, but each woman can choose the style that looks best on her.

Free Form: If you have no control-freak genes whatsoever, consider put this decision into your bridesmaids' hands completely. Maybe you want everyone to wear a sheath, or something in a shade of pink or black, but beyond that you're comfortable with leaving it up to your maids to choose. They'll probably be grateful (this way they can control how much they'll spend, too), as long as they are all pretty confident about dress buying and/or have firm ideas of what looks good on them. Some attendants get thrown for a loop if they don't get *any* guidance from the bride, so be sure to give them *something* to go on.

Going Shopping

Once you've got the big wedding-dress search out of the way, it's high time to start looking for your bridesmaids' dresses. Ideally you want to start looking about six months before the wedding; it'll take a few months for the dresses to come in if you custom-order them, and you want to be sure you'll have time for alterations and to deal with any problems (wrong color, wrong style) when they arrive.

Remote Maids and Measurements

An attendant across the country from you needs special dressing attention.

Call or e-mail her to get her ideas on what she'd be up for wearing (and what she's totally *not* into).

Send her pictures of dresses you like (or look at them online together) to see what she thinks of them. If you can, send shots of your honor attendant or another bridesmaid in one—all the better!

Ask her to send you her measurements (bust, waist, and hips). She can do them herself at home or go to a tailor, seamstress, or dress shop in her area to have them done there.

Order her dress along with the rest at your store (so they'll all be from the same dye lot) or select a dress from a national chain or catalog that she can purchase on her own.

When her dress comes in, call to let her know. Then ship it out to her.

Ask her to have her alterations done by a local tailor, seamstress, or dress shop.

Dress Contract Points

☐ Designer, style, and style number(s)
☐ Color of each dress
☐ Delivery date
☐ Total cost
☐ Deposit paid and date balance is due
☐ Additional fees (alterations, ironing, etc.)
☐ Refund and cancellation policy

Where to Look: Bridal salons almost always carry bridesmaid dresses as well. Some have separate rooms or even stores solely devoted to bridesmaids. You also can find maids' dresses at bridal warehouses, eveningwear stores (so many are identical to cocktail dresses these days), and in special-occasion dress departments at big department stores.

Whom to Shop With: You might want to go alone first to see what's out there, take along your honor attendant so she can test-drive dresses you like. If possible, try to take all your bridesmaids along on at least one shopping trip, so they'll feel like they have a say in what they'll wear.

Alterations: Once the gowns arrive in the shop, every bridesmaid needs to go in for a fitting; as with the bride's gown, the shop probably can take care of any alterations—taking in the waist, bringing in the shoulders, hemming the skirt. The shop will call the bridesmaid when the altered dress is ready, so she can go in to try it on again and make sure it fits.

Shoes: Many brides ask their maids to buy dyeable shoes to match the color of the dress. Many national chain shoe stores carry these, in styles from pumps to strappy sandals. You (or the maid) simply brings in a swatch from the dress, and the store matches the dye of the shoes to the color of the gown. Or you may be able to find ready-made shoes in the right color (or in black or silver). Maids can all wear the same style, or the bride can choose to let them each decide will be most comfortable.

Go to Appendix B for contact numbers for bridesmaid dress and shoe manufacturers.

Clothing Your Wedding Kids

When it comes to kid attendants' clothes, keep in mind that for little boys and girls who want to run around and play at the reception, comfort and practicality are key.

Junior Attendants

Preteen maids and groomsmen can wear the same dress or formalwear as their older counterparts. If your bridesmaids are wearing something a little less than appropriate for a twelve-year-old girl (a seriously plunging neckline, for example), put her in a more age-appropriate style in the same color or in a complementary shade.

Group Discounts

If the bride and bridesmaids' dresses are ordered at the same store, you (and/or they) may receive a discount, or free alterations. Some formal wear stores will rent the groom his tuxedo free if all the groomsmen rent at the same store. Ask before you order.

Check Appendix B
for contact numbers
for top child atten-
dant clothing
manufacturers. For
more on child
attendant roles, go
to Chapter 5.

ASK CARLEY

His Mom in White??

Q: His mom wants to wear a white dress! I feel like she's trying to show me up. What should I do?

A: First of all, it's just not *possible* to show up a glowing, gorgeous bride, so don't stress out too much over the situation. Your best bet here is to resort to some good old-fashioned etiquette: Let your fiancé talk to his mom and gently let her know that it's not appropriate for anyone but the bride to wear white. She may simply not be aware of this, or maybe she just didn't consider that it would upset you. Then you might ask your mother to give his a call to let her in on what she's planning to wear, since moms often discuss how they each are dressing for the wedding. If all else fails and you have a good relationship with her, don't be afraid to talk to her yourself.

Little Girls

A general rule of thumb: A flower girl's dress should echo the styling of the rest of the bridal party or the bride's dress, whether with color, style, or length. Shop with your flower girl and her mom (who probably will buy the dress, unless it's a gift from you). She'll look adorable in any pretty party dress. White is the most common color choice, but it can be any shade you—and she—like.

Sweet dress styles for little girls include short or long sleeves with full skirts and satin sashes; white organza pinafores over velvet dresses; all-over lace confections in white or colors with satin ribbons; or simple straight dresses, perhaps to match simply styled bride's and bridesmaid gowns. These darling little outfits, especially those made expressly as "flower girl dresses," can be pricey—be sure to check out the little girls' department at your favorite department store, and shop in local children's shops, too. Don't forget shoes—pretty ballet slippers or black or white patent-leather Mary Janes will match any choice you make. Floral hair accessories like headbands, wreaths, and combs are fun, too.

Little Boys

Traditional choices for ring bearers or pages are satin and velvet suits with short pants, often in dark colors, such as navy or hunter green. Or how about dark-blue jackets, white shorts, and blue or white knee socks? In England, little boys wear white in weddings. For summer, a seersucker or linen suit might be cute—or put the tiny guy in a little sailor suit, which you'll find in just about every children's clothing store. There's the "please, no mini tuxes" school, but you might find little boys in grown-up formalwear endearing (hey, if the flower girl gets to wear a bridal-gown replica . . .). Check to see what local department stores, children's specialty shops, and even men's formalwear stores have to offer.

Fashion Tips for Mom and Pop

Parents get gazed at quite a bit on wedding day—they should love what they're wearing.

Moms

It's a big day for your moms, too—they're concerned about wanting to look great. The best way to help them do this? Don't instruct them about what to wear or forbid them from wearing something. Moms should wear what they feel most beautiful and comfortable in. Since your mothers are two women with different personalities, the best look on each may be quite different, and that's okay. What you can do is help them with their decision by offering guidelines—suggest colors and styles that will go well with the overall look of your wedding. Each mom should wear a shade that suits her.

Moms usually dress with similar formality. This guideline simply ensures that one mom doesn't feel uncomfortable or embarrassed. Generally, if the bride's mom wears a floor-length gown, the groom's mom should, too—a pantsuit in a formal fabric like satin or velvet with wide pant legs will also do. If they seem paralyzed by indecision, this old etiquette rule might help: The bride's mother selects her dress first and fills the groom's mother in on what it looks like, so she'll have an idea of what *she* should look for. But we've been to plenty of weddings where the moms weren't dressed a bit alike—and each looked out of this world.

Log on to The Knot's Bridal Search (www.theknot.com) to browse through thousands of bridesmaid and mother-of-the-bride dresses.

Dads

Dads have wedding dressing pretty easy. Here's the drill: If the groom and groomsmen are wearing tuxedoes, cutaway coats, or tail coats, the dads should, too—especially if you're also asking guests to dress way up. Even if the boys aren't going black tie, dads can feel free to don a tux for the big day. That said, formal suits in appropriate colors (black, navy, charcoal for evening or winter; navy, brown, beige for summer or daytime) are great. Just remember to give each dad a boutonniere—that's what'll tip guests off as to his special status.

Guest Dressing

Wedding guests basically dress as they would for any other social event held at the same hour and in the same season as the wedding. Most guests are comfortable using that guideline, but if anyone asks you, give them some suggestions.

For example, if it's a spring brunch or luncheon, a pretty suit or floral dress would be appropriate for women; a light-colored suit and/or shirt and tie for men. For evening, depending on how formal the wedding is (guests often take their cue from the formality of the invitation and/or where the wedding is being held), the dress code is cocktail dresses for women and dark suits for men. If you want your guests to dress to the nines, have "White tie" or "Black tie" printed at the bottom of the reception invitation. If you want to let guests know they *can* don tuxes and cocktail dresses but don't *have* to, make it "Black tie optional" or "Black tie invited."

Black used to be taboo for women at weddings, but these days a black dress is perfect for evening—for female guests *or* bridesmaids—just as it is for a night at the opera. However, female guests should still stay away from white—the bride's color—and should try to avoid off-white and ivory, too. Brides, if a guest slips up on this one, try not to let it bug you. The person may just not know. And if she *is* trying to show you up (the witch!), don't let her get to you (or see that she got to you, at least). Trust us, you'll look *way* more fabulous.

Deciding Which Meal to Serve

Choosing a Caterer

Talking to Your Caterer

Making the Menu Memorable

Hot Menus from Cool Chefs

Serving Drinks

Cut to the Cake

The Food Chain

Chances are you'll spend almost *half* your wedding budget on the reception meal. Your choice of chow not only fills the tummies of friends and family who have come to see you wed; it also helps give your party personality and taste (pun intended). Guests probably won't remember the flowers the next week, but trust us, they'll recall the food. So, how to make your wedding meal worth the memories? First off, don't think your only choice is between chicken and beef. In this chapter we'll let you in on a few of our favorite feasts and give you some tips and tricks to keep them tasty.

Deciding Which Meal to Serve

Before you choose the menu, you need to know which meal you're serving, right? This depends mostly on when your reception will be: breakfast (9:00–11:00 a.m.); brunch (11:00 a.m.–2:00 p.m.); lunch (12:30–3:30 p.m.); tea (3:00–5:00 p.m.), cocktails (5:00–7:00 p.m.); dinner (6:00–9:30 p.m.); dessert (9:00–10:30 p.m.)—or even a cruise ship–style midnight snack (11:00 p.m.–1:00 a.m.).

Budget also influences what you serve, of course, and the price of your spread is set by a variety of factors. Generally, breakfast or brunch will cost less than dinner (because the foods involved take less effort to prepare). But other issues affect your bill, too—namely the day of the week your party is held, how much food you actually serve, how formal the service, how expensive (read: talented/popular) the caterer, and how costly your chosen ingredients. (Caviar is going to run you more than cocktail weenies, no matter when you serve it.) Buffets generally cost less than served meals, although equipment, such as buffet tables, pans, serving utensils, and heating/cooling devices, actually can make the final bill comparable. Be sure to get prices for each element of your ideal meal; if it's too pricey, you may be able to boil it down by a little creative substitution—using chicken instead of shrimp, serving foods at room temperature instead of steaming, or changing the time or day or service style.

Buffet

Whether for breakfast, brunch, lunch, or dinner, a buffet offers your guests a full meal *and* the chance to choose exactly which foods and how much of them they want. Your buffet can be hotel-style formal or all-you-can-eat-smorgasbord casual. You might choose to have staff creating crêpes or pasta dishes while guests watch or just have food set up in large serving dishes. You decide whether or not to assign tables.

Pros: You save money on wait staff since guests do their own legwork. Guests can tailor the meal to suit their taste buds. Food stays hot (or cold) longer because it waits in heated containers (or on ice) until it's time to eat. Food preparation can double as entertainment.

Cons: You may have to rent all the buffet equipment yourselves. Elderly or physically challenged guests may have trouble maneuvering. Long lines may force your guests to wait awhile.

Tea

Afternoon tea encompasses aspects of both a buffet and a seated meal. You can serve food on tiered stands on reception tables, where fancy scones, pots of jam, finger sandwiches, and fussy pastries will double as edible centerpieces. Or set up your spread buffet style. Offer three or four kinds of tea, ice water, coffee, and other favorite beverages. Hire waiters to pour, or make it self-serve.

Pros: Your guests will be floored by your taste and class. Older guests will adore your mellow sophistication—so much so that no one will realize that tea is far less expensive than a full meal. The reception will be shorter, which means you two get the entire evening alone together!

Cons: If you want hours of boogying to a rockin' band, a tea is not the party to do it at. It many be a little too "precious" for some crowds. Anyone expecting a full meal may walk away hungry (or start nibbling the doilies); be sure to note "tea reception" on your invites. It may feel rushed or insufficiently monumental for the scope of the event.

Cocktails

At a cocktail reception, you offer a slew of hors d'oeuvres instead of a full meal, and guests stand and chat while holding small, snack-laden plates and trying to balance their wineglasses. The variety of snacks depends on the length of the party. A good rule of thumb: For

Delicious Discounts

Ways to save some dough on your dinner:

- Stationary appetizers (crudités, cheese and crackers, olives, bread with spinach dip) cost less than passed hors d'oeuvres, which also require wait staff.

- Choose chicken instead of beef, or pasta instead of scallops. Simpler vegetables—broccoli instead of asparagus—cut costs, too.

- Cut down on courses. Do you really need soup *and* salad?

- Think ethnic! Mexican, Indian, Italian, or Chinese food is fun and much cheaper per person than traditional wedding fare.

- Consider a breakfast, brunch, or tea to save money on food and labor. Serving Bloody Marys and mimosas will save on alcohol. People also drink less liquor at these times of day.

a two-hour party, serve at least six different kinds of hors d'oeuvres; for a four-hour affair, at least nine. Hors d'oeuvres are either arranged on tables or passed by waiters.

Pros: A classy, low-cost, low-stress option. You don't have to spring for silverware (other than those frilly-topped toothpicks). You don't have to pay for dozens of tables complete with centerpieces, chairs, favors, and place cards (though you do need a few serving platforms and a smattering of small tables and chairs for guests who want to take a load off). You can skip the extensive breakdown crew. Cocktails tend to take less time than a full reception, meaning you're out the door and on your way to Tahiti sooner.

Cons: Without all the dancing, talking, bouquet-tossing, and so on, your wedding may feel like less of a big deal (but then, that may be exactly what you're after). The standing-and-chatting approach may be less comfortable for older guests than a sink-into-a-chair soiree. Guests may drink more than they would at a full meal, so liquor costs may be higher.

Seated Meal

At a seated breakfast, brunch, lunch, or dinner, guests are served by waiters. All other things being equal (food cost, time of day), this is the priciest option. But for some, it's seated dinner or starve. There are four approaches; as you'd expect, the more formal the service, the more frightening the price.

- Family-style: Each dish is delivered to the center of the table; guests pass them politely (or grab and hoard, depending on your family).
- American service: Plates are prepared in the kitchen and servers bring them out to the tables.
- French service: Waiters prepare food on stands set up next to the tables, and then serve individual plates.
- Russian service: White-gloved waiters carry each course on a large tray and serve guests directly from it.

Pros: Guests feel pampered. They can relax and sit comfortably, without having to lug plates, stand in line, or fret that the roast beef will be gone before they get their turn at the carving station. Less work for guests means more time to talk (particularly about how gracious and *classy* you are for serving a seated meal). You can keep better tabs on how the party flows.

Cons: Guests may never leave their chairs or talk to anyone other than their seated neighbors. The party may feel too stiff or formal for your taste. It may take a long time for the meal to be served and finished. Food might get cold because of such meticulous (and time-consuming) service. You may spend some *big* bucks.

How Much a Head?

Per-person catering cost depends on the type of meal. Chicago caterer Wendy Pashman's approximate starting price to feed 100 guests:

Seated brunch: $75 per person
Lunch buffet: $75 per person
Tea: $50 per person
Cocktail reception: $60 per person
Seated dinner: $100 per person
Dinner buffet: $80 per person
Dessert buffet: $12 per person

Dessert Only/Postnup Snack

The dessert-only party and the late-night snack have their origins in the church-hall cake and punch soiree. Even if you serve only a mint-chocolate-chip ice-cream cake and champagne in a box, you're still officially wed!

Pros: Saves you money! The dessert-only reception is the most economical, easiest, and fastest option (unless you decide to import all the chocolate for your 200-pound wedding cake from Belgium). Appropriate any hour of the day. (When is it ever the *wrong* time to eat cake? Or drink champagne, for that matter?)

Cons: Guests won't linger for long; you'll be disappointed if you want everyone to make a fuss over you for hours. You and your guests may wind up bouncing off the walls like the Energizer bunny on speed from too much sugar or leave the party still hungry. (Again, make sure your reception invite says "dessert.")

Choosing a Caterer

Now that you've decided what type of meal you want, you're ready to find the right person or company to execute your culinary plan. There are a number of ways to go.

An On-Site Chef

If your venue comes with its own caterer, your choice may be limited—to *him/her*. This isn't necessarily a bad thing—some of the most beautiful sites come with the region's best chefs. If you'd prefer having a bit more say over what your guests eat, ask if you can augment the meal by bringing some of your own dishes. Or see if the chef will prepare a special family recipe (or just something you both adore) along with the customary spread. You may be able to adapt the regular meal a bit, or choose only the chef's best dishes.

A Catering Company

If you don't have to use the on-site caterer (or there isn't one), call in a pro—a professional caterer who has done hundreds of weddings and already has worked out all the kinks. To find a caterer, ask everyone you know for recommendations. Ask your venue. Consult other recently married couples. Make a list of potential caterers, and then give each a call. Narrow down your appointment list to include those caterers who you: (1) like over the phone; (2) are available on your date; and (3) are willing to prepare the kind of meal you're craving.

Then it's on to the fun part: free food! You'd never buy new shoes without trying them on—why should you hire a caterer before sampling his/her wares? Ask to taste the offerings of every caterer you're considering. It's standard practice for caterers to prepare a meal just for you two or invite you to a group tasting (during which time you might meet other soon-to-be-weds and possibly learn of better or more-appropriate-for-your-reception caterers). Never say no to a caterer's meal—you're about to embark on one of the most expensive ventures of your lives, so accept all the free food you're offered! Besides, you're far too busy to cook—and every meal you sample may give you more reception food ideas, whether you work with that caterer or not.

The Restaurant Route

You met at a charming French bistro on the corner. Your eyes locked over your matching plates of foie gras and you were hooked. Obviously, you must have French food at your wedding—ideally that first dish you shared together. Is it possible? *Mais oui!* Ask your special place if they cater weddings. Many restaurants have catering departments or are willing to handle large affairs straight from their kitchens. The bistro may even be the perfect sentimental site for your soiree!

FRANCES AND JOE
August 26
Charlottesville, Virginia

WHEN FRANCES AND JOE started planning, they realized that to have the wedding dinner they wanted with all the people they loved in attendance, they would have to be creative. For only $2,500, including alcohol, they had a delicious buffet for 110. How'd they do it? A talented friend and a small army of their closest pals, instead of a caterer, prepared and cooked the food the day before and the day of the wedding. "We didn't need or want a fancy sit-down dinner. We knew we could ask our friends to help us cook and put it together, and we knew that they would be happy to eat casual food," Frances says.

On the menu: chicken on skewers with Thai peanut sauce and gazpacho for starters, along with a big green salad. The main course: a pasta-and-chicken dish served with green beans and sun-dried tomatoes. The alcohol was carefully chosen wine, local beer, and champagne for toasting. For dessert, everyone ate cake.

"The most important thing about our wedding was that we wanted everyone to come," Joe recalls. "Preparing our own feast with friends was the best way we could make that happen." Besides, close friends felt lucky to spend a lot of prewedding time with the bride and groom and to play an important role in their celebration.

A word of caution: Even if dinner for two is divine, the same meal for 200 may not be. Clearly, it's easier for a kitchen to turn out small portions than huge ones. Ask how the restaurant handles big events—how many cooks are there? How many waiters will serve? What's the lag time between preparation and presentation? How will your favorite dishes be affected? Can you have a buffet? What recommendations does the chef have?

Do-It-Yourself Catering

Whether it's a budget decision or sentiment, pure and simple, if your mom (or dad, or brother, or college roommate) loves to cook and is willing to do it, you may decide to ask him or her to prepare the meal. The do-it-yourself approach works best if your wedding is small (under fifty people; cooking takes time, and you don't want Mom to miss the party because she's grilling tuna kebabs in the kitchen), at a private home (the easiest place to pull this off), and you have full confidence in your cook's culinary skills (i.e., your mouth waters just thinking about it).

Sit down together to create a menu and a schedule of what needs to be prepared when. Empty your refrigerator to store dishes, and have some friends' refrigerators ready to be turned into storage units if needed, too. Make your cook an official member of the wedding party. (Mom already is, of course!) Get her a thank-you gift (and maybe a special apron or cap to use on wedding day, too), and let her know that the fantastic feast is her wedding present to you two.

Some tasty and less time-consuming options for do-it-yourselfers include:

The Italian Feast: Your Tuscan grandmother wants to cook? By all means, *let her.* Start with red wine, then serve the antipasti and loaves of Italian bread with olive oil. Move on to pasta, then the entree (something easy like eggplant parmesan). Top off your wedding cake with a little gelati—and don't forget the cappuccino.

The Barbecue: Think hot-off-the-rack chicken breasts, steak kebabs, hamburgers, or seafood and vegetable skewers. Serve salads (pasta, Caesar, potato) on buffet-style picnic tables. Don't forget the watermelon and a couple of kegs of local beer.

Get Some Help

Even if you are preparing the food yourselves, make sure to hire wait staff, even if it is just neighborhood college kids. You'll need the helping hands for serving and cleanup duty.

Getting a Head Count

Once you've found your caterer (or restaurant, or cook), let him/her know the size of your guest list. You'll need to hand your caterer an exact head count (based on invitation responses) about two weeks before the wedding. Likely your caterer will plan to prepare 10 percent more food than it looks like you'll need, just in case there are late additions (unless your budget is too tight to do this).

Don't forget to include your wedding vendors in the final dining tally—the DJ, bartenders, and photographer need to eat, too. Don't worry about feeding them if it's a short, informal affair (under three hours). Otherwise, plan *something* for these people to eat, even if it's deli sandwiches. (Some hungry vendors may put mandatory meals in the contracts you sign with them.)

Going Greek: Take the Mediterranean mezzo, or appetizer platter, and make it an entire meal. Or give your cook a break—order platters directly from your favorite Greek or Lebanese restaurant, and ask her to handle the setup. Serve stuffed grape leaves, baba ganoush, humus and pita bread, tabouli, sliced grilled chicken, lamb, and Greek salad.

Other Convenient Cold Cuisine: Roasted, sliced filet mignon served with horseradish sauce; seared tuna; baked or poached salmon; grilled zucchini and eggplant; a salad of sun-dried tomatoes with mozzarella and basil; wild rice; pasta salad; shrimp cocktail; elegant condiments like cornichons, olives, and capers.

Lotsa Leftovers

Don't waste food. Donate extras to a soup kitchen. Make arrangements ahead of time.

Talking to Your Caterer

After you've chosen the caterer right for you, it's time to talk business (unless it's your mom, of course). Not all food providers work the same way, so pay close attention.

Questions for Your Cook

- Does your caterer have a license? This is really important—having one means the caterer has met local health department standards and carries liability insurance.
- Does the meal come full service or no-frills? Will the caterer provide tables, chairs, plates, even napkins, silverware, and salt-and-pepper shakers? Or do you have to rent place settings and/or other equipment yourselves?

The Catering Contract

Your contract with your caterer or restaurant should include:

☐ The date and time of your party, including the *exact* location and room. (You don't want someone else's 400 guests noshing on your canapés!)
☐ The type of service (cocktails, buffet, tea, dessert, seated meal—French service, etc.) and the staff-to-guest ratio.
☐ The exact menu.
☐ What liquor is being served (if the caterer is handling it).
☐ The cost and payment schedule; when the final balance is due.
☐ The date the caterer needs a final head count.
☐ The name of the catering-company representative who will be on hand during the wedding (this should be the person you're working with); the name of an acceptable substitute should an emergency arise.
☐ Contact information for morning of wedding (cell phone number, for example).
☐ Any sales taxes, gratuities, overtime charges, bar, or extra-waiter fees.
☐ The cancellation/refund policy.
☐ Proof of license (liability insurance)

- Will the caterer provide wait staff? How many people will each waiter serve? (Or how many people will work the buffet?) Will the caterer set out those cute little place cards and centerpieces you created, or do you need to do it?
- Who will oversee the event on your wedding day?
- Will the caterer arrange the food attractively on the buffet or on plates? Can you see photos of previous presentations?
- Are there extra charges, such as a security deposit, sales tax, gratuities, bar fees?
  - Will the cook be willing to include a recipe you provide, like a special family dish or some sentimental appetizer? Can s/he prepare vegetarian or kosher meals for just a few of your guests?
  - Will the caterer provide alcohol, or can you handle the bar separately?

Aphrodisiacs

Why not incorporate some of these romantic foods into your wedding feast?

- Artichoke
- Asparagus
- Avocado
- Basil
- Black beans
- Chilies
- Chocolate
- Edible flowers
- Figs
- Grapes
- Honey
- Oysters
- Pine nuts
- Rosemary
- Strawberries

Making the Menu Memorable

As a kid, you may have believed that green beans grow in a can, all meat is hamburger, and macaroni and cheese is a square meal (the square box = square meal philosophy). But these days, you know better (as do your guests). Fine dining is a national pastime. Whether you're planning a simple cocktail reception or an elaborate seated meal, your wedding is one more chance for your food-crazed family and friends to eat. Here are five great ways to make your menu terrific. Even if your caterer is doing all the work, being in the know will help you make better choices.

Think Seasonal

Great cooks plan their menus around seasonal food—whatever's freshest that month or season. Your favorite summer tomato salad, for example, just won't be as juicy in January; pasta with a rich tomato sauce would be a better winter bet for tomato lovers. Save the fresh salad for a summer party, when you might make it a produce feast—tomatoes with mozzarella and basil, grilled zucchini, prosciutto-wrapped figs and melon, huge mixed-lettuce salads, chicken with fresh raspberries, and drippingly ripe peaches. Ask your caterer and culinary pals what's fresh when; see if you can incorporate those foods into your wedding-meal vision.

Go Regional

Another great way to guarantee freshness (and authenticity, too) is to choose regionally grown or raised food. You've got a better shot at finding ocean-fresh lobster in Maine than in Minnesota, for example. Hometown food is also a great way to personalize your party and introduce your guests to the local cuisine, especially if you're having a lot of out-of-towners. Give them a taste of authentic Southern barbecue, Chicago deep-dish pizza, New England clam bake, or a total Tex Mex menu.

Consider Temperature

One of the biggest problems with party food is the lag time between preparation and presentation. That creamy seafood in puff pastry looks great in the kitchen, but by the time it gets to table 23 the cream may have soaked through, creating a gooey, chewy mess. For a large reception, choose food with a long shelf life. And think seriously about going with a buffet rather than a seated dinner. Buffet food can be kept hot over chafing dishes or cold over ice, reducing the oven-to-table time and helping preserve flavor.

Liven It Up

To *really* shorten the kitchen-to-mouth time, go with food preparation stands in the dining room. Chefs prepare much of the meal live, right in front of your guests. Some ideas:

- Raw bar: Oysters are shucked and kept on ice.
- Pasta station: Guests choose their sauce and watch as their pasta is tossed.

International Eats

Where is it written that you must have filet mignon, salmon mousse, and chocolate-dipped strawberries? Yes, those are amazing eats, but you also can decide to make your meal a global adventure by serving ethnic cuisine. Ethnic foods often are prepared in large quantities, meaning your price per head may go *way* down—and your guests will have a ball getting a taste of another culture.

Chinese: A traditional Chinese wedding banquet has ten courses! Any restaurant will provide you menu options, but here are some musts: Start with prepared meats, shark's fin soup (sweet and sour is always a substitute), and small stir-fried dishes. Exotic entrees can include lobster with ginger and garlic, abalone, sizzling beef, and sesame chicken. Make sure to end with a noodle, as it ensures long life. A bowl of fortune cookies on each table is always a welcome touch.

Eastern European: If you're Polish, Czech, or Russian, serve caviar and chilled vodka shots for hors d'oeuvres, followed by hearty, beat-the-cold, meat and potatoes—potato knishes, pierogies, and pastries.

Ethiopian: To take this less-traveled culinary road, serve a huge spread of spicy vegetables, eggs, meats, along with spongy bread to scoop it all up.

Indian: Serve vegetable and banana samosas as hors d'oeuvres, followed by vegetarian, chicken, and beef curries. Put generous platters of rice and a variety of breads on each table. Make sure to offer plenty of mild dishes for the less intrepid diners!

Mexican: Start with "seven-layer" dip—layers of beans, guacamole, sour cream, and cheese, topped off with olives. Fajitas and tacos are always crowd pleasers. Serve rice and beans buffet style, and put baskets of chips and bowls of salsa on every table. Toast your good taste with margaritas.

Spanish: Serve tapas (small appetizer-size dishes) for a dinner-by-the-bite buffet. Also offer heaping bowls of paella (a mixture of rice, sausage, vegetables, and seafood) and arroz con pollo (chicken and rice flavored with saffron). Wash it down with sangria.

Thai: Serve chicken and pork satay (skewers of grilled meat dipped in a peanut sauce), followed by heaping dishes of pad thai, chicken and beef curry, vegetable dishes spiced with ginger and lemongrass, and sticky rice.

- Omelette or waffle stand: Dishes are made to order, with self-serve toppings.
- Sushi station: Chefs slice and roll fresh hand-rolls.
- Crêpe table: Cooks flip and fill sweet or savory crêpes.
- Burrito bar: Guests choose their tortillas and fresh fillings (chicken, beef, scallops, spinach, or rice and beans).
- Grill: Barbecued chicken, pork, ribs, and vegetables are prepared on request.
- Tepanyaki station (a.k.a. Japanese barbecue): Guests choose raw meats, shrimp, veggies, noodles, and sauces and watch it get stir-fried.

Hot Menus from Cool Chefs

Choose dishes or preparations you like and see if your caterer can create something similar.

Black-Tie Barn Buffet

Chef Waldy Malouf, The Rainbow Room, New York City

Appetizers:
Asparagus with Morels in a Champagne Vinaigrette
Salad of Snap Peas and Baby Carrots with Shallots and Dill

Main Courses:
Local Apple-Smoked Trout with Horseradish and New Potato Salad
Moroccan-spiced Baby Lamb Chops

Cheese:
Large Platter of Hudson Valley Cheeses and Bread
(Old Chatham Sheep's Milk Cheese, Egg Farm Dairy Hudson Cheese, Coach Farm
Goat Cheese, Egg Farm Dairy Cheddar)

Extras:
Country Loaves, French Baguettes, Rosemary-Olive Bread

Dessert:
Strawberry-Rhubarb Compote with Madeleine
Lemon Curd Tartlets and Champagne Truffles

Rock-and-Roll Wedding

Chef Amin Hossain, Hard Rock Cafe, Worldwide

Passed Hors d'oeuvres:
Hard Rock Minihamburgers on Poppy Seed Buns
Cold Assorted Brochettes of Vegetables, Swordfish, Ham and Cheese
Breaded Coconut Chicken Served with Mango Dipping Sauce

Cold Buffet:
Assorted Cheeses (Jalapeño Jack, Cheddar, Swiss, Gouda, Brie, Fresh Mozzarella, etc.)
Seasonal Vegetable Display with Assorted Dipping Sauces
Homemade Guacamole with Tricolor Chips and Salsa
Assorted Antipasto Spread with Cocktail Bread

Hot Buffet:
Hot Brie with Toasted Almonds and Fresh Berries, Served with Cocktail Crackers
Smoked Spinach and Chicken Dip with Tricolor Corn Cups
Sesame Chicken with Roasted Bell Peppers
Sauteed Shrimp and Vegetables over Wild Rice

Carving Station:
Smoked Prime Rib au Jus with Horseradish Sauce
Smoked Turkey Breast au Jus with Cranberry Mayonnaise

Salad Bar:
Dijon Chicken Salad
Saffron Rice Salad
Tortellini Salad
Fresh Mozzarella and Plum Tomato Salad
Macaroni Salad

Dessert:
Chocolate Fondue with Fresh Strawberries
Cold Sliced Amaretto Pears Topped with Zesty Lemon Cream
Fresh Baked Mini-Tiramisu with Fresh Raspberries
Seasonal Passion Fruit Display

Traditional Latino Wedding Meal

Chef John Arminio, Tito Puente's Restaurant, City Island, New York

Appetizers:
Ceviche (Shrimp and Scallops Marinated in Lime Juice with Spices and Herbs)
Avocado Salad with Tomatoes and greens
Oysters and Clams on the Half-shell
Scallops Ramacchio (Scallops Marinated in Teriyaki Sauce, Wrapped with Bacon and Grilled)

Main Course:
Pernil (Roast Pork)
Honey-Rum Chicken

Extras:
Maduros (Sweet Plantains)
Arroz con Gandules (Yellow Rice with Pigeon Peas)
Tostones (Deep-Fried Green Plantains), Served with Mojito (Olive Oil and Garlic Drizzle)
Cuban Bread

Desserts:
Cocoa Flan
Très Leches Cake
Mango Mousse
Cuban or Puerto Rican Coffee made with Anisette, Lemon Rind on the Side

Seaside Seafood Spread

Chef Michael Mina, Aqua, San Francisco

Salads:
Grilled Lobster and Heirloom Tomato Salad
Cured Sardine and Arugula Salad, in a Mint Basalmic Vinaigrette
Calamari and White Bean Salad with Shaved Red Onions
Artichoke and Rock Shrimp Salad, in a Chardonnay and Garlic Vinaigrette

Raw Bar:
Hog Island Oysters Served with Red Wine Mignonette
Cherrystone Clams Served with Prepared Horseradish
Poached Gulf Prawns with Lime Cocktail Sauce
Scallop Ceviche

Main Courses:
Lobster and Crayfish Paella in a Spicy Chorizo Broth
Crab Tortellini in a Smoked Tomato Sauce
Citrus-Poached Sole with Steamed Asparagus
Whole-Roasted Steelhead Salmon with Quince Foie Gras Stuffing
Coquille St. Jacques with Mushroom Mornay Sauce

Extras:
Truffle Potato Gratin
Horseradish Mashed Potatoes
Braised Chanterelles with Fennel Jus
Sauteed Baby Spinach
Sweet Roasted Bell Peppers
Marinated Grilled Eggplant

Table Settings 101

When you're chatting with your caterer or reasoning with the party-rental people, you need to know how to talk table settings. Here are all the pieces you could possibly need, what they're called, and where they're supposed to go.

Desserts:
Classic Root Beer Float with Chocolate Chip Cookies
Citrus and Strawberry Shortcake with Mint Ice Cream
Chocolate Hazelnut Torte with Mexican Chocolate Ice Cream
Spiced Apple Crêpes with Brown Butter Sauce

Serving Drinks

Weddings mean raising a glass, making a toast, imbibing the bubbly. For most couples (and guests, too), they mean enjoying a few drinks along with the rest of the festivities. Setting up the bar takes a bit of planning on your part. As always, you've got options.

The Open Bar

An open bar is the most gracious approach—no guest should have to pay for *anything* at the wedding—but it's also the most expensive. Guests can order any drink on the planet, and you (or your parents) pick up the often-hefty tab at the end of the party. Your bartender will count all the used and partially used bottles and charge you accordingly.

The downside of an open bar is pretty obvious. Because there's no limit, people may drink like guppies—and you may be concerned about a friend or uncle famous for imbibing. If the idea of confronting the issue is just too excruciating, point out any problem people to the bartender; s/he should be experienced enough at monitoring people's intake to able to smoothly offer soda when the time is right.

The Limited Bar

With a limited bar—probably the most popular option—you offer a selection of drinks (beer, wine, and mixed vodka drinks, for example) and/or set specific consumption times (say, cocktail hour, the toasts, and an hour after dinner). Consider having waiters pass drinks on trays rather than having guests go up to the bar. You'll have to *pay* for those waiters, of course, but you'll probably save money on alcohol, and fewer guests will go overboard—the fewer waiters, the longer it will take everyone to get served. If you decide to limit the amount of time the bar is open, make sure to have waiters circulate during dinner to refill glasses of water and soda.

Another sneaky way to limit alcohol is to serve a special drink that fits your party. If you're doing the *Great Gatsby* 1920s thing, serve Manhattans. If it's a brunch party, go with mimosas (champagne and o.j.). For a late-night, black-tie affair, think champagne punch. Mixed specialty drinks let you make a style statement, use less expensive brands of alcohol, tie into a theme—and limit consumption.

Drink Up

How much liquor will you need for a hundred guests? Talk to your bartender, but here are some averages:

- Beer: 2 cases
- Whiskey: 1–2 liters
- Bourbon: 1–2 liters
- Gin: 2 liters
- Scotch: 3 liters
- Light rum: 2 liters
- Vodka: 6 liters
- Tequila: 1 liter
- Champagne: 1$\frac{1}{2}$ cases
- Red wine: 8 bottles
- White wine: 1$\frac{1}{2}$ cases
- Dry vermouth: 2 bottles
- Sweet vermouth: 2 bottles

Keep Booze at Bay

Have someone watch over the bartender's bottle-counting process. You don't want any mistakes—unintentional or otherwise.

The
Food Chain

193

The Cash Bar

Don't have a cash bar unless you have a really good reason. (There really isn't one.) You don't invite people to your house for dinner and then charge them for butter, right? Trust us on this one. It's not a good cost-cutting solution—way too controversial.

A Dry House

If you, your families, and most of your guests don't drink alcohol, it's fine to skip it. Your bar can serve sparkling water, sodas, and nonalcoholic mixed drinks instead. If you want some bubbly to toast with, just serve glasses of champagne when it's time, or go for sparkling cider or grape juice.

Cut to the Cake

Of all the wedding food you choose, cake just takes the . . . er, prize. Why have a wedding cake? The tradition dates back to ancient Greece, where newlywed couples would share crushed sesame cakes to ensure fertility. In the Middle Ages, guests crumbled wheat cakes over the couple's heads, again to wish them good fortune and children. The wheat cake concept slowly evolved into a sweet, edible dessert cake in sixteenth-century England. The French then one-upped the English, introducing the tiered, sugar-covered, cake as art that we know and love today.

Serving It Safely

If you plan to serve alcohol in a park, private home, or anyplace else without a liquor license, check your homeowner's insurance policy to make sure you're covered against liability.

Who Makes it?

Your caterer might whip up your wonder cake or point you toward a talented baker. Or take matters into your own hands and head for the nearest bakery or specialty store to order a custom cake. And there's always the down-home method—make it yourself, or ask a cherished relative to reprise her famous chocolate-peanut-butter-marshmallow-creme creation.

Got a Sweet Tooth?

You don't *have* to serve a dessert in addition to the wedding cake. These days cakes are so yummy and alluring that they're dessert in themselves. But if you're dessert lovers and want a sweet table—go for it!

The Options

Chances are, your parents had a two- or three-tier white wedding cake with a mini bride and groom on top. But your newlywed friends might have gone with a five-tier cake crowned with fresh flowers, a chocolate-covered cheesecake, or a flat cake shaped like an armadillo. Today's wedding cakes come in a variety of shapes and sizes.

Grand Style: Have a professional wedding-cake baker create a fantastic, seven-tier cake with a spun-sugar couple on top, smooth, round-edged fondant icing, and a cascade of fresh flowers spilling down the sides. (If you go this route, you'll probably pay by the slice; average cost: $4.50 per. Certain reception locales or caterers also may charge a "slicing fee.")

Back Room Cake: Hire a professional wedding-cake baker to create a small but fantastically festooned confection to display, plus several large, less expensive sheet cakes of the same flavor to slice in the back and serve. A good option if you've got tons of guests.

Personal Style: Hire your favorite baker (the one who does your birthday cakes and holiday pies) to create the cake of your dreams.

A Taste of the Past: Replicate your parents' cake for a nostalgic nod of respect. (You'll want to put a picture of them cutting theirs on the cake table to complete the effect.)

Theme Cake: Make your cake match your party style—a stack of books for the heavy readers' reception, a big ladybug for a garden party, a cowboy boot for the highbrow hoedown.

Multifaceted: Along with your cake, have a make-your-own-sundae bar or a dessert table with a variety of sweets—eclairs, petit fours, miniature tarts, and cannolis.

The Groom's Cake

That other, smaller confection you may have noticed sitting quietly off to the side at wedding receptions in the past (especially in the South) is taking center stage these days. Grooms are getting creative, ordering their cakes in the shapes of soccer balls, golf clubs, or briefcases (those lawyers). And while the groom's cake used to be darker and heavier (chocolate or, traditionally, fruitcake) than the main wedding cake, today it can come in any flavor. Some couples decide to slice and serve it at the reception, along with the wedding cake, while others slice and box it for guests to take home. (Legend has it that a single woman who sleeps with a slice of groom's cake under her pillow will dream of her future husband.)

Now that you've got all our hot tips, you're ready to cook up a fabulous reception feast. Bon appetit!

Cool Cake Toppers

- A tree sapling (to plant at home later)
- Fresh flowers
- Marzipan fruit or figurines
- Tall tapered candles
- A framed photo of the two of you
- Mini flags from your home countries (or football teams)
- Glass Christmas ornaments (of snowflakes, doves, or angels)
- Sparklers
- A gingerbread bride and groom
- Your favorite cartoon characters
- Candy

Which Blooms to Use?

Reception Flowers

Finding a Fabulous Florist

Ceremony Flowers

Other Decorations

Flower Power

Who can resist the perfection of flowers, a pleasure-fest for the eyes, nose, and heart? Flowers are 100 percent romance—it's no big surprise that they have always gone hand in hand with weddings. Blooms can be an awe-inspiring backdrop for the ceremony, the perfect accessories for your big-day clothes, and gorgeous centerpieces (and conversation pieces) for the reception. But where to begin with all the amazing options? Choose your all-time favorite flowers, incorporate blooms based on color, or bank it all on their special meanings. Flowers have so much power that they even can *be* a wedding theme. (A daisy wedding sounds darling, no?) You really can't go wrong in this department, so find a great florist and have fun with it!

Which Blooms to Use?

You already may have definite ideas of your own regarding your wedding flowers. Maybe you're thinking tons and tons of orchids everywhere. Or you're more of a minimalist, and you just want simple pots of tulips on the reception tables or the wedding party carrying single lilies. No matter what you choose, of course, it'll be beautiful—that's the nature of flowers, right?

Floral Features: What to Look For

Consider these factors when choosing your wedding blooms.

Durability: If you're getting married during the hot summer months or need your flowers to last a long, long time (perhaps for the duration of your weekend celebration), steer clear of blooms that wilt easily. These include gardenias, lily of the valley, tulips, and wildflowers; ask your florist for other no-nos.

Originality: Roses, carnations, baby's breath, and gladiolus are quintessential wedding blooms. We're not saying don't get 'em, but think about incorporating some other, less-common flowers, too, for a super-unique look.

Color: Flowers that match your wedding colors or play off them in an interesting way are gorgeous.

Scent: In case you haven't noticed, many flowers have strong fragrances. Of course, that's one of the reasons everyone loves them, but consider how appropriate the scent will be for your wedding. (Take into account ventilation, the preferences of favorite family and guests, allergies.) Go with mostly gentle smells. Scents imprint a strong impression on the memory—which you want—but sometimes they can be overwhelming—which you *don't* want. Fragrant blooms include freesia, lilies, lilacs, tube roses, and gardenias.

Availability: Local, in-season flowers should be your mainstay. For starters, you're assured freshness—which means extra beauty. In addition, these are the blooms that will be the most affordable, which means more flowers for less money. Consult local florists or connoisseur friends about what's blossoming in your wedding region around the time you'll be tying the knot. Try to make those flowers the crux of your bouquets and decorative arrangements; use them as party favors placed in slender clay vases; incorporate them as the main elements of large structures such as huppahs, arches, and oversize wreaths.

Exotica: We're not going to tell you to give up on your favorite exotic flower. Keep in mind that imported blooms can be expensive, but if you adore birds-of-paradise, include several stems in your bouquet and centerpieces. If you *must* have lilies in December (your honey brought you a cluster on your first date), we understand. All we're saying is that by using seasonal fare as your base, you'll be able to maximize your flower-buying power and indulge your wildest floral fantasies.

The Root of It All: Flower Meanings

If you're sentimental, you might choose your blooms by what they symbolize. Here's the lowdown on some popular wedding flowers (as well as when they're in season):

- Anemone (fall to spring): Expectation
- Baby's breath (year round): Innocence
- Calla lily (spring/summer): Magnificent beauty
- Camellia (spring): Perfect loveliness
- Carnation (year round): boldness (pink), love (red), talent (white)
- Chrysanthemum (year round): Wealth, abundance, truth
- Daisy (year round): Share your feelings
- Freesia (spring/summer): Innocence
- Gardenia (year round): Purity, joy

Floral Lore

Brides in ancient Rome carried bunches of herbs to symbolize fidelity and fertility. The Greeks used ivy to symbolize indissoluble love. Brides today carry floral bouquets as a symbol of fertility and bounty.

- Gerbera daisy (year round): Beauty
- Holly (winter): Foresight
- Iris (spring): Faith, wisdom
- Lilac (spring): First love
- Lily (summer): Truth, honor
- Lily of the valley (spring/summer): Happiness
- Magnolia (spring/summer): Love of nature
- Orange blossoms (fall): Purity
- Orchid (year round; imported): Love, beauty
- Rose (year round): love; red—"I love you"; white—"I am worthy of you"
- Stephanotis (year round): Marital happiness
- Sunflower (fall): Adoration
- Tulip (spring): Love, passion

How to Huppah

Jewish couples say their vows under a huppah, a canopy that symbolizes shelter and the couple's new home together. The canopy can be decorated with (or wholly constructed of) flowers. In Israel, huppahs are usually a swatch of cloth hung between four poles and held up by close friends or relatives. Build your own with your fave quilt or a gorgeous piece of satin or organza: wrap ivy, ribbons, and flowers around the poles.

Ceremony Flowers

Traditionally, the entire wedding party—and other special guests—carry or wear flowers on wedding day. The traditional arrangements include the following.

The Bridal Bouquet

The bridal bouquet, of course, is the most in-the-spotlight flower arrangement, carried by the bride during the ceremony—and sometimes tossed skyward to the single women at the reception. On average, you'll spend $75 to $150 on this bouquet, depending on the size, the flowers, and the style.

Keeping Flowers Fresh

Have your flowers delivered boxed with cellophane and well misted—that way they'll look fresh through your ceremony and reception.

Bouquet Styles

For the bride, maids, and flower girls:

Classic Bouquet: A dense bunch of blooms anchored in a bouquet holder, wired, or hand-tied (the most of-the-moment option).

Nosegay: A small, round cluster of flowers, all cut to a uniform length, which was all the rage in Victorian times and is enjoying a renaissance today. Usually made with one dominant flower or color, nosegays are wrapped tightly with ribbon or lace for a delicate effect. Or you can go all-out Victorian, inserting the nosegay into a silver carrying cone.

Beidermeier: A nosegay made up of concentric circles of different flowers for a somewhat striped effect.

Composite: A handmade creation in which different petals or buds are wired together on a single stem, creating the illusion of one giant flower.

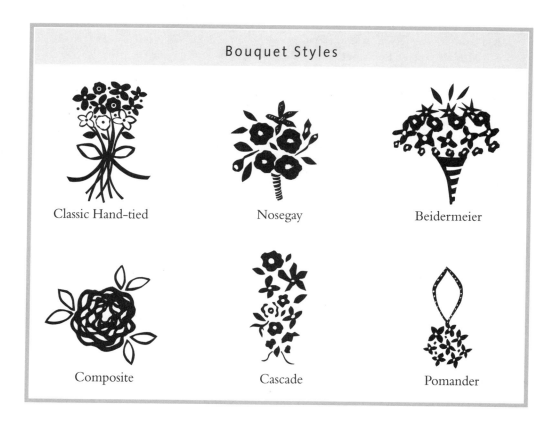

Bouquet Styles

Classic Hand-tied

Nosegay

Beidermeier

Composite

Cascade

Pomander

Understated Blooms

Bridesmaids can walk down the aisle carrying a single, stunning stem—such as an orchid, sunflower, or calla lily—instead of bouquets.

Cascade: A waterfall-like "spill" of blooms and greenery that's anchored in a hand-held base. Looks like a miniature floral train.

Pomander: A bloom-covered ball suspended from a ribbon, perfect for child attendants. (Flower girls may carry a basket of petals instead.)

Bridesmaids' Bouquets

Usually smaller than the bride's cluster, bridesmaids' bouquets play off of—and showcase—her bouquet by complementing its color, shape, or type of flowers. These arrangements will cost about $40 to $75 per attendant.

Groom and Groomsmen's Boutonnieres

Boutonnieres consist of a single bloom or bud (or several small ones) attached at the left lapel of the jacket, worn by the groom, his attendants, ushers, and the bride and groom's fathers. If you like, the groom's can stand out from those worn by the other men. (You might echo the dominant flower in the bride's bouquet.) Boutonnieres cost about $3 to $5 each.

Corsages for Moms and Honored Guests

Choose pin-on corsages or the kind with a band attached to wear at the wrist for your dot-ing mothers—and possibly grandmothers, aunts, great friends of the family, and any other special people—to wear during your ceremony. Cost: $15 to $20 a pop.

Other Floral Arrangements

You may want to add some flower power to your ceremony site itself. Depending on where you'll wed and your budget, this can range from lavish to simple. Popular floral decorations include:

- A central altar/stage arrangement or two large vases on either side of where you two will stand
- Flowering huppah (Jewish bridal canopy)
- Blooms fastened onto pews or chairs (every two or three rows for cost-effectiveness)
- Flower or ivy chains draped between seats
- A lush wreath on the entrance door
- Large potted plants or flower arrangements to delineate the cere-mony area (when it's the same as the reception site or outside)
- A blooming arch for the wedding party to walk through

Think Color, Size, and Shape

Don't choose the bridal and at-tendants' bouquets without re-gard to style of dress or body shape. A delicate nosegay will get lost against an elaborate, ruffled dress, for example, and a small bride will be overshad-owed by a massive cascading arrangement.

Think like an interior designer when you're deciding on ceremony flowers. Is the ceremony site large or small? Ornate or plain? If you're get-ting married in an exquisite mosque, the architects have done you a good turn by providing you with a magnificent backdrop; pare down the flowers so as not to dis-tract from the building's beauty. If you're marrying in a church around a major holiday such as Easter or Christmas, the sanctuary already may be fully decorated for the season—lucky you! Likewise, if you're marrying outside, especially in a garden setting, you'll likely save a bundle on blooms and greenery.

On the other hand, if you're having a nondenominational ceremony in a banquet hall or are sprucing up your uncle's living room, you may need some extra help from Mother Nature; think about a stunning floral construction, such as a rose petal–strewn aisle or a sun-flower-entwined arch under which to say your vows.

ASTRID AND CHRISTIAN

November 2, New York City

ON THE MORNING OF Astrid and Christian's wedding, the bride wasn't relaxing in a bathtub preparing for her big day. Instead, she and Christian were struggling with the roof of the floral huppah he had designed and built.

"I was complaining the whole time," Astrid says. "Everything was happening at the last minute."

Christian, an architect, had designed an elaborate floral runner and huppah for their wedding. The huppah design had a similar structure to a project they had worked on together in architecture school. The runner was made primarily of rose petals. Although the couple hired a professional florist for things such as table arrangements and reception decorations, Astrid and Christian—with the help of his sister—built the huppah and runner themselves.

"The most incredible thing about the flowers was their fragrance. As we walked down the runner it got more and more intense," Astrid says.

Although at several moments throughout the process Astrid wished they had let a professional florist take over, in the end she was happy with the way it was done.

"In retrospect, I was glad we did it. Constructing the huppah together that morning became symbolic to us. It was the beginning of building our life together."

Reception Flowers

Guests may not spend enough time at your ceremony site to fully appreciate the flowers there, but they'll spend the entire reception checking out the blooms. Centerpieces will be in closest range, but there are tons of other ways to dress up your reception room florally.

The Centerpieces

You can create pretty bouquets of mixed flowers, whimsical topiaries, or clusters of small vases with single stems inside. When designing your centerpieces, take into consideration:

> **Your Room:** High ceilings are best complemented with tall floral centerpieces, such as angular glass vases holding sprays of long-stemmed roses or lush bouquets placed on raised silver platforms (so guests can see each other). Small spaces need tight, bright arrangements that liven up the room without distracting.

> **Your Theme:** If you're having a hoedown, arrange clusters of wildflowers in old-fashioned jars or pretty pitchers; for a Victorian-inspired affair, opt for round bouquets of muted tea roses with antique lace wrapped around the vases.

> **Your Taste:** Are you sticklers for coordinated decor? If so, use the same centerpiece at every table, with a slightly more lavish arrangement for the head table (wherever you're sitting). Do you like a cozy, more cluttered look? Give your florist a variety of different vases that you picked up at flea markets; ask him/her to play with three or four different arrangement types that will create a mismatched but arty feel.

> **Your Budget:** Tight on cash? No problem. Go for maximum effect by doing the unexpected. Use little hot-pepper plants—in shades of red, orange, and yellow—as take-home centerpieces. Or place one or two gorgeous sunflowers on each table, surrounded by a cluster of gold candles.

A Rose at Any Other Time . . .

Timing is everything, especially when it comes to buying red roses.

- Near Valentine's Day (not ordered in advance): $18 per stem
- Near Valentine's Day (ordered well in advance): $8 per stem
- Any other time: $3 per stem

Other Decorative Floral Touches

You also may accent key reception areas—the entrance, the cake table, buffet stations—with floral bouquets, wreaths, or blooming boas. Visit the reception site with your florist so s/he can get a feel for how you might want to decorate. But don't feel confined by *conventional* uses of flowers. Some of our favorite wacky-but-wonderful flower uses:

- Real flower petals as cake decorations
- Sprinkling edible flowers, such as nasturtiums, hibiscus, roses, orange blossoms, pansies, marigolds, geraniums, squash blossoms, mimosas, and chamomile, in salads and drinks—lemonade, iced tea, and rum punch—or using them as garnishes on entrees and desserts
- The bride sporting tiny blooms in loose hair, wearing a splendid head wreath, or tucking a stem behind her ear

Arrangement Themes

Flower arrangements aren't just about pretty blooms; they're also about *style*. When you're choosing your ceremony bouquets and your reception centerpieces, keep in mind some of our favorite "themes":

A Whiter Shade of Pale: All-white bouquets have long been a popular wedding style, but the modern take plays with variations of off-white blooms for a deeper, richer look.

Off-Kilter: Predominantly white bouquets and arrangements can look stunning when you mix in one other color, such as blue violets or yellow tulips.

Serene Simplicity: A small nosegay created with one type of bloom is elegant and understated.

Victorian: Choose dense arrangements of such flowers as roses, Queen Anne's lace, delphinium, sweet peas, and peonies. Bouquets or vases decorated with organza or lace recall the Victorian era.

English Garden: Duplicate a garden with loose clusters of wildflowers, heather, ivy, lilacs, and lavender.

Herbal Accents: Fragrant herbs such as rosemary, thyme, and mint make a splash in wedding arrangements.

Brash and Bold: Colorful arrangements of unexpected, clashing blooms look modern and uncontrived.

- Wearing dramatic floral boas or leis (both of you!)
- Giving a dethorned rose to each guest upon arrival—and having a mass tango-fest!
- Topiaries instead of vases of blooms
- Giving bulbs tied in tulle with a bow or small potted plants like African violets as favors
- Placing pressed flowers (or autumn leaves) beneath sheer tablecloths
- Using large candles with dried flowers in the wax as centerpieces
- Draping ivy interlaced with flowers from the ceilings

They Work Hard for the Money

Labor costs make florist bills bloom. Trim them by opting for less labor-intensive arrangements—simple vases of seasonal flowers as center-pieces rather than elaborate wreaths. Also nix any elaborate blooming structures—gateways, window frames—that will take a long time to set up.

Finding a Fabulous Florist

Make a good florist your wedding gift to yourselves. As with all vendors, it's important to find one who is reliable, capable—and within your price range. But you also want a florist who is open to your ideas and who has an overall taste you respect. Your gown and tux are going to turn heads, that's a given, but you want the overall "look" of your wedding to make an impression, too—and your florist is a key player.

An important issue to hammer out before you hire someone is your budget. There is no limit to what you can spend on lavish blooms—$200 bouquets all around, a lush tea-rose huppah, vases of cut tulips as favors, wreaths of dried wildflowers in every bathroom, a floor-length floral boa to wear at your 1920s-inspired reception—you get the picture. But most people have a limited flower budget. A visionary florist should be able to come up with a magnificent concept that won't bust your piggy bank. It may mean scaling back here and there, but look on the bright side: Minimalism in design is *in!* So check out the phone book, ask your friends, and call floral associations for names of florists near you. Put together a list of people and make those appointments.

The First Meeting

- Describe your attire and the wedding party's, or show the florist pictures or fabric swatches of what you'll be wearing, so s/he'll be able to suggest flowers that match your style.
- Show photos of your ceremony and reception sites.
- Map out any other salient details, such as theme, color scheme, floral allergies, and flowers that have special significance to you. Also, show any adored flower images you've found in magazines or your cousin's wedding album.
- Have the florist go into the nitty-gritty of the options available given your budget. Cover everything from the bridal bouquet to reception centerpieces; name specific flowers.

The Second Meeting

- Your florist presents an exact proposal, itemizing the number and types of arrangements, the exact kinds of flowers to be used, and the cost for materials, as well as setup and breakdown.
- S/he shows you sketches or small models of complex orders, such as a flowering gateway for your outdoor ceremony, the perfect

Setting Up

Don't assume your florist will have access to your ceremony and reception site early on the big day. (S/he may need several hours to set up.) Make necessary arrangements—get written permission and a key, if need be—to ensure that everything is coming up roses before you hit the aisle.

Floral Contract Points

Don't even think of signing on the dotted line unless all these items are included in your flower contract:

☐ The date, times, and locations of your ceremony and reception.

☐ An itemized list of all the flower arrangements you're buying, from bouquets to centerpieces, with exact names, amounts, and colors of flowers being used.

☐ Acceptable flower alternatives (in your price range) should a specific bloom be unavailable on your wedding day; also include unacceptable substitutions, if any.

☐ Arrival times for setup at the ceremony *and* reception sites.

☐ Addresses where bouquets and boutonnieres should be delivered, if not to your ceremony site (home, for example).

☐ The name of the florist who will be on hand during the wedding (should be the person you're working with); the name of an acceptable substitute.

☐ The cost and payment schedule; when the final balance is due.

☐ Any sales taxes, gratuities, overtime charges, or delivery fees.

☐ The cancellation/refund policy.

nosegay bouquet, table topiaries (little flower trees or other ornamental arrangements), or the special "medieval" arrangements you discussed.

- You should now make adjustments to both your floral budget and plan, making sure the two meet. For example, you may choose to throw in another $300 so your arrangements will be more lush, or decide to ax that floral hula hoop that you thought would make a splash at your Hawaiian-themed reception but is upping costs greatly.
- You'll sign a written contract that outlines the agreed-upon plan. (See "Floral Contract Points," earlier.)

Trim Your Floral Budget

- Focus on one eye-catching, strategically placed ceremony arrangement rather than multiple, smaller floral clusters.

- Transport ceremony blooms to the reception, where they can work a second shift. Ask your florist or a trusted attendant or friend to oversee the move.

- Use large clusters of simple, inexpensive flowers to make a lasting impression. (Dense bunches of Queen Anne's lace with variegated ivy can be stunning. Potted flowering plants are another great option that people also can take home.)

Blooming Questions

Things to ask about a potential florist:

- Has s/he done many weddings?
- Can you see photographs or live examples of past work? (If no, cut to the door.)
- Will s/he supply you with references?
- Does the florist's style—and the overall look of the shop—make you gag or drool?
- Does s/he listen intently to your floral reveries, chiming in with useful suggestions, or does s/he brush you off and tell you what you *really* want?
- How big is the shop, and ultimately who will be carrying out your wedding-day flower plan? (In big shops, it's *not* a given that the owner will take care of you; make sure you get to know—and trust—the person who will.)
- How many weddings is the florist handling on the same day or weekend as yours? If s/he is handling multiple accounts, is there enough staff and time to go around?

Other Decorations

Flowers are just one—albeit hugely important—part of your wedding decorating toolbox. According to your taste and overall wedding theme and style, you can also incorporate a variety of other decorations.

Candles

The perfect romantic lighting option: Place candles on each table and throughout the room. There are so many stunning and affordable variations out there today that you can color-coordinate candles with flowers, your dress, even the main course. You also can play with the fragrances of scented candles or opt for floating candles that look gorgeous reflecting dim light. Majestic candelabras will add drama to a room; traditional lanterns holding candles will transform any site into a cozy, old-fashioned inn.

Tulle

This light-as-air fabric can be draped artfully over tablecloths or chair backs or hung from the ceiling in clusters for cloudlike columns. Glue-gun dried flowers or ivy to the material for a pretty accent. Other fabrics, such as organza, gauze, and satin, are also beautiful reception-decorating choices. They can be used for a huppah or archway for the wedding party to enter through or spread elegantly on the ground to create a magical aisle.

Ribbons and Bows

What's a wedding without ribbons and bows, after all? They can be attached to chair backs, wrapped around vases, mounted on the walls at regular intervals (large ones), and otherwise used to wrap up the general "look." Use a variety of colors around cloth napkins for a spontaneous, festive look.

Balloons

Sure, some people consider them childish, but balloons are lots of fun. Steer away from balloons in tight indoor spaces (too claustrophobic) but go nuts in high-ceilinged rooms or outdoors, with metallic or pastel-colored helium balloons attached to chairs or arranged in clusters.

Streamers

Use streamers artfully as filler to make the room seem more cozy and festive. Streamers draped from the ceiling will glow nicely in dim candlelight.

Work It: Overall Design Ideas

Coming up with a decorating scheme for your reception can be hard as nails. If you're having trouble, begin with a central idea and expand your plan from there. Here are some starters.

A Personal Touch: Decorate personally with beautifully framed pictures of the two of you—together and apart, childhood and current—on each table; guests will get a kick out of making the rounds to see you at all your cute (and not-so-cute) stages. Another great idea is to incorporate favorite objects in the decorations. Throughout your engagement, pick up vintage vases, place settings, and candlesticks that appeal to you. So what if they're mismatched? If you have enough diversity, it will look like an intentional—and thoroughly hip—design choice. And be sure to play off your favorite colors and flowers.

Period Decor: If you adore a certain era, go with it. For example:

What a Resource

You may be able to get decorations like balloons, streamers—even decorative arches and pillars—from your florist.

German Candle Custom

In traditional German wedding ceremonies, both the bride and groom hold candles decorated with flowers and ribbon.

Italian Ribbon Custom

Italian families tie a large ribbon across the front of the church door to symbolize the wedding bond.

Don't Overdecorate!

Remember that the wedding's about you two getting married, not how elaborately you can spruce up a room.

- Medieval: Candelabras; lush arrangements on iron stands; dried flower wreaths as centerpieces; parchment place cards with calligraphy; feather quills mixed into floral bouquets; bowls of gold chocolate coins placed about the room.

- Victorian: Lace tablecloths with mauve or blue place settings; lush centerpiece bouquets accented with antique ribbon; large dried-flower topiaries at the corners of the dance floor.

- '20s/Flapperesque: Potted palms and ferns; tall, tapered candles; incense burning for that smoky atmosphere; single-tone floral arrangements; a black-and-white color scheme; floor-to-ceiling sheer draperies.

- '70s/Disco Fever: Disco balls as centerpieces set off by many small candles; metallic tablecloths with brightly colored place settings; balloons and skinny streamers on the dance floor; a smoke machine.

Go to Chapter 3 for ideas on how to spotlight the season with your wedding decorations.

Far-Out Fest: Latch on to one *really* original idea and brainstorm around it. For example, you want to party amid clouds of ephemeral bubbles? Give guests soap-bubble containers as favors and put them in a blowing mood by hanging shimmering spheres from the ceiling, applying iridescent polka dots to sheer tablecloths, and scattering round confetti on the floor.

Photography

Focusing On a Style

Hiring a Hot Shot

Photo Types and Twists

Videography

Zooming In on a Genre

Hiring a Video Pro

Picture This

Your wedding is going to be gorgeous, scrumptious, and fabulously one of a kind. It would be mean, mean, mean of you not to leave a piece of it for future generations to ogle and coo over. And it would be cruel to yourselves not to ensure you have timeless mementos of this spectacular affair. Did we forget to mention that your parents might never speak to you again if you don't present them with some keepsakes of the big day? Unlike the work of your other wedding vendors (music, flower arrangements, dress, cake), photographs and videos are not things you can hear, smell, taste, or even see at first—you don't really know what you're getting until after the fact. That means careful research and pickiness regarding professional skills, artistic style, and personal demeanor are extra important. Luckily, we're here to help you out.

PHOTOGRAPHY

Photographs are quintessential wedding keepsakes. They speak volumes about the atmosphere and style of the big day and your and your guests' emotions. Arranged artfully in an album, photos narrate the story of your wedding, from your dress-up sessions—including your honey's contortions while trying to knot a tie—to the last revelers getting cozy on the dance floor.

In order to get photos that will best reflect your personal style—and make you feel warm and fuzzy for years to come—arm yourself with some basic information about what different photographic styles are available, where to find a talented pro, and when (and how) to get perfect shots.

Focusing On a Style

More and more photgraphers are hopping on the wedding bandwagon. The cream of the crop are those who are truly excited about the idea of shooting weddings and who bring some personal flair to their work. In order for their style to work for you, however, you two need to figure out what you want. Below, the basic style options.

Photojournalistic Style

By far the hottest trend in wedding photography (it's also our favorite style) is to shoot the affair as if it's a news event. Applying the rules of documentary photography, a professional working in this vein will attempt to make herself a "fly on the wall"—observing the goings-on, capturing them in the lenses, but keeping interference to a minimum. S/he will make a buzz only when s/he wants to coordinate the formal, must-have shots you told her/him to get; otherwise, s/he'll be hovering around capturing candids that reflect what you and your guests were really doing and feeling.

    Pros: The pictures you get will capture small details (your little cousin asleep under the cake table, you and your honey sneaking a kiss on the verandah) that might be overlooked by a more formal approach. They also will convey an emotionally charged authenticity (sweating dancers, smudged makeup caused by crying) that will bring back strong recollections of the big day. They'll be way more evocative—and beautiful—than portraits could ever be.

    Cons: This authenticity can mean that your hair won't be perfect in every picture and that you might be making silly faces—after a shot of tequila or while entertaining your little nephew. (We don't think this is a real problem, though, since you'll still look beautiful thanks to that just-married radiance.) There's also a chance that the photographer will not capture images of important guests because they didn't capture her/his attention. The photojournalistic approach also might end up being a little more expensive since you'll want the photographer there for more time.

Photo Lingo

Some technical terms you should know:

Small-format camera: The standard, uses 35-mm film. Most of your wedding photos will be snapped with a small camera. Make sure your photographer has one or two extra loaded cameras so s/he won't miss any shots to reload or because of a technical problem.

Medium-format camera: This one uses slightly bigger film, which means prints tend to be a little clearer. It's essential that your photographer have a medium camera on hand for formal portraits; you'll probably want to blow them up, which means you need an extra-crisp image.

100–200 ASA: Standard-sensitivity film. 100–200 film is perfect for snapping shots in sunlight, well-lit indoor spaces, or with a flash. Bring along some extra rolls in case your photographer runs out.

400 ASA and up: Light-sensitive film, ideal for shooting in darker interiors, such as a church or a candlelit ballroom. Make sure one of your photographer's cameras is loaded with this stuff.

LISA AND MICHAEL

June 4, Westchester, Pennsylvania

AS A LITTLE GIRL, Lisa loved looking at the sepia-tint pictures of her parents' formal wedding. To document their own wedding day in such a way that their children would be able to picture it, Lisa and Michael wanted to find a photographer who would do something special.

Lisa contacted photographer Rob Fraser, who is known for his photojournalistic approach. "I just loved his photos. He doesn't do any formal, stilted poses. Almost everything is spontaneous, candid," Lisa says. Fraser shot both color and black-and-white film, the color capturing the vibrancy of the day, the black-and-white adding a nostalgic feel. Because Fraser does not take posed shots of each table of wedding guests, he suggested an alternative to Lisa and Michael. In the mansion where they held the event, Fraser set up one room with a white backdrop, where guests could go and pose—or cut up—while he shot photos. "Some people were really goofy," Lisa says, "and those are the fun ones. Also, people could group themselves however they wanted—for instance, all the college friends could be in a shot together." Afterward, Fraser hand-developed the black-and-white film, adding a sepia tint, which provided Lisa with a wedding album much like her mother's.

Formal Style

Formal wedding photography focuses on posed portraits of you two, your attendants, and your extended families. The photographer will gather people together in groups for organized shoots against a backdrop s/he deems worthy (and you like). The formal approach also pays special attention to etiquette, capturing traditional "moments" such as the cutting of the cake, the signing of the Ketubah, and the garter toss.

Pros: You'll have elegant shots of all your close relatives and friends, which make wonderful thank-you gifts. Formal portraits also make timeless family heirlooms to display in your living room and to pass on and on and on. Formal-style photographers often use soft focus and other tricks of the trade to ensure you're looking flawless.

Cons: Posed portraits can have a contrived quality. The focus is on perfection rather than the chaos of the moment, so photographers have to take lots of shots of the same thing to get the *flawless* shot; that means you spend more time posing. Your photographer also may miss the more exhilarating and entertaining moments of your wedding while s/he's directing group shots away from the action.

Artsy Style

Photographers can be like painters, using film as a canvas and adding dramatic flourishes to create a bold impression. Artistic photographers employ a variety of tricks, from double exposure (an image of your honey slipping the gold band on over a close-up of your family tartan pattern) to visible borders (a strip of action shots that have been blown up with the film's original sprocket holes visible, for example). Artsy photographers also can touch up black-and-white shots by adding sepia tones or color to one specific detail (your pink bouquet, yellow candles).

Pros: These photos—pieces of art, really—will make great decorations in your house, on your desk at work, and on thank-you cards. You'll be able to savor not only the uniqueness of the moment you got married but also your one-of-a-kind shots.

Cons: A photographer who's really into special effects might put more emphasis on visual pizzazz than on the emotional context of each moment.

Color

Color film is the most popular option for photographers, largely because printing costs are much lower than with black and white. Many couples choose to have most of their photos shot in color.

Pros: Great for capturing all those details you toiled and troubled over: the lavender, lime, and cream centerpiece bouquets, the rainbowlike assortment of fresh fruit on the buffet. Color photos precisely record what things looked like (the sky's "mood," people's flushed cheeks, your hot-pink cake). They can capture the real flavor of your party: the blur of colors on the dance floor, the red noses of giddy (and tipsy) loved ones.

In Living Color?

"I like to shoot in color because it shows the emotional temperature of the day, such as a chill in the air. I like black and white because you see the essence of the picture first and foremost, the people and the emotions. Both have their charm."

—**John Dolan,
N.Y.C. wedding
photographer**

Cons: Leaves a little less to the imagination. Color pics sometimes look so vivid and clear that they almost seem fake. Your photos may also seem more dated in ten years, since details such as the exact color and look of the bridesmaids' dresses will be so clear. Blemishes and imperfections also may be more visible than with black-and-white film.

Black-and-White

Classy, romantic, and gorgeous, black-and-white shots have long been the preference of upscale photographers and discerning to-be-weds.

Pros: Pictures have a timeless, elegant quality, reflecting the magic of the event. There's also something dramatic and emotional about black-and-white photographs—the sheer power of the moment isn't overshadowed by a bright color or standout detail. (Bonus: Flaws are less apparent so you and yours look super-glam.) Black and white is perfect for ceremony shots (because it really captures the awesomeness of the happening) as well as formal portraits of you two, your wedding party, and family.

Cons: You'll miss many of the most thought-about details of your wedding: the color scheme, decorating touches. Black-and-white packages are often more expensive, too.

Visual Variety

Since each photographic style has unique charm, we believe that the most memorable photo packages include some of each, combining invaluable portraits of you with your new family, informal snaps of your guests whooping it up, and perhaps several special-effects shots that have special meaning to you and your honey. That's also how we feel about the infamous black-and-white vs. color debate, by the way. The two film choices are like ying and yang, Ben & Jerry, night and day—each completely great but even better together.

Hiring a Hot Shot

Once you have an idea of what style you're looking for, it's time to seek out a photographer who can deliver. As with all wedding vendors, your best bet is word-of-mouth. Ask relatives, friends, and newlywed couples for referrals to talented pros. The Yellow Pages are a good standby if you're having trouble finding someone; of course, you should exercise extra caution in checking the person's work samples and references. Other places to look to if you're still not turning up any leads: bridal salons, wedding consultants, even catering-hall managers—they've worked with countless photographers.

What Photos Cost

Sample photography package price list:

- 4 hours, 1 album: $2,000
- 7 hours, 3 albums: $3,000
- All day, leather-bound albums: $4,500

While your best bet is going with an experienced *wedding* photographer, there's no rule against hiring hot shots with other specialties (a fashion photographer whose work you admire, a local newspaper photographer), an amateur photographer fresh out of school, or even a friend. In each of these cases, take extra care checking that the individual knows what's involved in this assignment and has the necessary skills. Look at pictures from similar projects that required similar skills (journalistic reportage on a society function or a fashion shoot that took place in a crowded restaurant), including dealing with people doing unexpected things and working with naturally occurring light (lamps, candles, sunlight) as opposed to spotlights. Also check that the person owns (or can rent) several backup cameras; like the pros, a nonwedding photographer should be prepared in case of camera meltdown.

The Big Picture: What to Look For

Things to ask yourselves before you say "I do" to a photographer.

Do We Like Her Book? Check whether the person has mastered the basic photographic skills by looking at her "book," a collection of greatest hits. (If a "professional" photographer doesn't have a book, that means she's either severely unorganized or full of it, neither of which is a good trait for a wedding photographer.) While you're flipping through, look for crispness of images, thoughtful compositions (does a shot look good the way it was framed, are heads chopped off, is there too much clutter in the frame?), and good lighting (beware of washed-out pictures where small details are blurred). It's also very important that you detect sensitivity in capturing people's emotions; make sure the photographer's subjects look relaxed, not like deer caught in headlights.

Do We Like a Wedding Album He Created? Examine a real-life wedding album the photographer created. You should be able to get a feel for the couple's wedding from their pictures: the style, the overall mood, the main players. If all you see are formal shots and you've decided you want the bulk of your photos to be candid, feel out whether the photographer is open to that. Ask him to explain his philosophy in putting together an album and see if it meshes with yours.

Finding Your Pro

Looking for a photographer? Log on to the Wedding Photographers Network (www.theknot.com/wpn). The best photographers get booked a year in advance so start looking early.

Picture-Perfect Contract Points

A glitch-proof photographer's contract should include:

☐ All locations where photographer will be expected to shoot, with exact addresses and starting times.
☐ Estimated number of hours to be worked.
☐ The name of photographer who'll be working for you and any assistants.
☐ The name of an acceptible substitute in case of emergency.
☐ Number of cameras that will be used, and which formats.
☐ Number of rolls to be shot (numbers for color and black and white).
☐ Number of proofs you'll receive.
☐ Other package details: number of completed albums, special-request shots.
☐ Schedule for delivering proofs and final package, as well as length of time negatives will be kept.
☐ Total cost.
☐ Overtime fee.
☐ Cancellation/refund policy.

Do We Get Good Vibes? This may be the most important question. Is the person excited by your vision when you describe it? When she makes suggestions, does she present them in a clear and respectful way? Is she rude? Is she timid? Does she laugh like a hyena? In order to get the best photos, go with a hot shot who has a firm grasp of social graces but is assertive enough to go out hunting for great images and who puts you at ease. (She will be shadowing your every move, remember.)

Flash These Questions

If you determine that a photographer's skill set, style, vision, and personality are A-OK, it's time to get some specific information.

Will You Do a Switcheroo? Make sure that the photographer whose work you've seen and loved is the one who will show up to your wedding. Larger studios have several photographers on their roster.

How Do You Determine Price? You won't be able to nail down an exact dollar amount until you're sure of what you want and how many albums you need. However, get a general range based on the number of prints you think you'll want (usually a hundred or so). If the photographer is way out of your price range, try to whittle away extras (the album itself, enlarged portraits) or cut down on hours to find the price that's right. It's a good idea to shop around, but we don't recommend skimping on your wedding photos—they're the most durable thing you'll spend your money on; unlike a cupid-shaped cake or cream satin stilettos, you'll have them forever.

Your Friend, Your Photographer

Planning to hand the camera to a friend in addition to a professional—or in lieu of one? Offer friend photogs these suggestions from Rob Fraser, a New York photographer who specializes in creative camerawork. (Keep them in mind when choosing a pro, too.)

Shoot Between the Moments: You may want a traditional group shot of the wedding party, but why stop there? Fraser's found that great times to shoot are when people are getting ready for and breaking up after a formal photograph.

Go with a Wide Shot: Why make every shot a closeup? By varying the distance of your shots, you'll be able to capture both the intimate moments and the overall feeling of the event.

Shoot with Selective Focus: By using a shallow depth of field, a photographer can focus sharply on a face while making the background fuzzy; alternately, s/he could focus on a distant object. Isolating subjects in their environment can create great shots. Flip through some fashion magazines and pay close attention to the photography style, which often incorporates this technique.

Use Natural Light: Traditional wedding photography blasts everything with a hot flash. But reality isn't always quite that bright. Ask your photographer to re-create real changes in brightness by using available light instead of a strong flash for every shot.

Use Juxtaposition: Predictable shots can be jazzed up simply by adding some human involvement. Fraser once shot a bride and groom kissing by the cake while a little girl is stealing a piece.

Do You Develop the Film? This is the norm with black-and-white pics, but many vendors now farm out their color processing to megalabs. While this will mean less ouch to your wedding budget, it also means that the quality of your photos may not be as stellar. If you can swing it, pay for someone who takes the do-it-yourself approach across the board.

What's Our Plan of Action? Schedule a follow-up meeting where you'll talk about specifics. Together you'll decide how many hours your photographer will spend at your wedding and discuss which specific shots you want (your entire wedding party and you, the garter toss, your honeymoon limo driving off into the sunset) and don't want (the cake shot, the schmaltzy posed kiss).

What Are Our Numbers? Hammer out how many rolls of film your photographer will shoot, how many proofs (sample developed pictures) you'll have to choose from, and how many prints will be in your final package.

What's Your Negative Policy? Most photographers save negatives for a year or two, during which time you can order extras. If you're moving (or live) far away or think you'll be needing more copies for years to come—it's going to be the Wedding of the Century, after all—consider buying the negatives at some point.

Photo Types and Twists

You two look dashing. Your guests look delightful. The flowers look fantastic, the food, scrumptious. Wouldn't it be a disaster if you didn't get this stuff on film? Pull up a chair and study our list of traditional wedding shots and the rundown of some of the best images to snag. (All of these go for wedding video must-haves, too.) A professional photographer probably will suggest many of these on her/his own; if a friend or family member is doing the photographic honors, this should be their guide. Of course, your wedding is going to be delightfully different, therefore, we're sure that you'll add a few of your own essential pics to the master list.

Bridal Portrait

Chapter 1 walks you through the process of composing and submitting newspaper announcements with photos.

Traditionally, the bride would go to a photographer's studio one to three months before the big day to be photographed in her wedding gown (perhaps even holding a replica of her big-day bouquet). While this practice is becoming less and less common—except down South, where the bride's portrait often is displayed at the reception—some women still choose to pose for this formal shot so they can include it with their wedding announcement. Our modern spin on this idea is to have a professional picture of the two of you (with or without wedding clothes) taken about two months before the wedding; you can use the photo for newspaper or sent announcements, wedding invitations, even thank-you notes.

"Day-Of" Portraits

Happy Couple: A posed picture of the two of you on your big day is a must-have. If you're not superstitious, take this shot before the ceremony, when you're all dressed up and ready to go. It's a nice together moment before you venture into the spotlight and means you'll have less to worry about once the festivities begin. More often, though, people pose for this shot in the moments right after the ceremony. That's fine, too, because you'll have that new-lywed glow and be thankful for a moment apart from the crowd. Your photographer should take a number of shots in different positions; you two relax and smile. Add a personal flair to your big-day portraits by having them printed in a special technique that gives them a brownish, antique sheen (called sepia-toned) for a romantic memento, or by posing in a spe-cial locale, such as your favorite park or on your car. Be playful—some-times the best couple pictures are those where you're acting goofy, lovey-dovey, or downright nutty.

Shoot for a Mix

Don't feel pressured to take tons of formal portraits just be-cause your parents are urging you to. Compromise. Have your photographer shoot the basic formals—you two, you and your families—and spend the rest of the time doing can-dids.

Wedding Party: Take some shots with your wedding party, girls and boys separately and then everyone together, either before or directly after the ceremony. (Or you can step out for a bit during the reception if you'd rather.) You'll also want shots of you two and your two honor attendants and shots of each of you with your attendant (bride/maid of honor, groom/best man). Remember: There's no rule that you have to be stiff and still; hug each other, tell jokes, do the chicken dance.

Family: Photos of each of you with your parents and siblings—taken before or after the ceremony—are a must. Both of you together should be in a portrait with each of your immediate family members, and there should be one big picture of both families together (with you two smiling smack in the center).

Ceremony Action Shots

Shots of your ceremony—beginning with your arrival and ending when you leave—are the meat of your wedding album. Classic pics include the groom waiting at the altar, the wed-ding party and then the bride and her escort going down the aisle, and ceremonial high-lights (jumping the broom, exchanging rings, signing a marriage contract). Also get a shot of the entire crowd from where the two of you stand during your vows and several reaction shots of special guests crying/laughing/gasping/fanning themselves/sleeping—they tell the real story of the moment.

ASK CARLEY

Don't Make 'Em Wait!

Q: We want our photographer to shoot quite a few formal portraits and the ceremony, but we hate the thought of making our guests wait for us to show up at the reception. What to do?

A: Having your cake and eating it too is a snap in this situation. You definitely don't want to make peo-ple entertain themselves for hours while you pose for photos. It's perfectly acceptable to shoot some por-traits *before* the ceremony; in fact, it's when everyone will be looking sharpest. (It also may help soothe your nerves to snuggle up with your honey preceremony.) Or have your photographer pull you and fellow posers away from the reception for ten or fifteen minutes to shoot your must-have portraits. It will be a breath of fresh air, figuratively if not literally, and you'll all be at peak excitement level.

Must-Have Shot Sheet

Some wedding moments you don't want to miss on photo and/or video. (If you're more comfortable, enlist a trusted friend for behind-the-scenes shots.)

Getting Ready (before the ceremony)

- Your clothes, hanging in the closet or over a chair
- Bridesmaids doing bride's hair and makeup
- Full-length shot of bride with gown checking herself out in mirror
- Groom getting ready with Dad and pals (tying the tie is a classic)
- You two chatting with/crying with/hugging your parents and siblings preceremony
- Mom helping bride with one last detail, such as veil
- Dad whispering last-minute advice to groom
- Each of you ready to go—at the door
- Making your way to the ceremony (in backseat of limo, hailing cab, walking down the street)

The Ceremony

- Guests streaming into the site
- Ushers escorting guests to their seats (you get to see if they did it right)
- Closeup of the groom's adorably nervous mug waiting for his other half
- Flower girl and/or ring bearer walking in (how cute!)
- Gorgeous bridesmaids going down the aisle
- Closeup of bride just before making her entrance
- Wide shot of altar or canopy
- Wide shot of audience during ceremony, from bride and groom's point of view
- Closeup of your hands as you exchange the rings
- The kiss: zoom in!
- You two coming up the aisle, guests' smiling faces at your sides
- Congrats shots: you two hugging, laughing, crying with good friends

The Reception

- Bride and groom arriving (make it dramatic—your faces through the dark glass of limo, you two at top of staircase, pushing through a curtain)
- Receiving-line moments
- You two knocking back some champagne with your best friends
- Your parents whispering to each other during dinner
- Kids playing with balloons and streamers or sneaking a nap
- You two dancing (maybe with a slow shutter speed so the movement blurs the image a little)
- The musicians or DJ doing their thing
- Bride laughing with her bridesmaids
- Groom dancing with maid of honor
- The dance floor going nuts (again, slow-shutter speed could be effective)
- Bride and groom feeding each other cake (no smashing allowed)
- Closeup of your uncle making a toast
- The bouquet toss (perhaps a shot of just the flowers and outstretched arms)
- You two leaving, waving from the backseat

Reception Candids

Pictures of you and your guests mingling, munching, and moshing will bring you the most joy and laughter. Apart from totally spontaneous shots (give your photographer lots of freedom to roam and snap precious moments), reception highlights like the cutting of the cake and dances with your moms and pops also should be memorialized. It's also a great idea to encourage guests to shoot their own candids—which you can mix with pro pics in your album—by placing disposable cameras on their tables and asking them to leave them for you later.

VIDEOGRAPHY

Whether a wedding video is a must-have is still open for debate. It really depends on what you and your honey like and want and the budget you're working with. There are *many* compelling reasons to have your wedding videotaped: You'll get to see a lot of live action that you may have missed because you were off greeting guests/tending to those butterflies in your stomach/polka-ing with Gramps. You'll also have a vivid record of the sounds of your wedding—your processional music, your best man's hilarious toast, the cacophony of guests chatting and laughing—as well as key moving images, such as your dance with your mother, your honey's goofy line dance with her bridesmaids, the bouquet-toss pileup.

But before you plop down the $800-plus that it will cost you to hire a professional videographer, ask yourselves whether: you want to accommodate—and listen to—yet another camera person at the event; it's really important to you to have a real-time recording of your wedding (say, for someone who can't make it); if you're gonna watch the thing more than once. If you can afford a video without having to cut back on your photography package—or you've got an offer from a video-savvy friend—go for it! Don't feel badly, however, about only doing the photo thing; pictures are more durable and evocative anyway.

Photography Trends

- Fast-speed film (good for shooting in dim light)
- Black-and-white pictures
- Candids over posed pics
- Behind-the-scenes shots
- Images of guests reacting
- Different-size photos in an album (quarter page, full page, etc.)
- "Storyboard" album (an overall narrative concept)
- Detail shots
- Library-bound albums in soft leather or quality fabrics

Zooming In on a Genre

As the stars of your own made-for-TV movie, you have a few options in the style department. Before you begin shopping around for a videographer, figure out which directorial approach most appeals to you.

Documentary Style

Your wedding is covered like a major news event (which it is, of course), blending real-time footage; voice-over commentary from you two, friends, and family; and on-screen interviews with key guests.

Pros: Very entertaining to watch, this style plays up the highlights of the big day.

Cons: You'll typically need two cameras to create a good, newsy tape, which will be more expensive and more intrusive. If done right, the editing process is quite elaborate, as well—using lots of audio editing and montages (multiple-scene sequences)—which again means more money.

Oscar-Winning Ideas: Get your videographer to shoot talking-head interviews with people near and dear to your heart; their comments will be moving and funny, no doubt. Go chronological: Record the proceedings from when you're getting dressed until "The End," perhaps even giving your videographer some honeymoon footage to edit into the mix.

Memory Lane

This format incorporates past home videos, shots of childhood/college/courtship photos, and commentary from close friends and relatives to create a holistic vision of your relationship—with your wedding as the main event.

Pros: Finally you'll do something with those dusty homemade reels your father keeps in the garage. Plus you'll have a quirky, sentimental synopsis of your life to view on anniversaries, birthdays, even during together time with your future kids.

Cons: If done wrong, this could smell worse than Roquefort cheese. Again, this approach requires lots of postproduction work (editing, captions, voice-overs), so it's going to cost you.

Oscar-Winning Ideas: Divide the first part of the video into two separate, titled sections, one about each of you. Then start the couple section with a montage of pictures of you together while your fave song plays. Have your parents, friends, and siblings talk about what they thought of your honey when they first met, memories they have of your early days, sweet things you've said in confidence about each other.

Rough Cut

This is unedited footage of your wedding: live, raw, uncensored. And it's probably the route you'll be taking if you're having a friend or relative shoot the event, unless they have access to editing facilities.

Pros: Cheap, cheap, cheap. You'll get spontaneous outbreaks and raunchy hilarity à la *America's Funniest Home Videos* and lots of other images you probably would have never seen in a shorter, edited format.

Cons: Your hands are going to be sore from doing all that fast-forwarding. It's not that your wedding wasn't exciting; it's just that you really did need to *be* there to get the full sense of splendor.

Oscar-Winning Ideas: Have a ready-made script for the videographer of certain shots and interviews s/he must get so that the video has some rhyme and reason.

Freedom to Film?

Don't assume your videographer will have total artistic freedom at your ceremony. Some places of worship do not allow bright lights and may place restrictions on your vendor's movement. (S/he may not have access to a behind-the-altar audience shot, for example.) Check with your officiant about rules.

Hiring a Video Pro

Finding a good videographer is not as difficult as finding a contact lens in a haystack, but it still requires some effort on your part. Since your videographer is someone you really need to trust and like, it's extra important to check the person out carefully. As always, ask around for glowing referrals or consult your wedding photographer (if you've already hired one) for some hot prospects. Find a pro who's in your price range, comfortable with the genre of your choice, and an all-around nice person.

Making the Cut: Questions to Ask

Even though we all watch lots of TV, it still can be hard to judge what makes a video good or bad. Ask prospective videographers if you may see a few tapes of their wedding work and ask yourselves some questions.

Does This Person Have Basic Technical Skills Down? Images should be bright and crisp, not dark and grainy. Faces should be natural-looking, not shiny or washed out by too much light. Edits—cuts from one shot to another—should be seamless. Don't forget to listen for good, clear sound quality (no hissing or buzzing; sound level should be steady from scene to scene).

Does S/he Have Good Storytelling Instincts? Scenes should be put together in a coherent, logical fashion. Selected clips should be "best of" material (ergo, not boring). You also want your videographer to be a good interviewer who gets great quotes from friends and family. Make sure the people being interviewed on the tapes you're watching seem happy and comfortable, not besieged or annoyed. (That probably means the videographer is inappropriately pushy or familiar.)

Straight-to-Video Contract Points

When you're signing a contract with your videographer, make sure it includes:

- ☐ The wedding date and arrival time.
- ☐ Names and addresses of all locations where videographer will be shooting.
- ☐ The videographer's name.
- ☐ The name of an acceptable substitute in case of emergency.
- ☐ The hours they'll work.
- ☐ Number of cameras and assistant videographers (put in writing that they will bring at least one backup camera).
- ☐ The hours of raw footage they will shoot.
- ☐ The total edited time of your finished tape (Get about five minutes of live footage for each edited minute, or two-and-a-half hours of footage for a half-hour video).
- ☐ Any editing features or special effects you've agreed upon.
- ☐ Total cost.
- ☐ Fees including overtime rates and cost of additional tapes if you want them.
- ☐ Date the final video will be ready.

Looking Supermodel-Slick

The wedding paparazzi want a piece of you two! And *you* want to look like stalkable celebs, if just for one day. To say "cheese" in the best possible way, follow our gouda ideas and brie-liant suggestions— you'll look like runway pros.

Smile: Bearing your pearly whites definitely increases your odds of taking a good picture. Besides, the act of smiling alone has a calming effect that will translate into cool-looking pics. Don't force it; think of a funny joke your sister just told you or steal a peek at your jokester father.

Pick a Side: Don't sit on the fence; find your "good" side. Stick a pencil in your mouth, holding the center of it between your lips so it's parallel to the floor. Look in the mirror at the distance between the pencil and your eyes. You'll notice that one of your eyes is actually closer to the pencil—this indicates the shorter side of your face. In this case, shorter is *better.* Try to point that side toward the camera as much as possible.

Strike a Pose: Take a look at a Victoria's Secret catalog. *(Yes,* those are mostly fake.) The models usually position their bodies toward the camera at a forty-five-degree angle, then turn their heads to face the lens directly. Notice that their hips are pushed slightly forward and their shoulders are pulled back. The foot closest to the camera points toward it while the other remains parallel to it. This all makes them look fab—practice in the mirror for your trip into the limelight.

Do Something: Pictures can look funny if the subjects are stiff, awkward, and unnatural. The best way to avoid looking like a dweeb is to grab hold of the person next to you (especially if it's your sweetie!) and show some affection. Throw an arm around a friend, plant a kiss on your uncle's cheek, laugh and hold up your champagne flutes.

Eye It: We know you're scared of blinking, but don't widen your eyes—it'll give you a creased-up fore-head. To look naturally alert, shut your eyes quickly before a shot and then open them.

Hold Your Chin High: The best way to beat the dreaded double chin is to stand up straight and pull your head up.

Hair Dos: Keep your hair away from your face, so you don't look messy. Brush bangs aside with your fingers before a shot and tuck stray pieces behind your ears.

Sun Block: Stay out of direct sunlight. The sun shadows your face in pictures, making your nose look bigger and your eyes smaller. Head for a bright, not blazing, spot.

Do We Like His/Her Personality? You want to hire someone with super people skills who will make your wedding day better, not bleaker. Avoid pushy types whom you just know are going to be elbowing your grandparents aside to get a "money" (exceptionally good) shot. Also steer clear of videographers intent on convincing you that you need a crew the size of that employed on the set of *Titanic* to get a decent wedding video; they probably are more concerned about their bank account than your needs and desires.

Does This Person Have State-of-the-Art Equipment? Take note of the quality of the picture and sound, but also ask to take a look at the professional's camera and editing facilities. You may not be techie wizards, but you'll be able to tell if the equipment is time-worn or relatively shiny and new. Steer clear of so-called pros who use outdated VHS or 8-mm cameras (the quality of the images is quite poor) or Betacams (they need a lot of light, which means you either have to go with darker images or intrusive spotlights). In-

Photo and Video Storage Tips

Keep photos and videotapes somewhere that maintains a moderate temperature and humidity level, away from direct light.

Videos should be stored upright (on end) in their cases and away from electronic equipment such as stereo speakers, which have magnetic coils at their centers.

Remove the clip at the back of your video so you don't record over it by mistake.

Keep a second copy of your video and the negatives of your photos in a fireproof box made especially for photographs and negatives.

Chapter 21 briefs you on super hair and makeup.

stead, find a videographer who uses a S-VHS camera or, better yet, a single-chip Hi-8 camera that combines professional controls with lower-light capabilities—perfect for shooting a wedding.

Getting your hands on a good wedding photographer and videographer will enhance the beauty of your big day, because you'll be able to enjoy those precious moments with friends and family—and all the fleeting wedding-day emotions—for years to come. Doing thorough groundwork about your options and prospective hires is somewhat time-consuming, but it's the best wedding present you can give yourselves. Who doesn't want to be immortalized looking model-gorgeous and being the center of attention? Those wedding images will be lifelong pick-me-ups, reminding the two of you how luminous, lucky, and loved you really are.

Face the Music

Like your favorite flick, your relationship has a soundtrack. During your time as a twosome, you've adopted certain songs as your own and shared your favorites with each other in the shower. Your musical repertoire is one of a kind, reminding you of all the wonderful times you've had together. Unveil this fantastic compilation to the world at your wedding.

Wedding music is an art. Incorporated into your ceremony and reception, it punctuates dramatic entrances and exits, augments the overall mood of your celebration, adds to the romanticism of the affair, and, of course, gets you and your guests shaking your booties! Whether you're classical music buffs or top-forty junkies (or one of each), the music you choose will personalize the festivities. It's time to add rhythm and soul to your wedding!

CEREMONY MUSIC

Start your wedding off on the right foot by including music in your ceremony. Ambient sound—whether generated by a klezmer (traditional Jewish) band, a bagpiper, a string quartet, or a group of African percussionists—can create a mood of breathless anticipation, entertain guests as they wait for your smash entrance, up the romanticism and spirituality quotient, and soothe frayed nerves. While in the past, many a couple's ceremony score was solely a classical composition, we also love the idea of allowing your ethnic heritage, personal taste, wedding theme, and level of romanticism, playfulness, and unconventionality to play a role in your ceremony-music selection.

Music-Deserving Moments

Music can be used throughout this monumental event, from the time your early-bird guests arrive to the moment you're outta there. Get hip to the traditional components of ceremony music so you can decide what's for you and when you actually prefer the sound of silence.

The Prelude

The music that's played first—the prelude—is there to distract and entertain guests until the ceremony officially begins. Prelude music should start when the doors to your site open, no later than twenty minutes before the start time on your invites. (There are many early birds out there, and a lot of them are your relatives.) Depending on how many guests you've invited, how long it takes you to tie a tie, or how many times your honey has to reapply her lipstick before facing the world, you may have to plan for as much as forty-five minutes of music here.

Many musical choices are appropriate, from distinguished concerto excerpts by Bach, Chopin, or Handel to mellow jazz standards to covers of sweet R&B hits. You want to choose music that will mask awkward silences—as guests settle in their seats next to total strangers—but won't overshadow the energy of anticipation.

Establish a mood or theme with your prelude; remember, it's your invitees' first sensory impression of your wedding (along with the aroma of the flowers and the look of the site). For a fairy-tale affair, have a harpist make some heavenly music; for a casual beach ceremony, have a band play acoustic versions of Beach Boys' and reggae tunes; for a candlelit evening wedding, choose something mystical, such as Gregorian chants or Enya's haunting New Age songs. Even if you're not incorporating music anywhere else in your ceremony, do it here—a solo flutist, violinist, or pianist is a low-key choice.

Greatest Hits: Handel's "Water Music"; Saint-Saëns' "Benediction Nuptiale"; Bach's "Suite in D"; Haydn's "Violin Concerto in A."

The Opening Act

Have a soloist or choir belt out a classic hymn or song, a gospel standard, even a pop hit at the end of the prelude, right before the processional begins. It captures guests' attention and gets them focused for the big moment.

The Processional

The pièce de résistance of your ceremonial concert, the processional is the music playing as you and your wedding party make your grand entrance, whether down the aisle, through your floral canopy, or parachuting down from the sky.

Think drama. Often a march is chosen—played by an organist or trumpeter—to keep you and your entourage movin' on forward like shiny, suave soldiers. However, any music (or instrument) will do as long as it's monumental and bold. Personalize your processional music by selecting an acoustic version of a song with sentimental value to you as a couple—your first dance, your parents' processional tune—or that shows off your ethnic heritage.

Greatest Hits: Purcell's "Trumpet Tune", Mozart's "Wedding March" from *The Marriage of Figaro;* Beethoven's "Ode to Joy"; Pachabel's "Canon in D Minor."

Ceremonial Accents

Many couples choose to have music played to accent key moments during the ceremony (the exchange of rings, the breaking of the glass) or as actual elements of the ceremony itself, along with readings. Any tune is appropriate, from classic pieces such as Schubert's "Ave Maria" or Handel's immortal "Hallelujah Chorus" from *Messiah,* to folk songs such as "Amazing Grace" and the "Irish Wedding Song," to popular tunes such as "One Hand, One Heart" from *West Side Story* or Stevie Wonder's "You Are the Sunshine of My Life." Have pieces performed by a vocalist or an instrumental soloist/ensemble.

Since this is the most emotional stage of the entire affair, put some soul into it. Add some heritage, have a talented friend or relative sing an original tune, or have a particularly meaningful song performed. One of our favorite ideas is incorporating a group singalong; print the words of a hymn, folk song, or pop favorite in your ceremony program and have your guests double as performers for a true feeling of group harmony. Don't be afraid to make your ceremony longer by incorporating songs; if your hearts are in it, music can only add to the moment.

The Familiar Wedding Tune . . .

The traditional "Here Comes the Bride" is actually the "Bridal Chorus" from Wagner's opera *Lohengrin*. Some Catholic churches will not allow it because it's a secular composition; many rabbis frown on it because of the composer's well-documented anti-Semitism. And if you're at all superstitious, you might want to steer clear—it was written about a union that goes super-sour.

Personalized Ceremony Tunes

Incorporate one or more of these elements into your ceremony music:

Ethnicity: Use traditional musical instruments, such as a sitar (India), mandolin (Greece), fiddle (Ireland), or a digeridoo (Australia). Play national folk songs during the prelude.

Religion: Have a choir lead everyone in a hymn or religious tune; hire a gospel group or klezmer band; incorporate a Buddhist chant.

Wedding Theme: Match the musicians to the time period (fife and drums for a medieval affair; jazz trio for the 1920s). Select theme-appropriate songs, such as the Who's "My Generation" for a '60s wedding or Billy Ray Cyrus's "Achy Breaky Heart" for a country-western shindig.

Site Characteristics: Take musical cues from your site. Dramatic organ music goes well with a large Gothic church; a folk singer is perfect for your grandparents' living room; a string quartet goes hand in glove with a formal garden.

"Your" Songs: Choose tunes that have your honey's name in them (Elton John's "Daniel"; the Beatles' "Michelle") or bear special meaning for both of you (your first slow dance, something from the movie soundtrack you wore out on your first road trip together).

The Season: Play seasonal or holiday songs during the prelude and postlude: "Summer Time" for a July wedding, "Singing in the Rain" for spring, Christmas carols.

Greatest Hits: Thank heavens we're all so different—there is no top-forty countdown here. Be free.

The Recessional

The bride and groom should go out with a bang. The music that plays while you're walking back up the aisle together should reflect the giddiness of your just-marriedness and get guests revved up for the celebration to follow. Even if you're not technically leaving—say your ceremony and reception are in the same place—have your musicians play a show-stopping number once the rigmarole is over in honor of the big change that's just taken place. Again, classical music (like Widor's "Toccata" from Symphony No. 5 or Elgar's "Pomp and Circumstance") is a popular choice, as are upbeat contemporary songs.

Greatest Hits: High-energy pop hits—such as the Sister Sledge's "We Are Family," Kool & the Gang's "Celebration," and James Brown's "I Feel Good"—make radical recessionals.

Postlude

Keep the good vibes going with more love-happy and spirited music playing as guests file out of the ceremony site, or—if your entire wedding is taking place at one location—as they make the transition into chow and cha-cha time. You could have your musicians stick around a little longer or play a CD. Figure on fifteen minutes' worth of fun, celebratory tunes.

Greatest Hits: You two singing a duet of "We're Off to See the Wizard"—just kidding. Think happy and you'll bring down the house.

Fast Forward

If you're using CDs or tapes for ceremony (or reception) music, create a playlist for the person in charge. Write down the names of the songs and the track numbers; make sure to provide extra backup songs in case things take longer than planned. If you're using tapes, make everyone's life easier—cue 'em.

Ceremony Music Options

Before you book that steel drum band or campy, drag-queen barbershop quintet, you need to assess your site and find out about any religious (or other) restrictions on music, discuss your personal taste, and find songs and instruments that are music to both of your ears.

Musical Restrictions

Your first step in determining what style of music in general, and which tunes specifically, you can include is to investigate whether there are any pertinent restrictions you should keep in mind.

- Check with your officiant about religious restrictions on *what* you can play. Some places of worship will not allow secular songs (many Catholic churches) or forbid music completely (Quaker and Orthodox Jewish wedding ceremonies).
- Check with the ceremony site's musical director, if there is one. These coordinators can clue you in to limitations regarding *who* can perform at your ceremony.

Obviously, their preference is for you to hire in-house musicians; there may even be rules prohibiting outside performers. Be diplomatic if you want to farm out music duties; one smoothing-of-ruffled-feathers tactic is to consult the musical director about which pieces to choose. It's not only flattering, it's the smart thing to do—s/he probably has a better grasp of appropriate songs than you do.

- Consult the authorities in charge if you're tying the knot in a public place. When it comes to a city park or county beach, there may be time-of-day restrictions on playing music or limitations on noise levels. You may, for example, have to forgo that electric guitar riff you had planned in favor of an unplugged, acoustic tune.

Sounding Out the Options

In terms of *who* you want making music at this important event, you have a wide variety of options, from a solo guitarist to a large choir. Before you track down referrals to specific musicians, decide what it is you want. This will depend on several things.

Site Acoustics: The sound of a delicate harp will get lost in a bombastic cathedral; a chorus of bagpipes could be deafening in a small space like your living room. If you're getting hitched at a conventional site, such as a house of worship or banquet hall, consult people there about what works in the space and what doesn't. If you've selected an unconventional site, such as a forest clearing, experiment with a battery-powered cassette player and imagine what type of volume level you're going to want once the space is teeming with gabbing guests.

Specific Tunes You Want Played: Classical compositions won't have the impact you want played on a fiddle, say, and Stevie Wonder on an organ just ain't funky. We're not saying you can't be creative (a string quartet rendition of Celine Dion's pop hit "Because You Loved Me" could be awesome), but if you have specific pieces you want played, envision in your mind's ear who's going to be able to play it successfully and who isn't.

Your Music Budget: The dollar amount you've allocated to wedding entertainment must cover both ceremony and reception music. If you're flush, anything goes, but if—like most of the free world—you have some limitations, keep the musicianship simple, with a solo performer or a small ensemble (or even prerecorded music). Since *you two* are the feature ceremony attraction, you can afford to scale back the backup help here. After all, the reception is where you really need a hand in keeping the guests happy and engaged.

Music to Your Ears

In general, ceremony music is best kept simple. After all, you don't want it to overshadow the intrinsic emotional intensity of the vows. Go for a focused sound rather than flashy bells and whistles. Some of our favorite options for ceremony music:

Keyboardist: A classical pianist or organist can do it all, from soothing prelude tunes to a dignified processional to jazzy, upbeat postlude music.

Trumpeter: A soloist or a horn combo can add either regal solemnity or peppy rhythm—or both—to your ceremony, depending on what music you ask them to play.

String Quartet: Strings are pitch perfect for classical compositions; they also add romantic elegance to contemporary selections.

Harpist: The ideal choice for a small, romantic ceremony or springtime vows in the garden. Hire two harpists—to sit and strum at either side of the altar—for larger affairs or an accompanying flutist for a baroque tinge.

Blues Guitarist: The sound of a slide guitar is urban-romantic; it creates an all-American, down-to-earth, ultra-cool atmosphere. A mix of blues, jazz, and American classics can be played at different stages of your ceremony.

Vocalist/Choir: *Homo sapiens'* vocal chords are a beautiful instrument, say we. Hymns, gospels, pop hits, and classical compositions offer a wide array of feelings for the various stages of your ceremony.

Folk Singer: Like the troubadour of yore, a folk singer/guitarist has a unique, intimate, and sentimental aura. Scout local coffeeshops or performance spaces for a musician who touches you; perhaps even commission an original song for the occasion.

Jazz Combo: Have a trio, quintet, or singer/standing bass duet add some soul to your ceremony. Jazz standards create a sophisticated, glamorous atmosphere that's oh-so-romantic.

Musical Notes

- Don't book ceremony musicians before you check into the religious, cultural, and logistical restrictions at your site.

- For outdoor sites, look for a flat stage area and electrical outlets so that you and your musicians know what extra equipment (generator, stage, etc.) you need. This applies to your reception entertainers, too.

- If your ceremony will be outdoors and you've hired classical musicians, make sure they're sheltered. Violins, flutes, and harps are delicate; the slightest drizzle can put an end to the performance. If you want the music to go on, be sure to provide a tent or roof of some sort.

Hiring Your Music Makers

As with all wedding vendors, you want to make sure that you really, really know what you're getting for your music money. Hearing is believing. Once you've gotten the names of some good ceremony musicians (from friends, newlywed couples, your clergy, site coordinators, a wedding consultant), make sure you get a chance to listen to them play. Many performers today have recorded tapes of their craftsmanship, a good place to begin, but there is no substitute for seeing a live performance. Ask about sitting in on an event they're doing—whether a wedding or not—to find out if you like what you see and hear.

Pitch-Perfect Topics to Cover

Once you've zeroed in on some choice musicians, you'll need to talk about a number of issues.

Vision: Explain what you're thinking about in terms of musical selections. See if they respond openly and get excited. If there's a song you really want to incorporate and they don't know it, they should be willing to learn from sheet music you provide them. If they're resistant to the idea, find out if it's because they think it won't work with the instrument (they are, after all, more in the know than you; ask them to come up with some do-able alternatives of a similar style) or just *because,* in which case: Keep looking.

Schedule: Is the performer available on the day of your wedding? Will he or she commit to an early-morning ceremony or a midnight one? Most important, make sure your musicians are hip to the idea of showing up at least an hour in advance on the big day; be wary of people who tell you there's no need because they just need "a few secs" to get ready.

Fine-Tuned Contracts

When it's time to seal the deal with your ceremony musicians, get it in writing (if you've been paying attention, you already knew this, star pupils). Be sure to include:

☐ Exact date, arrival time, location.
☐ Equipment needed—chairs, music stands, amplifiers. If the musicians are bringing their own, record any extra charges.
☐ Attire. You should have a say in what your performers wear, according to your overall ceremony vision.
☐ What they will play when. Write in a clause that ensures their flexibility should you need them to play longer (during the prelude, for example); talk to them about some B-list songs should they need to fill time.
☐ The names of the exact musicians who will play at your ceremony, plus the names of acceptable substitutes should there be an emergency.
☐ Fees and overtime rates.

There are always last-minute glitches, and you want your musicians to be good and ready long before the first guest arrives.

Price: Ceremony musicians can charge anywhere from $50 to $150 an hour, less if they're students. This typically is a per-performer fee, so the more elaborate you're going, the costlier. Make sure you're in the know about all extras; ask whether there's a two-hour minimum (not uncommon) and how much they'll charge you if you end up needing them to put in overtime. If you're having trouble finding what you want with what you have to spend, scale back your plans or enlist the help of musical friends and relatives in lieu of wedding gifts.

RECEPTION MUSIC

A party without music is like low-fat potato chips: decidedly unsatisfying and *no* fun. Good tunes help create a celebrational mood, get your guests loosened up, and even provide easy conversation fodder for awkward moments when people have nothing to say to each other. ("I just love Neil Diamond, don't you?" "Oh, yeah!")

Your reception is your opportunity to play *all* your fave songs that weren't appropriate for your ceremony, wow the crowd with any amazing dance moves you've patented, and generally let your hair down. Music is the fuel that keeps the party train chugging.

Band vs. DJ

There are two major parties in the reception entertainment scene: live ensembles playing original numbers, covers of popular tunes, and/or traditional standards and disc jockeys spinning records, usually in an eclectic mix of styles. Live music is seen by many as the traditional, dignified uncle with good taste; DJs as the younger, hipper, less-refined cousin. We can honestly say that both options can be spectacular or sorry; it all depends on the talent of the performer/s.

In a perfect world—where money is no object—to-be-weds probably would choose a little of both: a live band to please upright guests alternating sets with a DJ who'll excite the club kids. Heck, in an ideal universe you'd have your very own Weddingpalooza, with a variety of acts—a big band, a Latin house DJ, a folk singer, a punk band—in different rooms. But since you probably don't have unlimited funds to spend on your merrymaking, most likely you'll opt for either the band *or* the DJ, each of which has its pros and cons. Whichever route you go, remember that top talent will be booked up to a year in advance; the sooner you make reception music arrangements, the better.

Bring on the Band

Many bands and orchestras specialize in wedding receptions, but your favorite local rockers also can be the entertainers at your wedding. The important thing is that the performers are fun, excited, sensitive to the crowd, and open to all of your suggestions.

Pros: There's something about the liveness of a band that's infectiously energetic. If they're good, they can get a crowd moving like nobody's business. A charismatic bandleader also can be a great master of ceremonies.

Cons: Generally more expensive than a DJ, a band also loses in the man vs. machine department—they'll peter out before a sound system ever does. (You'll have to pay extra for alternates to play during band breaks.) Also, even the most open-minded of music ensembles does not have the repertoire of a standard disc jockey, who can easily tote around stacks of different albums.

Cocktail Hour/Dinnertime Music

During the first hour or two of your reception, mingling, talking, sipping (of cocktails), and nibbling (of food) are going to be the greatest hits. You want the music playing to be:

Soft. The decibel level should be such that chatting is a breeze. The better your guests get to know each other at this stage, the more fun the rest of the party will be.
Romantic. Slide smoothly from your emotionally charged ceremony into your reception festivities by starting things off with lots of love songs.
Relaxing. Help everybody kick back.

If you can afford it, hire a string quartet, jazz combo, or harpist/flutist duo in addition to your main reception performers (perhaps the same people that played during your ceremony). A pianist/torch singer is another option—and very hip in today's cigar-happy, martini-worshipping world. If you don't want to spend the money (and energy) necessary to book an additional act, simply ask your band or DJ to think "mellow" for an hour or so. Request instrumental music, whether classical, easy listening, or jazz. Or ask your DJ to play "lounge" and "ambient" music, decidedly modern, laid-back, and oh-so-groovy club favorites.

AMANDA AND JAY
November 2, New York City

"WHEN JAY AND I were discussing where to put our wedding dollars, we decided that the band and the photographs would be the top two priorities, and we're very glad we did that," Amanda says. "A good wedding band doesn't just play music—they really run the reception; the band we chose, 747, did a terrific job. The bandleader is great at keeping a party going, and they played the most amazing, endless horah—almost every guest at the wedding was dancing!" Friends who had been to a lot of Jewish weddings told the couple it was the best they'd ever seen.

"I think one of the really fun things about our reception was that Jay and I both sang, which people weren't expecting," Amanda continues. Jay and four of his groomsmen—who all happen to be musically talented—borrowed the band's instruments and played "Every Breath You Take" to Amanda. Later the bride and groom sang a duet: "Let's Stay Together." "While we sang, everyone crowded around us, and by the end of the song, everyone was singing the chorus with us," Amanda remembers. "It was beautiful."

Disc Jockey in the House

DJs are becoming the increasingly popular option for weddings. They also are becoming more sophisticated, collecting a balanced and eclectic mix of musical styles conducive to all-ages affairs.

Pros: DJs are generally cheaper than bands. You also have more control over the sound of the songs—whatever your favorite recordings are, you can have 'em played—the variety of musical styles, and the length of the party. (Experienced DJs have enough tricks up their sleeve to last through a party that goes all night long; bands, understandably, can't play for much longer than five or six hours.) When DJs take breaks, they can play a great compilation record to keep the party going.

Cons: Disc jockeys do seem a little less personal than bands; for example, they can't time the song to match your dancing style during your first dance (and you worked so hard on that over-the-shoulder, through-the-legs move) or improvise to accommodate sweet surprises (your kids joining in the dance with you all excited, for example). The worst of them are also really cheesy, playing tired party songs, wearing sequined vests, and making goofy comments.

Hiring Your Reception Entertainers

Good word-of-mouth is music to your ears. However, nothing compares to observing performers in action when it comes to finding a band or DJ that really can rock your (and your guests') world.

Get Your Hands on a Band

Bands that specialize in weddings can be tracked down by asking for referrals from newlyweds you know, your site coordinator, your wedding consultant, or another in-the-know vendor. You could, of course, hire a bar band you've seen and loved; be extra-diligent about telling them what you want and need since they won't be as familiar with wedding protocol.

Let the Music Play

Some local branches of the American Federation of Musicians (212–869–1330) keep records of area musicians who play special events; call for referrals.

What to Look For: Go see the band in action, preferably at a similar function (although a club gig or videotape will do). Watch how the musicians interact with the audience: loud, gaudy, rude, and peacocklike strutting are bad; pleasantries, enthusiasm, and flexibility (playing audience requests, for example) are good. You also might want to look for an act that can play a wide variety of styles if it's important to you to get *everyone* up and hopping. When you see a band you like, schedule a meeting with the leader and discuss the type of music you'll want them to play as well as whether you want him/her to coordinate the reception "happenings," such as announcing the cutting of the cake and your major dances. Make sure s/he reacts with enthusiasm and openness.

What It'll Cost: A four-piece ensemble generally will charge between $1,000 and $4,000 for four hours of work, although prices can be significantly higher at peak times, in major cities, and for top talent. You generally will have to put down a 20 to 50 percent deposit. (Don't put down more than half of the total cost.)

Questions to Ask:

- If you listen to/watch an audio- or videotape of the band, is it recorded live or studio produced? Is the sound technically enhanced? You want to hear how they *really* sound.
- How would they describe their style?
- No matter what their repertoire is, can they play other songs important to you, such as a horah or other ethnic classics and favorite pop hits?
- If you have an original or esoteric piece you want played, will they learn it and how much lead time do they need? What do they charge to arrange it?
- How many musicians are in the band? How many vocalists? Are there different options as far as how many musicians/instruments you can hire?
- Would you need to rent any instruments (a piano, for example)?
- Does the band use techno-tricks such as sampling? (You may or may not want these.)
- Will the band bring its own sound system? How large a room can it accommodate?
- Can the bandleader or another band member act as master of ceremonies?
- Who will do the setup and how early will they do it?
- Does the band have another gig before or after yours? Is the band prepared to play overtime?

Band Contract Points

- ☐ Date, exact time, and location of the reception.
- ☐ Band's starting time and estimated total hours.
- ☐ During which stages of the reception they'll be playing (cocktail hour, after dinner).
- ☐ How many breaks they can take and whether taped music will play during that time.
- ☐ The names of the band members who will play and what instruments they're bringing.
- ☐ The names of acceptable substitute musicians in case of emergency.
- ☐ Emcee duties, if any.
- ☐ Commitment to play key songs.
- ☐ What equipment the band will bring and what you need to provide, including chairs, stage, amplifiers, speakers, etc.
- ☐ What they should wear.
- ☐ Whether you'll be serving them meals (some bands have this written into their contract).
- ☐ The negotiated rate, plus hourly overtime fees.
- ☐ Cancellation and refund policy.

LISA AND MILES

October 13, Brooklyn, New York

WHEN LISA AND MILES met, she was preparing a dance piece choreographed by a mutual friend to music that Miles had composed. They got to know each other during the rehearsals, and the relationship grew from there. For their wedding, the couple decided to compose their own dance. "It was a way for us to express our love in a very personal and creative way, especially because music and dance are so much a part of who we are," Miles explains.

To prepare, they took ballroom dance classes, to learn how to dance together—"*and* to get me up to speed," says the groom. They decided on a waltz—again, Miles composed and Lisa choreographed. Dur-

ing the months before the wedding, the couple rehearsed in complete secrecy, since they wanted it to be a surprise.

"Beforehand we were afraid that we would be nervous performing in front of everyone, but when it actually happened we felt so comfortable holding each other and moving together that nothing else mattered," Miles says. "Many of our guests let us know that they cried through the whole dance because they were so touched by how personal it was."

The Way to a DJ

The best method for finding a good party DJ is, as usual, word of mouth. You also can call local dance clubs you like—and even radio stations—for references. Some of the best DJs work for professional entertainment companies that hire a fixed roster of spinmeisters—check your Yellow Pages or local magazines for listings.

What to Look For: Attend one of the DJ's events, if possible, and see that s/he skillfully reads the crowd, is polite, and takes requests. At the very least, you should have a face-to-face interview where you explain which musical genres you like, specific songs that are on your must-have list, and information about the demographics of your guests (ages, ethnic groups, hipness factor). Make sure the DJ is attentive and sharp, asking questions that show s/he comprehends the situation. You may even want to ask to see the person's record collection; have him/her pull albums from the different genres you're into. It's a must to get phone numbers of other couples who have used the person's services; you want to make sure s/he is familiar with wedding protocol and etiquette and is sensitive to the sentimentality of the event.

What It'll Cost: Fees range from about $200 to $1,000 for a four-hour reception, with higher prices on the weekends, during heavy party months, and for big-name DJs, such as radio or club celebs. You also will pay more for more elaborate equipment (better speakers, for example) and a backup DJ.

Toning Down the Entertainers

Don't forget to talk to your DJ or bandleader about how little or much you want *him/her* to talk. You may want him/her to give your guests cues at big moments ("Ladies and gents: It's cake time!"), but that's probably all. This is one of the important reasons to see the performer in action: You don't want to be stuck with a blabbermouth.

Questions to Ask:

- Will the DJ or the agency check out the electrical requirements and acoustics at your venue, especially if s/he hasn't worked there before?

DJ Contract Points

☐ Date, exact time, and location of the reception.
☐ DJ's starting time and estimated total hours.
☐ During which stages of the reception s/he will perform.
☐ How many breaks they can take and whether taped music will play during that time.
☐ The name of the DJ(s).
☐ The name of an acceptable substitute in case of an emergency.
☐ Emcee duties, if any.
☐ Commitment to play key songs (and *not* play certain songs you hate).
☐ What equipment the DJ will bring and what you need to provide.
☐ What s/he should wear.
☐ Whether you'll be serving him/her a meal.
☐ The negotiated rate, plus hourly overtime fees.
☐ Cancellation and refund policy.

- What does the equipment look like? Does the DJ need a draped table for the CD player?
- What size are the speakers, and can they be camouflaged?
  - Does the DJ plan to use any funky lighting?
  - Is s/he comfortable with the emcee role as well as spinning tunes?

Who'll Spin the Disks?

At 1–800–Disc–Jockey (www.800discjockey.com/index2.htm), you can type in your area code and find local DJ listings.

Home-Grown DJ

If you're really tight on cash, take the do-it-yourself approach. Make great mixed tapes, or, better yet, borrow a 200-CD changer from a high-tech friend. Rent a high-quality sound system (your reception site might have one) and put a trusted friend or two in charge of the music. As long as you nab decent speakers, you're set.

Getting Everyone Groovin'

Any good band or DJ knows that there's an art to playing music. Like a well-constructed play, a party has a beginning, middle, and end. Your reception playlist should manipulate the audience skillfully, building up momentum and excitement with crowd-pleasing hits, providing an ample crescendo of the wildest and most party-friendly of tunes, and then winding things down with smooth, soulful, and sexy music. There are, as well, some super-important acts (your dances with each other and with your parents) that merit super songs.

Today's radio airwaves are awash with different types of music, from Harry Connick Jr.–mellow to Prodigy–hyper, from Celine Dion crooning to Puff Daddy rapping. For your reception, especially if most of your guests share your taste, you might choose one overall sound—hiring a reggae band or a country-western DJ, say. Most likely, however, you'll ask your musicians or DJ to play an eclectic mishmash of tunes. That way you have more of a chance of making *everybody* happy (all right, almost everybody—as far as your Uncle Simon is concerned, Duran Duran is the only band worth its weight in solid gold) and ensuring that your dance floor is permanently crowded.

The best wedding bands and DJs know that genre-bending is the key

---

ASK CARLEY

Getting Your Tunes Played

Q: A lot of people have told us they had trouble getting their band or DJ to play the songs they wanted. How can we avoid this?

A: Our number-one tip: Talk to other couples who have used the performer to make sure that s/he's the play-what-*you*-want type. Then take a few extra precautions. Print out a list of your must-have songs and at what stage of the party you'd like them played, if you have a preference. Give your DJ/bandleader the list well in advance of the big day so s/he can get hold of sheet music or recordings. Then put one of your friends—someone who's assertive and knows music—in charge of monitoring things during the reception. Your delegate should have your must-have list and be willing and able to coax your vendor into playing your songs.

to success. Even if you've enlisted the services of your favorite alternative-rock act, they should be open to going mainstream here and there, playing some Beatles or Aretha Franklin. Check that your DJ carries a potpourri of different records, so that even if you've asked for a predominantly hip-hop repertoire s/he'll be able to mix in some Kool & the Gang and Rolling Stones for variety's sake. Every genre has its charm and distinct way of moving people.

ASK CARLEY

Intergenerational Dancing

Q: We're inviting guests of all ages to our wedding, and we want there to be much dancing at the reception. Help!

A: No problem. What you need to focus on with your band or DJ is *variety*. Ask them to play songs that span a variety of decades, from 1930 Big Band standards to today's hits. Start the party off with songs so popular that everyone will know and enjoy them. Think Beatles, Elvis, Tina Turner—the major league. Disco classics, swing, and salsa are also intergenerational favorites. As the evening progresses—and presumably your less dance-happy relatives and friends of the family bid you adieu—feel free to shift into serious party mode, playing more dance, house, hip-hop, or alternative rock. With a healthy dose of sensitivity and open-mindedness, Frank Sinatra and Nirvana *can* coexist.

Dancers of the World Unite

Sure, organized dances are dorky, but with the right mix of good people, good champagne, good vibes, and good tunes, they also can be wildly entertaining. Depending on your musical tastes—and coordination—there are many different dances to do.

Country Western: Texas two-step ("Forever and Ever Amen" by Randy Travis); West Coast Swing; cha-cha; El Paso; Sweetheart Schottish; square dance ("Turkey in the Straw")

Ethnic Flair: horah (Jewish); depke (Greek); jig (Irish); tango (Latin America); tarantella (Italian); Highland fling (Scottish); polka (Polish)

Pure Goofiness: limbo; conga line (Cugat's "The Conga" or Barry Manilow's "Copacabana"); chicken dance; macarena

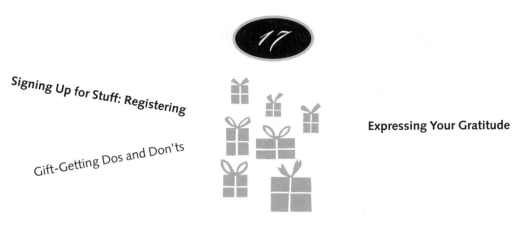

Giving and Getting

Well, it looks like you've hit the jackpot with this wedding thing: Weddings equal gifts galore. From your engagement announcement to beyond your big day, you'll to be showered with presents as loved ones celebrate your commitment. That means it's time to brush up on your knowledge of giving and getting.

Daydreaming about, registering for, and weathering the downpour of gadgets, trinkets, baubles, and cold, hard cash you'll get during the next year or so is one of the perkiest perks of engagement. What's really great, though, is the intense show of love and support these gifts represent. With their presents to you, your friends and family are blessing your union and contributing to your blissful future. Those thoughts are the best gifts of all—and a great motivator when it comes to penning those thank-you notes.

Signing Up for Stuff: Registering

Today's most popular present-related wedding tradition is, of course, the bridal registry. (Why it's called the bridal registry is beyond us—men use toasters, too!) This modern practice gets the happy couple prancing around a store (or a Web site), identifying objects that they would really, really like to own; having the retailer keep a record of these coveted items; passing on the word of where they've registered to family and close pals; giddily waiting as guests scout their choices and decide what to spring for; and receiving a bunch of packages containing their carefully selected treasures.

If registering sounds like winning the grand prize on a wacky game show, that's because it kind of is. You're big winners in the lottery of love, and registering is your reward.

Lest you think, however, that registering is a tacky fishing-for-presents tactic, remember that the most compelling reason for doing it is to help *your guests* in the daunting process of choosing gifts that you'll love and actually use. Sure, your closest friends and relatives probably have a good idea of the perfect wedding present for the two of you, something that will blow your socks off. But most people—those who aren't familiar with your board game fetish or your love of African art—need a hand. By registering (or at least making your gift preferences known to a select group of people who can discreetly spread the gospel), you're not dictating exactly what a guest should get you but rather offering a wide variety of suggestions guaranteed to make your day. Even if she chooses to be original and go out of registry, you've given her a good idea of the kinds of stuff you like, want, and need.

How to Do It: Registering Rx

Setting up a gift registry is not brain surgery, but there are some fundamental laws that will make the process go smoothly. With a little research, advance planning, and attention to detail, you two can quickly become bona fide gift gurus.

Time It Right: It's a good idea to set up a registry soon after your engagement, in time for all those prewedding bashes. In general, department stores suggest you firm up your present plans six to nine months before the big day. But since most gifts actually are purchased closer to your wedding, it makes sense to register even if you have only two months or less left— just get the word out lickety-split. On the other end, if you have more than one year to go before your big day, *don't* register right away; items you select now could go out of stock, even be discontinued, by wedding time.

Know Thyselves: Classic home accessories such as formal place settings, silverware, and fancy bed linens are customary registry items (and sweet things to have), but that may not be your bag. Maybe you've been playing house for a while and you already own all that stuff. Or perhaps you're into minimalist decor or eating out every single night of your lives. Luckily, today's couples have a huge range of options when it comes to registering, from contributions toward a dream honeymoon to handsome hardware tools. Whether you're going the major department store route or registering at a funky local boutique, sit down as a team and figure out what type of stuff you want to focus on. This will cut down on leg cramps caused by too much time spent wandering the aisles and paper cuts resulting from excessive catalog skimming. Having trouble finding a route that makes both of you smile? Set up two registries—one for his gourmet cookware, one for your outdoorsy gear.

Get in the Know: Once you've narrowed down your options, get some important info on your dream store's registry policies (or how it can

Register at Home

Exhausted from trolling the aisles in search of the perfect stuff to register for? Register online—it's super-convenient! At The Knot's Wedding Gift Registry (www.theknot.com) you can sign up for everything from a tent to fine china, from Colombian coffee to bath towels. You'll make your guests' lives easier, too; they can shop from home. Call 1-888-WED-KNOT (888-933-5668) for information.

We Can't
Give It Back

Don't register at a shop that has unreasonable return deadlines. You don't want to get back from your honeymoon and find out you're stuck with four electric toothbrushes, useful as they are.

accommodate you if it doesn't have an established program). To figure out if what it's got is going to work for you, ask lots of questions:

- How do they keep track of the registry? Ideally, you want the store to use a computer database, so gifts can be checked off your wish list as they're bought.
- Do they accept credit-card purchases by phone or fax? If you have lots of guests coming from far away, you want them to be able to use your registry easily. The shop should be able to fax your guests your wish list and take their orders from a distance.
- Do they ship? Your best bet is a retailer that can arrange direct shipment of your gifts to an address you give them (yours, your honey's parents, etc.) so guests are spared a trip to the post office or the hassle (for them *and* you) of bringing gifts to the reception.
- Do they allow for easy refunds/exchanges? Even with the best technology in place, you may end up with duplicates and triplicates of some items. (You're also entitled to change your mind about those orange mohair drapes.) Make sure you're not stuck with them.
- How long will they keep your registry list? Make sure it stays in the store's system for at least a year after your wedding day, because that's how long guests have—etiquette-wise—to buy their gifts.

Get the Goods Now

When you register, make sure the items you're selecting are not way back-ordered and that the store has them readily in stock. You don't want to wait until your one-year anniversary for that leopard-print bed set (grrrrr!).

ASK CARLEY

No Gifts, Please!

Q: We want to put "please no gifts" on our invites because we disagree with the obligatory gift tradition. Are we tacky or rude for doing this? Are we the only ones who just want our guests to spend our special day with us?

A: Writing "your presence is your present" (or some such) on your invites is a nice way to let guests know that their attendance is the most special part for you—and that you don't want or expect gifts (which, by the way, are common but *not* mandatory). There are many good reasons for not wanting more stuff in your lives; you're not freaks. Perhaps you've been living together for a while and feel you have everything you need. Maybe you're getting married in an exotic location or are planning on a full week of wedding events and don't want your guests to have to spend yet more.

At the same time, recognize that most guests will *want* to get you a gift, something to help you begin your marriage with a bang. People derive joy from giving. While it's not tacky or rude specifically to ask for no gifts, it may make some guests feel awkward. One option is to spread the no-present-please word through close friends and relatives instead of jotting it on the invites. You also could indicate that you'd like guests to make a donation in your name to a favorite charity, so they still feel like they're doing something that makes you happy.

Grace Yourselves: The Traditional Registry

A classic registry includes essential items for a distinguished home, most important of which is the fine dinnerware that a freshly engaged couple (much like yourselves) probably doesn't have yet. We're talking about china, crystal, sterling silver, the works. Even if you think of yourselves as more Cap'n Crunch than caviar, there are some compelling reasons to consider registering for elegant tableware:

It looks great and adds instant pizzazz to any dinner party.

It's perfect for romantic, candlelit dinners for two. (Just remember to clear the table before you hop aboard for—umm—dessert.)

It makes you two bona fide adults.

It can be a beautiful decorative addition to your home—china hung on walls or crystal showcased in a glass cabinet is très elegant.

It's expensive! Might as well let someone else pick up the tab!

If you decide that you want to go the formal dinnerware route, here's what you're looking for:

China: Select a pattern that both of you like, in either procelain or bone. Don't be turned off by visions of your grandmother's cluttered birds-castles-hares-and-fierce-warriors china design; today's fine dishes come in a wide variety of styles, including many simple and chic options. Register for up to twelve five-piece place settings (dinner plate, salad plate, bread and butter plate, cup, and saucer) plus twelve rimmed soup/salad bowls. You also may want to sign up for some matching service pieces (large bowls, platters, a tea set, etc.).

Stemware: Today's crystal designers are keeping the young and hip in mind when doing their thing, carving out sleek and stylish designs. Or you can go the ultra-ornate, romantic crystal route. Register for up to twelve each of water goblets, white wineglasses, red wineglasses, and champagne flutes as well as other barware, such as double old-fashioned glasses, highballs, martini glasses, and a pitcher.

Flatware: The crème de la crème of cutlery is made of sterling silver, which is sparkling, elegant, gorgeous. Regular flatware, made of stainless steel, is slightly less expensive—and has the advantage of being dishwasher-friendly. Whatever you decide, you'll find a wide variety of cuts, ranging from classic curvaceous to modern flat; just find one that just makes you want to stick it in your mouth *now!* Register for up to twelve flatware settings (dinner knife, dinner fork, soup spoon, salad/dessert fork, and teaspoon). You also may register for serving utensils (large spoons and forks, a gravy ladle, a cake server, etc.) and butter spreaders.

Sealing the Deal: After you've selected the gift-registry program/s for you, make sure that it's organized in a way that makes your—and your guests'—lives easier.

- Ask for a registry form on which to indicate your desired objects. Either with the help of a store consultant (usually available at big retailers) or on your own, tour the store, Web site, or catalog, recording things you want. Include as much detail as possible for any given item, including color, stock number, pattern, size, and number of items where appropriate (these are usually part of the registry form).

- After you've done your picking and choosing, get a master list. Scan it carefully and correct any errors. Make sure the mailing address where you want your gifts to go is clearly indicated.
- Remember to get the name of a contact person when you are setting up your registry, possibly the registry consultant who guided you through the store. You want to deal with someone who'll know who you are when you call.
- Throughout your engagement, ask for periodic printouts of your registry list to keep tabs on the process, especially after each wave of gifts arrives (engagement party, shower, etc.). Cross off any purchased gifts the store didn't catch. It also should be possible for you to add more items to your list if you find that your generous loved ones are cleaning out your registry.

Gift-Getting Dos and Don'ts

As you can imagine, there's a lot of etiquette surrounding wedding gifts. There's the don't-include-registry-cards-in-invites cardinal rule, the write-thank-you-notes-or-else edict, and, of course, the be-tactful-about-returns law. We trust your healthy, sensible instincts, but we're sure you'll be happy to glean some more wisdom from our vast wedding experience. Here, then, is what we think about some sticky gift subjects.

Money, Money, Money: Cash Gifts

Let's say every single engaged couple in the country were to cram into a huge stadium and we were to ask them (over a high-power loudspeaker system) to raise their hands if they wanted to get cash, cool cash as their wedding gift. Our hunch is that there would be a whole lot of arms in the air. Obviously, there's a good reason for this enthusiasm—more and more young couples already have been living on their own (or together) for a while, and they may own all the plates, towels, sheets, and forks they could ever want. Engagement may be the first time they start thinking seriously about their long-term financial goals—financing a dream honeymoon, buying a house or a cool set of wheels, building up adequate savings for retirement—and some meaty checks would certainly help out.

If you've got dollar sign–gift aspirations, the first thing to remember is *not* to put your wish for moola on your invites. Instead, tell close friends and family that cash is your gift preference; they'll spread the news when guests ask them. Guests who give you checks will either mail them or bring the loot to your wedding, in a card. (Appoint a responsible friend to keep the money on his/her person.)

Consider Guests' Budgets

Register for gifts in a variety of price ranges, with an emphasis on the $50 to $100 range. It's fine to choose some super-pricey pieces perfect for group gifts, but nice-but-reasonable choices like vases, kitchen appliances, pillowcases, and wineglasses will make you happy without turning your loved ones into paupers.

Create a Registry

If a shop the two of you love doesn't have a registry program, approach the manager and see if you can work something out.

- Photocopy your wish list.
- Ask the manager to keep master list near the register and check off gifts as they're bought.
- Make sure the store can accept credit-card orders over the phone.
- Check in regularly to make sure list is being updated, see if you need to add items, and so on.

Weddings
in the
Real World

244

Go to Chapter 25
for tips on getting
your financial house
in order.

The most important things to remember about cash gifts are: (1) don't impulse-spend; (2) stash your money away in a joint bank account or, preferably, a high-interest mutual fund; (3) have specific goals in mind so you won't be tempted to fritter your bounty away on run-of-the-mill bills *(not* romantic). Decide together that you want any money you receive to go toward a down payment on a house, your annual vacation fund, the biggest stereo system you can get, or another major investment. You may want to enlist the help of a recommended financial planner after you come back from your honeymoon so s/he can tell you how best to put your money to work for you.

GAYLE AND IRA
July 13
Benton Harbor, Michigan

WHEN GAYLE AND IRA were planning their wedding, they were looking for the right way to address an issue that was important to them—the fact that they could legalize their commitment when their lesbian and gay friends could not. "We were looking forward to this wonderful day," Gayle says, "and all the love and affirmation you get from everyone, and we found it painful that we would be gaining rights and privileges that our friends are denied."

The couple decided to address this through an unusual "registry": They included cards in their invitations requesting that gifts be in the form of donations to Lambda Legal Defense Fund's Marriage Project, a task force working toward legalization of gay marriage in the United States. "It's a very small step, but it felt important," Ira says. It also helped make their wedding a very personal expression of their values and their shared vision of the world.

Present Potholes: How to Deal

Not every gift you receive is going to be perfect, despite your loved ones' best intentions. Deal with these duds with grace, honesty (okay, white lies), sensitivity, and—most important—gratitude.

Broken Gifts: If the present was shipped by a store, you should be able to get a quick replacement by calling the customer service department. If the package was sent by givers directly, check for a postal insurance stamp. If there is one, simply mail the gift back, with a note of thanks and an explanation, and your friends will be reimbursed by the post office; then they'll rebuy and resend.

If the gift was neither sent by the store nor insured, it's your decision whether to inform the giver of the mishap or not. If you have a hunch the gift was bought using a credit card or carries some sort of insurance policy (i.e., the givers are wise/cautious/credit card-happy), do tell, because they can get an exchange easily and would be sorely disappointed if you didn't get to enjoy their present! However, if the piece looks like a one of a kind or you suspect the giver is creditless, you don't want to make your guest feel like she has to get you *another* gift; send a normal, gushing thank-you note. If you're asked later where the gift is, you always can blame your own personal clumsiness in its demise.

Duplicates: Sometimes—in the case of place settings, bath towels, and margarita glasses—doubles and triples aren't a bad thing. You can stash them away for when their kin break, tear, or wear. However, in the case of sterling silver tea tray, for example, one *is* enough. The great thing about exchanging duplicate gifts is that givers usually will never know you did it. Since you are keeping one of the thing, whatever it may be, you can conveniently attribute it to *all* of the givers (not at the same dinner party, though). If two close friends got you the same thing, however, honesty is the best policy. If asked about the gift, explain you received doubles and show your friend the fab replacement gift you got instead.

Unwanted Wares: It's not broken or duplicated, it's just ugly (not your style). When it comes to exchanging gifts like those Eskimo salt-and-pepper shakers and that Velvet Elvis, be sensitive. If the giver is a close friend or relative who probably will be visiting a lot, you

Great Monetary Gift Traditions

- China: Guests give the couple money at reception in red envelopes.
- Italy: The reception ends with a receiving (or is it parting?) line, in which guests are given a box or satchel of candies in exchange for envelopes of money.
- Poland: Guests "buy" a dance with the bride to contribute to the couple's honeymoon fund.

ASK CARLEY
Cancel the Gifts!

Q: If the wedding is called off, do gifts already received have to be returned?
A: Yes. All engagement, shower, *and* wedding gifts, as well as any money, should be sent back to the givers in the case of a breakup. However, if it's been a long time since you got the gift, if you've used the thing, or if you know the giver really well and think s/he would want you to keep it, it's definitely your call whether to return or not to return.

may want to bite the bullet and keep the gift (bringing it out only on visitation days) for your communal happiness. It's fine, however, to exchange a gift from someone who is unlikely either to come over or to get his/her feelings hurt. In any case, do not mention exchanges in your thank-you notes.

Cashing In?

Make sending out thank-yous for cash gifts a priority. The envelopes and cards money comes in are easy to lose, and guests may fear you didn't receive their present if they don't hear from you promptly.

Go to Chapter 9 for info on ordering your thank-you notes and other stationery.

Expressing Your Gratitude

One of the wonderful things about getting married is witnessing your loved ones rallying for you and pulling out all the stops to make your big day huge. It's incredible the amount of love, generosity, kindness, support, and even out-and-out sacrifice they display during this period. It's of utmost importance, we're sure you'll agree, to show your gratitude for all this devotion. Here are some pointers on giving thanks where thanks is due.

Thank-You Notes

All right, then, brace yourselves. As fast and loose as we are about all this etiquette stuff, we are definitely *not* letting you off the hook in one department: thank-you notes. Simply put, you've got to thank every single gift-giver. No exceptions! Not optional! Engagement, shower, and wedding presents all apply. Limber up those wrists—it's thanksgiving time.

Who? We are only going to say this once—*both of you* are responsible for sending out thank-you notes. We don't care how bad your handwriting is or how much stress you're under at the office, the gifts you've received were intended for both of you and the karma police insist you both reciprocate. In order to establish equality on this front, divvy up your thank-you list. You send notes to *your* friends, family, and family friends; your honey does the same for his/her posse. Guests who "belong" to both of you get split down the middle.

Why? Because it's the nice thing to do, the right thing to do. Thanking people for their gifts reassures them that you got what they sent. And since most people have their gifts shipped (unless we're talking about engagement party or shower goodies), your thank-you cards are their only way of knowing you actually received the goods.

Organized Gratitude

Keep a copy of your invitation mailing list and record every gift you get, as you get it, next to the giver's name. That way you can be sure of writing thank-yous that are accurate, descriptive, and personal—and you'll have your guests' addresses at your fingertips.

When? Etiquette says you should send out thank-yous within one month of receiving a gift (even less time than that when you receive something *before* the wedding). We'll give you a little more leeway; we're hip to how hard it is to juggle your jobs, your busy social life, and honeymoon recovery. Don't get your hopes up too high—we're giving you a few more weeks, not years. You have two months from the time you get back from your 'moon to send out those notes. If you each put aside fifteen minutes daily (or every other day) toward this end, you probably can bang them out at a rate of ten a day. Besides, it'll be fun together time for the two of you. (Play tunes, drink wine/hot chocolate.)

How? Traditionally, thank-you notes are written in blue or black ink on simple ecru sheets or folded cards that match your invites. Consider having your stationer create cards with your married name/s or monograms, a pop-up ape holding a "thank-you" banana, colors that match your vibrant reception decorating scheme—or make them yourselves! Whatever you do, remember to purchase/create plenty of cards—you don't want to run out.

What Should They Say? Quite simply, a thank-you note expresses how grateful you are for a gift. The essential thing is to personalize each note by naming the present and addressing your unique relationship with the giver. It doesn't have to be a work of genius; a dash of humor and a sprinkle of loving sentiment are all you need.

Even if the gift wasn't (how shall we say) a "hit," and you're planning to exchange it or sock it away in the dark recesses of your junk closet, still allude to it in your note. You don't have to lie and say you're going to put that Godzilla rug smack in front of your fireplace, but you can say you're sure it will be all the rage at your next cocktail party. Make each guest feel like the effort in selecting your gift was duly noted.

You also should be specific when thanking someone for a gift of money; give as much detail as you possibly can about how you plan to put the generous gift to use (as part of a house downpayment or second honeymoon, for example).

The Gifts You Give

Some people's roles in your wedding were, undoubtedly, much greater than just showing up and getting you a groovy gift. Whether their contribution was of money, time, or just old-fashioned running-around-doing-stuff energy, they deserve extra-special thanks for making your wedding the best that it could be. Buying gifts for these amazing individuals should be one of the most enjoyable parts of your wedding planning, a time to let your creative juices flow.

Family: Although it's easy to take them for granted, chances are your folks (and/or your siblings, grandparents, and other close relatives) were an indispensable part of your wedding brigade. Whether they contributed to your budget, scoped out vendors, or provided you a shoulder to cry on, let them know how grateful you are for their support by giving them a personalized gift at your rehearsal dinner or in a more private meeting just before your big day.

Many gifts are appropriate for your parents, from extravagant (a second honeymoon/weekend getaway) to sentimental (a blown-up wedding picture in a nice frame). For other family members, gifts of wedding mementos are great, from lockets with your portrait inside or framed reception snapshots to scarves in your wedding colors and CDs featured heavily during your reception party. If you're strapped for cash, sometimes the nicest thank-you for relatives is the honor of being the first people invited over to see honeymoon pics/slides. Cook up a tasty meal (served on your brand-new dinnerware) and make a festive evening out of it. If your parents and your honey's are friendly, invite them over together—and kill two birds with one lasagna and slide show.

Attendants' Gifts

- Spa certificates
- Champagne and caviar
- Picnic baskets
- Cufflinks, jewelry, and money clips
- Swiss Army knives
- Tickets to a game or play
- Silk or flannel pajamas
- Beer of the month club
- Cigars, flasks, lighters
- Journals, photo boxes, stationery
- Beauty basket, bath soaps, perfume

Go to Chapter 6 for all you need to know about prewedding thank-you fests.

Attendants: They calmed your nerves, did your bidding, chatted up your parents' friends. Let's not forget those prewedding parties they helped organize. Give each attendant a gift of gratitude; go a little bigger for the honor attendant and best man. The rehearsal dinner is again a good time for giving, or you can throw a bridesmaids'/attendants' party shortly before the wedding. (We're highly in favor of a special fest exclusively for these hardworking troopers.)

You can go the traditional route and give your attendants something they can wear on the big day, such as cuff links, earrings, bracelets, or silk cravats. You can get everyone an identical item or (our preference) personalize the gifts; for example, your boating friend gets anchor cuff links, financial man gets dollar signs, actor boy gets masks. It's also cool to get your attendants something that has nothing to do with your wedding but everything to do with their enjoyment, such as ritzy bath product baskets or martini glasses.

Out of Town Guests: It's not compulsory, but we just love the idea of showing your devotion to friends and relatives who've made a long haul to come to your wedding. Place a goodie bag or basket in each hotel room before your guests show up. (Ask the hotel early on about distributing your gifts to your guests' rooms.) Our favorite out-of-towner gifts: small wine bottle and box of truffles; guide to the city and a disposable camera; gift bag of small bottles from a bath shop; certificate for a massage (or another amenity) at the hotel; a gourmet fruit basket.

Yourselves: Why not give yourselves a hand for all the hard work, the love, sweat, and tears you poured into making your relationship—and your wedding—such a rip-roaring success? On wedding day, exchange gifts that express your gratitude, devotion, and passion; a mushy card is a must. Getting a wrapped package on the morning of your wedding will help take your minds off the nerves and put an extra bounce in your step. Give your honey an outfit s/he's always wanted, a piece of jewelry, a book with an inscription, a spa certificate, expensive cigars, and the like. Have a private give-and-get session before you start getting ready.

Hosts with the Most

Don't forget to thank all your wedding party hosts (your honor attendant, your neighbors, or your coworkers) with a gift and grateful note. Flowers, wine, or a gourmet food basket are all good choices.

Anniversary Gifts

1st: Paper. Deluxe stationery set, hand-bound photo album, antique book of love poems, gift certificates.
2nd: Cotton. Luxurious bathrobe, chenille sweater, sexy undergarments, pajamas.
3rd: Leather. Cool pants or coat, nice bag or briefcase, fancy organizer, exquisite belt.
4th: Linen. Luxury bedding, nice summer outfit, a hammock.
5th: Wood. Hand-crafted bowl, antique chest, trip to the woods, rocking chair.
6th: Iron. Wrought bed frame, fancy candlesticks, gym membership (iron abs and buns).
7th: Wool. Cozy blanket or shawl, month's worth of warm socks, trip to Wales. (Lots of sheep there.)
8th: Bronze. Deluxe cookware (bronze, copper—close enough), sculpture, piece of jewelry.
9th: Pottery. An art class, certificates for mud mask (and other spa treatments).
10th: Aluminum: Set of fancy silverware, unique choker, durable hiking boots, fireplace tools.
Other important anniversaries: 15th—Crystal; 20th—China; 25th—Silver; 30th—Pearls; 40th—Rubies; 50th—Gold; 60th—Diamonds.

Fending Off Your Family

Managing Money Madness

Passion Patrol

Religious Rifts

The Challenge of Change

Fighting Right

Cures for Cold Feet

Love Patrol

At first, getting engaged seemed like the perfect culmination of a passionate romance. It added a new sheen to your usual routine. Work passed more quickly. You walked around in a haze of just-engaged joy. Your copy of the *Kama Sutra* became downright dog-eared from use. But then . . . the details of wedding planning came slamming down like a meat cleaver, cutting right through your relationship.

Welcome to engagement. While getting married is the first step to an eternity of sublime togetherness, the actual planning process can be so tension-ridden that it threatens to tear you apart. Wedding planning brings life's five major flash points speeding toward you all at once—family, money, sex, religion, and change. And the resulting arguments and doubts can put a strain on your relationship. We're here to help steer you through the labyrinth of engagement-time tension and get your relationship back on the freeway of love. Read on.

Fending Off Your Family

Your mom wants the reception at her country club. Your honey's dad wants it at the restaurant he owns stock in. Your honey thought maybe you'd hold it at the bowling alley where you had your first date. And none of them understands why you're being driven nuts! Will the Number-One Wedding-Planning Stress Factor please stand up? Let's hear it for families. Weddings are rarely just about the couple getting married. If you're getting flak from your folks that's causing you two to tangle, try these solutions.

Present a United Front

Wedding planning has a way of pitting people against each other—even madly in love to-be-weds. Decide how you feel about various elements *together,* before discussing them with your family. Even if your parents are paying for the wedding, your honey's opinion should matter most to you (along with your own). Don't let your parents think they can get their way by cornering you alone. And don't promise your mom a full seated dinner in a hotel ballroom unless you check it out with your partner first (who, it turns out, had his heart set on hot dogs at the park).

Focus the Interference

The two of you should decide what you do and don't care about. (Big dress? Yes! Big band? Whatever.) Then talk with your parents about which elements they feel strongly about. Ask for their help with those things that are more important to them and less so to you.

If they're helping pay, you might ask them to foot the bill for specific items—such as the band, the bar, and the food—rather than underwriting the whole thing, allowing you to maintain some control. Or reconcile yourselves to planning the ceremony and letting them go wild with the reception. And comfort yourselves with the fact that you can live your lives exactly as you want to *after* the wedding.

Don't Betray Each Other

Trying to appease the parents—at the expense of your sweetie—can make your future spouse feel like a second-class citizen. Family loyalty should not mean dissing your honey. Don't let yourself be pressured to reveal a confidence, expose an insecurity, or make a plan that you know conflicts with your honey's belief system. If you find yourself fighting with

---

ASK CARLEY

Shy of the Spotlight?

Q: I love the idea of being married, but I hate the thought of being the complete focus of the party on wedding day. The anxiety is making me tense and mean. Is there a way to avoid being the center of attention during my wedding?
A: Not entirely—but if it really freaks you out, there are ways to minimize it. First, admit your discomfort to your honey (and apologize for being snappish!). Together you can figure out ways to handle your stress.

Some suggestions:

Have a couple's shower so he can share the limelight.
Skip the whole "dining-on-stage" head table thing. Sit at a regular, floor-level reception table.
Make your first dance a family or all-couples affair.
Let your family and friends know that you'd like to keep a relatively low profile, so they don't plan a surprise party, stage a two-hour toast-a-thon, or send a congratulatory strip-o-gram to work.
Share the spotlight with others. Include special people in the ceremony (as readers, performers, speakers, child attendants) and the reception (dance leaders, toasters, greeters). Make it a cast of dozens, rather than your star turn.

your sweetie about something you don't actually care about, figure out who else is in the room (in your head, rather). Once you're married, "looking out for number one" means watching out for yourself *and* your partner. Start practicing now.

Go to Chapter 20 for more help with family.

Managing Money Madness

First-place wedding flash point—money. Just because you love each other doesn't mean you like each other's fiscal policies. Your expectations and approaches to the green stuff (not to mention the amount your parents can contribute) may vary greatly, particularly if you come from different backgrounds. How can you avoid conflicts over cash?

Agree on a Budget

Face it—there's *never* enough cash. But you can have an awesome wedding with whatever you've got in your coffers. Set an objective, *joint* budget and stick to it. Put your money into a shared pot, and forever after refer to it as *Our* Budget. No pointing fingers or subtly inflicting guilt. This is Your Budget, and you've both got to deal with it.

Reconcile Family Fortunes

If your honey's family owns the Chrysler Corporation and your family owns . . . a car, you quite likely learned different ways of dealing with dough. When you find yourselves fighting over finances, stop. Back up. And look at the issue objectively. Are you really ready to kill each other over the relative merits of caviar versus chili? Or are you defending your family's honor ("They may not be well off, but they're honest!") while your honey is championing his clan ("They're not crooks, just smart!")? This isn't about which family is better or which of you is right. You had different experiences, and you need to devise a joint financial approach that works for you both. Talk about the ways your families dealt with money, what you liked and didn't like. Chances are you both learned some pretty valuable tactics that you can combine to create a new and improved fiscal policy.

Separate Money from Emotion

We've all done it—mistakenly judged one's commitment by his/her willingness to spend C-notes. If you're putting 20 percent of your income toward the wedding and your honey isn't, you might feel that her reluctance to pay means she's only lukewarm about the marriage. She, meanwhile, may think your willingness to drop a bundle on a heated buffet means you're not serious about planning for future needs.

Take a look at the offending person's financial past. If her behavior is consistent with her track record, that's a good sign that this is a question of loot, not love. Talk with the tightwad (sorry, financially responsible partner), or spendthrift (um, live-for-the-moment one) calmly about her approach. Really listen. And then try to explain that her spending policy is making you feel unloved. See if there are nonfinancial ways you each can express your commitment to the marriage. By separating money from emotion, you've got a better shot at dealing with both elements more sanely.

Go to Chapter 4 for help creating a wedding budget you both can live with.

CAROLYN AND MATTHEW
September 7, New York City

"A PRENUPTIAL AGREEMENT is an uncomfortable thing to discuss, so I think it's important to see how your partner responds to the issue," Carolyn says. "I asked Matthew one night at dinner, and luckily we felt similarly about it." The couple knew they would have a prenup, but, says Carolyn, "When we finally did the agreement it was extremely stressful because we left it until a few days before the wedding, which is the *worst* time to do it. You're feeling so happy and romantic and a prenuptial agreement is cold and harsh."

Although it was sobering, Carolyn says she found the experience ultimately empowering. "Women often are not brought up to think about money. If you have a career, however, and you're going to have children, you need to think about issues such as 'What happens if I give up my career?' You're not just protecting yourself, you're protecting your children." Carolyn acknowledges that as a romantic, she finds the idea of a prenuptial agreement somewhat sad but that, in reality, it has helped her relationship with Matthew. "It opens communication about important issues and makes you talk about things like your will, which you might not talk about otherwise," she says. "It's not for everyone, but it is something the couple needs to agree on."

Passion Patrol

Sex is one of the most important intimacy builders in a relationship and, sad to say, one of the first things to go when people get overwhelmed. Desire is a complex mix of emotion, attraction, and straight-out libido—a delicate brew that can get out of balance when you're stressed out, exhausted, angry, frustrated, or scared. Not to mention busy. Juggling the many tasks of getting married can leave precious little time for doin' the nasty.

Your pending wedding adds some unique pressures to your bedroom life. You may wake up in a cold sweat, staring down those big questions: "Will our sex life grow bland once we're wed?" "Will we still find each other attractive?" and "Is our sex really good enough to be the only sex we have, as long as we both shall live?" Not to mention, "What if we don't do it well together?" for you first-timers.

Relax. A lot of married couples we know say that their sex lives actually improved *after* the wedding. They grew more comfortable with each other and gained the confidence to spice things up with experimentation. As they say, practice makes perfect. Meanwhile, the planning process can take a big bite out of your love life. Here are some ways to bite back.

Procrastinate and Be Blissful

When it comes to putting the passion back in your love life, a little procrastination can go a long way. Here are our scientifically proven remedies for plummeting pleasure; they also can be used preventively.

Movie and Make-Out: Take the afternoon off work (tell your boss it's an emergency—not a lie, technically) and go see back-to-back screenings of two hot new flicks (or romantic oldies). Buy a jumbo popcorn-and-soda combo (hey, you'll save $1!) and a pack of Twizzlers. Before the previews, practice your synchronized licorice-eating skills (nibble from opposite sides). Sit in the back so you can sneak in plenty of smooching.

Healthy Healing: Save up and book full-day spa treatments for both of you on your next free Saturday. Wake up early, have a lavish breakfast, and surrender yourselves to hours of massages, facials, and wraps. See if the spa can seat you next to each other for treatments. (Strapped for cash? Opt for a do-it-yourself spa at home.)

Recycled Fun: Tool around the closest flea market, garage sale, or antique and collectibles store. Play the $5 game: You each have five bucks to buy a gift for the other, not a penny more. When you're done rummaging, go to a bistro or diner and exchange presents.

Play Games: Pull out your dusty board games (or go buy brand-new editions), stock up on soda, beer, and munchies, and spend an evening in hot competition. You'll work out any couple "issues" you may have and be reminded that two is better than one. (Solitaire sucks!) Ah, yes—any one of these venerable games can be adapted to the Strip variety.

Afternoon Delight: Take a long lunch break and meet at your favorite secret spot—in the middle of a bridge, on a park bench, on the observation deck of the tallest building—for an afternoon rendezvous like in some steamy French film. Bag a lunch and a bottle of wine for your clandestine date. After a few long, passionate kisses, head back to work, truly refreshed.

Use Your Mouth

To talk, that is. Discuss your fears, concerns, and sexual preferences. Give each other guidance. Read a few good manuals. Be open about your issues. If you have different ideas (religious or otherwise) about the role of sex or different levels of desire, talk about those, too. The nitty-gritty of creating a killer sex life takes time and communication.

Make Time for Sex

Too busy to have sex? Take a break and *just do it*. If the stamps don't get stuck tonight, they'll stick tomorrow. Be flexible. If you're too tired at bedtime, make love in the morning. Or right before dinner, after *Friends,* or on your lunch break. There's no right time (or place) for sex. Make a standing sex date, if you have to, to ensure you fit it in. (Thursday, at seven. In the bedroom. Be there.) And when you get the urge to bring up a great centerpiece idea during foreplay, bite your tongue.

First-Time Fears

Waiting until after the wedding to do the deed? No wonder you're nervous. Discuss your fears with your sweetie. Plan to go very slowly on that first night, and remember that sex gets better as you grow more comfortable with each other. If you don't see fireworks on your wedding night, it doesn't mean you never will! You'll have to keep on trying. (Not a bad deal!) For you, the work of creating a compatible night life will come after the wedding.

Religious Rifts

Planning your ceremony can bring up all the major how-will-you-handle-religion questions—where you'll worship, how you'll raise your kids, where you'll spend holidays. If you have different religions, these issues can take on the complexity of an international summit. But even if you share the same religion or spiritual beliefs, you may not share the same level of intensity or involvement. Small differences may start seeming like chasms. How do you keep religion from ripping you apart?

Respect Each Other (and Yourself)

You go to church every Sunday; your sweetie refuses to step inside a chapel. You fear she'll ask you to stop going, while she's afraid you'll try to pressure her to join the church choir. What do you do? Make a pact to maintain your individual feelings about faith. You continue to go to church, alone or with family and friends. She'll worship as she sees fit. No pressuring each other to change. Don't turn your back on your beliefs—but don't expect her to do so for you, either.

Whose Beliefs Are These?

Your parents are worried you'll abandon the faith they taught you once you marry "that heathen," and you're letting their fears affect you? Stop, and take some time to figure out which beliefs are yours—and which are theirs. You don't have to live according to their practices, and neither does your sweetie. Let them know that your beliefs are *your* beliefs— not theirs or your partner's—and you can manage your own faith, thank you very much.

Make a Plan for the Future

You want your kids to go to Hebrew school (or weekly Marxist theory classes) and he says absolutely not? Now is the time to talk about how the two of you will deal. Map out a game plan. By figuring out where you stand as a couple, you'll be better able to field questions from others.

Go to Chapter 19 for more help dealing with interfaith headaches.

The Challenge of Change

Even if you've been dating since high school, getting married is a major threshold to cross—your lives will be different forever after. It's normal to feel anxiety in the face of so much change—even when something better is about to come along. Change is pretty much the major life stress factor. (Right up there with divorce and moving, which you also may know something about.) If fear of change is giving you the jitters, read on.

Have That Last Fling

As you feel your single life slipping through your fingers, you may find yourself clinging desperately to old habits, suddenly aching for activities that grew boring years ago. (All-night club-hopping? A slumber party with the girls? Party on!) The good news is, that's your fear of change speaking, not some latent desire to regress. Go ahead and indulge yourself. (In moderation, of course—you can't handle hangovers the way you used to!) Fill your sweetie in on your plans, and ask him to be patient with your bout of temporary insanity. If your honey is the antsy one, encourage him to hit the town. Give each other space. Chances are, you'll both remember exactly why you put your past behind you in the first place. (Were clubs always this smoky? And loud? And expensive?)

Recognize That Change Equals Loss

Every time you make a major life change, you're going to feel some sense of loss; it's one of those quirks of human nature. And a wedding is a big bucket of change. Gaining a permanent partner also means losing your single status. Moving in together also means leaving your bachelor pad behind. Marrying the Prince of Monaco also means kissing your summers backpacking across Europe with your three closest guy friends good-bye.

Acknowledge your feelings of loss, but don't confuse them with regret; they don't mean you're making the wrong decision. Feel sad about what you're giving up, and then focus on what you're gaining. You might even mark this rite of passage in some fun, silly way—turn your little black book over to your best pal with grand ceremony, or write a guide on the fine art of flirting (based on your years of experience) to present to your little sister. Whatever you need to do, try not to take these feelings out on each other.

How's Marriage Different from Living Together?

If you have been living together, you've already made a lot of the changes that can come with marriage. (He's learned to differentiate between potpourri and party mix, usually; she tolerates Howard Stern.) But if you think nothing more can change when you tie the knot, you may be surprised by some of these factors:

Your sense of stability: You always can move out of a live-in arrangement, and you've probably thought about it at least once. But lots couples who lived together first say that marriage closed this escape hatch, really solidifying their sense of being a team.

The way your in-laws/parents treat you: Parents tend to see a live-in as a transitory fixture and avoid making an emotional commitment. Once you're married, however, they may come running over with that emotional Welcome Wagon.

The way acquaintances/strangers treat you: You may suddenly garner more respect among your conservative work mates/fishing buddies/shop clerks. Saying "I must go meet my wife" carries greater clout than "I've got to go get my girlfriend."

The way your honey's insurance policy treats you: Bring on those benefits!

Your legal status: Yep, it's time for the joint tax return, the merged bank account—physical factors that reiterate the seriousness of your union.

Your expectations of your spouse: You may discover an untapped marital routine lurking in the back of your brain. "Dinner is at six, damn it!" you find yourself saying. "Be at the table, napkin under chin!" Or "It's time for you to go get a *real* job now, Messenger Boy!" Try to use these last months of living together as a "practice marriage" to avoid being clobbered by your own unexpected expectations after the wedding.

Stay Single *and* Be Married

Fearing your individuality will dissolve into your couplehood? You're not alone. Keeping your own identity intact can be one of the toughest challenges of making the big hook-up. Create some boundaries for yourself. Set up a once-a-week gin game with the girls. Sign up for that ballet, accounting, or karate class you've been thinking about. By working to maintain your own interests and friends, you actually help make your marriage stronger.

Fighting Right

What happens when all these stress factors bear down on you at once? The big explosion. The showdown. The ultimate match. We're talking big-time fighting. It may seem like you disagree on absolutely everything about your wedding—from the ceremony site to the honeymoon—and your fighting tactics have reached new lows. (You've slammed the door so many times, the frame is wobbly.) And then there are all these decisions to make, enough cause for constant conflict even if you weren't feeling so much pressure. All this strife may even make you wonder if you'll actually get along for the long haul.

The good news? All of this potential fighting material provides a great test case for how you'll handle problems later on. While life may not be a dress rehearsal (according to the great bumper-sticker soothsayer), wedding planning is. The important thing is not to avoid conflicts but to learn how to handle them—*now.*

ALISON AND CRAIG
September 6, Rhinebeck, New York

"THE PROBLEMS IN OUR relationship didn't go away just because we got engaged," Alison says. "In fact, after the engagement they seemed all the more important. For example, Craig and I don't fight well. He'll just storm out and come back two hours later. I like to talk things over right then and there. Before we got engaged, it bothered me. But afterward, it became the biggest deal in the world. I'd think to myself, do I have to live with this man doing this to me for the rest of my life?"

How'd they resolve it? "We slowed down and remembered the reasons why we're getting married in the first place," Alison says. "That we love and complete each other, not to mention that we have a unique ability to crack each other up. All that put our problems in perspective. But we're working on them, too. I try to give him the space he needs, and he promises to resolve our fights as soon as possible. And I talked to some of my married friends—it turns out that each of them went through a similar period early in their engagement."

Communicate, Don't Sublimate

He's sulking in the corner, or she's flinging dishes across the room, and you don't know why? You're not mind-readers—the *only* way to understand each other's needs and neuroses is to talk about them. Voice your feelings clearly and not critically. Often the difference between a discussion and an argument is a matter of style. Follow these tips to keep your disagreements civil (and your makeups fast and steamy).

Skillful Problem Solving

"Pay less attention to what's wrong—to how many problems and disagreements you have—and more attention to how you resolve them. That's what will carry through into the marriage. If you work through problems by brainstorming and coming up with new solutions, that's a good sign."

—**Jane Campbell, Ph.D.,**
Houston-based therapist

- Chill out before you begin discussing a sensitive topic. No one is reasonable when ticked off.
- Adopt the same-side-of-the-table approach. Before you begin, say "This isn't you against me. If we're having a problem, it hurts us both. We're on the same side of the table here." Make the problem the enemy, not each other.
- Don't insist on solving a problem before you go to sleep. The later it gets, the more irrational you get. Go to sleep. (Try to kiss each other first.) There'll be plenty of time to fight in the morning (and, chances are, a lot less reason and inclination to do it).
- Write it down. Afraid you'll forget your points? Jot notes and then go through each item together. It'll help keep you from interrupting each other, which can cause even more hurt and anger.
- Take the "I feel . . ." rather than the "You did this . . ." approach: "I feel like you're not interested in my opinion when you turn on the TV while I'm talking," rather than "You always turn on the TV when I'm talking because you don't give a damn about what I'm saying." By attacking your honey, you force her to defend herself. By expressing how you feel, you give her an opportunity to comfort you.
- Paraphrase for clarity. To make sure you understand her, listen to your honey, then repeat what she said in your own words. This not only helps you both clarify your complaints, it also shows that you're paying attention.

Learn the Art of Compromise

You're not always going to get your way, during the wedding or after. Acknowledge that you have different priorities. To reach a compromise, try the **XYZ** method:

- e**X**press the other's side.
- **Y**et . . . (Give your feeling.)
- **Z**ip it up. (Present a solution.)

For example:

X: I understand that you want a vegetarian buffet because you feel very strongly about animal rights.
Y: Yet my fear is that my meat-eating relatives will accuse me of being cheap.
Z: Maybe we could give my relatives the option to choose between a vegetarian *or* meat entree, and we can have all-vegetarian hors d'oeuvres.

Your backgrounds—religious, cultural, social—will affect how you deal with the details of your wedding and your life after. For help dealing with conflicts of difference, go to Chapter 19.

Fight Fair

There's no way to avoid fighting completely. It happens, and it's far better to get something out in the open than to let resentment build. A little tiff can reduce stress, but only if you fight fairly. No low blows or permanent scarring. Here are our tips for fair fighting:

- No manipulative tricks like crying fits or stomping off. You're both adults—act like it.
- If your sweetie says something that hurts your feelings, don't lash out with the meanest thing you can think of to say. Take a breath. And tell him he's hurt your feelings, instead.
- Temper your honesty. Too much bluntness can cut deeper than sharp words. If you think her parents are stupid bigots, don't say so. Think of way to address the problem their bigotry creates instead.
- Always attack the problem, not the person. "I'm worried that this invitation wording will confuse people" is an issue you can address together. "What are you, nuts?" is just an insult. No name-calling. *Ever.*
- Don't ask for proof of love. Yes, your sweetie may make a sacrifice or decision to do something because she knows it will please you. But she'll do it voluntarily. Love is *not* a bargaining point. Sentences like "If you really loved me, you'd agree on a swing band" are not about love but manipulation.
- Recognize that it takes two to fight. It's almost never *all* one person's fault.

Bridezilla vs. Couch Monster

It's possible (okay, probable) that you aren't experiencing wedding obsession to the same degree. We hate to stereotype, but the fact is, a lot of times women become just a *teensy* bit more interested in the details than men do. Unequal distribution of labor and concurrent bridal wacko-ness can build resentment on both sides. What to do?

Find Out Why He's Not Helping: Chances are, he is not just a big lazy lump. A lot of guys don't participate because they feel unsure about what to do or don't feel welcome.

Find Out Why She's Obsessed: Likewise, she's probably not a *total* control freak. What's causing her mania? Is she trying to please anyone other than the two of you? Is her parents' recent divorce making her even more nervous? People often go crazy trying to control details as a way to address a feeling of powerlessness in some other area.

Divvy Up Duties: You, Great Planning One, might as well take the lead. Assign specific tasks to your less-than-enthusiastic planning partner. Be very clear about what he should do. We're not recommending you become a dictator—just give him tasks he'll be interested in. But make sure he has all the info *and* your true support to do it.

Cures for Cold Feet

All this stress and fighting making you think about calling it quits? You're obsessing about all the things that annoy you about each other and wondering if s/he's really the one? If you're racked with doubts about the wisdom of this wedding, look at them seriously. There's a difference between healthy doubts, which everyone has, and real warning signs. Chances are your cold feet just mean your relationship needs some TLC. Here's how to tell.

What Are You Questioning?

Is it your honey, or the idea of marriage? If you love your honey as much as always but you're waffling about the whole wedding thing, your relationship isn't in jeopardy. You've good reason to question a wedding. We live in a country where half of all marriages end in divorce, a factor that can make anyone skeptical about the lifetime-commitment aspect (especially if your family is in the split-up camp). We're a generation of broken commitments. Who's to say that yours will be different?

You're to say. Your relationship is a private affair, completely under your control. It has nothing to do with failed marriages around you. You create your own shared vision of the ideal marriage, and live within it. Talk about what you want from your marriage. Ask each other—and yourselves—the hard questions: What do you like most, and least, about each other? What factors make you think you'll be happy together? What is really important to you in life/love? Look to role models—other couples with relationships you admire—for inspiration. Or, for some outside input, consider going to a couple's counselor to talk out your doubts. As we said earlier, change always makes people feel uncomfortable.

ASK CARLEY

Calling It Off

Q: I thought this was the guy for me—but now I know it's a bad idea to get married. What happens if I call off the engagement?

A: Unfortunately, not all love stories are meant to be. The planning period is a trying time for every couple—people chicken out, discover huge incompatibilities, and sometimes even drive each other away. What you don't want to do is lose yourself in a cloud of anguish and despair. There is, however, some difficult business to attend to. First off, the ring. We think you should return it. (Unless there was major foul play involved, in which case, think *Melrose Place* mean!) Why would you want such a reminder of the engagement? It's also respectful to return any family heirloom, ring or otherwise, given to you as gifts by your ex-fiancé/e's relatives as well as any other gifts you both received.

Depending on how far into the wedding preparations you are, you'll also have to cancel all vendor agreements and site reservations. We hope you signed contracts that will let you get at least 50 percent of any deposits back. (There's no etiquette about being reimbursed for your loss if your fiancé broke up with you, so don't hold your breath.) If invitations already have gone out, recall them by sending out rush notes ASAP. (You don't need to delve into the sordid details of your romantic meltdown, just let everyone know the wedding won't take place.)

Once you take care of all the unpleasant details, book a full-day session at the spa, take in a movie with some friends, or go paint the town red!

Whose Doubts Are These?

Your parents think you need to be with someone more like you, while your friends keep subtly suggesting that you find someone funnier, smarter, prettier, richer, or more ambitious. Your job is to figure out what *you* want. There is no formula for a perfect relationship. Happy couples range from having nearly nothing in common to sharing essentially every aspect of their lives. Regardless of how much others try to impose their vision of a perfect union on you, all that matters is that the two of *you* agree on what works.

If you're doubting your choice for any reason—too poor, too rich, too young, too old, too lazy, too obsessed with work—figure out whose doubts these are. Are *you* worried about never having enough money for an annual Carnival cruise and a maid three days a week, or are your parents the ones with that concern? Try to comfort your parents, kiss your honey, and then carry on with your planning.

Testing the Waters

Celtic couples used to live together for a year and one day before officially being considered wed. This "trial marriage" was a way for the couple to see if they could reconcile their differences before making that final commitment.

Differences and Your Relationship

Different Worlds, One Address

Compromise 101

Family Friction

Fair-Weather Friends

Combining Cultures

Maybe you two grew up next door to each other, or you're high-school sweethearts. Perhaps your beloved is from another generation or from a country on the other side of the world. You may have grown up in the same town or state but in different religious or cultural communities.

No matter how different or alike your backgrounds are, you're still coming to your marriage from two different places. The chasms some couples have to cross may be larger and wider than they are for others—your families or friends may be less than supportive of your decision to marry "outside the community." But for everyone, marriage should mean reveling in your differences, not letting them create conflict between you. It's important to come up with good problem-solving solutions now—both for your wedding and for your life after the party.

Differences and Your Relationship

You may be soul mates, but you're not the same person. It sounds obvious, right? But it's something couples in love don't always address. Even if you grew up next door to each other, your families probably used different brands of toothpaste, drove different cars—and related to each other in different ways. We know that you love each other deeply and that nothing could pull you apart. But we also know that the stress of wedding planning—with its focus on tradition, family, and endless financial minutiae—inevitably can bring differences to the surface, where they may simmer for weeks or escape in spurts of steaming insults, shouts, and tears.

If you come from different religions, races, countries, generations, or (it sometimes seems) galaxies—these disagreements may be more profound, looming over an otherwise serene horizon like a huge monster from one of those old black-and-white horror films. Every once in a while, you may even find yourself pondering the wisdom of this marriage.

Relax. Prewedding disagreements do not necessarily mean postwedding unhappiness. It's perfectly normal to have a few fights. After all, you're planning a profoundly private event that all your friends and family will watch (the ceremony), followed by a party that's supposed to express your personalities *and* double as the best bash your circle has ever seen, meanwhile juggling your disparate belief systems, religious values, and social styles. It's no wonder you're feeling some stress.

On the other hand, wedding-planning disagreements *can* indicate larger, underlying conflicts. Which makes now the perfect time to identify your primary areas of friction and to develop good problem-solving skills for the big day and all the days after. The truth is, everyone has conflicts, but that usually doesn't mean you should call the whole thing off.

In our experience, conflicts of difference tend to arise in three places: between the two of you, among your families, and with your pals. Learning to deal with them will help you live happily ever after (not to mention saving you thousands of dollars on therapy, late-night phone calls home to Mom, and dozens of boxes of chocolate doughnuts).

Different Worlds, One Address

You may be the Man from Atlantis, while your honey's the Daughter of Frankenstein, but once you're married, you both become the Atlantis-Frankensteins (metaphorically speaking). This isn't about my way or your way. It's got to be our way, or—sad to say—the highway. Marriage is all about compromise. How do you create your own new family, incorporating both your beliefs?

Admit It: You're Different

Don't pretend you're exactly the same. Bring up those uncomfortable, maddening, frustrating differences now. Don't shy away from them or attempt to sweep them under the entertainment center and hope they go away. Issues confronting you now—which religion

---

Issues That Need Resolution—Soon

You want to raise your kids Catholic; your honey doesn't believe in organized religion.
You assume you'll both keep your jobs; your honey assumes women stop working once they're wed.
You plan to avoid your families if they give you grief; your honey values family above all else.
You plan to spend every dime you both make; your honey plans to scrimp and save until retirement.
You plan to keep all your friends, including those of the opposite sex; your honey thinks men and women can't be just friends.

should permeate the ceremony, or how much wedding money to spend—will still be there when you return from your honeymoon—which religion to raise your kids, or how to spend your hard-earned cash.

We're not suggesting you spend all your time dwelling on your differences. You obviously share the most important thing—your love for each other, and the desire to spend your lives together. But accepting the fact that you have differences will allow you to move toward resolving them.

SHIRLEY AND MATTHEW
July 26, Greenfield, Indiana

SHIRLEY AND MATTHEW'S was a self-proclaimed "Emily Post meets John Deere" wedding, between a groom who grew up on the farm and a city-girl bride who was born overseas (the Netherlands). They joined their two different worlds and created a new family in the process.

After the couple had been dating for two years, Matthew was ready to propose, but he wasn't asking just for himself. Matthew decided to include his son, Evan, right from the start. Matthew told Shirley that he and Evan, who's ten, wanted to know if she'd spend the rest of her life with them. Shirley said yes.

At the ceremony, in addition to exchanging vows with Matthew, Shirley promised new stepson (and best man) Evan that she'd take good care of him. The couple's first dance was to "The Maker Said Take Her" by Alabama. "The song was on the radio a few months before we got engaged, and Matthew kept going on and on about how much he liked it," Shirley says. In it, a man talks about how God told him the woman he was with was the one for him. Matthew confided in Evan about his intentions then. "So Evan knew for months that Matthew was going to ask me to marry him, and he kept the secret!"

Clarify Your Expectations

A lot of people have one set of expectations for their lover and an entirely new slew of requirements for their spouse. It may be fine for your boyfriend to be a starving artist, but your *husband* better damn well bring home the bacon. Or maybe you love having a girlfriend who wears miniskirts and high heels, but you think a *wife* should dress "respectably." Different backgrounds tend to widen the expectation gap when it comes to planning your wedding and your future; the two of you may have different assumptions about the role your families should play, who will handle the social calendar, even whose job it is to take out the trash. Bring those assumptions into the open now.

Bang Out Your Beliefs

A lot of fights over nitty-gritty wedding details actually boil down to underlying beliefs. If you haven't already, talk about your views on religion, sex, money, kids, and family. Are there specific points of contention that make you want to gnaw your finger down to the knuckle? Bring them up now! All this talking isn't a way to exhaust each other into agreement. You don't have to agree on everything. But it will help you figure out which beliefs you share (money, religion, favorite houseplants), which issues you disagree on (children, family, which is smarter—cats or dogs), and what your individual opinions are on each of the disputed points. If you know where you each stand, you can make informed, effective choices about both big and little things. Knowledge is power in the game of life—and blissful wedding planning, too.

How Not to Avoid Stuff

Make uncomfortable wedding-planning discussions as pleasant as possible by setting up "an appointment" to talk and then heading to your favorite place to do it. Take yourselves to dinner afterward.

Go to Chapter 18 for more on healthy communication skills.

ASK CARLEY

The Parents Are Coming!

Q: Help! My honey's parents are coming from India for the wedding, and then they're staying with us for *three months.* They plan to stay in our bedroom, while we sleep on the couch. Haven't they ever heard of the Holiday Inn? My fiancé said, "You people in this country are so cold. You don't care about anyone beyond yourselves." So I said, "You're hopelessly enmeshed in your family. Why don't you grow up? And tell them not to be so inconsiderate." Now we're not speaking to each other. (Which is a big problem, since we're in the middle of choosing caterers.) We love each other, but what do we do?

A: First of all, stop making this personal! Your honey was obviously raised to value his family *very much*, and in a very hands-on way. You were clearly brought up on the more independent plan. Locate these difference within the broader context of your cultures—and normalize relations by understanding their cultural base. These are two different belief systems you're dealing with. Once you recognize that it's not mere personal stubbornness, you can begin to arrive at a compromise. Maybe they stay with you, but for a shorter length of time.

Compromise 101

Ah, conflict resolution. There are several different ways you two can come to a compromise on the various issues that are coming up right now. At least one of the following approaches should work for any conflict.

Do Both

You want a Catholic wedding. Your honey wants a Jewish wedding. You decide to blend both traditions into one ceremony. Or you want to go to your parents' house for Thanksgiving. Your honey wants to go to her parents' house for Thanksgiving. You decide to take turns—your parents' one year, her parents' the next.

Do Something Else Entirely

You want a Catholic wedding. Your honey wants a Jewish one. You decide to go Unitarian; still religious, but not filled with emotional/familial landmines. Or you want to go to your parents' house for Thanksgiving. You honey wants to go to her parents'. You decide to have Thanksgiving at *your* house, and invite both sets of parents.

Do Neither

You: Catholic. Your honey: Jewish. After talking about it, you realize that neither of you really wants all the rigmarole of a religious wedding. You decide to bag the whole debate and have a fabulous civil service on the beach. Or, You: Thanksgiving dinner at your parents' house. Your honey: Dinner at her parents' house. After some discussion, you discover that you both hate turkey and both of your families spend every Thanksgiving fighting. You decide to go out for Mexican food instead.

Talk This Way

Try this method of discussing differences—with your beloved, parents, friends, anyone:

1. Show empathy and understanding for the other person's position.
2. State what you feel yourself.
3. Indicate what you'd like to see happen.

Healthy Mental Attitudes

Consider that differences can be good: Rather than viewing differences as monsters you must kill, adopt the attitude that they are challenging, invigorating, and stimulating.

Look at issues through your honey's eyes: When resolving issues, don't try to force your spouse to *prove* his love. Think of what you can do to show yours instead. Healthy couples go out of their way to do things that they know will make the other person happy.

Wear rose-colored glasses about your partner's uniqueness: In lasting relationships, couples see their partner's quirks as charming. You probably already see your honey's bizarre behavior in the best possible light (and adore him/her because of it). Make a habit of continuing to do so.

R-E-S-P-E-C-T: Don't go back on your agreement to respect each other's beliefs. If you're secretly hoping your beloved will give up his/her religion after a few years with you, you're going to be in for some heartache down the line. Get it out in the open. If you've agreed to maintain your differences, no fair going back on that.

LYNN AND BEN

October 8, New York City

LYNN AND BEN planned their wedding to incorporate both of their faiths—he's Jewish, she's Episcopalian. "We wanted to celebrate both but also recognize the two different traditions," Lynn says. Because the couple did not want to choose one religion over the other, they decided to hold both their ceremony and reception at the Americas Society in Manhattan. "We liked it because it had no religious affiliation. We wanted an intimate place that would give us a close sense of family and friends," the bride says. "It was perfect."

While Lynn and Ben put aspects of each religion into their ceremony, they chose a nondenominational officiant. "We worked very closely with him on different elements of the ceremony," Lynn says. "The vows we wrote had universal themes that could be applied to both of our religions."

The couple hopes that the blending of faiths will carry into their marriage. "We plan on continuing to honor both religions," the bride says. "We want to celebrate our backgrounds as much as we can."

Family Friction

Of course, differences and conflicts don't always stop with you. If you're marrying outside your religion, race, socioeconomic background, or suburban subdivision, you may be getting plenty of unpleasant, unsupportive, downright negative feedback from your family about now. So how, exactly, should you respond to this kind of familial "support"?

Show Affection, Not Rejection

A lot of parents view their child's choice of a "different" partner as a direct hit, a rejection of them, a slap in the face to all that they've taught you. If your parents are feeling defensive, rejected, and rebuffed, there's *no way* they're going to listen to why your honey is so great. Tell them how much you love and value your own religion (or race or culture) first. Assure them you're *not* turning your back on what they taught you and that your children will learn it, too. Let them know that you want their support. If you convince them that you value their opinions and beliefs, you have a lot better chance of them laying off of yours.

Go to Chapter 20
for more help
dealing with family.

Give Your Folks the Floor

Let your parents voice their opinions and give you their advice (even if only *they* consider it "advice"). Then ask them what conflicts arose during their own wedding planning. How did their families react to news of their engagement? If they had it to do over again, what would they handle differently? What "truths" have they learned about marriage? Find out their concerns. Really listen.

Talking to your parents accomplishes three things: (1) It lets you know what their issues are so you can address their real fears; (2) it gives you ammunition to diffuse future attacks effectively; and (3) it shows respect. Asking their opinion is a form of honoring them. It gives them the sense that you value them, which can go a long, long way toward helping them stop undervaluing *your* decisions.

Accept a Little Disapproval

If there are some points on which they just don't, or won't, agree with you—guess what? They don't have to. They can harbor different beliefs or a different view of how you should do things. And you still can go about your business as usual, aware of their disapproval but loving each other anyway.

Keep the Door Open

We believe (as do most therapists) that you should try to keep your family in your life as much as is humanly possible. If your parents are giving you flack, don't resort to the silent treatment. Alone in your living room, that disapproving comment can start to feel like an avalanche of rejection. By keeping in contact, you've got a better shot of maintaining your perspective and remembering that this dispute is only a part of your relationship with them.

Accepting your family—foibles and all—is part of accepting yourself, really. Of course, that doesn't mean that you need to take abuse. If you get together to go over your guest list and the talk turns into a rousing round of "Criticize the Kids," get out of there (gracefully) and return later, when everyone has calmed down.

If your parents are the ones shutting *you* out, we still advise keeping your door unlocked. Go ahead and send them a wedding invitation anyway. They very well may turn around and show up at your wedding.

Set Boundaries

Even if your parents' input feels too painful to endure, you should try to keep them in your life, *with limits.* If, every time you get together to discuss ways to include both families in the wedding, conflicts arise or pot shots are taken, try your best to keep them involved in your planning, but do it by telephone. Or control the discussion by asking for input on specific items *only* and then changing the subject. Let them know, if you have to, that you'll stick around until you hear *one word* against your beloved, and then you'll slip out the back. You're adults now. If you choose to keep your family in your life (which we hope you do), you can set the terms.

Fair-Weather Friends

If you're choosing an "unconventional" path, recognize now that at various times during your life together, you'll probably receive unpleasant, unsolicited feedback from the narrow-minded world out there. The following is some ammunition to help you through it.

Decide Whose Opinion Matters

It's important to distinguish between prejudices spouted by perfect (or rather, imperfect) strangers and acquaintances and genuine concerns raised by good friends and family members. The clerk at the Stop 'n' Go casts a sideways glance at you because you're black and she's white? Who cares? You don't owe that clerk any explanation for how you live your life.

If that store clerk is your best friend, though, his opinion will be harder to dismiss. You've heard it a million times but we'll say it again anyway: If someone is really your friend, she's not going to turn her back on you because she disagrees with your choice of a life partner. On the other hand, give your good friends a chance to say their piece. They may really be concerned about you and only trying to help. Hear them out and then make your own decisions.

What Will the P's Think?

"Give up on the idea that everyone is going to be enthusiastic and positive about everything you do. Children think that they should receive 100 percent approval from their parents for everything, and that's a myth. Generally, people adjust, slowly. A lot of parents may not be excited about a marriage to begin with, but they get over it."

—Jane Campbell, Ph.D., Houston-based therapist

Go to Chapter 20
for more help with
friends.

Questions to Answer Now

What religious or cultural traditions are you going to use in your wedding?
Are you going to address your differences in your vows or readings?
How are you going to get your families to mingle at the reception?
What religion are you going to raise your kids?
How can you turn your back on all we've taught you?
Aren't you afraid your kids will be teased because you're different races?
How are you going to handle random prejudice?
Isn't s/he old enough to be your mother/father?

Assess Your Commitment

If others' opinions really make or break your day, now is the time to realize that. The world isn't going to change during your ceremony. (Though it's true that peoples' opinions may change over longer periods of time.) It may help you to think of yourselves as pioneers. If you can't hack that role, admit it now. Be honest about who you are and how committed you are to this relationship.

There's no rule that says all happily married couples must share the same religion, background, skin color, or age group. What they do share, however, is respect for each other. View your differences as the assets they are; two great cultures to draw from, two backgrounds to tap, and plenty of zesty conversation fodder for the rest of your lives.

Knowing Me, Knowing You

Get to know your honey's culture better. Learn her native language, read books about her background, or take a class in her culture or religion. Cook foods from her home country or plan a vacation there. Embrace both cultures—you've got two great traditions in your lives.

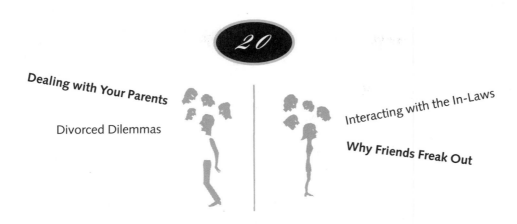

In-Laws and Outlaws

As you embark upon this final frontier of togetherness, don't be surprised to find just about everyone in your lives crammed into the space capsule with you. You may have believed marriage was a private affair between the two of you, but unless you're secretly eloping (which may sound like a pretty good idea right about now), announcing your wedding likely will inspire everyone you've ever met to rev up their opinions and let them loose. Not everyone will be thrilled with the way your new status impacts them—nor will they all keep their feelings to themselves.

Fact is, your personal ceremony *does* affect others. It not only joins two families who may not have much in common (other than you two), but it also changes the relationships you've created as single people. If the behavior of relatives and friends seems bizarre, here's a little insight that may help you deal.

Dealing with Your Parents

At the head of the line of potential interference stand your parents—those people you love who, come wedding time, may take to making your life a living hell. They might be questioning all your decisions, insisting that you do things their way, or exploding into angry harangues with no apparent provocation. (They also may be the most helpful people around, but we're just looking at their less lovely traits, for now.) Why are they acting so strangely? They have good reason. Tying the knot is a huge rite of passage—for you and for them. Getting married is the final act dividing the adults from the kids, especially in your parents' eyes. And since their main role in your life, to date, has been to protect you—their precious cub—from the outside world, watching you take adulthood for a test drive can be pretty unsettling—more so than other transitions, because it's the one that makes their usefulness wane (and their mortality wax). But you can, and should, help make the transition smoother.

Go to Chapter 5 for ideas on how to include your dads in your wedding preparations.

Look at the Subtext

Is this family feud *really* about the color of the napkins? Probably not. Fights over frivolous details tend to mask some other struggle—they're the symptoms, not the cause. Rather than arguing endlessly about trivialities, get to the root of the problem. Here are a few common "hidden" conflicts that may be motivating your parents' bizarre behavior.

A Slipping Sense of Control: As your parents feel their influence on you becoming less crucial, they may become obsessed with micromanaging every detail of your wedding, instead. If you respond by screaming "I don't need your dumb old ideas anymore!" you're adding fuel to the fire of their sense of lost significance. Instead, assure them that you love them and still value their opinions. As out-of-left-field as it may sound, acknowledging their importance in your life may help them ease up a bit. If not, tell them you'd like to handle some of your wedding tasks yourselves and see if they'll turn any over to you, or consider the joy of letting someone else do all the work while you just slip on your dress and tux and attend. You'll have plenty of details to deal with once you're married.

Whatever you do, *don't* get defensive. You don't have to prove that your decisions are sound or your choices sane. You're going to get married, regardless of who chooses the flowers. The ultimate power (of growing up and moving on) is in your hands.

A Desire to Rewrite Their Past: Perhaps your mom didn't have her fantasy ballroom wedding, and she's decided that you damn well will. Never mind that you want a civil service and a backyard barbecue—this is her chance (in her mind) to right that earlier wrong.

This is pretty tough argument to win. Mom is not being logical; she's spewing emotion. *Of course* this is your wedding, not hers. *Of course* she's had a happy marriage, despite her "failed" wedding. But as anyone who has ever been in a fight knows, a logical rebuttal just skips right over the surface of a cauldron of seething feelings. Try to unravel her tirade, instead—figure out what part of her dream nuptials she's sorry she missed. Chances are there's a common thread you can work with.

Fear of How It Will Reflect on Them: Some parents are hyperaware of their place in society. If you get married in the back of your VW van, they know that Mrs. Goodbloom of the Flower Club will lord it over them for years. Peer pressure among parents? It happens. If your parents are pushing you to have a Trump-style wedding when all your lives you've been strictly Simpsons (as in Homer), they may have status woes.

Thanks for the Memories

Ask your parents about their wedding—what they wore, served, danced to. Take a look at their wedding photos. Not only will you help ease parental tension by showing your interest in and respect for them, but you also may get some great ideas for your own wedding.

ASK CARLEY

Who Gets to Plan This Thing?

Q: My parents are paying for my wedding. Does this mean they have the final say on *everything*?

A: If your parents are doing the Lord of the Wedding dance, do your best to accept it. There's no rule about who has the final say—and we'd hope they'd give *you* the honor, since it is your wedding—but those with the cash can always take it back. (And you might consider being a bit indulgent toward a set of parents willing to foot the whole bill!) If you can't handle their incessant demands, try asking them to pay for specific items rather than underwriting the whole wedding.

This is some pretty warped thinking, but you may not feel comfortable confronting them directly about it. Instead, see if you can figure out which status symbols are critical to them. This will give you an idea of what elements you should try to be flexible about. And question your own motives, too—make sure you're not opting for a down-market affair just because you know it will embarrass them. This is the time to try to heal old wounds, not gain the upper hand. If your parents have always been status-conscious, you already know what to expect from them. Try to let their "needs" figure into your planning. Two words: Humor them.

How to Cope

Even if you've figured out why your mom or dad is acting so strange, you still have months of planning ahead of you. Try these conflict-solving tactics to make the process more fun.

Apply the Five-Year Test: Whenever you feel yourself about to explode over some disputed detail, ask yourself how much you'll really care about this five years from now. "Your bridesmaids *must* wear the same dress or the whole wedding will be ruined!" your mom screams. "I refuse to dress my friends like Barbies. I'd rather kill myself!" you scream back. Stop. Breathe deeply. And ask yourself, "Will I really care about their dress five years down the road?" If you work in the fashion industry, you might. Otherwise, probably not. Is it worth the grief? You decide.

Give Each Time You Take: Every time you win a round, make sure Mom gets something she wants, too. Or offer up a tasty tidbit first to help you gain ground. For example, Mom wants the matching dresses. And you know she also wants the men to wear tails. Say something like "What if we dress the men in tails, to keep it formal, but put the bridesmaids in assorted styles?" Or: "How about tails for the guys, the same color and material for the girls, but each in a style that flatters her figure?"

Soften Them with Sweetness: Like the give-when-you-get approach, kindness can carry you far in the game of compromise. If you hurt someone's feelings, you're not only fighting an opposing opinion, you're also paying reparations for your slight. Keep everything cozy. Assure your parents that you think they have great ideas and want what's best for you. Actually listen to their points (which you actually may agree with sometimes, in spite of yourself). Then calmly state yours.

No Love Lost?

Q: My parents are ripping into my fiancée, and I don't know what to do about it. I love her, but I love them, too.

A: Your parents may be criticizing your choice for several reasons. Perhaps they feel dismissed, as if you prefer her over them (an immature stance, but a stance nonetheless). Perhaps they fear she's the wrong one for you. Perhaps they just like to criticize. The solution depends on their motivation, of course. But try these tactics:

Listen to their complaints, *alone.* There's no reason for your sweetie to sit through a character assassi-
nation. Hear them out and really think about the issues they raise. If you decide their points are sound,
you've got some serious thinking to do.

Focus inward, not outward. Make sure you're not putting so much energy into defending yourself and
your fiancée that you fail to look inward at your relationship to be sure it's really what's right for you.

Explain your side. If their complaints are invalid, explain why, *calmly.* They may genuinely not have noticed your sweetie's good points. Give them a chance to see her through your eyes. But if you've chosen
someone unlike them for a good reason (such as they're bigots and your sweetie's not), steer clear of the
flash-point issues and focus on the traits of hers that they'll appreciate.

Help them get to know her better. Take them out to dinner as a couple. Invite them to your honey's art
opening/bowling league final match/handball championship. Start with light, brief activities that you
know they will enjoy or that let them see your sweetie as you do.

Set boundaries. If your parents refuse to change their minds, it's time to create some rules. Your loyalty
has to be to your new relationship. Tell them you love them but no longer want to hear complaints about
your honey. Continue to include them as much as possible in your wedding planning, but only in ways
that don't hurt you or her.

Make a Life Plan

"If you figure out some
guidelines for what your life
together is going to be like and
then share that with your
parents, you should have an
easier time dealing with them,
both about the wedding plans
and about your marriage."

—Joan Hawxhurst,
editor of *Dovetail,* a
newsletter for Christian/
Jewish couples

Stop When Things Get Heated: If the discussion becomes a dia-
tribe, take a break. Good solutions rarely arise from mud-slinging contests.
Excuse yourself. Take a walk. And then resume talks in a better mood.

Divorced Dilemmas

If you've got two sets of parents, you also have twice as many people whose ten-
der feelings you can hurt. If your plethora of parents is adding angst to your planning, try these tactics.

Make Them Feel Valued

Let's face it, if you grew up with your mom and stepdad, there were probably nights when your biological dad sat home alone in his living room
thinking about how his children were being raised by another man. During
a wedding, everyone's insecurities become more pronounced. And when
you've got more than two parents vying for your affection, they can be hypersensitive about
how you treat them, how you address them, and how you include them in your wedding.

Go out of your way to make everyone feel important and wanted. We know you're busy, but a little extra warmth now will save you a lot of unwanted grief later (like next week). It's worth the time to call your dad (or mom, if she's the more distant parent), or drop a note. Think about the good times you've had together, and bring them up. While you're at it, be extra-nice to your mom and stepparents, too.

Include Them All

Find specific ways to include *all* your parents. Ditch the traditional breakdowns and assign your own roles. Maybe you'll have a father/daughter dance, stepfather/daughter dance, *and* a stepmother/daughter disco number. Maybe you'll ask your biological dad to lead you down the aisle and your stepdad to lead the toasting. However you divide the tasks, focus on each person's job when you talk to him/her, stressing how important it is to you. Your goal is to make each parent feel honored.

Where will all these steprelatives sit? Go to Chapter 7 for the skinny on ceremony seating, Chapter 8 for the essentials on reception seating charts.

Beyond the wedding details, you may need to assure your parents of their continued role in your new life, even if it takes a little adjusting of old roles. Make a date for lunch with Mom and Dad and talk about *them,* for a change. Or see if Mom is up for that weekly yoga class you want to join. Changing a relationship can be awkward—with parents or with friends. But stick with it; once you establish your new roles, you'll be back on smooth ground with your folks.

Discuss Wedding Roles Early

Lay out the plan way ahead of time so everyone has a chance to adjust and to voice any objections. Go over the proposed ceremony structure, seating arrangements, toasting order, and the like. If someone opposes a specific element, ask for an alternative that would make him more comfortable. If you're afraid your ceremony plan (speech, seating, etc.) is going to make a parent squirm (or make a scene), talk to her about it *now.*

Go to Chapter 5 for new ways to include your assortment of parental types in your wedding.

Interacting with the In-Laws

Leaving a Parent Out?

If you don't want to include a parent in your planning—you don't have a good relationship or any relationship at all, say—that's okay. Just be aware that the person may approach you about it. Think about how you'll respond and whether there's any way to include him/her that won't make you uncomfortable.

Your honey is so unique—the way she folds socks instead of rolling them into balls, how she makes gallons of chicken soup and then instantly freezes them "for later." Where'd she ever get such charming quirks? From her parents, who apparently do things quite differently from yours. And while her family's unusual ways probably seemed charming while you were dating, those same quaint traits and differing tastes can drive you nuts during wedding planning.

Accept That Both Ways Can Be Right

Even if her parents do seem like extras from *One Flew Over the Cuckoo's Nest,* they did manage to produce that fabulous being known as your fiancée. Their ideas can't be *all* bad. Try to be open-minded about their views, and look for ways they might benefit you. They're tightwads compared to your free-and-easy folks? Let them help you sketch out a budget. Embracing them does not mean being disloyal to your own family. You have room to include them all in your heart (and wedding).

Don't make it into a me-against-them struggle. There's no need to compete. You already won; your fiancé obviously chose *you*. Pushing him to "side" with you on wedding stuff will create stress, not closeness.

Have Realistic Relationship Expectations

You don't have to love her parents. You love her—that's enough. But you *do* have to be considerate and pleasant. Unfortunately, there's no magical instant-friendship formula. You'll get to know them as time goes by and you spend more time together. If you want to speed things up, invite his mom out for lunch. Or see if her dad could go for a round on the golf course. Chances are good that you'll become close. You've already got one very important thing in common—your love for your sweetie.

Address Potential Conflicts Now

If they're homophobes, bigots, or rabidly antismoking, for example, and your family is, well . . . one-third gay and primary stockholders in RJR-Nabisco, things are bound to be tense. Have your honey tell her folks about your family's background long before the wedding, even if it makes you nervous (since you know how they feel). They probably had no idea

---

Sibling Rivalry

Sibling rivalry doesn't automatically cease just because you're grown up. We know some very nice grandparents who have managed to keep their sibling struggles alive and well. If your siblings are less than loving, try to:

Be the adult: To change long-established behavior, one of you has to start acting differently—and we nominate you. While you can't change other people, you'd be amazed at how easily you can change someone's reaction by adjusting your own actions. Talk to your sibling. Explain that you're individuals and that what one of you does is not a reflection on the other. Focus on him. Be a friend to him. If he can't handle hearing about your love life, don't force it on him. Don't get dragged into juvenile shouting matches.

Include, don't exclude: On the flip side of the sibling rivalry issue is displaced sibling syndrome. If you and your sis have always been close, your gain may feel like her loss. And it just may be—you always turned to her for guidance, but you've just replaced her with your sweetie. It's up to you to go out of your way to include her and find a role for her in your new family. Talk to your spouse-to-be about this; she may have suggestions of ways to welcome your sister (like setting her up with her brother).

Recognize a pattern: If you've always been the one to get the girl, the grades, or the goods, your sibling might view your wedding as one more example of how you always come out on top. Old perceptions and resentments are hard to change. It's probably not your honey that's ticking her off, but you and your damn good fortune.

they were offending you by voicing their opinions. A lot of people just repeat the same old stock prejudices without really listening to themselves or considering how their audience feels.

If they're strongly committed to their point of view, your honey should let them know that he expects them to curb their words around you and be on their best behavior during your wedding. Let your family in on your in-laws' beliefs, too. By letting everyone know what to expect in advance, you give them time to adjust their attitudes (or at least their behavior) now—not at your wedding.

Confront Your Own Folks

If your parents seem to be competing for worst in-law-of-the-year award or have elevated meddling into an Olympic sport, your best bet is to separate and each confront your own. You have more experience with your folks, while he knows best how to handle his. Try to be as kind as possible while clearly expressing your loyalty to your soon-to-be and your plans.

JENNIFER AND LEN
June 12, Washington, D.C.

JENNIFER AND HER MOTHER practically came to blows over who would officiate her and Len's ceremony—Mom wanted an Episcopalian minister, but Jennifer didn't. "I felt like the ceremony was our thing," she says. "We already had our officiant picked out—and he wasn't Episcopalian."

So how'd they resolve it? "Well, we talked about it," Jennifer says. "And I realized that she felt like her side of the family wasn't being represented in my wedding in any way. Like we were completely excluding her heritage, which I obviously didn't want to do." In the end, Jennifer and Len kept their original officiant and also had an Episcopalian minister speak about Jennifer's heritage. "It actually made the wedding much nicer and more personal," the bride says.

Top-Ten Family Q and A's

Most of the wedding "etiquette" dilemmas to-be-weds tell us about have to do with family conflicts. The following are some common problems and our best solutions. As always, use what you can, and otherwise rely on your common sense.

Q: Is it okay for my mother to give me away at my wedding? My father expects to, but he hasn't been a part of my life since I was two.

A: It's absolutely appropriate for Mom to give you away. The larger issue is breaking it to your dad. It's understandable to feel uncomfortable with having him as your aisle escort if he hasn't been a very big presence in your life. Tread carefully, and try to break it to him gently, even if you don't feel "gentle" about it—you don't need big blow-ups right now—and enjoy walking with your mom.

Q: My father recently remarried—but told me two weeks after the wedding. I now have a stepmother and a stepsister, neither of whom I'm very fond of. I would love for my father to attend my wedding, but do I have to invite his new wife and stepdaughter?

A: Since your dad didn't tell you he had remarried until two weeks *after* it happened, you probably don't feel like being super-gracious to him right now. But *not* inviting his new family to your wedding isn't the answer. That's only going to cause bad blood between you and your dad—and these other two people who, like it or not, are now family. You probably have enough to stress about, right? Why not be a bigger person and invite them all. If they come, great—it's not like you have to sit and talk to them all day. You'll be busy enough to just say a kind hello and go about your business.

Q: Should I invite my ex–parents-in-law? We became very close after my divorce and they are loving grandparents to my six-year-old son. However, their son, my ex, is a total jerk (they freely admit this), and I am afraid they may feel uncomfortable around my new family and old relatives who hate their son.

A: Especially if it will comfort your son to have his grandparents at the wedding, it's totally acceptable to invite them. The matter of whether they will be comfortable is something they need to consider. Talk to them about it before you send out the invites—say you'd really love to have them there for you and your son, and that your continued relationship with them means a lot to you, but you understand that they might feel awkward about it. Let them think about it and make their own decision.

Q: My oldest son is getting married next fall. I love his fiancée and I'm thrilled. The only problem is that my son, whom we adopted at birth, wants to invite his birth mother (whom we recently found) to the wedding. I have always been grateful to her for giving life to my son and making the decision to give him up for adoption, but I do not want to share this day with her. I want him to be happy, and this is his day, but she was not there for the zits, mumps, broken hearts, tears, etc. When he realized I was upset by the idea he immediately dropped it, but now I feel guilty!

A: You said it yourself: You want him to be happy, and this is his day. Your feelings are totally understandable and normal—you raised him, and you feel that it's your right to be the mother of the groom on his wedding day. What you need to remember is that you *will* be, whether his birth mother is present or not. Any relationship he builds with her is not going to compare to or replace his relationship with you. Talk to your son about your feelings—tell him you're feeling like his birth mom is going to take your place at the wedding, even though you know that's foolish. Let him reassure you. And then give him your blessing and let *him* make the decision about whether to invite his birth mom or not.

Q: My parents are divorced and both are happily remarried. Both couples regularly attend family gatherings, although my mom and dad amicably avoid each other as much as possible. My mom wants to walk down the aisle with my father and me. Is being given away by both parents okay from an etiquette standpoint? (I wouldn't mind.) They do make the effort to get along.

A: How great that your parents are willing to coexist, even if they really don't have much to say to each other these days! This alone is helping you to avoid wedding stress, trust us. There is absolutely nothing improper about having *both* your parents walk you down the aisle—in fact, it's the norm in Jewish weddings. (You even could consider having your fiancé's parents walk *him* in, as well—but they don't have to if you'd rather meet him at the altar!) Just make sure Dad is cool with walking with you and Mom, and you're in business.

Q: My parents can't stand my fiancé's parents (and vice versa). They also don't like my fiancé. They think I can find someone better. My parents (mostly my father) even went as far as saying that if we did get married, they would not come to the wedding or support it. I'm hurt, and I don't know what to do. We're not getting married until two years from now, but it's like a war when I want to talk about the wedding. It's putting a strain on our relationship, too, and I do not want to lose him.

A: The key here is your time frame. The wedding's not for a while, so maybe the actual marriage part doesn't have to be at the forefront right now, either, as far as your parents/families are concerned. Instead, concentrate on your relationship—and let your parents know that you love this person and you hope they will come around and be happy that he makes *you* happy. It's always tough when your parents don't support what you're doing or don't approve of the person you've decided is the *one*. But ultimately, you're the one who has to make the decision, with or without their approval. All you can do is let them know you hope they will change their minds and then quietly show them that you've made the right choice.

Q: I've already decided that my stepfather, who raised me, will walk me down the aisle. My real dad has not shown the slightest interest in my wedding. He even called my mom and questioned her about my fiancé and said he really didn't think he was the one for me. Anyhow, my dad's wife threatened my relationship with him if he didn't walk me down the aisle. Please help!

A: It's always difficult when you've got a stepdad whom you love and respect and a real father who—well, who's your father. But it sounds like you've made up your mind to walk with your stepdad, and rightly so—if he is the person who has really been a father to you, then he should be the one to escort you to the altar. As far as your real dad, our best advice as far as deciding how much (or if) he should be involved in the wedding is that you should make your decisions about that based on how *you* feel about *him*, not because someone else told you what to do. Perhaps it would help to sit down with your real dad and talk it out. Remember that it's *your* wedding day, and call upon all your family members to try to coexist for your sake.

Q: I had a huge falling out with my future brother-in-law. Okay, I hate his guts. I really don't want him in or at our wedding. My fiancé knows his brother is an idiot, but he's still his brother, after all. How do I approach him with the idea of his brother not being invited? And if I have no choice, how do I deal with that loser being there?

A: No one wants someone they detest at, much less in, their wedding. But you're right, no matter how much of a moron this guy is, he's your fiancé's brother, and you are going to be related to him soon. We'd advise against telling your honey you want to bar his bro from the wedding—it will only make things tense between the two of *you*. It's fine to let your fiancé know how you feel about what happened between you and his brother, and that you feel far from close to the guy and would prefer not to have any more contact with him than is absolutely necessary. But uninviting him will only make things worse for everyone. Instead of focusing on the problem, just dismiss it. There are going to be plenty of people at your wedding whom you are going to want to hug and kiss and pay attention to. Focus on them, and put the brother out of your mind.

Q: My fiancé's parents went through a messy divorce, and his sisters and mother hate his dad. His sisters say we should have two ceremonies, one for their mother's side and one for their father's side of the family. I think this is an unfair demand!

A: It's definitely an unfair demand, and you can only hope they were kidding! There's no reason you have to put on two ceremonies to placate everyone. As for what to say to them: "We're sorry you feel that way, but we really want everyone to put aside their differences and come to our wedding. We're inviting both sides of your family, and we hope everyone will attend and be happy for us." They may be upset, but hopefully they will be able to deal on your wedding day.

Q: My father is remarried, and my stepmother refuses to be in the same room with my mother. I find her attitude unreasonable. What do I do?

A: Sounds like your stepmother is acting freezing cold. You're right that she's being unreasonable. It's your wedding, and of *course* your mother is going to be there. Duh! Talk to your dad and see if he'll talk some sense into his wife, or talk to her yourself if you feel comfortable. Just tell her you're sorry she feels the way she does, and you hope she will reconsider and be there on your big day.

Why Friends Freak Out

Naturally, all of your pals are thrilled with the news of your engagement. They're calling you up with congratulations and sending fruit baskets. For your single friends, especially, the news of your union is like a shot of adrenaline: "It can happen!" they're all saying, popping the corks on the vintage champagne that they've been saving for just this kind of monumental occasion.

Um, right. Unfortunately, friends may get pretty bizarre around engagement time, too. Gaining a spouse shouldn't mean losing a friend, but sometimes even people you count among your closest buddies seem to turn on you the moment they hear your blissful news. What should you do?

Your Bliss, Their Bummer

Fact is, your good news might feel just a *teensy* bit negative for them. When you change from a bar-hopping, all-night-partying stud muffin into a happily married guy, it's a loss of lifestyle—and possibly bar companion—for your friends. People react to loss in different ways. For the most part, they don't call you up and say, "Hey, man, I love you. I really hope you'll still be my buddy now that you're getting a wife." Instead, they may withdraw or become combative or angry. They probably don't even realize they're doing it.

Accept that your gain might be a loss for others, and be sensitive to their feelings. Don't pretend everything is the same. You're *not* going to go out for all-night beer brawls any more (at least not every weekend). You probably *will* start making more couple friends. But that doesn't mean you're going to ditch your best pals. Assure your friends of your continued commitment to them *and* your to-be.

Redefining Your Relationships

Friendships change when situations do, and you can't always tell who will weather the transition, or in what way. But you *can* make the decision to keep a VIP (very important pal) in your life. Make a dinner date with your friend and talk about what your marriage means to each of you. Discuss ways you think it might affect your friendship, and come up with a plan. You might decide to sign up for that dance class/basketball league/croquet team you've been discussing, ensuring that you'll spend Wednesday nights together. Or agree to double date with any of her prospective beaux, rather than going out to the bars with her to find them. Getting all those fears out in the open (yours and hers) and addressing them can actually bring you closer.

Are You Wedding Obsessed?

All right, admit it. Somewhere way, way back in your mind, you fear that maybe you're contributing to your friends' abominable behavior by becoming an obsessed bride-to-be whose unending fascination with her own wedding overshadows all other issues and people in existence. How do you diagnose this sickness? And what do you do?

Survey Your Sensitivity: Your best friend has been trying to find Mr. Right for years. Now that you've found *your* dream guy, do you start every sentence with "Thor and I think . . ." or "Thor and I are going . . ." or "Thor says . . ."? You're acting a little self-absorbed. (Okay, a lot.) Be sensitive to your friend's insecurity and feelings of frustration/unfairness. She doesn't need to know everything Thor thinks. Whenever you feel yourself saying the Th-word, stop and ask about her life instead. We're not saying you should never talk about your sweetie again. But to break the habit, he's subject non gratis for a while.

Even if your friend is happily married/partnered herself, a steady diet of wedding and nothing else can turn the best of buddies into zombies. It's just not that interesting to everyone else. Even we wedding-world enthusiasts can find the subject just a little bit unfascinating every once in a while. Don't lose your perspective.

Examine Your Expectations: We've all heard stories of horrible bridesmaid behavior. And yes, sometimes your wedding party, or a specific member, can turn on you. But we've also heard of brides who ask their ten best friends to spend $300 each on an unflattering dress they'll never wear again and then expect a shower as grand as the reception. Your bridesmaids don't have parents footing the bill. And they do have lives beyond your wedding. Are you making realistic requests? They're supposed to be your *friends*. How about a little friendly concern for their finances here?

And what about the dress itself? You know how picky you are about your clothes. How would you like to squeeze into the exact wrong cut and color—and then pay for it out of your vacation kitty? Are you choosing a dress that's going to make half the party look like sausage casing? Get their opinion on what they're going to wear.

We know it's hard to turn a critical eye on yourself when it seems like that's just what everyone else is doing. But take the time to look at the situation from others' points of view. If you find you've been acting a bit monstrous, it's not too late to change. Invite your attendants over for an apology and a pizza. And then talk about something else!

Unfinished Wedding Business

Getting Gorgeous

It's All in the Timing

Last-Minute Craziness

Having a Ball

The Countdown

You've picked out outfits, pounced on bargains, pounded out vendor contracts, and pored over every detail of your wedding. It's two weeks and counting until the big day. While there are a few last-minute wedding details to attend to, this is the time to savor the moment. No matter how diligent you are, there are always going to be big-day glitches, curve balls, even boo-boos—and that's what will make your wedding unique and wonderful. No amount of obsessing will ensure against surprises, so you might as well just kick back. Trust yourselves—the groundwork you've done and the capable vendors and loved ones you've enlisted to help will ensure that your wedding is fabulous.

Unfinished Wedding Business

By this point, the bulk of your wedding planning has been taken care of. What's left for a couple to do? Mostly tweaking, finessing, and confirming plans with guests and vendors. These tasks can be dispensed with swiftly if you throw yourselves into them with gusto.

The Guest List and Seating

Now's the time to find out, once and for all, who's coming and who's not. The first thing to do just after the two-week mark is to call up people you've invited who haven't sent in their R.S.V.P.'s yet. Simply inquire whether they plan to attend. Divvy up the calls with your honey—each of you can phone the guests you're closest to—and you should be done in no time. (Try not to chit-chat or it *will* take forever.) Once you have your final head count, let your caterer or banquet manager know.

Depending on the kind of wedding you're having, you may or may not want to assign your guests reception seats. If you've invited under fifty to a lowbrow buffet, it's fine to let things fall into place spontaneously. You also don't need to worry about a seating chart if you're having cocktails or a casual brunch or lunch. On the other hand, if you're serving a seated dinner and your guest list tops a hundred, do yourselves a favor and make a plan. You'll cut down on the overall chaos, keep potential feuds at bay by separating dueling parties, spare your guests the discomfort of feeling like they want to "save" spots and shoo strangers away, and make everyone feel like you've thought of them (especially once they see those nifty place cards and out-of-this-world favors).

Once you have your final head count, nail down how many tables and chairs you're going to need. If you haven't already, ask your banquet manager or maitre d' how many guests each table will seat comfortably. Now you're ready to map out your seating chart.

Draw your reception floor plan on a large sheet of paper, using circles or squares to designate tables, and start penciling in names. Another alternative is to number the tables in your head—for example, deciding that the tables next to the entrance will be 1, 2, and 3, from right to left, and so forth—and use a separate index card to write down the names of guests assigned to each table.

Try to strike a balance between familiar faces and acquaintances. Every person at the table should know at least one or two of his/her neighbors, but consider adding some fresh faces, as well. After all, the essence of a wedding is bringing people together and taking a leap, neither of which is reflected in seating people who all know each other together. This is an excellent opportunity to get your relatives acquainted with your honey's, build bridges between your childhood and "adult" friends, and even play matchmaker.

Go to Chapter 8 for more reception-seating details.

Your Marriage License

One of your most important eleventh-hour missions is getting your marriage license. This state-issued permit to marry is proof that you two are fit to marry each other (i.e., officially single, divorced or widowed, and of legal age). You get it by going in person (*both* of you) to city hall, the city or town clerk's office, or the local marriage license bureau. Call the appropriate office in advance to find out about operating hours and whether you need an appointment. Also ask which documents you need to bring along; typical requirements include a birth certificate, photo ID, passport, and divorce papers or death certificate (if divorced or widowed).

Timing is of the essence when it comes to getting your license; most states have both a waiting period between the time you get the license and the time you actually can say your vows as well as an expiration policy that dictates how long license is valid. In other words, a marriage license allows you a specific window of opportunity. So it's crucial to find out the rules in the state where you're getting hitched. If you're getting married in a state other than the one where you live, you'll have to wait until you arrive in your wedding town/city to get your license. Be sure to leave time for this crucial task.

Have You Been Tested?

Some states require you to take a blood test in order to get a marriage license. Call the marriage license bureau or county clerk in the town where you'll wed to see if you need one.

Vows Abroad

Q: We're getting married out of the country. How do we find out about marriage license requirements there?

A: Call your wedding country's embassy, consulate, or tourist office. First off, make sure nonresidents can even get marriage licenses. (We're hoping that you've already got this covered.) Then get the low-down on specifics: which documents and medical tests you need, how long it will take to process the paperwork (so you can time your arrival accordingly), whether you need witnesses, and special requirements for a religious ceremony as opposed to a civil one. (Check Appendix B for requirements in some of the most popular foreign wedding destinations.) Get everything you need in order and pack it in a safe place. Bon voyage!

Your Vendors

You and your wedding vendors already have hashed out all the specifics and signed a contract. Now let them do their thing without breathing down their necks. (You screened these pros carefully—trust your instincts.) That said, you definitely should check in with each vendor during the last two weeks to answer any last-minute questions, make sure preparations are on track, and get the reassurance you need.

We suggest one phone call at the two-week mark, a call (or visit) during the final week, and a final ring the day before the wedding to reconfirm arrival times and other important points. Have contracts on hand so you can go over what needs to be done in an organized fashion. Make sure, however, that your tone is friendly and helpful rather than suspicious and bossy. If you can, leave this final call to a trusted friend or family member who's capable and willing (Mom, you're a saint) so you don't have to tie yourselves in knots over any last-minute glitches.

Guest Hospitality

Now's the time to do the prep work that makes out-of-town guests feel welcome. Check with the hotel/s where they've booked rooms to make sure all is well. Make a round of phone calls to find out how and when your faraway guests are coming into town—if you can swing it, hire a car service to pick them up at the airport or train station, or arrange to have nearby family and friends fetch them in shifts. Make sure everyone has rental-car info, too. On the day before the wedding, drop off gift baskets, itineraries, and maps in your guests' hotel rooms.

Go to Chapter 17 for instructions for putting together guest welcome baskets.

Last-Minute Vendor Questions

- Ingredients: Do they already have the specific blooms, liquor brands, fresh fruit you ordered? If your picks are unavailable, what replacements will be used?

- Legwork: Have labor-intensive, complicated tasks been completed?

- Access: Is your vendor all set to get into your site(s) ahead of time?

- Equipment: Does your vendor have everything s/he needs?

- Schedule: They know crucial arrival times, right?

- Assistance: Is there anything you can do to help?

Honeymoon Preparations

These final fourteen days are the perfect time to shore up your honeymoon plans. Get a printout of your itinerary, if you haven't already. Reconfirm your flight and hotel reservations about five days before takeoff. Do any last-minute shopping. Pack several days before your wedding, so you'll have one less thing to fret about.

CINDY AND WAYNE
June 21, Livingston, New Jersey

"WE HAD A FOURTEEN-MONTH engagement—plenty of time to plan a wedding," Cindy says. "I had worked for a bridal magazine, and I'd hired a wedding consultant. With our experience, I figured we could practically guarantee that the day would come together smoothly. For the most part, it did—until the last ten days." The bridesmaids' dresses had arrived several weeks late—the wrong dresses—and the shop had to make a last-minute rush order. In the meantime, after a third round of alterations, Cindy's veil still did not look the way she wanted it. The seamstress assured her that she would fix the problem, but it wouldn't be ready until the day before the wedding! As if that wasn't enough, Cindy realized that one of her wedding shoes didn't fit: "The foot I had fractured when I was nine was swollen—probably from all the running around I was doing—and I couldn't put on my right shoe." Finding a new pair took her to ten different stores.

Everything went swimmingly on the big day, however. "I kept thinking that the mayhem that ensued before my wedding was due to the fact that we were getting married on a full moon and the summer solstice," Cindy says. "Little fairies somewhere were having a ball watching me go crazy! Even with all the knowledge and help that I had, I learned that things will go wrong, and you just have to find a way to deal with them."

Getting Gorgeous

In order to ensure your big day is as stress-free as humanly possible, plan how foxy you're going to look well in advance.

Killer Clothes

At the two-week mark, you should each make a final trip to meet with your big-day clothier. Brides should make sure their dress fits as it should and that they've got all their accessories (even if you've gone the off-the-rack, do-it-yourself route, it's still essential that you do a full dress rehearsal); grooms renting a tux should firm up plans, get alterations done, and arrange to pick up their outfit the day before the wedding. Make sure to hang your clothes in protective plastic covering so they look perfect for wedding day; keep all accessories together in one place.

While we're on the subject of clothes, let's talk about your bods. If you want to look your best in your out-of-sight garb, it's essential that you keep up—or step up—your fitness regimen during the final countdown period. Even if you feel insanely hectic, the benefits of a brisk, half-hour walk (to the florist's, say), a bike ride, an aerobics class, ten laps in the pool, a session with a personal trainer, or an afternoon of in-line skating are way too great to pass up. Try to fit some form of aerobic activity in six times during the last two weeks. (Sex counts as half an activity, you'll be happy to know.) If you're wearing a sleeveless gown, girlfriend, consider doing some upper body exercises, whether it's pushups, bicep curls, or chest lifts. Getting physical not only will help you look toned and beautiful, it also will add radiance to your skin, lift your spirits, and boost your energy level. You'll wear your wedding clothes with look-at-me confidence.

Clothes Call: The Dressing Checklist

The Bride
- ☐ Dress
- ☐ Veil/headpiece
- ☐ Shoes and hose
- ☐ Strapless bra or bustier
- ☐ Slip/petticoat
- ☐ Slimmer/underwear
- ☐ Garter
- ☐ Gloves
- ☐ Jewelry
- ☐ Purse

The Groom
- ☐ Tux/Suit
- ☐ Bow tie, long tie, or ascot
- ☐ Shirt
- ☐ Vest or cummerbund
- ☐ Socks
- ☐ Shoes
- ☐ Undershirt/boxers
- ☐ Cuff links
- ☐ Studs
- ☐ Suspenders
- ☐ Tie tack

Hair with Flair

Two weeks before your wedding is the deadline for getting your hair dyed, highlighted, or permed. That's so you leave time for the color or curls to tone down and, knock on wood, fix any mistakes. If possible, also schedule a trial styling session. (If you're getting a full head of braids or another complicated 'do, a verbal consultation will suffice.) Firm up plans for the big day the next time you and your stylist meet. (Grooms: You, too, may want to get your hair cut professionally no later than a week before the wedding, so you're looking as sharp as can be.)

When you meet with your hair stylist, talk about a 'do that's right for your face, suits your personality, and complements the clothes you're going to wear on your big day. (Take a Polaroid of the outfit if you can.) Things to consider:

Make a Match: A bride's hair should complement her gown, not compete with it. For a chic look, try slicking back the hair or pulling long tresses into a tight chignon. A modern, informal look gets added spunk from jeweled barrettes or a narrow headband. For a romantic look, either wear your hair au natural (sprinkles of small flowers take well to curly hair) or tie it back loosely.

Use Your Head: If a headpiece is part of your getup, find an effective way to attach it to your hair. Wide-toothed combs aren't going to cut it with straight or fine hair; have the store replace them with finer combs. Wavy and curly hair are more suited for headpiece staying power—use bobby pins, barrettes, or combs. If you'll remove your veil for the reception, make sure the 'do you choose goes well both with your headdress and without.

Shine On: The most important aspect of a bride's (and a groom's) hair is shine. Straight hair by nature tends to have more sparkle, but flyaway problems can ruin the effect. Try rubbing a sheet of Bounce (fabric softener) directly on your hair and headpiece, or spray them with an antistatic spray. For wavy and curly hair—which are prone to brittleness and dullness—slather on a moisturizing product before you begin styling, then use a shining serum to gloss.

Wedding Day Makeup

Even if you normally wear nothing but a bit of mascara or a dab of lipstick, you'll want to get more made up for your wedding—pictures, pictures! Schedule a rehearsal with your makeup artist or your department-store counter of choice. (Perhaps on the day of your bachelorette bash; after you're done, ask your pro to tone it down a little and—presto—you're ready to paint the town red.) If you're doing your own face or having a talented friend do the honors, plunk yourself down for a practice session. Stock your big-day makeup bag no later than the one-week mark. (This is a great time to indulge in some top quality products.)

Your Big-Day Makeup Bag

- Lipstick, lip liner, mascara, eyeliner, blush—for touchups

- Pressed powder (to maintain perfection)

- Blotting tissues (to minimize shine)

- Lip gloss

- Moist towelettes

- Perfume (and some of your honey's cologne, if he asks nicely)

- Hair spritz or moisture mist

Tips for a Perfect Face

"If you don't wear a lot of makeup on a regular basis, don't show up with a full face of makeup on your wedding day. Your wedding makeup has to last all day, but that doesn't mean that you should apply *more*—it actually means that you need to take your time applying it. Use powders—easier to use than pencils—and concentrate on defining the lines: your lip line, your eyelids, your brows."

—Mitchell Behr,
New York City
bridal stylist

Beauty Countdown

This step-by-step beauty schedule will have you looking fabulous come wedding day:

Six Months Before

- Want to grow your hair out or try a new color or cut? Experiment now.
- Get serious about your skin care. Start a good cleansing, nutrition, and stress-relief regimen.
- If you don't already, start exercising! A few sessions with a trainer may help to jump-start your routine.

One to Two Months Before

- Find and meet with a makeup artist for a trial run.
- Or get a makeover at a department-store counter and purchase any products you need now (so you have time to practice).
- Take your veil to your hairstylist to try out big-day 'dos.
- Have your eyebrows professionally shaped. Why not? It's your wedding!
- Test out at-home masks or a salon facial. (Don't risk an allergic reaction on your wedding day.)
- Moisturize! Soft and silky elbows, hands, and feet are a marriage must.
- Want a sparkling smile? Cut down on tea and coffee and try a whitening toothpaste.

Two Weeks Before

- Eat right. Load up on fruits and veggies; nix the salt and fat.
- Drink lots of water and exercise, exercise, exercise.
- Get your final haircut or trim.
- Touch up your haircolor or perm.
- Do a full big-day hair trial before your final dress fitting. (If you're not happy, now's the time to speak up!)

One Week Before

- Avoid overindulging in salty snacks and alcohol at those fab prewedding parties.
- Have a bikini wax and a final eyebrow shaping.
- Remind your man to get his final trim.
- Get a massage (if you can afford it; if not, ask him to do the deed, and give him one, too).
- Get a final facial. (Do not wait until the day before to do this!)

One Day and Counting

- Drink lots of water! (Have we made ourselves perfectly clear?)
- Deep-condition your hair.
- Have a professional manicure and pedicure.
- Take a long, relaxing bath.

Don't Worry, Be Happy

Want to know the cardinal rule for looking and feeling your best on your big day? Three words: relax, rest, and rejoice. Honestly, happiness is the most effective beauty secret in the world, with sleep, wholesome food, and exercise close runners-up. During these two weeks, make time for the following.

Romps with Your Friends: Make the most of your bachelor/bachelorette bash, but also make other dates with those closest to you, like a trip to the mall to hunt for earrings followed by a scary movie, a Sunday afternoon chill-out in front of the television, a group workout session topped off by a whirlpool and sauna powwow. Be silly, carefree, crazy.

Get-togethers with Out-of-Town Guests: All those great people are coming from afar to be with you on your wedding day. You'd be passing up a rare and special opportunity if you didn't spend some time with them. Greet them with a prewedding cocktail party, invite them over for a casual dinner, join them for a sightseeing tour, drop by their hotel rooms for some intimate conversation, have afternoon tea and snacks together. Chat, catch up, laugh, reminisce.

Intimate Moments with Your Honey: During the final stages of your engagement, you may have neglected one another, even had petty fights because of the mounting pressure. Now's the time to hang out, babble, and snuggle, so come wedding day you two will be a loving, winning team. Hit the gym together, book a table at your fave romantic restaurant, go to the movies.

'Twas the Night Before Wedding . . .

It's the eve of your wedding. The butterflies in your stomach are having a field day. These ten quick fixes will calm your stomach (a little) and help you sleep easier.

1. Be prepared. Lay out all your clothes and accessories so that they're ready to put on or transported to your ceremony site.
2. Watch the Weather Channel so you know what Mother Nature has in store for you. If it looks like rain or snow, alert your wedding party and relatives and ask them to bring umbrellas, space heaters, whatever. You can't change the forecast, but you can work with it.
3. Get an at-home massage. If you're only going to get rubbed down by a pro once in your life, this is the time to do it.
4. Have a nutritious carbohydrate-heavy, low-salt dinner (pasta, gourmet sandwich). You need all the energy you can get.
5. Drink a cup of herbal tea. It soothes the stomach and will help you sleep.
6. Enjoy a laid-back rehearsal dinner with your attendants and family. Whatever you do, don't stay up too late; the idea is just to take your mind off the looming dawn.
7. Whisper sweet nothings in your honey's ear. They'll be much appreciated.
8. Meditate. Spend half an hour completely alone. Play soft music, light candles, stretch, hum, pray. Calm yourself with thoughts of how lucky you are.
9. Pamper yourself. Take a luxurious bath, soak your feet, slather your body with moisturizer.
10. Order a wake-up call—just in case your alarm clock lets you down.

It's All in the Timing

The sun's up. Your vendors are getting ready to do their thing. Your mother's having a cry. Your sister's overslept (again), and your best man woke up with a hangover (again). It's all come down to this. The big day. Just a few more hours until all eyes are on you two. To make this time most manageable, sit down together a few days before the big day to write out a schedule of exactly what's going to go down when. This timetable will not only keep your whirling head in check; it also will be a useful tool for your wedding party and vendors, helping them plan and prepare for what they need to accomplish. (Don't go insane over sticking to this schedule—it's supposed to be helpful, not stress-inducing!)

Whether your vows are scheduled for when the rooster crows or when the stars come out, certain just-before-the-wedding preparations are universal. Each couple will add their own unique flavor, quirky rituals, and personal freakouts to the list. Here are some things you should *definitely* work into your schedule.

Early Preparations

Get alert, excited, and prepped—this period can last from two to eight hours, depending on your ceremony start time. It's time to:

- Wake up. Lie in bed gathering energy for a few minutes—you're gonna need it.
- Take a long shower or bath.
- Have breakfast. Eat your favorite things; you don't want to test your tummy with anything exotic today. Hold off on the coffee and tea refills, but hydrate yourself with lots of water. If your wedding is scheduled for late in the day, consider organizing a casual breakfast or brunch for your wedding party and immediate families—a team huddle before game time.
- Relax. If you're having a morning ceremony, take fifteen minutes or more to just chill. If your wedding isn't until the evening, fill your time with fairly routine day-off activities: jog, go for a drive with friends, get a pedicure (or barbershop shave) with an out-of-town pal. *Don't* obsess all day long!

Last-Minute Preparations

The two to four hours before show time are spent getting ready, *really* ready:

- Get your hair styled. Brides: It's also makeup time for you and your bridesmaids.
- Dress with the help of your attendants. Hang out with your crew to calm nerves.

How to Be Punctual

Make sure you leave enough time for the big-day essentials:

Bride's dressing: 45 minutes

Bride's hair and makeup:
40 minutes

Bridesmaids' makeup:
20 minutes each

Groom's dressing: 30 minutes

Bride's arrival at ceremony site:
20 minutes early

Groom's arrival at ceremony site: 40 minutes early

Couple and wedding party shots with photographer:
1 hour

Keep It Clean

Brides: Wear a button-down shirt when you go to have your hair and makeup done so you don't have to pull it over your head when you change.

Chapters 7 and 8
give you info on
what typically
happens, and
when, during the
ceremony and
reception.

Something Old, Something New . . .

This wedding tradition (old, new, borrowed, blue) is from an old English rhyme. This is possibly one of the most-fun last-minute wedding tasks—especially because you usually get help from your parents and attendants.

Something Old: The idea is to carry a token of the past into this new phase of your life. Go for: a locket with a childhood photo or your parents' wedding portrait; an antique necklace, bracelet, or pair of earrings that's been handed down in your family; an inherited book of prayers or poems (read from it during the ceremony); a piece of your security blanket or a family quilt sewn into the hem of your dress.

Something New: You're being reborn as a married chick—the idea is to celebrate the novelty. Go for: brand-new lingerie; a sparkly tiara or pair of barrettes; a daring new haircut or color (one that you've tested out, of course).

Something Borrowed: Marriage is about community, both your tight family unit and your wide support circle. Give it a nod by wearing something that belongs to a loved one. Go for: your mom's or sister's veil; your best friend's earrings; your niece's charm bracelet; gloves made from lace from your grandmother's wedding gown.

Something Blue: The color of fidelity, blue Curaçao, and other good stuff. Go for: blue toenail polish; baby-blue heels; bluebells scattered in your bouquet or tresses; a navy satin purse; sapphire earrings.

● Pose for formal portraits. Unless you're totally opposed to seeing each other prewedding, this is a great opportunity to get shots of you two with your wedding party and families out of the way. That way you can go straight to the party after your ceremony, or at least get there more quickly.

Now You See Me . . .

Some say it's bad luck for the bride and groom to see each other before the ceremony. We say it's bad luck to do something just because it's tradition. Go with your gut—breakfast together might be just what you need.

It's Showtime!

Time to walk down the aisle, say your vows, kiss, greet guests, and, most important, have lots of fun. In your timetable, jot down your estimated ceremony start and end time and reception arrival time. The rest of the to-do will flow from there!

Last-Minute Craziness

Murphy's Law says there's always going to be a big-day glitch (or two). Problems will arise on your wedding day, some serious, some silly. Most will work themselves out; some you'll never even know about.

Emergency Remedies

Here are some common big-day problems and our favorite quick fixes:

Heat Wave: If your idea of a perfect wedding does *not* include a mass meltdown, beat the heat with huge water coolers (and cups!) on hand at your ceremony and reception, heavy-duty electric fan action, and paper fans as favors. (Ceremony programs will double in a pinch.) For outdoor affairs, make sure there's ample shade by hanging fabrics among trees, setting up an airy tent, or supplying sun umbrellas to guests. Make sure air conditioners are on early enough to get your sites cool before the crowds arrive. This is particularly important for early-morning events.

Rain/Snow: Monitor the weather forecast the week before your wedding. If things look like they could get wacky, prepare yourselves. In case of rain, bring as many oversized umbrellas for your guests as you can, and move festivities indoors. (That backup site we recommended comes in handy *now.*) For snow, hire a plow operator to clear access roads and parking lots (or make sure your sites do), rent four-wheel-drive vehicles to transport guests, and bring space heaters to your sites. In both cases, stock up guest bathrooms with grooming products so they can repair weather damage, and play appropriate songs, such as "Singing in the Rain," "It's Raining Men," and "White Christmas" during your reception.

Sick Relative: If a close family member falls ill and is unable to attend your wedding, the show should go on (unless, of course, things look really, really bad and you're too upset). Your loved one probably would want it that way. Find ways to include this person in the proceedings. Have him/her pen a piece you'll read during the ceremony; have your officiant lead a prayer for his/her recovery; play the absentee's favorite song during your reception and dedicate it to him/her; have a friend "broadcast" the ceremony to him/her by cell phone during your vows. Send flowers and a card on the morning of your big day and then make sure to visit your loved one at some point before you leave for your honeymoon.

Wedding Emergency Kit

Put together a bag of "tools" to keep you two fresh and gorgeous, help you solve potential predicaments, and generally keep things together. (After pulling everything together, entrust it to your attendants.)

Breath mints/spray (or a small toothbrush and tube of toothpaste)
Safety pins
White masking tape (for wayward hems)
Small brush/comb
Clear nail polish (for inevitable stocking runs)
Krazy Glue (for shoe heels, decorations, even jewels)
Tissues
Aspirin
Smelling salts
Ponytail holder/bobby pins/butterfly clip (in case your hair does a double take)
Cellular phone (borrow one if you don't have your own—it's essential for tracking down vendors, guests, or other lost parties)
Tampons/sanitary napkins
Static-cling spray
Power Bar/Fig Newtons/bag of pretzels (even to-be-weds get hunger pangs)

Tight Ring: It fit perfectly in the store (and two days ago!), but between the heat and nerves your fingers have grown to monstrous proportions. This common ailment can be prevented easily by running your hands under cool water and coating your ring fingers with Vaseline just before the ceremony to ensure a smooth, easy glide.

Fainting Guest: This is a highly emotional event for you and yours, and depending on the season it can get hot in that church, so it's not uncommon for someone to pass out. Don't panic. Attend to the fallen guest (this is your once-in-a-lifetime chance to yell "smelling salts, smelling salts!"); once the person has revived, have him/her sit with head down until s/he feels better.

Drunken Guest: Every party has at least one guest who goes overboard. Have one of your assertive attendants on sober (okay, almost sober) duty to take care of disruptive behavior. If necessary, have a designated driver take beyond-drunk guests home or back to the hotel. In general, it's a good idea to close the bar an hour before your reception ends, so people won't be *able* to have one for the road.

Hangover: Drink lots of water from the moment you wake up. Amazingly enough, greasy foods will help calm your stomach (presumably they absorb the alcohol), as will a bottle of Coke. Take a long, cool shower and pop some aspirin if you need to.

Zit: You wake up the morning before the big day with visions of hundreds of fawning guests, only to find there's a new neighbor on your face. Zap it with a blemish ointment like Clearasil, being careful to avoid contact with the rest of your skin so you won't end up with a dry, flaky patch. On the day of the wedding, use concealer to hide it.

Keep in Touch

Take a contact list with the numbers of all the critical people—vendors, attendants, family—along to the wedding. Go to Appendix A to get started.

Vendor Problems

Careful screening and contract-writing are important preventative measures against vendor mishaps. However, even the best of vendors can—and do—slip up.

The Big Picture: On your wedding day, it's too late for your vendor to undo the damage if s/he brings the wrong order, sends a less-qualified replacement, shows up late or never, or otherwise fouls up your agreement. In the short run, you need to:

- Take a deep breath.
- Point out to your vendor the items or services that are not satisfactory.
- Try to track down a vendor missing-in-action.
- Either return unsatisfactory orders or get a verbal commitment to be compensated financially.

If you have a clear and precise contract and have paid your deposit using a credit card—we can't emphasize the importance of this enough—you are fairly safe as far as getting your money back in the case of a no-show or a fouled-up job. Either your vendor will do the right thing by reimbursing you, or your credit card company will take up your case if you dispute a charge. Worst-case scenario: You take the out-of-line "pro" to small claims court.

Immediate Fixes: All is not lost if you don't get what you expected from your vendor. Even the worst screw-up can be covered up with a little help from your friends and a bit of initiative.

- Food: If the caterer brings food you don't want—or nothing at all—order in lots of pizzas, Chinese food, deli salads, or other goodies. Have friends and relatives run out for hors d'oeuvres platters as well as soft drinks, cakes, and anything else you need. Who knows? Your makeshift cuisine might be an even bigger hit than the catered fare would have been.
- Flowers: If your florist botches things up, raid the nearest farmer's market for the day's best blooms. Send some attendants to a local flower shop to buy as many bouquets as you can afford; ask relatives to bring vases by as soon as possible. Balloons and streamers are quick-fix decorative fillers.
- Music: Ask a musical friend to tote along his/her instrument in case your ceremony musicians don't show. You also can buy a wedding-music tape and play it on the site's stereo system or your own boom box. Play mix tapes made by you and your friends should your band or DJ not show; appoint a groovy friend to monitor CD changes. Arrange in advance for an alternate stereo system should the need arise.
- Photography/videography: If these crucial pros are no-shows, have someone run out to the drugstore for tons of film and get the word out for everyone with a camera (or camcorder) to go crazy. Ask a particularly talented photographer friend to do you the honor of shooting your formal pictures.
- Transportation: If your limo never arrives, it's time to hail a cab (they'll stop in a sec for a chick in a wedding dress) or hitch a ride with the bridesmaids or Mom and Dad.

Having a Ball

Your big day will come and go like a beautiful, blazing comet. If all you're doing is obsessing, worrying, and fretting, you'll miss its fleeting glory. In order to make your wedding a truly special event, you two need to revel in it, milk it, seize it by the horns. Focus on the excellent things—your honey's smile when you're pronounced husband and wife, your adoring guests, the scrumptious food, watching your friends dance—not the glitches or slip-ups. Not only will this make your big day better and put your attendants and guests at ease, it'll also be good practice for marriage—and life (i.e., always look on the bright side). Ways to really savor the day:

- Take a minute to write in your journal on wedding morning.
- Tell your parents you love them.
- Get in the middle of a group hug with your best friends before the festivities begin.

- After the ceremony, retreat with your honey to a quiet, private place. Kiss, gaze into each other's eyes, and tell each other how happy you are.
- Chat with friends and family you adore but hardly ever see.
- At some point during the reception, grab your honey's hand under the table and squeeze it tight.
- When you take a pit stop during the party, look at yourself in the mirror and smile.
- Eat something even if you're nauseous with nerves—it will keep your stamina up.
- Shake your bootie on the dance floor. Tango with your baby. Lead a silly line dance. Twirl your nephews and nieces around. Twist with Grandpa.
- Toast all your guests.
- When the reception's in full swing, stand back for a couple of minutes and just take in the sights and sounds.

Forget the preparations, the decisions, the agonizing, the coordinating, the orchestrating, the finessing. Your most critical task at this point is having the time of your lives. *This* is what it's all about: love, happiness, fun, good friends, and family. Oh, yeah, and how simply amazing your sweetie is.

Leaving the Wedding

Where to Next?

BRIDAL SUITE

DO NOT DISTURB

Let the Games Begin

The Big Morning After

The Big Night

You've come this far. The hors d'oeuvres are chosen, the reception room's set, the gifts are pouring in. In other words, everything's going exactly as planned. But then there's a moment. A fleeting flash of quiet introspection amid the organizing storm when you dare to ask yourself, "Isn't there a higher meaning to all of this?" Well, yes. In addition to all the partying and planning and parental gratification, your wedding night does have a deeper, more intimate purpose. It's about leaving your friends and family behind, disappearing into a cloud of birdseed and tears. Welcome to the big night.

The big night is the opposite of everything that happens on your wedding day. It's the first time in that twenty-four-hour period when you're actually allowed to blow off the concerns of anybody and everybody besides your new husband or wife. It's your moment to finally be alone.

Leaving the Wedding

The first step in any newlywed couple's big night is, literally, out the door. You've got to ditch the party—leave the reception behind and get to your next operational staging area (hotel, airport, seaside bungalow). This is actually more difficult than it sounds, since, as the stars of this event, you'll be surrounded by anywhere between 5 and 1,500 of your nearest and dearest, all set on getting a piece of the action (a few moments with you) before you bail out the door. You've got to give everybody their due. In fact, these days a lot of couples actually stay until the bitter end of the party to make sure they've spent time with each and every guest before they slip away to do you-know-what.

But still, there will come a moment when it's perfectly acceptable to flee to your getaway vehicle. Which brings us to the first important big night element that you need to plan ahead for: transportation.

Getaway Pointers: Notice we just said getaway *vehicle,* not getaway *car.* That's because there's no rule, law, or wedding etiquette dictating that you have to hop into a white stretch limousine for your party departure. The only necessary transportation stipulations are that your ride must (1) move and (2) match your exacting aesthetic, comfort, and snob-appeal requirements. Assuming that you've probably got a pretty good handle on the whole physics of motion thing, we'll move right on to part (2).

Like everything else about your wedding, the way you leave should complement your personal style. Considering that it's how your guests will remember you riding off into the sunrise of your love (we can't believe we just wrote that), it pays to put a little creative thought into the decision. But remember, it's also going to be one of those images that lives forever in your wedding album—so it pays equally as well to show some tasteful caution. That said, here are some of our favorite big-night ways to move on.

The Classic Approach: Truth be told, you can't go wrong with a stretch limo. It's simple, elegant, and fits everyone's picture of the storybook way to end a perfect wedding. What it may lack in originality a stretch limousine more than makes up for in sheer class and reliability. When you buy quality, you only wince once.

Need a Ride?

Where's a good limo when you really need one? Call the National Limousine Association (800–652–7007) for a referral, or check their Web site (www.limo.org) to find a nice stretch near you.

Getting Stretched

A limousine departure from your wedding reception is classic, classy, and, face it, more comfortable than the backseat of your uncle's Tercel. If you're going to rent—as opposed to buy, borrow, or steal—keep the following in mind:

Reserve at least six months in advance. A last-minute limo search is more likely to net you a car that says "Take us to the mortuary!" than something long and weddinglike.

Shop around. Call more than one service and compare prices. The national average is around $50 per hour plus a 15 percent tip.

Check the car out in person. One person's luxury is another's fuzzy dice. While you're there, also ask what the driver will be wearing. (For this event, appropriate means black jacket and tie, not a Winger T-shirt and jeans.)

Sign a contract. You'll want the full terms in writing, including total price, deposit, overtime, cancellation policies, and confirmation of all dates, times, and locations.

Haggle for extras. A TV's nice, but champagne's better. Work the charm and see what they'll throw in gratis.

Consider the color. If you're not a stickler for all things white, black and silver limos generally cost 10 percent less.

Make sure the driver knows where he's going!

Get Personal: What better way to end the public part of your wedding—and begin the private part—than to ride away in/on something that's uniquely you? A tandem bike for loving cyclists or hot-air balloon for likewise loving balloonists, say. The sky's the limit (pun intended) as long as your choice gets you to your desired destination in one piece. In other words, think twice before choosing to in-line skate or bungee-jump.

The Old School: If you're looking to add a little character to your departure but still want something on the traditional side, consider the several charmingly old-fashioned options. A horse and buggy is probably the most romantic way to take off on a warm summer evening, and it makes for a great photo op. For longer rides or colder weather, a Bentley or Rolls-Royce limo is the perfect best-of-both-worlds getaway car. Both have tons of class, lots of original charm, and were *made* for sipping champagne in the cushy backseat.

Where to Next?

You've figured out how you're going to leave the reception—now you've got to find a place to go. Depending on what your honeymoon plans are, there are several options for where to spend your first night together as husband and wife.

The Honeymoon Suite

Without a doubt, the most common big-night destination is a nearby hoity-toity hotel. The night is earmarked as one of the most memorable of your life, and special, fancier-than-normal surroundings can set the perfect tone. As we all know, however, all hotels were not created equal—even the four-star kind—so it's important that you do a little prewedding reconnaissance and select your lodgings with care. Consider these points as you formulate your battle plan.

Is the Joint Actually Nice? Reputation is one thing; firsthand inspection is another. Just because a hotel is famous doesn't mean the rooms are habitable and the service is friendly—all-important components of a successful big-night environment. Take a look for yourself.

Is the Room Fully Stocked? Do a walk-through of the room and check for: (1) an inspiring view; (2) a squeak-free, king-size mattress; (3) a fully stocked minibar; (4) a clean tub (preferably with Jacuzzi jets) large enough for two; (5) a cable-equipped TV (with adult pay-per-view options); (6) room service.

What Can You Scam for Free? Most hotels worth their Bibles offer some sort of upgrade or thoughtful freebie for newlyweds, from a chilled bottle of bubbly to a better view or larger suite. If you don't feel comfortable asking, get one of your parents or friends to call and talk to the manager.

Gotta Fly Now

If you're one of those daring couples jetting straight to your honeymoon location, you won't be able to enjoy the comfort of a cushy hotel room immediately, but that doesn't mean you've got to suffer like any other anonymous airport slob. Au contraire!

IRENE AND TUCKER

June 15, Philadelphia, Pennsylvania

AS THEIR WEDDING RECEPTION began to wind down, Irene and Tucker didn't make the traditional grand exit and subsequent dash to a nearby hotel room often performed by newlyweds. Instead, the party's end was only the beginning of their big night. "Our family got tired about 1:00 A.M., but we weren't ready to say good night," Irene says. Instead, the couple and about fifteen of their closest friends went dancing at a club in downtown Philadelphia. "All of our faraway friends were in town—we didn't want to pass up the chance to spend time with them," Irene explains. "We danced until five-thirty, when we couldn't walk any more. It was a blast."

Irene and Tucker didn't think there was anything strange about not spending their first night as a married couple alone. "I wouldn't have wanted to be anywhere else," the bride says. "The only thing that was a little strange was walking into a club with about 120 bobby pins in my hair. I'm sure people thought I looked a bit bizarre."

The first step to a comfy newlywed flight is booking with a reputable airline. This is your honeymoon, after all—don't skimp and try a bargain-basement carrier. When you arrive at the airport, notify the ticket agent of your newlywed status—feel free to flash your marriage license, rings, the smear of wedding-cake frosting on your lapel, or any other convincingly authentic items—and ask if you can wait for the flight in their VIP lounge.

If you're flying coach, ask if a first-class upgrade is possible. The better the airline, the better your chances of flying up front with the genuine swells. If there's room, you're almost guaranteed to get first-class seats, and maybe even a bottle of champagne to boot. This trick works both ways if you're returning from a country that subscribes to a Westernized understanding of marriage (monogamous, licensed, free of sacrificial offerings), so feel free to push your luck.

Let the Games Begin

So you're now safely ensconced in your big-night destination. Whether it's a swanky local hotel room or a Mediterranean villa, one thing's for certain—now it's time to get down to business.

Like peanut butter and jelly or milk and cookies, your wedding night and S-E-X are inseparable elements. You can't have one without the other. Well, you can, of course, but that's not the point. The point is, this is your big night together. The first time you and your loved one will lie side by side in bed as legally bound partners for life. So whether it's your first time or the higher-number-than-you-can-possibly-calculate time, this is your moment to consummate the marriage bond.

Now, we're going to leave all the technical details to your parents or high-school sex ed teacher and assume that when it comes to doing the deed, you know which end is up. Same goes for the more advanced positional variations and physiodynamic options at your disposal. What we *are* here to discuss are the best ways to set the mood, calm the nerves, and make the most of this once-in-a-lifetime romantic moment.

There are two kinds of big-night couples: Those who have done "it" before and those who've been holding out courageously. If you're a member of the former, your mission is making the evening a special, loving experience that stands out from all your prenuptial liaisons. If you're a member of the latter, skip down a couple of paragraphs, because, well, *we need to talk privately.*

Make Yourselves Crazy

If you and your honey are, well, a little ho-hum about getting it on lately, consider declaring an official sex-free week right before your wedding. It might be just the thing you need to recharge the batteries.

Old Pros

Okay, so big deal, you've done it a couple dozen/hundred/thousand times together already. That doesn't mean your big night has to be a paint-by-number affair. It can (and should) be something extraordinary that you'll both remember with a loving smile, thumping heart, or at least a long, lustful laugh. Think of it as a milestone in your relationship: a chance for you

The Big Elopement Night

So you've opted for the no-frills wedding—no reception, no church, no family struggles, just you, your beloved, and a judge (or maybe an Elvis impersonator). Might we suggest some options for your no-fuss wedding night?

Hire a cab or a limo to drive around town all night. Get busy in the backseat.

Go camping in a remote spot near a lake, beach, or hot springs. After you finish gazing at the stars (and into each other's eyes), go skinny-dipping.

Visit a casino and use half the money you would have spent on a reception to play with. (Invest the other half.)

Stay up all night drinking and dancing. Consummate your marriage at dawn.

Pick the one place in the world that you've always thought was the most romantic (a tree in your backyard, the Empire State Building, the Eiffel Tower), and go there to drink champagne and pledge your love to each other.

Go to the airport and buy the cheapest or most convenient round-trip ticket to a romantic place. Hop the next plane out.

Tell all of your friends that you're leaving town and hole yourself up in your apartment for the week. Unplug the phone and don't check your e-mail.

both to strip off your clothes, get under the covers—or the nearest palm tree—and reaffirm how much you truly mean to one another.

Your wedding ceremony was probably nice and meaningful, but unless you tied the knot on a remote Himalayan mountaintop, odds are it wasn't history's most private exchange of vows. Now's your chance to make it intimate. The first thing you have to do is set the right mood.

Rub-a-Dub-Dub: Weddings generate lots of things for the modern couple—presents, in-laws, and sensible shoe–wearing marriage counselors, to name just a few. But most of all, weddings generate stress and fatigue—two things that have no place in a successful big night: Tired, tense couples aren't generally that into sex. The best remedy, of course, is a nice warm bath for two, with all the trimmings.

Picture this: A big bathroom, the lights out, and your favorite mellow music on the stereo. Scented candles surround a tub filled to the brim with bubbles. Add one ice bucket, a bottle of good champagne, and two crystal flutes, followed by two naked bodies—that would be you two—and a tube of body paint. Okay, the body paint is optional, but everything else is practically mandatory for a perfect chill-out-and-let's-get-sexy atmosphere.

Once you've toweled off, you should be relaxed and ready to get cozy in your honeymoon bed. At this point, you can proceed in one of three ways.

Suspension of Disbelief: Since your wedding is, in fact, the start of a new phase in your relationship, you can think of the big night as your chance to begin again as freshmen in the sex department. Think of it as your Madonna makeover. Even though you're old pros with one another, your wedding night is the best excuse yet for recapturing that virgin moment when you touched each other for the very first time. Don't just hop in the sack and go at it as usual. Invest in a little prep time. Anything that contributes to the unexpected and makes you a little nervous is good. It sounds kinda stupid, we know, but if you can re-create some of those first-time jitters, you're in for a pretty good time.

Been There, Done That: Celebrate the fact that you already enjoy a pretty rockin' sex life together. Use your big night to review some of the highlights—sort of a greatest-hits compilation of your wildest moments. Props are essential here. For example, let's say one of your best memories is doing it under the Eiffel Tower. Pack some croissants and French wine and relive the experience. Bring a little surf music and sunscreen for those summer break sex-on-the-beach memories. If you'd like to add some variation to your old routine, mix things up a little. Instead of going the kissing-touching-intercourse route, vary the order and throw in a couple of moves that you haven't used since high school. (Hint: The tongue isn't just for kissing anymore.) Enough said.

Unexplored Territory: For the daring, the big night can be the perfect time to introduce some new and interesting predilections into the relationship. You know, the *kinky* stuff. Since your wedding night is the start of a new chapter in your love affair, it's ripe for exploration of the unknown sexual territory that you have yet to traverse as a couple. We're not going to get into specifics here—we're already blushing—but we will recommend packing some naughty toys along with the lingerie and scented candles. A few words of caution: Don't go overboard. If your fiancé has expressed a repressed desire to be "bagged and gagged," by all means, bring along the handcuffs. But unless you've had some sort of prior communication, avoid anything that even barely crosses the line between kinky and federally offensive.

Get Yourselves Ready

Don't neglect to spend a little extra time on grooming before you take off for your wedding. A pedicure, manicure, and nice clean shave (we're talking both sexes here) will do a lot to help set a positive mood for the action to come on your big night.

First-timers

Now for the moment you've all been waiting for. What can we possibly say to those of you who have dutifully held out until this big night to do it for the first time other than: You made it! Congratulations! Sure, it was a long haul, but the end (and the beginning) is now in sight. That doesn't mean the pressure's off yet, though. As you're obviously well aware, the first time is a pretty heavy-duty event. How will it start? Who will do what? Will it be good? So many unknowns and so many questions, to which we have one single answer: Don't stress.

It's Not That Big of a Deal: Really. Compared to meeting each other's parents or buying a diamond ring, having sex is a cakewalk. In fact, it's the icing on the cake of your wedding day. It may sound incredibly trite, but it's true.

It's Only the First Time: And it definitely won't be the last. The first time in the sack is almost always an awkward experience. It takes awhile to get in sync with your partner and figure out what makes each of you tick. That's why you've got about a couple thousand more times to get it right. This is merely the first night of the rest of your amazing sex life.

The big night is for dipping your toe in the water. You've got the rest of your honeymoon—and an entire life together—to learn how to swim.

It's Fun: We take part of number two back: There is no one "right" way to have sex. There's an infinite amount of "right" ways—in fact, anything that feels good is right enough for us (as long as you're both still breathing when you're done). The key is to have a good time and enjoy the fact that you're finally able to do *anything you want* with the person you love more than any other person in the world. This is the moment to unpack all your fantasies.

You're Allowed to Open Your Mouth: For speaking, among other things. Just as with everything else wedding related, good communication is the key to great pillow talk. Since you're new to this, talk to each other to figure out what is, and isn't, working. Ask questions. Express your fears. When something feels *really* good, say so. The whole communication thing is especially important if you're a "mixed" couple (one of you is a virgin, the other's not). In this case, it's crucial that the more seasoned partner offers up words of encouragement to help soothe the other's fears and insecurities.

You Don't *Have* to Do It

After the longest day of your life—a day of primping and performing and schmoozing and boozing and emotional excitement and withdrawal—the big night might end up being all about the irresistible desire just to pass out. At the end of a long wedding day, most couples are so exhausted that the last thing on their minds is getting hot 'n' heavy under the covers. No sweat. Literally. This is the fate of tons of newlyweds who are passionately, romantically, eternally in love with one another but just can't summon the energy to get it on first thing postreception.

The reason we're bringing this up is that we don't want you to feel like not having sex on your big night means something's wrong with your relationship, or that it's a bad, lazy sign of things to come. It's not. It's merely a sign that you're too pooped to party and need to save up your energy for some *really* good lovin' once the sun comes up. That doesn't mean, however, that you should just lurch into your hotel room and pass out with your wedding clothes on. No, you may not be up to the task of a full-blown hanky-panky session, but you *can* have some fun before you go comatose.

We've already mentioned the importance of a really cozy bath for destressing after the wedding. If you don't think you're going to light the fireworks later, the bath is a good place to give each other a sexy rubdown at least. Then again, you don't have to be wet to rub your hands all over each other. A light massage with some body oil or lotion is always a pleasant predreaming treat, too.

One more thing: Never underestimate the power of cuddling.

The Big Morning After

Good morning! It's your first full day of being married! So what next? You could (1) spend the next twenty-four hours in bed with the phone off the hook and have room service deliver really flat foods (crackers, American cheese, Pop Tarts) that will slide under the door, or (2) jump up at the crack of dawn and go hang out with your family and friends. It's a matter of personal preference, of course, so do whatever floats your boat. In either case, don't miss out on the opportunity to have your first round of wake-up sex as a married couple.

Wake-up sex on the big morning after is your chance to do it just because you feel like it. You've had a chance to sleep away all the wedding exhaustion, and now you're ready to go at it again and again if you like. Or not. No pressure, no expectations, no reason to get out of bed until you want to. It's like waking up to a whole new world. Unlike wedding morning, you're not worrying about getting to the ceremony on time or who's going to pick Uncle Murray up from the airport. All you've got to think about is each other . . . and, of course, whether you want to do it one more time in bed before getting up for your first official round of married shower sex. Decisions, decisions.

Honeymoon Highway

How often in life is it encouraged—all right, *demanded*—that you drop everything and rush off to the most romantic spots on earth to while away the days in unabashed bliss? Once— right now, on your honeymoon. This is your chance to take the biggest trip of your lives (to date) and splurge to your hearts' content—with everyone's deep approval and warm good wishes.

Go to Chapter 24 for help planning your trip.

There's only one rule: Take the trip of *your* dreams. Talk about what kind of vacation floats your boat (cruise?), makes your hearts soar (a B&B high in the hills?), or sends goose bumps down your spines (an Arctic adventure?). Or maybe you're just ready for a good old-fashioned beach honeymoon. Banish that six-letter "B" word from your mind; budget has no place in your honeymoon vision (yet). Just get your dream trip in sharp focus; we'll help you figure out how to foot the bill in Chapter 24.

So what are the options? Here's a sampling of some of our favorite spots.

The Best Beaches

Calm breezes, sandy beaches—it's a classic honeymoon scenario. A beach vacation can be Ritz-Carlton chic or Ritz-cracker casual. It can be quiet and deserted—just a strip of sugar sand, swaying palms, and thee—or Bay-watch–meets–Spring Break boisterous. You decide what type of sand scenario says "romance" to you. Whichever way you go, you'll find miles of

> **Honeymoon Love**
>
> Newlyweds used to drink mead, a honey-based wine, for their first married month, or "moon"—honey + moon = honeymoon. This fermented brew of honey, water, yeast, and spices, originally created by medieval monks, was used to ease any postwedding tension (and help the couple get busy in the bedroom!).

excellent beach right here in our very own hemisphere—meaning you don't have to cross the globe to get good sand. The one drawback of the sun-and-surf approach is that it's weather-dependent. While we know you'll think of something to do if it rains, plan to hit your tropical isle of choice when hurricanes generally don't. Here are some of our top beach spots.

Kauai, Hawaii

The least developed of the Big Four Hawaiian islands (Hawaii, Kauai, Oahu, and Maui), Kauai lets you experience Hawaii's legendary lushness without tons of T-shirt shops, traffic, or tourists. After an easy five-hour flight to Honolulu from California, it's a quick hop on an interisland airline to this westerly wonderland.

Why You'll Love It: Possibly the most romantic island in the world, with green mountains, crashing waterfalls, and geyserlike water flumes shooting over rocks. About as exotic as you can go and still get the Sunday *Times.* Peaceful. Serene. Awe-inspiring.

When to Go: Year round (December and January are the rainiest months).

Must-Dos: Hike Waimea Canyon (called "the Grand Canyon of the Pacific") to see plants that grow nowhere else in the world. Take a helicopter tour around the island for an aerial view of the rivers, waterfalls, and the stunning cliffs of the Na Pali coastline. Snorkel at Ke'e Beach. Stroll through the town of Hanalei. Pig out at a Hawaiian luau. Learn the art of massage together at the Hyatt's Anara Spa. For info, call the Kauai Hotline at 800–262–1400.

Anguilla

This little-known, formerly British island has what many consider the best beaches in the Caribbean—and the most private. Chances are you'll see more goats than people on your trip.

Why You'll Love It: Dozens of beaches (thirty-three coves, to be exact) with white sand, aquamarine water, and no one but you and your beloved anywhere in sight. Charming, English-speaking locals. A totally quiet, private hideaway that feels like a deserted island—but with room service. A short ferry ride from the stores, restaurants, and bustle of St. Martin/Sint Maarten, the half-French/half-Dutch island visible on the horizon that's as bustling as Anguilla is calm.

When to Go: December–August.

Must-Dos: Take off your watch. Discover a different isolated cove every day. Explore the island by bike. (Ride on the left side of the road!) Have fresh snapper at Ernie's. Eat conch stew. Drink plenty of rum punch. Snorkel, swim, and snack at Shoal Bay. Check out Moorish-style Cap Juluca (the choicest resort), Malliouhana, or the all-inclusive Casablanca. Or rent your own villa for even more alone time. For info by mail, call the Anguilla Tourist Board at 800–553–4939, or log on to www.candw.com.ai/~atbtour.

Puerto Vallarta, Mexico

Once a quiet fishing village on Mexico's Pacific coast, Puerto Vallarta hit the headlines after the Elizabeth Taylor/Richard Burton film *Night of the Iguana.* The duo reportedly fell in love while on location here, inspiring millions of star-struck lovers to follow their footsteps to this beachfront town—turning it into the bustling resort/quaint Mexican village you'll find today.

When You'll Love It: Deluxe hotels, super-fresh food, and sizzling night life. Crooked cobblestone streets lined with funky, whitewashed adobe restaurants, indigenous crafts, and international boutiques. Genuine local color, despite the tourist comforts—look up from your cappuccino at a new, Seattle-style café to see fifty women in fuchsia feather head-dresses parading down the street. Safe and friendly. Most people speak some English.

When to Go: February–May (November–January is a bit rainier; June and July are hot day *and* night).

Must-Dos: Visit the Playa de los Muertos (beach of the dead—but filled with very lively sunbathers). Eat fresh fish grilled over charcoal pits on the sand. Buy silver, wood carvings, rugs and serapes from strolling vendors. Get turtle cream (a great after-sun mois-turizer) on the island in the Rio Cuale. Visit the recently restored *Iguana* set. Indulge in a Mexican version of fancy French food at the terraced gar-den of Café des Artistes. Snorkel, scuba dive, go deep-sea fishing. Walk hand in hand along the oceanfront *malecon* (boardwalk). Disco at Crystal. Sip Corona with lime at the bars. Call Mexico tourism at 800–44–MEXICO, or check out www.mexico-travel.com.

Less Can Be More

Lack the funds for your ulti-mate fantasy? Find a less-ex-pensive alternative with the same great features. Great beach? Caribbean instead of the South Pacific. Big city? Chicago rather than New York. Big nature? Yellowstone rather than Africa. Save up for that dream trip on your first (or fifth, or tenth) anniversary.

St. John, U.S. Virgin Islands

The U.S. Virgin Islands are American territory—no passports required. As for the status of your sex life before you arrive, that's your business. But we're betting that the sheer beauty of St. John (and your mad love for each other) will take care of that. The smallest of the three main U.S. Virgin Is-lands (St. John, St. Croix, and St. Thomas), it's also the most pristine.

Why You'll Love It: Two-thirds of the island is national park. Caribbean beauty with the comforts of home. Excellent snorkeling, hiking, biking, and swimming. Accommodations ranging from super-luxurious Caneel Bay (with its seven amazing beaches) to rustic-yet-romantic campgrounds at Cinnamon Bay and Maho Bay.

When to Go: December–August.

Must-Dos: Hike the Reef Bay Trail through forest and cacti, past an old sugar mill and pre-Columbian petroglyphs. Do the snorkel trail at Trunk Bay, an underwater "hike." Try "Snuba," a cross between snorkeling and scuba diving, at Cruz Bay. Shack up in an ecofriendly hillside tent overlooking the beach at Maho Bay or Cinnamon Bay for at least one night. Call the U.S. Virgin Islands at 800–372–8784, or see the site at www. stjohnusvi.com.

South Beach, Florida

Located on the southern tip of Miami Beach—an island connected to the city of Miami by "causeways," or long bridges—South Beach was the hot spot in the 1930s and looks to be the hippest beach resort once again at least through the millennium.

**Perfect Stretches
of Sand**

The ten most romantic beaches
in the United States, according
to Dr. Stephen Leatherman,
Ph.D., author of *America's
Best Beaches* (published in
conjunction with Florida International University, 1998):

1. Captiva Island, Florida
2. Hamoa Beach, Hana, Maui
3. Kiawah Island, South
   Carolina
4. Little St. Simons Island,
   Georgia
5. Kapalua, Maui
6. Santa Catalina Island,
   California
7. Keewaydin Island, Naples,
   Florida
8. East Hampton, Long
   Island, New York
9. South Nauset Beach,
   Chatham, Massachussetts
10. Bald Head Island, North
    Carolina

Why You'll Love It: A huge, palm tree–lined beach and the hottest nightlife in the country. Great Cuban cooking (and Miami's own spicy "New World" cuisine). Tons of shopping, from Lincoln Road's eclectic boutiques to the super upscale shops in nearby Bal Harbor. A chance to use your Spanish. Glamorous, completely renovated, pastel-painted Art Deco hotels from the 1920s and '30s facing the beach. Easy and cheap to get to. American with an international feel.

When to Go: October–April (May and June are less crowded, cheaper, and hotter).

Must-Dos: Take an Art Deco walking tour. Observe octogenarian Cubans playing dominoes on a card table in the shade. Stroll the strip with model wannabes. Have cocktails (or, better yet, a mineral bath at the spa—women only) in the trendiest-of-all trendy hotels, The Delano (or The Tides). Eat at Yuca and watch the Miami City Ballet rehearse right from the street. Dance it off to a salsa band at night. Call the Greater Miami Convention & Visitors Bureau at 800–283–2707, or cruise over to www.miamiandbeaches.com.

Adrenaline Adventures

Why not begin your marriage with heart-pounding excitement—on an action-packed honeymoon? For some, adrenaline is the ultimate aphrodisiac—making an adventure trip the perfect escape. Whether you go high-octane athletic or low-impact leisurely, find out the peak season for the sport you'll be doing, the safety record of your outfitter, and a list of supplies you must bring. If you're taking a group trip, be sure to ask how much privacy you'll have.

Biking in Ireland

Grab your hybrid cycle and hop on for a tour across southwestern Ireland. You'll peddle through County Cork and the small villages of Kenmare, Baltimore, Ballylicky, Inishannon, and Kinsale—a fishing town known as the "good food circle" for its numerous fine restaurants. This is a trip for experienced riders—we're talking hills, hills, hills.

Why You'll Love It: Steep mountains carved by glaciers. Medieval castles. Emerald-green fields. Sheep. Stone fences. Celtic ruins. Seaside towns with beautiful ocean vistas. Good riding on open spaces. Plenty of pub action at night.

When to Go: Late June–early August.

Must-Dos: Hit the pubs, even if you don't drink; locals in these quaint villages will see you bike in and want to chat (and buy you a beer). Drink Guinness on tap, Ireland's most popular stout. Dance an Irish jig to a live band. See tropical plants at Derreen Gardens on the Beara Peninsula. Call the Southern Irish Tourist Board at (800–233–6470 (212–418–0800 in New York) or check out www.ireland.com.

LESLEY AND TOMAS

June 24, Vancouver, Washington

SINCE LESLEY AND TOMAS lived four blocks from the ocean, they weren't particularly interested in spending their honeymoon lying on a beach and basking in the sun. "We're very active people anyway," Lesley says. "We wanted to mark our marriage with a totally new experience that we would never forget. We also wanted the chance to do lots of different activities." Tomas suggested they spend two weeks in southeastern Alaska. While there, the couple indeed did a little of everything: "We rode mountain bikes through the hills, we went kayaking and whale watching, and took a daylong boat excursion up Glacier Bay with a National Park Ranger."

Lesley and Tomas's first Alaskan experience certainly won't be their last. "It was amazing," the bride says. "Who else can say that on their honeymoon they watched two majestic bald eagles frolic on a windy beach off Icy Strait with the jagged, glacier-capped mountains of the mighty Fairweather Range in the background?"

Sea Kayaking in Vancouver

Dart among dozens of tiny islands and inlets along the coast of Vancouver in British Columbia, Canada's westernmost province. By day you'll paddle among whales, sea lions, and seals; by night you'll camp on sandy beaches or private islands in a tent for two or kick back before a roaring fire in a cedar-walled lodge.

Why You'll Love It: The two of you in your own slim boat, practicing teamwork as you paddle to remote inlets that a monster cruise liner could never reach. The thrill of crashing through wild waves in the icy blue water. Millions of spawning salmon streaming by your boat. Eagles overhead. Among the highest concentration of Orca whales anywhere in the world. (They're surprisingly gentle.) Dense forests. Pristine beaches.

When to Go: June–September.

Must-Dos: After your morning paddle, hike, play boccie ball, and watch the whales surface. Explore ancient Native American sites complete with totem poles and longhouses. Fish your own salmon for dinner and cook it over a fire. Dress in layers—days can be chilly. Call British Columbia Tourism at 800–663–6000 or check the Web at www.travel.bc.ca.

Skiing in Sun Valley

Swoosh to the "secret" ski escape of the rich and famous (Arnold Schwarzenegger, Jamie Lee Curtis, and Clint Eastwood have homes here). Idaho's Sun Valley has some of the best skiing in the West. You'll fly into the Sun Valley airport from Salt Lake City, Utah, and then head to one of the super-luxurious resorts.

Why You'll Love It: High-speed quad lifts and relatively short lines, meaning more time vertical. Spectacular views with awesomely clear, crisp mountain air. A remote location—secluded and romantic. Higher peaks than the East—Sun Valley's Bald Mountain ("Baldie" to locals) rises 9,150 feet. Some of the best-groomed slopes in the West. The chance to tan while you ski—more than 325 days of sun a year. Great food. The Sun Valley opera house. Outdoor ice-skating rink.

When to Go: February–March.

Must-Dos: Try cross-country skiing or snowshoeing. Snowmobile at the base of the Boulder Mountains. Lunch on the mountaintop at Seattle Ridge Day Lodge. Do a Friday night gallery walk. Take a horse-drawn sleigh ride to Trail Creek Cabin for dinner. Do Sunday brunch at the Sun Valley Lodge, followed by a dip in the outdoor heated pool. Tour the town of Ketchum, where the Hemingways live (and lived). Call the Sun Valley–Ketchum Chamber of Commerce at 800–634–3347 or check out www.visitsunvalley.com.

**A Honeymoon
You Can Handle**

Make sure you're familiar with at least one element of your high-adventure honeymoon. If you've never been on a boat, never seen Latin America, and never learned to speak Spanish, that weeklong Galapagos cruise may be too much adventure at one time. Consider staying at a great, land-based hotel instead (the Relais & Chateaux on Santa Cruz?) and day-trip to the islands.

Roughing It Resources

Backroads Travel (800–462–2848) is the most expansive soft-adventure company (140 destinations in 28 countries). Call for info on bike trips around the world as well as hiking, walking, and multisport adventures. For an adventure afloat in your own sea kayak around Vancouver (or around the world), call Northern Lights (800–754–7402).

For a scuba tour in Cozumel or 75 other places, call Adventure Express Travel (800–443–0799).

Diving in Cozumel

Dart with fish among the living reef in Cozumel, off the coast of Cancun on Mexico's Yucatan Peninsula, one of the Caribbean Sea's scuba meccas. (Its coral reefs were featured in Jacques Cousteau films.) You'll find beginner to advanced diving and a full certification course you can take during your trip.

Why You'll Love It: Mexico's best—easy drift diving in crystal-clear waters along tropical reefs with jewel-colored fish. Underwater visibility often exceeds 150 feet. An intact, living coral reef that's protected by the Mexican government. Lush tropical jungle by land; flora, fauna, and floating *thingees* by sea. Easy to get to and relatively cheap once you're there. Accommodations ranging from all-inclusives (with dive packages) to five-star resorts and small local inns. Dive boats pick you up and drop you off right at the hotel.

When to Go: December–August.

Must-Dos: Slip into your sleek new Scuba gear and check out the Yucatan's ancient underground caverns, called *cenotes,* in nearby Akumal. Take the ferry to the mainland to tour the Maya ruins at Tulum. See six species of giant sea turtles at the sanctuary on Isla Mujeres, off Cancun. Tour Cozumel's tiny town to see the local fishing boats. Sample Yucatan cuisine and super-strength margaritas at El Moro. Try Prima's super Italian food, made from hydroponically grown vegetables. Work it off in a disco. Call 800–44-MEXICO or log on to www.mexico-travel.com.

More Hot Scuba Spots

- Australia's Great Barrier Reef
- Belize
- Bonaire
- Borneo
- Costa Rica
- Fiji
- Grand Cayman
- Hawaii
- Honduras
- Maldive Islands (Indian Ocean)
- Micronesia's Palau
- Papua New Guinea
- The Red Sea

Disney World

Not your first thought when we say "adrenaline adventure"? What makes your heart beat faster than racing down a roller-coaster track at 40 mph, wind in your face, screams in your ears, cotton candy in your hair? Disney World remains one of the top honeymoon spots for those who like their action fast, shiny, and man-made. It's a natural vacation for honeymooners with kids—or with that kids-at-heart spirit.

Why You'll Love It: Forty-two square miles of activities—from raucous rides and wild animal safaris to super shows, cooking classes, and every sport imaginable. Surprisingly luxurious hotels with romantic themes (Polynesian, turn-of-the-century). Super spas. White-sand beaches. Beautiful manicured grounds. Complete cleanliness unlike anywhere else on the planet (except maybe Singapore). The chance to meet Mickey and Minnie. Escapism. Regression. Pure delight.

When to Go: Year-round.

Must-Dos: Ride everything. Get soaked at Splash Mountain. Grab a seat for the Jungle Cruise. Shiver through the Haunted House. Have a picnic lunch in the Wildlife Sanctuary. Ride the monorail to the elegant Grand Floridian hotel for a bodacious buffet. Sample super Mexican food at the San Angel Inn Restaurant in Epcot Center. If you're taking kids, drop them off at one of the Children's Activities Centers at night so they (and you) can live it up in an age-appropriate style. Go clubbing at Church Street Station and Pleasure Island.

See an over-the-top dinner show. Be prepared for lots of references to "Disney Magic." Plan ahead! Get a good guide, such as *Walt Disney World for Couples,* by Rick and Gayle Perlmutter (Prima Publishing, 1997), to help you navigate the World. Call Disney World's info line at 407–824–4500 or check out www.disney.com; for general info on all Orlando attractions, call the Orlando-Orange County Convention & Visitors Bureau at 407–363–5871 or see www.goflorida.com/orlando.

Urban Escapes

For some, nothing is more romantic than window shopping at Tiffany's, dressing to the nines for dinner at ten, and hitting the clubs around midnight. If you're set on an urban adventure, plan what to see before you go—so much to do, so little time! And see if you can get that friend of your cousin's former boss who lives there to give you some recommendations; nothing beats insider advice.

Super Spa Honeymoons

Your idea of working out is a good rubdown after a mineral bath? Take a spa escape for two. Some of our favorites:

- The Aveda Spa, near Minneapolis, Minnesota
- Canyon Ranch, Tucson, Arizona
- The Doral Gold Resort and Spa, Miami, Florida
- The Four Season Resort and Club, Irving, Texas
- The Golden Door, Escondido, California
- Grand Wailea Resort and Spa at Fox Run, Hawaii

New York City

You want to be a part of it—the glamour, the excitement, the fast pace. This is the Capital of the World, after all. There are more things to do on a single day in New York than you could possibly fit in all year. And crime is way down, meaning things are looking up for the ultimate urban vacation. You still shouldn't hang your purse on a parking meter, but you can walk just about anywhere in Manhattan safely, use Central Park, and zip about on the subway with ease.

Why You'll Love It: The latest fashions, the best restaurants, the coolest stores, the top theaters, the hottest cabaret acts, the hippest nightclubs, the trendiest bars, the most amazing museum collections and galleries—basically, the chance to put your finger on the pulse of the country (and reach deep into your pocket to do it). That feeling of being alive that comes from ducking out of the way of thousands of harried New Yorkers.

When to Go: Fall. Runner-up seasons: *very* late spring, summer, Christmas.

Must-Dos: See a Broadway or off-Broadway play. Window-shop along Fifth Avenue. Visit the Empire State Building, the Statue of Liberty, and Ellis Island. Check out the antiquities wing in the Metropolitan Museum of Art and then head over to the Guggenheim—a winding, white spiral tower of a museum designed by Frank Lloyd Wright. Watch daredevil in-line skaters in the skate circle in Central Park. Have a drink at Rockefeller Center's Rainbow Room. Lose yourselves among the West Village's charming, tiny streets. Check out Chinatown for hot noodles on the street ($1) and fake Chanel handbags and Rolex watches ($15–$35). Stroll across the Brooklyn Bridge and share bagels, lox, and cream cheese on the Promenade in Brooklyn Heights. For info, call the New York City Visitors Bureau at 212–484–1232, or the New York City Visitors Service at 888–692–2775. Or check out www.nycvisit.com.

For the most up-to-date info on great honeymoon destinations, plus tons of traveling tips, go to The Knot Online at www.theknot.com.

San Francisco

Latte lovers, unite! San Fran is up there with Seattle when it comes to sheer numbers of people walking around with coffee-to-go cups. This moderately sized northern Californian city on the bay combines big-time sophistication with the laid-back, dressed-down attitude of the West Coast. It's urban without being overwhelming.

Why You'll Love It: Candy-colored Victorian houses. Intensely steep hills rolling down toward the brilliant blue San Francisco Bay. Romantic in that windswept-hair, fog-rolling-over-the-mountains, panoramic-view-of-the-ocean-every-ten-feet way. The chance to feel like cover models for a steamy romance novel. People are polite. There's tons to do. And it's always spring.

When to Go: Year-round.

Must-Dos: Order steaming clam chowder in a sourdough bowl at the touristy Fisherman's Wharf and carry it to Pier 26 to dine while watching the sea lions sunning on the docks (free). Wander through Chinatown. Take the ferry to Sausalito. Hang out at a café in Berkeley. See the Exploratorium, Yerba Buena Gardens, the view from the Downtown Marriott. Shop on Union Square. Eat at ultra-cool LuLu. Watch the sun set from Coit Tower. Ride a cable car at midnight. Choose a romantic old hilltop inn with a fireplace and a canopy bed. Dress in layers! Call the San Francisco Convention and Visitors Bureau Visitor Information Center at 415–391–2000 or check out www.sfvisitor.org.

Paris

Let's face it—Paris is synonymous with romance. Whether you adore the art, the food, the fashion, or the French *(mais no,* we're not rude!), a seven-hour flight from New York will land you in the quintessential city of love and lights.

Why You'll Love It: Beautiful old stone buildings with garreted windows. Flower-filled gardens with rows of perfect trees. Countless outdoor cafés. Street vendors selling books, postcards, and Picasso prints. Breakfasting on croissants and café au lait. Steaming sugared crêpes. Museums galore. The river Seine. That misty pink sky like an Impressionist painting. *La vie elegant.*

When to Go: Fall, spring, summer (except August, when the locals are on holiday and the city is empty).

Must-Dos: Stroll along the Champs-Elysées, the Seine, the Boulevard St. Michel, the Jardin du Luxembourg. Stop every hour at a sidewalk café for coffee and a chance to practice your French. Eat ice cream from Berthillon on the Ile St. Louis. Visit the Picasso Museum and the now totally restored Louvre. (Don't even try to see it all in one day; you can spend hours merely admiring the architecture.) Head to Les Halles to see street performers. Swing-dance or hear jazz at Le Caveau de la Huchette on the Left Bank. Check out the clubs at the Place Pigalle. Call France On-Call at 202–659–7779, or try www.france-tourism.com.

Venice

This northeastern Italian city rises up out of the water like Atlantis, presubmerged. All that water reflects the sun against the Gothic-style architecture in the unique way Venice calls its own. Fly to the island airport and then take a water taxi to this amazing aquacity, small enough to cover by foot.

When to Go: Spring, fall (winter for a romantic, misty ambience).

Why You'll Love It: No cars; you take boats—or feet—everywhere you go. Water, water everywhere. Gondoliers who really do sing. Super shops where you can buy Venetian glass. Brightly colored laundry fluttering over winding streets. Ornate, gilded churches with mosaic ceilings. A charming hotel room overlooking a canal. Great food.

When to Go: Spring, fall (winter for a romantic, misty ambience).

Must-Dos: Feed the pigeons at the Piazza San Marco (St. Mark's Square) and tour the Basilica di San Marco. Walk across the small Bridge of Sighs and the large Rialto Bridge crossing the Grand Canal. Wander down tiny, twisting streets. Take a gondola ride. Eat *pannini,* flat cheese-and-prosciutto sandwiches, at a sidewalk café. Tour the Accademia, the city's best museum, across the Grand Canal from Piazza San Marco. Duck down a little alley for some smooching *al fresco.* Hire a motorized water taxi to take you to other islands. See the glassmakers of Murano. Call the Italian Government Tourist Board at 212–245–4823.

Québec City

The only walled city in this hemisphere north of Mexico, this terraced, nineteenth-century town carved into a cliff in southeastern Canada is like Paris, only hillier. And far cheaper to visit—with the dollar's current strength, all of Canada feels like it's on a 30 percent-off sale.

Why You'll Love It: Streets so drippingly romantic, you inevitably wind up making out in public. (The first French kiss on the continent is rumored to have taken place at Québec's Auberge du Trésor.) Perfectly preserved seventeenth- and eighteenth-century architecture lining cobblestone streets. The thrill of speaking French with the backup of everyone also speaking English. The feeling of living in a picture postcard.

When to Go: May–October (February for WinterFest if you're hardy as a polar bear).

Must-Dos: Explore Old Town by foot. Eat a boxed picnic lunch from Serge Bruyere on the Terrasse Dufferin—the huge boardwalk promenade behind the castlelike Chateau Frontenac on the edge of Upper Town. Take the glass-walled funicular down the 300-foot cliff to Lower Town. Buy an ink drawing of the city on the rue des Trésors. Dine at the quiet, charming Laurie et Raphael. In spring, have a maple-sugar feast at a *cabane à sucre* (sugar shack). Rent a car to tour the surrounding tiny, French-style towns, eastern British villages, and Montreal. Call Québec Tourism at 800–363–7777 or check out www.quebec-region.cuq.qc.ca.

Head Trips

A walking tour of ancient ruins, open notebooks, glasses, furrowed brows—rev up your brain while you recharge with an educational/historic honeymoon. Learning can be exhilarating, and downright sexy, if you know where to do it. To get the most out of your head trip, do some reading first, and consider hiring an expert guide the first day for an overview of the area. Don't forget to plan education-free hours—you'll need recess between all that brainwork!

Scottish Castle Tour

This vast, open country north of England is home to hundreds of castles, each holding its own piece of British history. Fly to Edinburgh, rent a car, and drive north, deep into Castle Country. Overnight in castles turned hotels. (You also could do a castle tour in England, France, Spain, Portugal, or Eastern Europe.)

Parlez-Vous What?

First time abroad? Consider a country where the natives speak English. It'll give you the thrill of an overseas vacation with the comfort of still having a bit of control. Good choices: England, Scotland, Ireland, Australia.

W h y Yo u ' l l L o v e I t: Everything you ever wanted to know about being a prince and princess. Rooms full of armor, antiques, and charters from the king. Rugged cliffs and purple heather. Friendly people (outnumbered by sheep, two to one). Shaggy, orange Highland cattle that are possibly the cutest cows on the planet. European without feeling foreign.

W h e n t o G o: May–October.

M u s t - D o s: See Glamis Castle (Queen Elizabeth's childhood home), medieval Huntingtower (complete with window slits and gun loops), and the ultraluxurious Crathes Castle and Gardens. Inquire about the ghost stories. Visit the town of Stirling (of *Braveheart* fame), site of Scotland's independence wars. Tour the creepy, narrow alley called Mary King's Close in Edinburgh—the site of some of the city's goriest chapters. Eat smoked salmon and cullen skink—a fish chowder that tastes better than it sounds. Pack a *Blue Guide* for historical briefing. Call the British Tourist Authority at 212–986–2266 or go to www.visitbritain.com.

Wine Lover's United States: Napa Valley

Stimulate your brain *and* palette with a wine tour of California's great grape-growing regions. Called the Tuscany of the United States, Napa Valley (and neighboring Sonoma) has one vineyard after another (more than 200, actually), most offering educational lectures, extensive tours, and guided wine tastings. About an hour outside of San Francisco, Napa feels ten degrees warmer and ten times more relaxed than the city.

W h y Yo u ' l l L o v e I t: Endless opportunities to sample wine and see how it's made. Golden hills covered with dark-green vines. Warm California sunshine. Small towns with pristine streets, perfect air, and subtle sophistication. Fabulous fresh food. Elegant small hotels and B&Bs.

W h e n t o G o: Year round (August–October is harvest and crushing time).

M u s t - D o s: Take the Napa Valley Wine Train through the valley for a narrated introduction to the region and a wine-cellar tour. Visit no more than three wineries a day—too much info (and wine) to take on more! Check out Sterling Vineyards, a touristy spot whose tram to the top of the hill and balcony overlooking the valley make it worth the crowds. Discern the difference between Chardonnay and Chablis. Take a mud bath for two in Calistoga, Napa's spa town. Have lunch at Auberge du Soleil for the best food and the most spectacular countryside view. (Check in if you can afford the $300-plus per-night room rates). Call the Napa Valley Tourist Bureau at 707–944–1558 or log on to www.napastyle.com.

Israel

This long, skinny, Mediterranean country about the size of New Jersey just celebrated its fiftieth anniversary. But you'll find landmarks dating back more than 5,000 years—as well as beaches, great restaurants, and active nightlife.

Why You'll Love It: About as romantic—and educational—as it gets. A chance to go back in time to experience the spirit of the Bible and get in touch with your religious roots. Sparkling beaches. Ethnic cuisine. Modern cities and ancient towns.

When to Go: Spring or fall.

Must-Dos: Walk through Jerusalem's Yemin Moshe, where quaint houses border cobblestone pathways in view of the Old City walls. Visit the Wailing Wall. Peer over Jerusalem from the Haas promenade. See Bethlehem. Eat an omelette at Kafe Kafit in the German Quarter. Tour the Russian Quarter's bars and discos. People-watch on Ben Yehudah Street. Take a boat to Tel Aviv, where you can shop on Sheinkin, sail, windsurf, and water-ski. Swim in the Dead Sea. Climb the famous mountain of Masada. Call the Israel Ministry of Tourism's Travel Information Center at 800–596–1199 or check out www.goisrael.com.

Explore Your Heritage

Travel to the town (or towns) where your family (or families) were born. Look in the town registry for names. Find family tombstones, streets, houses, stores. Interview your grandparents or other relatives before you go. Take photos, names, numbers, and other leads with you.

Mexican Colonial Towns

To learn about Mexican history and culture where it happened, head inland and upland to the Silver Cities—tiny towns founded by Spanish silver prospectors in the mid-1500s. Stay in San Miguel de Allende (150 miles north of Mexico City), the most Americanized of the colonial towns, and one of the prettiest.

Why You'll Love It: Beautiful, Spanish-style buildings with interior courtyards. Central squares, or *zocalos,* where townsfolk meet to chat, read the paper, sip coffee, and eat fried snacks coated with hot sauce. Funky museums. Genuine Mexican culture with little tourist activity. The sense of being very far from home.

When to Go: Year-round.

Must-Dos: Check into San Miguel's elegant Casa de Sierra Nevada, then check out the music, dance, or various art classes in the former courtyard convent Bellas Artes or at the Institute de Allende. Spice up your cooking skills at one of several different schools. Pick up *The Insider's Guide to San Miguel* for the lowdown on the leisure life. Visit the mummies in Guanajuato (an hour north) as well as the Don Quixote Museum and the Diego Rivera Museum. Hear the Cervantinos—strolling musicians dressed like sixteenth-century Spaniards. Try avocado ice cream in nearby Delores Hidalgo. Brave the bus ride to

Eco-Honeymoon

You're "Love me, love my planet" types? Take an eco-trip—one of the hottest options on the vacation front. But know what you're getting into before you go. "Eco" can mean "extra-rough." Err on the over-cautious side, and find someone who's been before you buy your tickets. For ideas, head to the library for back issues of *National Geographic Traveler* and *Adventure Journal.* Or take ours:

Stateside Safari: Head to Yellowstone National Park, the largest intact eco-system in the Lower 48. We're talking wall-to-wall (tree-to-tree) wolves, elk, moose, bison, bear, eagles, and deer.

Ecuador's Cuyabeno Wildlife Reserve: The world record-holder for biodiversity, Cuyabeno has more than 500 species of exotic tropical birds, 12 species of monkeys, freshwater dolphins, caiman, tapirs, peccaries, anteaters, and more than 277 species of plants.

The Galapagos Islands: The inspiration for Charles Darwin's *On the Origin of the Species,* this UNESCO World Heritage Site 600 miles off Ecuador's west coast has some of the world's unique wildlife: flightless cormorants, marine iguanas, equatorial penguins, giant tortoises, and blue-footed boobies.

Eco-Vacation Organizers

Adventure Associates (800–527–2500 or 972–907–0414)
Alaska Discovery (907–780–6236)
Colorado Trail Foundation—build and maintain mountain trails (303–526–0809)
Florida Oceanographic Society—explore Florida's coastline (407–235–0505)
The Great Plains Wildlife Institute in Jackson Hole, Wyoming (307–733–2623)
Journeys—trek around the world, stay with locals (800–255–8735)
National Audubon Society—cruises (212–979–3000)
Smithsonian Study Tours—folk festivals, research sites, natural wonders (202–357–4800)
World Wildlife Fund—conservation tours (202–778–9683)

Zacatecas (five hours farther north) to see the Mask Museum—more than 3,000 indigenous masks in a crumbling ex-convent—and buy popcorn roasted over an open flame and eat homemade potato chips. Stay at Zacatecas's Quinta Real, a full-service hotel built around one of Latin America's first bull rings. Fly to Mexico City or León and take a Primera Plus bus to San Miguel. Call 800–44–MEXICO for info or see www.mexico-travel.com.

Washington, D.C.

This swamp–turned–world capital on the Maryland side of the Potomac (bordering Virginia) is a world-class city and a surprisingly romantic destination.

Why You'll Love It: Awesome architecture, monuments, and statues. Great museums. The chance to learn about your country and reconnect to your childhood pride in the good ol' U.S. of A. Elegant hotels. Beautiful parks. Sophisticated nightlife. A short drive from pastoral countryside.

When to Go: Spring.

Must-Dos: See the cherry blossoms bloom (in April) along the central green, or

"Mall," and visit the Capitol Building; the Lincoln, Washington, Jefferson, Vietnam, Korean, and FDR memorials (a lot of memorials, but they're all fantastic!); and the Smithsonian museums (all free!). Tour the White House (good decorating ideas for your new home?). Visit Kennedy's Tomb, the Tomb of the Unknown Soldier, and the Women Veterans Memorial in Arlington National Cemetery. Take a mule-drawn barge ride down the old canal in Georgetown. See the giant pandas at the National Zoo. Rent a canoe and paddle out on the Potomac. Try African food in the sophisticated Adams-Morgan area, and listen to the city's hottest jazz. Call the Washington D.C. Convention and Visitors Association at 202–789–7038 or try www.washington.org.

Let Your Sign Be Your Guide

- Aquarius: India
- Pisces: Mediterranean
- Aries: Florence
- Taurus: Rural Ireland
- Gemini: New York City
- Cancer: Venice
- Leo: Prague
- Virgo: Paris
- Libra: Upper Egypt and the Nile
- Scorpio: New Orleans
- Sagittarius: Australia
- Capricorn: Moscow

Exotica

Berlitz books in your backpacks, creative cuisine (is that a pet or food?), places so exotic your friends have never heard of them—you've been everywhere and done everything. You're ready for the adventure of a lifetime before that lifetime adventure—marriage—officially kicks in. If you've got the time, the money, and the courage, make your honeymoon a voyage to the ends of the earth. And make sure to give yourselves time to look around once you get there!

Australia

This huge country, the size of the United States, is about as far away as you can go (fourteen-plus hours from the West Coast). Choose an area of reasonable size to cover on your trip—you couldn't "do" the entire United States in one week, so don't even think about it with Australia. You'll adore what you do get to see.

Why You'll Love It: Rugged landscapes and sparkling cities. Fresh air, beautiful people. Lush tropics merging with vast stretches of desert. Giant rocks rising in the Outback. British-style traditions mixed with a West Coast attitude. Plenty of places to hike, bike, dive, and drive. The chance to try a Vegamite sandwich.

When to Go: February–April, October and November (but it depends where you go).

Must-Dos: Check out Sydney, Australia's glamorous waterfront city with a healthy outdoorsiness, like a cross between L.A. and Seattle. Rent a boat at the Whitsunday Islands, on the southern edge of the Great Barrier Reef, to dive, snorkel, or just bob around. Explore the rugged northern territory, where you'll find aboriginal artists and the wild rock formations of Kakadu National Park. Climb to the top of the lighthouse at Byron Bay for a spectacular view of the ocean (and Mel Gibson's house). Take high tea at your hotel. For an Australian travel planner, call 800–DOWNUNDER. Also check out www.australia.com.

Bali

When you think of mystical palaces, aqua water crashing on jagged cliffs, natives wrapped in brilliant saris, and exotic food with names you can't pronounce, you're thinking Bali. This Indonesian island north of Australia is the original Enchanted Isle. While natives don't stroll around topless anymore, European tourists do.

Why You'll Love It: Pagodalike palaces rising from the water. Colorful Hindu festivals. Remote villages, each dedicated to a single handicraft. More things to buy for less money than you ever thought possible (jewelry, batik, puppets, paintings, baskets, carvings). Beautiful women carrying pyramids of fruit and flowers on their heads. Some of the planet's most luxurious new resorts (and rooms with their own personal plunge pools).

When to Go: Year-round (best weather May–October).

Must-Dos: In Ubud, the center of Bali's cultural tourism, take a walking tour of a working rice field, see a puppet show, and eat at one of the open-air cafés on the main drag, Jalan Raya. Visit the Puri Lakisan Museum to see all types of Balinese art. Head to the Bali Barat National Park for a sunrise hike/climb around the Gunung Batur volcano. Check out Penestanan, a quiet village twenty minutes by foot from Ubud. Tour super-commercialized Kuta (near the airport) to sample unique local cuisine at the food carts near the beach, get in some great surfing (or watch the pros do it), and stock up on batik paintings and jewelry to take home. Call 213–387–2078.

Tahiti

The 115 islands of the South Pacific nation of French Polynesia cover an area of ocean larger than Europe. Your seven-hour-plus flight from California lands in bustling Papeete, on the island called Tahiti. From there you can set out for your more remote piece of paradise. Locals speak French and Tahitian.

Why You'll Love It: French style on a tropical isle. Foliage-covered volcanic peaks. Deep mountain jungles. Brilliant blue lagoons with rainbows of fish and coral. Fresh roadside baguettes. Ripe-from-the-tree pineapples, papayas, and coconuts.

When to Go: Year-round (best weather May–October).

Must-Dos: Buy vanilla sticks, woven bracelets, and straw hats at the market in Papeete. Eat steak frites, followed by ice cream made from fresh vanilla beans, at a roadside *roulette*. Visit the Gauguin Museum. (He fled France for Tahiti, determining never to return, twice.) Climb among the ruins in Huahine. Learn the *tamure,* the island's provocative dance. Catch the ferry to Moorea (the inspiration for *South Pacific*'s Bali-hai) and take a jeep safari into the hills. Hole up in a thatched-roof bungalow on stilts over a clear lagoon in Bora Bora. Call the Tahitian Tourist Board at 800–365–4949 or check out www.tahiti-tourisme.com.

Rio de Janeiro

This Brazilian city is synonymous with sultry, sexy romance. An eight-hour flight from Miami puts you in another world—it's like Portugal with the heat turned *way* up.

Why You'll Love It: Huge humpbacked mountains. Miles of cream-colored beaches.

Sunny days. Nights like silk—soft, sensual, alluring. Gorgeous, gregarious locals called *cariocas,* or "exuberant people." Fabulous spicy food. Shopping. Music. All-night excitement.

When to Go: April–November (February for Carnival).

Must-Dos: Hit the beach at Ipanema, a local hangout where you'll see perfect bods in "dental floss" bikinis. Take the funicular to Corcovado, topped with the gigantic 125-foot-high statue of Christ the Redeemer. Ride a cable car to Sugar Loaf, Rio's postcard peak. Sip *Caipirinha* (a knock-your-socks-off concoction of sugar-cane liquor, crushed lime, and sugar) at an open-air café along Avenue Atlantica. Have an all-you-can-eat *churrascaria rodizio*—twenty kinds of meat served tableside by waiters wielding long skewers. Samba 'til you sweat at one of hundred nightclubs. Call the Brazilian Vacation Center at 800–342–5746 (in New York State, 800–848–2746).

Classic Cruises

If you spent your childhood glued to the tube during The Love Boat, we know where you'll be heading for your honeymoon. Just the two of you, the open sea, and 500 other passengers. (A martini, Isaac!) A cruise is like a floating all-inclusive resort with everything on deck—except all those great ports of call. Wherever you go, make the most of your time at sea. Order breakfast in bed. Stay up for the midnight buffet. Lounge at every pool, try every dance floor, and watch the stars in the sky from the deck late at night. Read up on your ports before you go—a little planning will let you make the most of your time on land.

Alaska

Get up close and personal with some of the country's most spectacular scenery and wildlife. Then tour northwestern cities like Seattle, Vancouver, Victoria, Ketchikan, Petersburg, and Juneau. Alaska is an ideal summer cruise destination.

Why You'll Love It: Glistening icebergs and glaciers. Land of the Midnight Sun phenomenon—almost constant daylight during the summer months. That last-great-place feeling—undisturbed nature at its most awesome. Glacier Bay National Park. Easy to get to from the West Coast.

When to Go: Mid-May to mid-September.

Must-Dos: Take the Inside Passage tour—the route between Alaska's western coast and a string of offshore islands—to see humpback whales and sea lions. Listen for glaciers cracking off jewel-blue icebergs into deep-green fjords. Eat salmon and tour the totems in Ketchikan. Relive the Gold Rush days along the boardwalks of Juneau and Skagway. See Czarist Russia–style architecture in Sitka. Check out slopes and cliffs of Valdez, called the "Switzerland of Alaska." Buy smoked salmon, carved wood totems and animals, Native American crafts, and masks. Don wetsuits for a whitewater rafting trip.

Who Goes There: Carnival Cruise Lines, Celebrity Cruise Lines, Crystal Cruises, Holland America Line, Norwegian Cruise Line, Princess Cruises, Radisson Seven Seas, Royal Caribbean. Call Alaska Visitors Information at 907–465–2010 or try www.state.ak.us/tourism or www.travelalaska.com.

Greek Islands

Cut through the crystal waters of the Aegean Sea to the Greek Islands—the world's most popular place to cruise. You'll fly to Athens and board your ship from the port city of Pireaus, for island-hopping, ship style.

Why You'll Love It: Whitewashed buildings covering steep hillsides. Unbelievable vistas. The history of Western civilization at your fingertips. Great Mediterranean food. The chance to wear next to nothing. English-speaking (often) locals.

When to Go: April–October.

Must-Dos: Wander among the ruins of the Temple of Zeus in Katakolon. Bronze on the beach in Mykonos. Sip a Greek coffee at an outdoor café and watch the sun play across the water. Eat *mezedes* (traditional appetizers) and drink licoricelike *ouzo* on Patmos, a strikingly rugged island that's home to shepherds and fishermen. Visit the birthplace of mighty Aphrodite—the Love Goddess—in Kithera. Climb the Acropolis in Athens. Explore the Palace of Grand Masters in Rhodes, set among olive and cypress trees. Climb to the top of Santorini for a view over the lost city of Atlantis. Learn at least one Greek word—we suggest *Opa!* meaning bravo, wonderful, hooray!

Joy Rides

Just the two of you on the open road, Dylan on the radio, and the late-afternoon sun in your eyes—a road-trip honeymoon is the ultimate joy ride. If you're planning to put the pedal to the metal for some serious postwedding togetherness, make sure to map out some must-see stops and leave plenty of time for wandering those old back roads. Plan where to stay for the first few nights, at least; this is a great opportunity to check out the charming inns across the country. Take along your Polaroid camera, your favorite tapes, maps, guidebooks, and two weeks' worth of conversation. Our top road-trip picks:

The Florida Keys: This string of islands is connected to mainland Florida (and to each other) by one smooth, two-lane highway. From Key Largo to Key West, you spin along the perfect strip of blacktop, watching the land falling away on either side. It's the open sky, the endless sea, and a feeling of freedom unlike anywhere else in the United States.

New England: Plymouth Rock, Salem witch trials, Ivy League schools, the Headless Horseman, Hester Prynne, the Boston Tea Party—they're here, in Connecticut, Rhode Island, Massachusetts, New Hampshire, Vermont, and Maine. Stay at some charming inns along the way.

Southwest: From New Mexico to Arizona and Nevada, this wide-open country is great if you *love* to drive. You'll see the southern edge of the Rockies and some of the most unusual land on Earth, including red rocks as tall as skyscrapers (but shaped more like some extraterrestrial habitation). See Native American culture, awesome natural monuments, the Grand Canyon, and Las Vegas. Experience the feeling of being part of the free-wheelin', fast-dealin' Wild West.

The California Coast: From south of San Diego to north of San Francisco, California's Pacific Coast Highway is the most spectacular stretch of road in the country. Wander slowly through flower-filled towns so beautiful you'll swear they're movie sets. Brilliant bougainvilleas the size of small cars bloom in the medians, the Pacific Ocean is right out your window, the weather is flawless, the towns are charming and historic, and the resorts are deeply luxurious.

Who Goes There: Costa Cruise Line, Crystal Cruises, Cunard Cruise Lines, Holland America Line, Mediterranean Shipping Cruises, Norwegian Cruise Line, Orient Lines, Princess Cruises, Radisson Seven Seas, Royal Caribbean, Royal Olympic Cruises, Windstar Cruises. Call the Greek Tourist Board at 212–421–5777.

The Caribbean

Can't decide which Caribbean island is for you? Choose a cruise and check out a handful. Most Caribbean excursions leave from south Florida (though there are other ports) and cover a collection of Caribbean countries, often including a stop at a private island.

Why You'll Love It: The bluest seas, the whitest sands, the greenest palms. Bubbling waterfalls. Exotic markets. Fresh fruit. The smell of cocoa butter. A very pared-down wardrobe (swimsuit, shorts, sunglasses, one fancy getup). Warm days, warm nights, warm people.

When to Go: December–August.

Must-Dos: Climb the Dunn's River waterfall in Jamaica. Bargain at the straw market in Nassau, the Bahamas. Learn to beat the bongo drums. Have an espresso at a harborfront café in French St. Martin. Take high tea in British Barbados. Bronze your bods on black sand in Grenada.

Who Goes There: Carnival Cruise Lines, Celebrity Cruise Lines, Commodore Cruise Line, Costa Cruise Line, Crystal Cruises, Cunard Cruise Lines, Holland America Line, Mediterranean Shipping Cruises, Norwegian Cruise Line, Premier Cruises, Princess Cruises, Radisson Seven Seas, Regal Cruises, Royal Caribbean, Royal Olympic Cruises, Windstar Cruises. Call the Caribbean Tourist Board at 800–356–9999.

Western Mediterranean

Board a cruise in the western Mediterranean and wake up every morning in a different country—from France to Italy, Spain to Tunisia. You'll fly to your departure city (the port depends on the cruise line you choose); airfare to Europe may be included in the overall price. Book a water/land package to spend a few days tooling around town before you hit the seas.

Why You'll Love It: A chance to see a handful of Europe's most beautiful cities and practice your Italian, Spanish, or French. A small circuit, meaning more ports of call, less time at sea. Maximum culture, minimum effort.

When to Go: Mid-May to late October.

Must-Dos: Eat pizza in Naples, birthplace of the pie. Tour the ruins of Pompeii. Light a candle in a Gothic church. Wander through the fourteenth-century maze of the Barrio Gotico (Old Quarter) in Barcelona. Take a tour of Gaudi's famous drippy architecture. Drink café con leche while watching Sardana dancers. Eat bouillabaisse (fresh seafood stew) in Marseille, France's oldest city. Bargain in Tunisian street markets. Peer at the illuminated manuscripts of the Koran. See the ornate Palace of Dar Ben Abdullah. Leave plenty of room in your luggage for souvenirs.

Chateaux to Go

For an elegant, privately owned inn with a top-of-the-line restaurant, look for a Relais & Chateaux property. This French-based organization is a loose affiliation of some of the most romantic small hotels on the planet. For info, call 212-856-0115 or browse the properties at www.integra.fr/relaischateaux.

Honeymooning at Home

Can't leave town just now? Even if you're planning your *real* honeymoon for next May, take a long weekend after your wedding for a whirlwind of intimacy and indulgence. For the perfect forty-eight-hour honeymoon at home, try these tips:

Make the weekend as romantic as possible, even if it means being downright extravagant.

Hire a maid to do a complete overhaul before you begin.

Fill the house with huge bouquets of fresh flowers.

Stock your fireplace with wood, your bed with pillows, your pantry with snacks.

Put new sheets on your bed.

Put Ravel's *Bolero* on repeat on your CD player.

Turn off the ringer on your phone. (Don't check your messages!)

Take a bubble bath together. (Turn off the overhead light and use fifteen candles, instead.)

Give each other a hand massage and manicure.

Pack a gourmet picnic for lunch at a local park or lake.

Book a half day at the local spa.

Dress up for a super-fancy dinner out (or order in and eat on your best new china and crystal). Have a limo pick you up.

Wear your sexiest lingerie and boxers to bed.

Rent a steamy video for super-late-night viewing.

Have chilled shrimp cocktail and champagne waiting for midnight snacks. (Or ingredients for gooey nachos, if that's more your style.)

Treat each other to breakfast in bed.

Do something only the tourists do. Visit the pretzel factory; ice-skate in the park; ride a horse-drawn buggy.

Plan a surprise for each other—a professional masseuse after dinner, a new martini shaker for cocktails; something battery-operated for the bedroom.

Take pictures! This *is* a vacation.

Who Goes There: Costa Cruise Lines, Crystal Cruises, Cunard Cruise Lines, Holland America Line, Mediterranean Shipping Cruises, Norwegian Cruise Line, Orient Lines, Princess Cruises, Radisson Seven Seas, Royal Caribbean, Royal Olympic Cruises, Windstar Cruises.

Norwegian Fjords

Whether you chug along in a huge ship or poke among the fjords in a private boat, cruising Norway puts you on top of the world—literally. If you take the big-ship route, you'll probably leave from Amsterdam or Copenhagen, stop in Oslo, and then head up Norway's west coast toward the Arctic Circle.

Why You'll Love It: Towering cliffs, shooting geysers, and ice-fringed fjords. Pure white glaciers topped with packs of penguins. Fairy-tale towns with red, yellow, and orange steep-roofed buildings lining the waterfront. Great gray mountains rising up behind wooden churches. Strange, desolate capes over which the sun never sets. Polar bears, reindeer, white whales, arctic foxes, and seals.

When to Go: June–August.

Must-Dos: Sail up the Oslofjord to Norway's capital city, Oslo—just like the Vikings. See the *Kon-Tiki* (the raft that Thor Heyerdahl sailed across the ocean) and tour the Viking Ships Museum. Buy Norwegian crafts in the town of Stavanger, the oil capital of Norway. Wander among the old Hanseatic Wharf in Bergen—a medieval shipping port. Drive up the wiggly *Trollstigen* (troll's ladder) to see crashing waterfalls and sheer mountains. Have a coffee in a hip café in Tromso—a city way above the Arctic Circle. Visit Hammerfest, the most northerly town in Europe, on Norway's northern coast.

Who Goes There: Bergen Line, Costa Cruise Line, Crystal Cruises, Cunard Cruise Lines, Holland America Line, Norwegian Cruise Line, Princess Cruises, Radisson Seven Seas, Royal Caribbean, Royal Olympic Cruises. Call the Scandinavian Tourist Board at 212–885–9700 or try www.travelfile.com/get/NORTRA.

B&B Books

- *America's Best Bed & Breakfasts* (Fodors, 1997)

- *Country Inns and Backroads, North America* (Birnbaum's, 1997)

- *The Official Bed & Breakfast Guide,* by Phyllis Featherson and Barbara Oster (National Bed & Breakfast Association, 1995)

- *The Official Guide to American Historical Inns,* by Deborah Sakach (American Historic Inns, 1996)

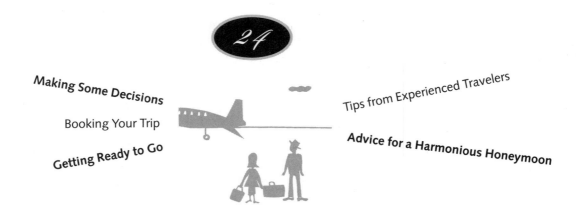

Making Some Decisions

Booking Your Trip

Getting Ready to Go

Tips from Experienced Travelers

Advice for a Harmonious Honeymoon

Honeymoon Helper

You've agreed on the perfect honeymoon place, bought the books, registered for that Louis Vuitton luggage you *had* to have. Now all that's left between you and euphoria are the details—booking the trip, packing your bags, and finding someone to feed Fido while you're gone. Here to help you with the nitty-gritty of honeymooning are our foolproof, fabulous trip-planning tips. Whether you're experienced globetrotters or novice travelers, you need a good grip on the rules and language of the travel world before you set out. We'll give you the inside scoop on everything you need to know to make your honeymoon great. So put on that calypso CD, make some rum punch (for inspiration!), and get ready to plan.

Making Some Decisions

By now you've done your destination research—you've read Chapter 23, talked to friends, checked out your newspaper's travel section, and surfed the Web for possible packages. But before you stroll into your travel agent's office and whip out your Gold Card, there's some additional information you need to have—namely how much honeymoon money you've got and how you want to spend it.

Getting the Most from Your Budget

So just how much will the trip of the century cost you? An average eight-day honeymoon costs between $3,500 and $4,000. That includes airfare, hotel, taxis, meals, alcohol, snacks, and souvenirs. Plane tickets and hotel costs suck up more than half of the total. But you're not the average couple. You're you. Use those figures as a ballpark range, then plan to spend less if you're driving rather than flying or staying for a shorter amount of time; more if you're planning to cross the globe and/or check into a five-star resort. Always overestimate honeymoon costs and leave padding for an unexpected splurge. Plan to take along a few hundred "safety" dollars and a credit card for emergencies—you never know when you'll blow the engine in your car or *feel compelled* to upgrade to the Cleopatra Honeymoon Suite.

If your budget doesn't live up to your dream trip, talk about your priorities and decide where to scrimp and when to splurge. Some couples don't care where they go as long as they can stay in the most luxurious room; others will sleep in a tent as long as they can go far, far away to pitch it. Talk about how you'll spend your time, what makes you feel pampered (expensive meals? in-room massage? a beautiful view?), and what you care less about. Since we're fully aware that you never have enough money for all your honeymoon dreams, here are our top tips for saving dollars:

Travel Like Kids Do

If you're under twenty-six, you can pay dirt-cheap student rates on air and rail fare as well as get discounted museum admissions in various countries. No student ID is required. Call STA Travel (800–777–0112) for info and help with booking, or check it out at www.sta-travel.com. Also try Council Travel at 800–226–8624.

- Go during "shoulder season"—the week or two before and after a destination's peak season. You'll save up to 40 percent on your room, avoid the crowds, and still get great weather. Ask your hotel or travel agent for specifics on your honeymoon spot.
- Get a second opinion. And a third. Prices vary widely.
- Start your research early. (Travel pros recommend nine to twelve months.)
- Check airfare from nearby cities: Newark rather than New York, Milwaukee rather than Chicago, Indianapolis rather than Cincinnati, Baltimore instead of D.C., Oakland or San Jose instead of San Francisco.
- Stay over a Saturday night for lowest fares.
- Beach bums? West Coasters, head to Mexico. East Coasters, think Caribbean. Midwesterners: either!
- Drive, don't fly.
- Check Amtrak's cross-country or regional train packages (800–USA–RAIL).
- See if you can use your employer's, AAA, or alumni association discount.
- Avoid hotel restaurants. Food tends to be cheaper (and better) at local joints.
- Tell everyone you're honeymooners and ask about specials. You may at least get an upgrade.
- Buy a package trip including air, hotel, and transfers. (See "Choosing Your Trip," below.)
- Use a credit card that has automatic trip insurance rather than buying separate insurance.
- Ask Dad (or Mom) if you can use the company's corporate condo in the Caribbean.
- Compromise. Stay an extra day by choosing a cheaper room. Or go high luxury for less time.
- Ask your parents to give you the gift of their frequent-flier miles.

Who Pays Your Way?

Q: Is the groom's family responsible for the honeymoon? We want to go to Thailand, but his parents don't have that kind of cash. Do we settle for Cincinnati?

A: Not unless you *love* the Reds, the Ohio River, and Skyline Chili. Traditionally, the groom's parents paid for the honeymoon (and the bride's parents funded just about everything else). But today the entire budget is up for grabs. If you have the cash, pay for your dream trip yourselves. If his parents feel the honeymoon is in their hat, ask them to contribute toward your Thai trip—by picking up the hotel tab, covering the airfare, or springing for new luggage (depending on their budget and interest) while you cover the rest. If they don't have the dough, and you don't, either, then it's time to think about a less exotic location, a shorter trip, or less luxe accommodations.

Choosing Your Trip

Now that you've got your budget in order, it's time to decide what type of trip to spend it on. Decide now how you feel about each of these options, and whether they figure in your honeymoon vision.

Package Possibilities: Packagers are companies that buy hotel rooms, airline seats, and other trip elements at a low bulk price and then combine them into one "package" deal. A package does not mean a guided trip in a tour bus. It just means you're buying all of your pieces of paradise together—air, room, hotel transfers to and from the airport, theater tickets, a boat tour, and so on. You'll see packages advertised in the travel section of your Sunday paper, or your travel agent might suggest some.

On the plus side, a package is easy to book and can mean big savings. But it also may mean a tiny hotel room. Some packagers cut costs by squeezing travelers into the hotel's lowest-end accommodations. If you see a package you like, call the hotel directly to find out just what category room you're reserving. Then call the package company to see if you can upgrade.

Tour Trips: A tour is a package that generally includes a guide and other travelers. It may be a huge trip with hundreds of people or a small, specialized group. You may *have* to take a tour if you're going somewhere remote, like a trek through the Himalayas. But think seriously before signing on. Not only can traveling en masse make it hard to get to know a place, but it also means forced togetherness with people other than your sweetie. This is your *honeymoon*, after all—do you really want to spend it with thirty members of the Akron Super Strikers bowling league? Of course, an organized tour does mean less planning—and you may want the security of that big group in a country where you don't speak the language. Some companies offer private tour guides for challenging terrain—at an equally challenging price. A private tour eliminates the presence of others, but it also nixes the substantial savings. We aren't saying tours are always a bad idea—just be careful.

Register and Sail Away

All you want for your wedding is a two-week cruise? Register for it! Call the Cruise Line Industry Association (CLIA) at 212–921–0066 to set up a "floating registry." For a land-locked honeymoon, try HoneyLuna (800–809–5862), a service that lets your guests choose which part of the trip to give—part of the airfare, room costs, even that welcoming champagne.

The All-Inclusive Option: You've seen the ads for all-inclusives—a love-struck couple sprawled on the sand, clad in bathing suits and wedding bands. Same couple, laughing over cocktails, snorkeling in chartreuse or fuchsia flippers, springing across the tennis courts in new Nikes. "What is this?" you've asked. "Camp for adults?"

Sort of. At an all-inclusive resort, you pay one price for your room, meals, entertainment, activities, and (sometimes) alcohol. Everything is within the resort's compound. These resorts vary in price, size, ambience, and degree of luxury—an all-inclusive can be a private, 60-room hideaway where you'll eat meals alone, albeit in a dining room with other vacationers. Or it may mean 300 other couples, a social director urging you to join in on games all day, and group meals. Some all-inclusives are "couples only," meaning it's just you two and a gazillion other lovers. You'll find all-inclusives throughout the Caribbean, in the Poconos, and, increasingly, in Mexico, Europe, and the South Pacific.

On the glass-is-half-full side, an all-inclusive is easy, easy, easy. You roll out of bed and start playing. It's impossible to get bored or lonely, and there are plenty of other people to swap wedding stories with. Because you pay one price, you can try every activity—from swimming, boating, parasailing and water-skiing to dining and dancing till dawn, without ever thinking about cost while you're there.

On the half-empty hand, staying at a self-contained resort may prevent you from getting to know the local culture. You *can* explore the island outside your resort, of course, but since you've already paid for all your meals and activities, you may not be motivated to. If you're not joiner types, a huge all-inclusive with "manufactured fun" (volleyball around the pool, couples-only Ping Pong contests) may be more annoying than entertaining.

Call for brochures and look at the photos; you should be able to tell what kind of vibes a place has from its promotional materials. Consider the activities, the rooms, the amount of privacy you'd have, and the cost. And try to talk to someone who has been there. Well-known all-inclusives are:

- Caesars Poconos Resorts (800–243–4141) are in Pennsylvania's Pocono Mountains, the original Land of Love.
- Club Med (800–CLUB–MED) has resorts worldwide (most in the Caribbean).
- Club St. Lucia and Club Antigua (800–777–1250) are affordable Caribbean resorts.
- Sandals (800–SANDALS) has couples-only resorts throughout the Caribbean. Log on to www.sandals.com.
- SuperClubs (800–859–7873) is a Jamaica-based company with packages through Air Negril.

Good Tour Operators

- Abercrombie & Kent: 800–324–7308, private guides to exotic places. Big trips. BIG price tags.
- Amelia Tours: 800–742–4591, upscale (read: expensive) group or independent tours.
- Contiki Tours: 800–CONTIKI or www.contiki.com., for people eighteen to thirty-five years old.

Touring Tips

The United States Tour Operators Association (800–GO–US-TOA) will send info about all its member companies and advice for selecting a tour or package. Check 'em out at www.ustoa.com.

Booking Your Trip

Unfortunately, you can't beam from the ballroom to the beach as in Star Trek. (If you can, call and tell us how.) You have to buy tickets (air, rail, or ship), and book a room for when you arrive. Whatever trip you take, there are a variety of ways to book it—and different prices depending on how you do it.

Using a Travel Agent

A travel agent can do everything from making your airline reservations to reserving theater tickets—saving you time and frustration. S/he also may save you big bucks by finding cheap fares, recommending less-expensive alternatives, or selling you seats on a flight his/her company has chartered (a service offered by some agencies). This service is free—agents get a commission from the hotel or airline, not from you.

What to Look For: Find an agency that specializes in your dream trip—luxury travel, cruising, the Caribbean, adventure—and an agent who's flexible and willing to work with you. But beware—travel agents vary in terms of experience and talent. Some have been everywhere and know next to everything. Others sit in their office and book trips to places they've never been, meaning you're getting tourist brochure advice, not firsthand experience. In general, don't go anywhere *solely* on the recommendation of a travel agent, unless s/he's actually been there.

What to Ask: When you call your travel agent, state your destination, dates, budget, desired room type, and any other preferences you have (an ocean view, kosher food, nonstop flights). The agent's working for you; tell him/her your needs. And get answers to any questions you may have, such as:

Destination Questions

- Is it safe? Are there areas to avoid?
- Can we drink the water and/or eat fresh foods?
- Do we need our passports, special visas, shots, or other papers?
- Is there a good taxi or bus system, or will we need a car to get around?
- What's the weather like during the time we plan to go?
- Do we need a converter for our hair dryer/curling iron/hand-held massager?
- Have you been there yourself?

All-Inclusives on the Web

- #1 Travel Network's All-Inclusive Resorts: www.1travel.com
- Quin Well Travel Service's All Inclusive Resorts of the Caribbean: www.quinwell.com
- Resorts Guide All-Inclusive Resorts: www.vacation-travel.com

Finding a Travel Agent

- Get a referral from a friend.
- Call the American Society of Travel Agents (703–739–2782) for a referral.
- Look in the phone book for an ASTA agent.

- Can we request special in-flight meals?
- How do we get from the airport to the hotel? (Are transfers included?)
- Will you reserve us a room with a view?
- Is there a special honeymoon package?
- Can we change hotel rooms if we're not satisfied? How much will it cost?
- Do you have any suggestions to save us money?
- What's your policy if we have to cancel?

Go to The Knot's
Aloha Travel
Auction at
www.theknot.com.

How It Works: Your agent will do some research and call you back with the possibilities. You'll probably have to decide whether to take a morning or evening flight, which airline to use, if you want to stay an extra day to get a better rate, and the like. Once you agree on the details, the agent will book the tickets and let you know when to pay (either by credit card over the phone or in person in the office).

Before you leave, your agent should give you the plane tickets, hotel confirmation numbers, a complete itinerary with phone numbers and addresses of all the places you're staying, his/her phone number in case you have a problem (an 800-number or a number to call collect), vouchers, directions, maps, and anything else you'll need.

If you've asked an agent for help, you are not obliged to book with him/her. If you

---

Travel Agent Talk

Talking to a travel agent makes you feel like you've already entered a foreign land. What the heck do all those terms mean? Here's our Glossary of Professional Travel Gibberish.

Hotel

EP (European Plan): Price covers room only
CP (Continental Plan): Continental breakfast comes with room
AP (American Plan): Three meals come with room
MAP (Modified American Plan): Breakfast and dinner come with room
Double occupancy: The price of a package if two people stay in one room
Rack rate: Retail rate for a room (what you get if you call the hotel)

Air

Bulkhead: The first seat in coach (the one with the tray table in the arm)
Exit row: The seat over the wing (more leg room, but the seat back doesn't recline)

General

Tariff: A tax, generally an added travel or border tax
Departure tax: A tax you pay at the airport to leave the country, usually about $10 to $15 (included in the price of some packages)

find a better deal by calling the airline or hotel on your own, book it yourself (or ask the agent to do it for you, but make sure s/he gets the same rate you were quoted).

Doing It Yourselves

If you have the time and inclination, you may be able to find better rates by booking your trip yourself—but only if you can stomach the prospect of spending hours on hold listening to the Muzak version of "Send in the Clowns." Booking on your own can be very time-consuming and frustrating, but it may be a good option if you're relatively experienced travelers who've read about a place (or talked to a friend who went) and have all the info you need. Stay organized: Keep track of phone numbers, rates, flight times, and pay-by dates in one notebook. There are several approaches for do-it-yourselfers.

Dial Direct: Call each airline directly and ask about dates, rates, and upcoming specials. For a list of hotels in your honeymoon hot spot, call the country's U.S. tourist board; then call the hotels directly, too. (Remember, if you're calling a charming little country inn deep in the Tuscan hillside, be prepared for a hotel operator who doesn't speak English.) If you dial direct, you're being your own travel agent; make sure to get all the information you'd expect from a pro.

Surf the Web: The newest do-it-yourself option, travel sites are popping up all over the Web, meaning you can do much of your destination research and booking at home, anytime, day or night. Most major hotel chains have Web sites, too, letting you reserve rooms,

Good Air Discount Brokers

Cheap Tickets: 800–377–1000
Mr. Cheap: 800–MRCHEAP

Glossary of Rooms

You'll probably spend a lot of time in your hotel during your honeymoon. Make it a room you love. Here's the rundown on rooms for rent.

B&B: While a bed and breakfast sounds romantic, it often literally means a bed in someone's guest room and breakfast. This is either incredibly charming or not private enough (walls too thin for you-know-what, an overly talkative owner). Check it out first or talk to someone who has stayed there.

Cottage: Usually an independent structure.

Inn: A small hotel, often privately owned. More privacy than a B&B; more romantic than a huge hotel.

Motel: Stands for "motor hotel"—usually means a roadside, low-rise building where you park your car near your room.

Suite: Officially two rooms—a bedroom and living room—separated by a full wall. A "junior suite" may have a comfortable sitting area rather than a complete second room. A "housekeeping suite" usually includes a kitchen.

Villa: An upscale take on the cottage—usually with a kitchen, maid service, balconies, and elegance. (You may have to stay at least a week.)

pay for them, and maybe even take a virtual tour of the grounds without ever leaving your desk. But make sure you know exactly what you want before typing in your credit card number!

Use a Discount Broker: Often your best budget bet, discount brokers, or "consolidators," are private companies that purchase air tickets or blocks of rooms in bulk and pass their savings on to you, much like trip packagers. Look for their ads in the travel section of your local newspaper. But unlike packagers, they sell individual trip parts at a cut rate (rather than the air/hotel/transfer approach); you put the pieces together yourselves, giving you total trip freedom. Wholesalers often have great last-minute (two weeks before departure time) fares and rooms far below the rack rate.

When calling an air wholesaler, ask what airline your potential flight is on; most work with major carriers *and* small companies. If you're not comfortable flying Coconuthead Express, say so. If you have doubts, call your local Better Business Bureau to make sure the wholesale company (or the airline) is legit. When calling a room wholesaler, make sure to find out exactly what type of room you'll be staying in. And again, get all the same info you'd get from a travel agent—destination details and company policy.

**Good Hotel
Discount Brokers**

Hotel Reservations Network:
800–964–6835
Players Express Vacations:
800–458–6161
Quikbook: 800–789–9887

Getting Ready to Go

You've got your tickets, reserved your room, and stocked up on all the sunblock, cool shades, and trashy novels you'll need. But if you're heading abroad, you may have a few extra pretravel steps to take.

Identify Yourselves

Whenever you travel out of the country, you have to pass through immigration and customs. You'll need to show your passport to get through. Call your local passport agency (check for yours under government listings in the phone book) or ask at your post office for info on how and where to get it. You also may need a tourist card, which the airline gives you on the plane.

Exceptions to the passport rule include Canada, Mexico, and parts of the Caribbean. While a passport is easiest, you can get in with a photo ID (driver's license or other ID) and proof of citizenship (an original birth certificate with raised seal or U.S. naturalization papers for Mexico and the Caribbean; the same items or a voter's registration card for Canada). The Dominican Republic also requires a $10 tourist card, which you buy at the airport.

If you're driving to Mexico, you need a temporary vehicle importation permit (except in the Baja peninsula and parts of the state of Sonora), available at the Mexican customs office on the border. You'll need your vehicle registration and a major credit card, in addition to personal entry requirements.

Just Charge It

If you're buying in a foreign currency, put everything on a credit card. You'll get the bank's official exchange rate, which is almost always better than that of a store, hotel, or restaurant. And you'll get an itemized record of exactly what you spend.

Some countries require you to have a tourist visa in addition to your passport. You get one from your vacation destination's consulate before you go. Countries requiring visas change all the time, as does the length of time it takes to get one. Ask your airline or travel agent about visa requirements as soon as you make your travel plans. Then call the country's consulate to double-check.

Immunization Alert

The more exotic the country, the greater your chance of contracting some equally exotic disease. If you're traveling to Africa, Asia, Latin America, or India, ask if your doctor does travelers' immunizations or can point you toward a local hospital or clinic that does. Call the Centers for Disease Control and Prevention hot line (404–332–4559) about the status of your destination, or check them out on the Web at www.cdc.gov.

Safety First

If you want to go to Peru, but you don't want to experience an attack by the Shining Path, call the U.S. State Department Travel Advisory (202–647–5225) for an update on global hot spots. Or check out their Web site at travel.state.gov/travel_warnings.html. State Department advi-

How to Stay Flush

Take your cash card with you! You'll find ATMs all across Europe, where you can get local currency as you need it and pay the same great bank rate. Withdraw in bulk to save on the sometimes *big* transaction fees. And make sure you have cash in your checking account—some machines don't offer the option of taking from savings.

Packing Like a Pro

What you bring depends on where you're going—from a fancy frock for dinner at the captain's table to hiking boots and a sun visor for a Galapagos trek. If you're unsure what wardrobe you'll need, call your hotel, cruise ship, or tour company. Or look in a guidebook to the area for advice.

Choose luggage that fits your trip—a garment bag for evening attire, a backpack for a European hike. Bring an extra duffel (or expandable suitcase) for all your loot.

Take clothes in colors easy to coordinate—navy, black, and white, for example, or beige, white, and tan.

Dump everything you might want on the bed, then take half of that. Or envision your trip day by day and plan an outfit for each day, repeating shorts, pants, and sweaters.

Slip shoes in plastic bags.

Wrap your white silk blouse or other easy-to-wreck items in the cleaner's bag to protect them.

Put things that spill in resealable baggies.

Put heavy things on the bottom of your bag, or over the wheels; delicate items go on top.

Label your luggage clearly with sturdy luggage tags.

Lock up your zippers and put the key somewhere you'll remember.

Pack important items in your carry-on, including *anything* valuable—tickets, passports, itinerary, jewelry, cash, medicine, ID, and phone numbers—as well as an outfit for the first day and essential toiletries. Airlines *do* lose luggage.

Make sure your traveling outfit is comfortable enough for hours on the plane.

Plan to wear bulky things, such as hiking boots, on board.

sories tend to be even more cautious than your overprotective mother. If an advisory says "Don't go," we say "Don't go." But if there's a slew of warnings for things such as pickpockets and theft in your ideal city, think about them in terms of your personal experience. If you're traveling to Rome from New York City, for example, chances are you've already got your urban defenses in place. If you live in a little house on the prairie, however, you're going to need to practice defensive touring. Wherever you go, use your common sense. If you're taking a walk alone on the beach in Nassau and some guy offers you a free ride to a secret cave on the back of his Jet-Ski, just say no.

Get Insured

Your honeymoon can cost as much as a new car. But before buying travel insurance to protect your investment, see if your credit card and/or homeowner's policy covers you if your luggage gets lifted, your trip is delayed, or you have to cancel. If not, you can buy a separate, trip-only policy. Call your insurer, or ask your travel agent for details.

Tips from Experienced Travelers

However you get there, you can take steps to make the traveling part more fun. Each mode of transportation has its own unique requirements. Here are our top tips for making getting there almost as good as being there.

Air Advice

While that plane is an essential part of your dream trip (you gotta get there), the actual flight can be pretty damn boring. Not to mention so dehydrating your skin may feel like a sun-dried tomato by the time you land. So what can you do to improve your in-flight experience?

- Try to book nonstop flights. Changing planes, while sometimes cheaper, makes for a loooong trip.
- Reserve special meals (vegetarian, kosher) ahead of time. Usually they're fresher than the standard fare and bear a closer resemblance to real food.
- Take moisturizing lotion for your hands and face.
- Drink a glass of water every hour you're aboard to keep from dehydrating.
- Dress in layers. Air on? Sweater on. Air on the blink? Sweater off.
- Have a sip of celebratory champagne, not the whole bottle. Alcohol contributes to dehydration.
- Save the coffee for the end of the flight. (More dehydration!)
- Contacts drying up? Take 'em out. Or make sure to bring saline.

And Your Name Is . . .

Even if one (or both) of you is changing your name, make all international reservations in your given names. You can't apply for a passport using your married name until after the wedding; keeping everything consistent will save you big-time headaches. And if you need a passport, make sure to apply 6 weeks before your trip.

Get Married, Get Miles

Pay for your wedding on a credit card that gets frequent-flier miles. Then cash in those air awards for that flight to Fiji. If you don't have a mileage-generating card, call your current credit card company and ask to enroll in its frequent-flier program. Need lots of miles? Switch your long-distance service to the miles-for-minutes program with the same airline.

On Board that Boat

Whether you're taking a 2,000-passenger cruise ship or a private yacht, rocky water can make landlubbers feel like deflated rubber duckies. Big cruises have some special factors to consider:

- In huge–cruise ship land, bigger does not mean calmer; just longer lines at the midnight buffet.
- Don't trust listed prices. Call the 800 number and pay less.
- Find out *exactly* what's included. (Food? Yes. Drinks, port charges, taxes? Yikes!)
- Consider an outside room—that little porthole of light can save a claustrophobic.
- Ask about the dress code. There's usually at least one formal night on board.
- Take a sweater and windbreaker for that chilly night air.
- Take along Dramamine and antiseasickness, acupressure "bracelets," just in case.
- Read up on the ports of call and plan what to see to maximize your land time.
- If you hate your room, tell the purser. You may be able to change it.
- Buy shipboard gifts at the end of the trip; cruise line gift shops often mark everything way down on the way back.

Road Rules

Good news, speed lovers—highway speed limits are back up to 70 mph in some states. But more speed means even more need for safety precautions. And while nothing beats a road trip for hours of alone time, too many days of staring at that white dividing line can make even the loviest couples feel like slapping each other. Road-trip tactics:

- Join your local branch of AAA (800–AAA–HELP) for free maps, guidebooks, roadside help (just in case), and a personalized Trip-tik with your ideal route highlighted on an easy-to-hold, flip-style map.
- Check the air in your tires, gas in your tank, and fluids in all those other, enigmatic under-the-hood vessels.
- Stock up on your favorite music, books, books on tape, and an Itty Bitty Booklight.
- Take sunglasses (and sunscreen!) for late-afternoon glare.
- Take snacks, but not a cooler of meals. Stopping for lunch is an important part of seeing the country.
- Forget your health regime. It's a scientific fact that nothing beats behind-the-wheel boredom like curly fries and a Dairy Queen Blizzard.
- Get enough sleep before heading out.
- If you get tired, pull over! This is not the time for a who-can-drive-the-longest-without-stopping or who-has-better-hand-eye-coordination-while-asleep contest.

Don't Leave Home Without . . .

- Birth control
- Bug spray, sunblock, anti-septic, anti-bacterial ointment (for an outdoor trip)
- Extra pair of glasses or contacts
- Film
- List of important phone numbers
- Money, one credit card, a cash card
- Notebook or travel journal
- Prescription medicine (in original bottle), aspirin, allergy pills
- Toothbrush
- Voltage converter (if needed in a foreign country)
- List of addresses for must-send postcards

Honeymoon Tipping Table

Here's how much to tip the people who make your honeymoon amazing:

Dining

- United States and Caribbean: 15 percent of total, pretax bill.
- Mexico: 20 percent of total, pretax bill.
- Europe and Canada: 10 percent of total bill unless it says "service included."
- South Pacific: No tip expected.

Travel

- Airport porter: $1 per bag.
- Train porter: At least $1 each night in a sleeper car.

Hotel

- Bellman: $1 per bag.
- Maid service: Leave about $1 on the nightstand each morning in the United States and the Caribbean. In Europe, it varies; ask at the front desk.
- Doorman: $1 for each service rendered (taxi hailing, door, bag carrying, etc.).
- Room service: About 15 percent of the bill in the United States, 10 percent in the Caribbean, nothing extra in Europe.
- Special service: If someone from the housekeeping staff brings you an iron or a bottle of champagne, give $1 or $2.
- All-inclusives: Check the info in your confirmation package for tipping suggestions.

Cruises

- At least $16 for each day aboard (management divvies it up for you).

Cabs

- United States: About 15 percent of the fare.
- Caribbean: About 10 percent, generally; no tipping in the Dominican Republic or the British Virgin Islands.
- Europe: Generally, just round the bill up to the nearest dollar; in Italy, Portugal, and Britain, go with the 15 percent rule.

Tour Bus Driver

- At least $4 per day for the two of you.

Tour Guide

- At least $5 per day for the two of you; if there's a group of you going in together, have everyone contribute about $2 per person, per day.

Instructors/Activity Organizers

- About 15 percent of the cost for water-skiing, Scuba, boat ride, horseback riding, tennis lessons.

- If you're renting, specify automatic or stick shift when reserving your car (especially in Europe, where stick shifts are standard).
- If you're headed abroad, ask AAA about an International Driving Permit or other needs.

Making Tracks

Whether you're taking an Amtrak across the United States, zipping through the Canadian Rockies, or riding the rails through Europe, going by train lets you see the sights without having to keep your hands on the wheel. Here're our tips for a terrific train trip:

- If you're taking a sleeper car to a faraway destination, pack a separate carry-on; you can't get to your checked baggage en route.
- Trains are far noisier than you'd expect—but your ears adjust and you forget about it.
- If you're training across Europe, hang on to your hat (and bag, purse, wallet, etc.).
- Pack snacks. Unless your train has a high-class dining car with a real chef, you'll be eating microwave meals from here to eternity (or wherever you're going).

Advice for a Harmonious Honeymoon

And now a word from our sponsor—romance. It's the ultimate reason to take a honeymoon, regardless of where you go. But romance isn't guaranteed to happen (though things like a hot tub under a moonlit sky, the sound of the ocean, and a big bottle of bubbly do help). Your attitude and actions really dictate how much fun you have. Here's our best advice.

Pack a Positive Attitude

There are always rough spots when traveling. How you handle them determines the quality of your trip. Constant complaining exaggerates the downsides, while ignoring imperfections and focusing on the positive will leave you both feeling like you planned the vacation of the century. Your goal—make sure your sweetie has a fabulous time. You not only guarantee that she'll love the trip madly (and you, of course), but you also protect yourself from getting into the traveler's rut of obsessing about the inevitable little glitches that can be so annoying. And keep your sense of humor intact! If your car's engine is overheating, and you have to run the heat to keep it cool, and it's August, and it's raining (meaning you have to roll the windows up), it could be a tragedy. Or it could be pretty damn funny.

Take Realistic Expectations

First time traveling together? Expect to learn a lot about each other. Even if you like to do all the same things at home, you may discover that you have very different travel styles. If he wants to hole up in the room and you discover you need to disco till dawn with all the new friends you've made, it doesn't mean you're headed for divorce court when you get home.

Be indulgent and supportive of each other. A rocky first vacation just means you need to plan another one soon.

Honeymoon blues? Believe it or not, a lot of couples spend the first days of their trip in the doldrums, depressed by so much calm after all the commotion. It's normal to feel in limbo—you just planned the biggest event of your shared lives and then left before basking in the afterglow. Spend your first day "debriefing" about your wedding—who wore what, who came, how it felt compared to your expectations. Then, when you've gone over every single detail, you'll be ready to start focusing on the fun in front of you.

Take a Little Time Alone

Don't feel obliged to spend every moment together. Even the most passionate, sex-crazed newlyweds need some time apart. Lie on the beach while she does yoga; have a cappuccino while he watches TV. A lot of long-married couples say they had more fun on a "second honeymoon" because they were able to relax and pursue their own interests occasionally.

Talk to Strangers

Yes, this is the opposite of what you learned in kindergarten. We're not suggesting that you hitchhike your way across Mexico. But the best way to get to know a place is to talk to those who live there. Ask the waiter for disco recommendations. Talk to that nice-looking couple on the beach. Ask the Scottish bank teller if she has a ghost in her house (guaranteed conversation-starter *anywhere* in Scotland). If you're at an all-inclusive, meet a few of your co-honeymooners. It not only enhances your experience of the place, but sharing a *little* time with others also gives you more conversation fodder and inevitably makes the trip more fun.

Honeymoon Snapshots

"Souvenir" does not mean "tacky mermaid made entirely of sea shells." It's French for "remember." Here are some great ways to remember your terrific trip:

Take photos. Enlarge your best shot and frame it for your office.

Write it down. There's nothing like a daily journal to keep your experiences alive.

Collect matchbooks. Every time you light a candle you'll think of that bistro on the Left Bank.

Buy a local-cuisine cookbook. Learn to make your favorite dishes.

Take a taste. Buy edible souvenirs—rum from the islands, chocolate from France, flavored honey or spice rub from Louisiana.

Breathe deeply. Focus on a scent during your trip—the lilac tree growing off your balcony, coconut-scented sunscreen, the incense burned in the Buddhist altars—and then re-create that aroma back home for instant sensual memories.

Name that tune. Buy the nightly steel drum band's CD.

Practical makes perfect. Buy crafts you'll use—pottery from Mexico, a wool sweater from Scotland, even a new bedroom set from North Carolina.

Plan a Surprise

Even if you're making all the arrangements together, you still can spring a romantic surprise on your sweetie. Call the restaurant ahead of time and ask for a bottle of champagne to be waiting at your table. Plan to get up early one morning and bring him breakfast in bed. Or return from your walk across the resort with a bouquet of flowers (just don't get caught picking them!). Think of anything romantic that you know she'll love.

Linger Over the Last Night

Plan something special for your last night—a moonlit cruise, a romantic dinner. Then talk about your favorite part of your vacation and ways to incorporate it into your home life. Love the hotel's predinner cocktail-on-the-balcony hour? Vow to make it part of your daily grind. (So what if your balcony at home overlooks the neighbor's garage, not the ocean?) Maybe you want to continue eating more fruits and vegetables, or sipping cinnamon-spiced coffee together in bed on weekends. Take a little bit of the luxury back with you.

Honeymoon Planning Calendar

12–6 months before: Talk about your dream destinations. Start looking for a travel agent, reading up on your favorite spots, and investigating costs. If you're taking a time-specific trip (Mardi Gras in New Orleans, Carnival in Brazil, New Year's Eve for the year 2000), book your room and flight *now*.

5 months before: Get your passport, visa, and immunization info if you're going abroad.

4 months before: Nail down your budget. Look for deals in the paper and online.

3 months before: Book your tickets, rooms, rental car, and so on. Pay necessary deposits.

2 months before: Find out about the weather and any dress-code or special attire requirements. Start shopping for your trip.

1 month before: Line up someone to feed your plants or watch your pets while you're gone.

2 weeks before: Pick up traveler's checks. Write down your airline, hotel, and rental car confirmation numbers, as well as traveler's check numbers.

1 week before: Give a copy of your itinerary to your folks or honor attendants. (They may want to surprise you with flowers in your room.) Change about $50 (if you're going abroad) to get you started.

A few days before: Pack your bags. Double-confirm international flights.

Day before: Confirm domestic flights.

Day of: Enjoy!

Back to the Future

Your first year or so of marriage is an intense, romantic period—a time to adjust to being together forever, for real. The foundations you lay during this period will ensure that your lifetime love affair unfolds like a fairy tale. Take the time to communicate, openly and honestly, about what you want from your new marriage, home, joint future, family—life. Make the important decisions about merging your money and setting goals for an idyllic future. (You know, when you'll be watching the sun set from your beach-house patio as you sip lime gimlets.) Invest energy in learning to live with—and love—your honey's quirks and making each day better than the one before. This is the wonderful world of marriage. Welcome!

Adjusting to Newlywed Life

It's not uncommon to feel a little discombobulated after your wedding is over. The period leading up to your nuptials was one nail-biting adventure after another. Your insides were all whacked-out with nerves and excitement. Friends and family couldn't shower you with enough praise and attention. You couldn't get enough of each other, despite the piles of your honey's dirty clothes strewn on the floor.

But now it's back to the real world, smelly socks, daily grind, grimy dishes, and all. Is this what married life is all about? Yikes. Feeling let down, annoyed, even panicked is *not* unheard of. But we're here to remind you that as a newly married pup, you are at the *beginning* of a great journey (perhaps the greatest ever), not the end. With a little prep work—on your own emotions, the relationship, and your ties to the outside world—you can get your psyche in check and your partnership rock-solid.

Postparty Depression

You two have just taken a serious step in your lives, the biggest of the big. You've promised to love and cherish and respect each other *no matter what*. Now the day-to-day of that promise—loud snoring, scheduling conflicts, meddling family—is starting to set in. To add fuel to the blah-fire, your engagement fanfare and big-day celebrity are but a blissful memory. It's natural to feel a little blue, perhaps even a little on edge.

Whenever you have a moment of despair, *do not* start downing Ben & Jerry's or lashing out at your sweetie. Instead, stop and say to yourself:

- "This is a healthy response. I'm letting go of the unrealistic expectation that every day will be filled with heart-pounding fun and excitement."
- "My blues are going to pass soon. My ego just needs to readjust to not being the center of attention every waking second."
- "My honey *is* my perfect match. It just so happens that s/he is also human."
- "Real life is real. So what if there are no life-or-death decisions to make, no trays of canapés at every turn, no revolving heart-shaped bed? There's the comfort of our daily routine, the time to hang out with our favorite friends, the happiness borne of a time-worn love affair."

Let Your Love Grow

In Switzerland, couples often plant a pine tree near their new home to symbolize fertility. Plant a tree together soon after your wedding—either in your own yard or in a nearby park or field. It's symbolic of the growth of your relationship, reminding you not to dwell on the past but on your wonderful future.

If you *must* watch your wedding video over and over and over, do so—but not at the expense of other activities. You may need to gorge yourself on nuptial memories to purge yourself of your desire to relive them. In the meantime, though, get on with the adventure. Depending on the amount of energy you invested in your wedding, your natural nostalgic disposition, and external circumstances (such as whether you enjoy your job and how often you work out), coming out completely from the shadow of your big day can take anywhere from a few weeks to several months. When you do, you'll realize just how much sunshine you've got in your life: your sweetie, your loyal friends and family, never mind that spanking-new silverware.

Got the Blues?

"While planning your wedding, try to keep things in perspective—otherwise the wedding takes on larger-than-life proportions. Everything else will suffer in the meantime, and afterward, of course you'll feel let down; the thing you've focused on for so long is over."

—Gerard Monaghan, president, Association of Bridal Consultants

Roommates for Life: Living Together

Whether you shacked up or not before you said your vows will have an impact on your adjustment to married life. If you've never cohabited, you're going to have to deal with the nitty-gritty roommate stuff: whether your mess-tolerance levels are compatible, how to cope with your different decorating styles, and divvying up household chores. Even if you've been there, done that, you're still going to have conflicts to solve, rules to lay down, and arrangements to set up to make your now-permanent partnership work. Compromise, patience, and humor are key. So is an active sex and social life—when you're having lots of fun, little disagreements are that much easier to handle.

Here are some issues you'll need to deal with to make sure that two's company.

Alone Time: You love your sweetie to bits. You love watching TV together, hosting cocktail parties together, taking showers together, even sorting out the recycling together. But every once in a while even *you* need some time apart. Retaining a certain separateness—keeping up with your own friends, interests, and hobbies—is essential to a healthy long-term relationship.

- So as not to hurt each other's feelings when you want private time—whether to go for a run, grab a beer with your buddies, or retreat to do some writing—talk about the things that you enjoy doing alone early on. That way your honey will know you're doing them purely because you like 'em, not because you're sick of him/her.
- Have one evening a week each when you get the house to yourself. That way you can have a quiet, chill-out night and do silly things that make you happy (paint your toenails, flip back and forth between every single ball game on TV, talk to friends long distance, blare music your honey hates).
- Establish do-not-disturb boundaries. Inform your honey of specific times—bath hour, Monday Night Football, meditation—when you want peace and quiet.
- Learn to be together apart. It's fun to be at home at the same time doing your own thing.

Company: It's lots of fun (and highly economical) to make dates with friends at your place. However, it's essential that you take your sweetie's schedule, plans, and feelings into consideration before you declare open house.

- Inform your honey of your plan to invite people over well in advance. That way you can avoid scheduling conflicts (work deadlines, book-club gatherings), and give your sweetie an opportunity to make alternate plans if s/he so desires.
- Invite joint friends or a mix of pals as often as possible. That way neither of you feels like a stranger in your own house and you'll liven things up by acquainting your friends with cool new people.
- Schedule single sex get-togethers on the same night. You want to have your pals over for an evening of beer and bonding? No problem. Tell your honey of your plan a few weeks ahead of time; not only will she be more than happy to organize a night out with her own pals, but she'll be thrilled that you're being considerate by giving her a heads-up.

Chores: There is no surer recipe for marital strife than lopsided household duties. Divide day-to-day responsibilities fairly and come up with an acceptable schedule for heavy-duty cleaning.

- Balance your strengths and weaknesses. For example, if one of you does all the cooking, the other should do the dishwashing.

- Compensate. If you don't have time—or an iota of inclination—to contribute to house-cleaning, make it up to your honey by footing the bill for a maid service periodically, regularly buying essentials like toilet paper and milk, or taking charge of car or yard upkeep.
- Make it fun. Put aside one day a month for scrubbing, mopping, dusting, and tidying. Blare music, take make-out breaks, and reward yourselves with dinner at a romantic restaurant.
- Establish no-can-dos. If scraps in the sink ruin your sweetie's day, you should know about it; make sure your honey's familiar with your dust phobia. Talk about your pet peeves and red lines early on in your marriage so you can avoid flare-ups.

Privacy: Establish boundaries early on for things you don't want touched or borrowed. While most things in your home are there to share, it's fair to keep some items completely for yourself, whether it's a journal, your favorite T-shirt, or a toothbrush. You don't want it to feel like there are dark secrets or lack-of-trust issues, though. Explain a mine-only object's sentimental value so your honey doesn't feel shut out and can fully respect your wishes.

Rules: Everyone has dislikes and particular quirks. In order to build a successful marriage, you need to be respectful of each other's wishes and—at the same time—committed to compromise and adaptability.

- Distinguish danger zones. It's important that you know of and respect your honey's hard-and-fast no-nos; for example, if cigarette smoke is your sweetie's number-one enemy, ask tobacco-puffing friends to take it outside.
- Find workable compromises. If your sweetie doesn't want cable (he hates the idea of wasting time in front of the tube) but you need your MTV, establish blackout hours when the television set must stay off.
- Forgive and forget. Transgressions are inevitable—you're two different (though equally exquisite) people. Learn to laugh about your crazes and flaws.

Becoming Family

In the soundtrack of your life, one record is getting a lot of play these days: Sister Sledge's "We Are Family." You and your honey are now officially a familial unit. Your sweetie's family is now officially *your* family. In addition to the busload of new cousins, grandparents, uncles, and nieces whom you've inherited, you're also officially stuck with your baby's friends—for better or for worse. Sometimes it's the more, the merrier. Other times you wish that you could make certain people—poof!—disappear. All in all, however, we think you've got a great deal: more support, more love, more greeting cards, more places to stay while traveling, all for the price of one "I do." If you play your cards right, all these family and friend matters can actually add joy to your life.

Two Become One: Creating a family with the person you love most in the world is the bee's knees. Now's the time to talk about what the notion of "family" means to you.

Celebrate your new, improved status by creating your own unique family traditions. Host an annual Earth Day brunch for your extended families, where you serve tasty organic dishes and gather donations to an environmental charity on a brilliantly decorated Money Tree; decide to pose for a portrait every year—on your anniversary; host a neighborhood July Fourth cookout.

If you two come from different ethnic backgrounds, devise ways to merge your different customs and to make them accessible to the other relatives. If one of you is fasting during Ramadan, say, throw a big dinner party on the last day of the holiday so both Muslim and non-Muslim relatives can celebrate the devotion and religious joy. Host an Easter dinner/Passover seder, and spend time talking about the historical relation between the two holidays.

Also remember that while it's great that you and your honey's customs and routines overlap somewhat with your extended families, it's also important to break apart sometimes to have quality alone time. Don't participate in every single family get-together. You now have the right—as your own family—sometimes to celebrate just the two of you. One Thanksgiving, for example, choose to stay at home and cook up—or order in—a romantic meal for two. Capitalize on the Christmas/New Year's break—and the chance to spend a full week together—vacationing in a tropical spot rather than visiting with the folks. Keeping to yourselves once in a while serves to make the time you spend with your—or your pumpkin's—family more special.

In-Law Issues: His parents, her parents—now they're all *your* parents. This is the time to discuss likes, dislikes, boundaries. Since you probably have different relationships with your folks, talk about how close you want to be to them, what you expect from them, how often you want to see them. Then the ancient art of compromise comes into play. Settle on general guidelines (that sit well with both of you) for the frequency of get-togethers, phone calls, and visits.

When problems arise, you should each take charge of setting things right with your respective families; your honey should not have to deal with antagonizing his/her in-laws (at least not this early in the game). You two are a team now, so if your father's having a key to your house or your grandmother's daily phone calls cramp your sweetie's style, they cramp yours, too. If you approach problematic situations with a respectful, cheerful, here's-a-great-alternative ("Use the key only for emergencies," "I'll call you from work"), there probably won't be any sparks a-flyin'. If there are, you'll all deal with them, as adults (which is, in case you haven't noticed, what you now are).

Friend Fine-Tuning: Coming up with arrangements that make both you and your honey happy is also important when it comes to your circles of friends. Talk to your sweetie about how often you'd like to have people over and go out socially. Hear out each other's concerns—bad-influence friends, not-enough-time-for-us worries—and offer reassurance.

Together Alone

"Married couples need to 'individualize.' If either or both spouses stay too connected to their nuclear families, they will become partial to that family's needs, and they won't be able to address each other's needs very well. Individualizing is a process—you'll figure out what your boundaries are as situations come up."

—Paula Popp,
Pittsburgh-based
therapist

Getting Your Affairs in Order

You've dealt with newlywed affairs of the heart; it's time to turn your attention outward and focus on some practical, logistical issues. You now need to deal with changing your name officially (if applicable), assessing your financial situation (savings, investments, debt, credit, insurance), and setting long-term goals, whether they are buying a house, moving to Paris, or just getting rich. (Good luck to you!) That may seem like a lot of work to do on topics that are uncomfortable to discuss, but with a balanced diet of love, patience, respect, honesty, and understanding, you can not only master these tasks, you can ace them. Also remember that the sooner you get these practical matters out of the way, the sooner you can kick back and bask in the splendor of your gorgeous new spouse.

Changing Your Name

One of the most important logistical decisions you two need to make—*before* you get hitched, ideally—is what to do on the last-name front. Once wives had no choice but to adopt their husbands' names, but today's couples have many options.

Wife Takes Husband's Name: The traditional way, which will make your old-fashioned relatives happy and keep the question-asking to a minimum. Many couples also see this choice as a sign of real togetherness.

Husband Takes Wife's Name: A twist on the conventional decision, especially cool if the man dislikes his last name or the woman is the only child of her clan. A pretty rare choice, though. And his family might be miffed.

Wife Takes Husband's Name (sort of): Some women choose to adopt their sweetie's name socially but continue to use their given name for business purposes, even legally. This is a good option if you are a professional who relies on name recognition for your livelihood.

You Both Keep Your Own Names: You've spent your lives "building a name" for yourselves; changing what people call you may be painful. Bonus: You'll avoid the long lines at the DMV. Drawback: You may have to deal with in-laws who question your reluctance to take "their name."

Join Hearts and Names: Adopting a double or hyphenated surname is an ultramodern option. A hyphen ensures that people use both names, although the bride might prefer using her given last name as a middle name. (Tina Brown becomes Tina Brown White.) Sometimes only the bride does the twin-tower last-name thing, but it's pretty cool if both of you do it.

Both Do the Switcharoo: You may decide to adopt a whole new name for yourselves. This is a good idea if your names don't go together (like Cherry Berry or Long-Dong) or if you want to revive an extinct family name. You could artfully combine both your last names (Warner and Yasser become Yasner, for example), or choose the name of a personal role model or one you just like.

Your final name decision probably will appear on your official marriage certificate. If you have changed your name/s, it's time to run a few errands to make your new identities official with the rest of the world:

- Contact the Social Security Administration (800–772–1213). Their automated system will talk you through the name-change steps; you'll get new cards for free. (Don't fall for companies that charge "a small fee" to do this; it's a scam.)
- Visit the Department of Motor Vehicles. This agency requires you to make a personal appearance when recording a name change. Bring a good book, every form of identification you can lay your hands on, and a bottle of water. *Don't* forget your original marriage certificate (with the official-looking raised seal).
- Tell the world. Once you have a social security card and driver's license in your married name, making the other changes should be fairly easy. Some institutions require only a phone call; others may ask for more (to see your marriage certificate, social security card, etc.). Here are the important people and places to notify.

    - Friends and family (send name change cards or thank-you notes on married-name stationery)
    - Banks and other financial institutions
    - Credit-card companies
    - Employers
    - Schools and/or alumni associations
    - Post office
    - Phone company
    - Registrar of voters
    - Passport office; and
    - Landlord.

> **Playing Doctor**
>
> Choose a doctor together to be your family physician. That way s/he'll be able to take both of your symptoms and conditions into consideration when making a diagnosis—a healthy approach.

Partners on Paper: From Bank Accounts to Insurance

Now that you've dealt with the name game, there are a few more steps on the proverbial paper trail.

To Merge or Not to Merge: One of the premier decisions of your young married life is whether to join your bank accounts. For decades it was the only way to go, but now it's common wisdom that every person should keep at least one fund in his/her own name. Joint bank accounts are still the best way to go when it comes to a household fund from which to pay rent, mortgage payments, bills, or furniture purchases, though. It will simplify your lives if you have a stable coffer—into which you each put a designated percentage of your earnings—from which you can both write checks. Consider each keeping a private account for entertainment, clothing, and other small purchases. Many a happy marriage has been soured by silly money fights that could have been avoided had both partners held on to a cash flow of their own. After all, how are you going to buy your sweetie all those "I love you" gifts if your funds are totally merged?

Rest Insured: Assess your insurance situation, eliminating duplicate policies and making your honey the beneficiary of any you keep. Every couple should have:

- Homeowners'/renters' insurance: You want to protect not only your home but all the things in it. Update your coverage to include all those excellent wedding presents you got.
- Medical insurance: If you both have an employer plan, choose the better policy and both use it. If one of you doesn't have insurance, marriage is definitely a bonanza for you—you're entitled to be on your spouse's policy. If neither of you have health insurance, get it *now*.
- Disability/life insurance: This is the cornerstone of every family's financial health, a way to ensure that your honey will be all right should disaster strike.

Will Power: At some point, you'll want to draw up a will or trust that names your honey as your beneficiary—why not now, when you're on a paperwork roll? Schedule a consultation with a good attorney (about $100) to draft a legal document that's right for you.

Fringe Benefits: Make your honey the beneficiary of your retirement accounts and any other investments you hold. (You could decide to name another relative as cobeneficiary, if you wish.)

Money Talks: Family Finances 101

Remember all the time, all the blood, sweat, and tears you put into your wedding? That same colossal effort should be invested in your joint financial life now. Money is a huge relationship maker or breaker; you want to be on the winning side. You will be, if you take some time to (1) figure out your goals; (2) commit to being honest and respectful business partners; and (3) create a practical financial plan. You don't have to know a ton about money matters; it's most important that you exercise your communication skills.

Even long-term sweethearts, who may have intimate knowledge of their honey's favorite cereal and *Star Wars* movie, often know nothing about their partner's attitude toward money and his/her financial aspirations. For some reason, money is still a taboo subject in romantic relationships—people are scared to mix business and pleasure. But guess what? A marriage is not only an emotional bond for life, it's also a financial partnership. Your home is your corporate headquarters, and you two are co-CEOs. Book a table at a nice, quiet restaurant (it'll dissipate the seriousness of the matter at hand) and have a heart-to-heart with your partner about your finances. (Repeat this conference annually.) Questions to address include the following.

Ground Rules: Agree from the get-go to make all major financial decisions (beyond buying a shirt, a vase, or tickets to a ball game) *together*. Discuss each of your financial strengths and weaknesses; set some short-term and long-term investment goals.

A Couple of Independents

Want to feel like you've really merged but still keep track of your own balance sheets? Make your honey a cosignator of your account—and have your sweetie do the same—so you maintain financial independence but still have access to each other's funds if the need arises.

Get Out of Debt

Now's the time to wipe your credit card clean of all wedding-related expenses. You want to remember the day as your happiest moment, not the event that ruined your credit rating.

Is a House in Your Cards?

You always assumed you'd buy a house or condo once you got married. But are the two of you ready to make a down payment? Obviously, your bank account balances are a major factor, but there are many others to consider.

Got good credit? Even if you have a pile of cash after your wedding, you'll still need to apply for a mortgage. If your credit reports are not squeaky clean—or if you're in major debt already—you may have trouble getting a bank to back you.

Ready to settle down? You should be relatively sure that you want to stay put in the place where you buy your property. Otherwise the financial and emotional hassle of buying and maintaining a house are not worth it.

Need a fresh start? If one of you moved into the other's place—and especially if the decor and aura still reflect that in some way—buying a home may be a smart relationship move. You'll be hunting for a space that's yours together and symbolic of your new status.

Have the handyman bug? Every home—no matter how new—needs some work, and when the place is yours, there's no landlord to call in. You'll need to sacrifice some leisure time to work on making your home sweet home sweeter, *or* have money in your budget to pay someone else to do the fixin' up.

If you do decide to take the plunge, look for:

A place well inside your price range. You should be able to make a sizable down payment; you don't want to be mortgaged up the wazoo.

A community where you both feel comfortable, safe, and happy.

A house that caters to your priorities. Must have a patio, a large kitchen, a master bedroom suite? Be ready to make compromises in less-important departments.

Something reasonably close to both of your workplaces.

A mortgage pro—someone who can help you through the process.

Debt: You should know about each other's outstanding debts, because they'll affect you both down the line if you apply for a mortgage, car lease, or bank loan. Spend some of your wedding moola on erasing debt (it's one of the best gifts you can give yourselves) or come up with a reasonable amount of money to put aside for payments every month. Then stick to it.

Credit: Consider consolidating accounts (one of you becomes a secondary signer) so that you don't have too many credit cards between you. Too much credit could hurt your chances of getting a bank loan down the road, not to mention the fact that it's a pain in the neck every month when you have a stack of bills to pay. That said, you and your honey should each have at least one credit card in your own name so that you maintain your individual credit ratings.

Savings: Tell each other about your cash situation. Give your honey the lowdown on any retirement funds—IRAs or 401(k)s—certificates of deposit (CDs), and savings ac-

Get a Life

All this financial talk is freaking you out? Check out *Get a Financial Life: Personal Finance in Your Twenties and Thirties*, by Beth Kobliner (Fireside, 1996).

Marriage Can Be Taxing

So much for family values. When Uncle Sam comes looking for your taxes come April 15, he's going to want more money from you now that you're married than he did before. The so-called marriage penalty is a quirk of the tax law that means most betrothed couples must pony up more than two single people with the same joint income. This is due to the difference in the standard (nonitemized) deduction a single vs. married individual can claim. In 1997, for example, a bachelor/ette could write off $4,150 of his/her income, whereas a married duo could write off only $6,900 (or $3,450 each). That means Uncle Sam gets a bigger bite of your paycheck now that you're hitched—and he didn't even send you a crystal vase or a toaster!

The marriage tax penalty does not have to hurt you too badly, though. First of all, if one of you makes *a lot* more money than the other, getting hitched might even work to your benefit, because the high-earner gets averaged by the lower-earner into a lower tax bracket. You also can lessen the blow by visiting an accountant to figure out whether you can start claiming itemized deductions (if one of you is self-employed, say), which allow you to shield more of your income from the tax man. In general, it's a smart idea to walk hand in hand to a local accountant during your first year of marriage to get pointers on tax-deferred investments, deductible charitable gifts, and other smart saving strategies. Your financial well-being is well worth the $200 or so a consultation will cost. Splurging for a tax software program is another good move; it will help you get organized for taking the do-it-yourself approach in future years.

All this tax talk got you down? Keep in mind that you don't have to pay a dime on any cash you got in honor of the big day. They're considered gifts, which means that Uncle Sam can't touch 'em. Hee hee!

counts. In general, you should try to put away three to six months' worth of your household budget as emergency money. We know it's easier said than done, but you won't regret devising a savings plan to get there as soon as possible—you'll feel an intense sensation of relief and security. Beyond that, the money you've put aside should be earmarked for future purposes that you agree upon, whether it's your first house or a trip to Bali.

Investments: As a young couple, the majority of your investments should be in equity-heavy mutual funds or stocks—the returns are big, and you have time to ride out market fluctuations. Decide together where to invest any wedding cash you have left. Research your options, and set up a joint mutual fund account in which you two deposit your monthly off-the-top savings (about 10 percent of your income). It's a very good idea to meet with a financial consultant for advice on meeting your goals and making wise investments.

Organization-Less Frustration

A designated file for storing W-2s, deposit slips, canceled checks, receipts, and any other important tax documentation will eliminate many arguments—and save you mucho grief come tax time. Also investigate top-notch money stress-reducing management software like Quicken (www.quicken.com).

Living Happily Ever After

Believe it or not, there will come a time when your honeymoon will seem like a distant memory, your wedding, a hazy, fabulous dream. You'll no longer sneak a desperate, passionate kiss every single time you walk by each other. Five-hour lovemaking sessions will be pushed aside for deadlines, dates with friends, and dirty laundry. There's less breakfast in bed, less mushy love talk, less by-the-book romantic intensity. You may find yourself wondering: Was it worth it?

We know there are times when marriage seems blah at best. Everything in life—even the cool stuff—has a downside. But brush aside the routine, the petty arguments, the responsibilities, and you're left with regular sex with a stunning partner, cozy weekend breakfasts, a friend for life, a confidant(e) who doesn't need background, and on and on and on. Being married is sweet and sexy, just like a chocolate-covered cherry. Whenever you need to remind yourself of that, follow our five-point guides to personal and marital bliss.

Five Ways to Rekindle Those Honeymoon Fires

1. Seduce your baby in a public place. Fondle under the table, whisk into the bathroom, grope up against the wall.
2. Give each other hot-oil massages.
3. Book a romantic weekend away in a bed and breakfast. Stay in your room the entire time.
4. Make a detour to a tried-and-true make-out point and get hot and heavy in your car.
5. Get into a set schedule of having sex every other day—no excuses. It sounds unsexy, but it will get you going—and once you start, you *won't* want to stop.

Five Ways to Remind Yourself Your Honey's the Best

1. Watch your sweetie sleep. Study that gorgeous face. Lift up the covers and feast your eyes on those sexy thighs, those strong arms, that perky bottom. Kiss your baby's forehead and feel a surge of love.
2. Ask your honey to run an errand for you, something that you could have never asked her/him to do when you were dating, like getting your stuff from the dry cleaner, shoring up dinner plans for when your parents are in town, making a bank deposit. Doesn't it feel good to have a true partner in this world?
3. Do the laundry for both of you. Fold your sweetie's sweet-smelling garments as you recall all the times you've seen him/her wearing them and all the times you've peeled them off.
4. Watch your muffin having a good time, giggling with friends, telling a joke, dancing, skipping in the rain. Remember that you are one of the things that makes your sweetie happiest.
5. Next time your folks call, get your honey on the line with them. Feel your insides gush as your darling chats your folks up with poise and charm.

Five Quick Breaks from Each Other (Or: How to Avoid a Fight)

1. Spend a Saturday afternoon alone at the movies. Buy your favorite snack. Don't be afraid to cry or hoot with laughter. Lose yourself in the fantasy of it all.
2. Go for a walk or a run in the park.
3. Get a massage at a local gym or spa.
4. Invite your best friend out for a coffee or cocktails. Talk about everything *but* your problems.
5. Eat alone at a diner. Take a book or the day's newspaper for company.

Five Ways Marriage Frees You

1. You don't have to spend precious time obsessing whether your honey is really committed—the answer's on your ring finger.
2. You can use your baby as an excuse to get out of invitations you really don't want to accept, such as dinner at a boring work colleague's home or a get-together with your pompous second cousins. ("Unfortunately, I'm not going to be able to make it. Shawn has already made plans for us.")
3. If someone creepy tries to hit on you at a bar/café/gym, the glint of your wedding band is just the thing to scare 'em off.
4. There's always someone to split time-consuming chores and errands with.
5. You no longer have to feel guilty about spending the night chilling at home because you might be missing something. You've already found what you were looking for.

Five Reasons Marriage Rules

1. You never have to go on a first date again.
2. You always have someone to celebrate the holidays with.
3. Every day's a sleepover—your best friend is also your bedmate.
4. Practice makes perfect—and that goes for sex, too.
5. Your Sunday-morning routine—reading the paper, walking the dog, sipping coffee at the neighborhood café. Sometimes you can never get enough of a good thing.

Appendix A:
Checklists and Worksheets

Your To-Do List

We've put together a twelve-month planning calendar because a year is the length of the average engagement, but you can start planning even earlier, or make it all happen in under six weeks. If you've got more time, you can linger over your initial decisions a little longer and you'll likely get first dibs on the best vendors (florists, photographers, sites, etc.). If you've got less time, start at the top of the list, get busy, and don't be as picky. Most important, don't panic. Your wedding will be fantastic regardless of your time constraints.

Twelve-plus Months Before

- ☐ Begin envisioning your wedding—formal hotel or friend's loft? Backyard barbecue or exotic beach? (Chapter 2)
- ☐ Pick preferences for wedding date and time and finalize after okaying with important guests, location, or officiant. (Chapter 2)
- ☐ Decide on budget and hash out who's contributing. (Chapter 4)
- ☐ Hire wedding consultant and/or ask for vendor recommendations from family and friends. (Chapter 2)
- ☐ Start a notebook/file folder to house all your wedding planning paperwork in one place.
- ☐ Begin working on guest list—decide on approximate size, get request lists from parents, create your own wish list (more realistic version to come later). (Chapter 2)

☐ Brides: It's never too early to start shopping for the dress. (Chapter 11)

☐ Begin looking for main vendors (caterer, photographer, musicians) and set appointments to review their work.

☐ Start looking for the officiant who suits your style and spirit. (Chapter 7)

Nine to Eleven Months Before

☐ Scout out ceremony and reception sites and book as soon as you see something you love that's available on your date. (Chapter 10)

☐ Choose attendants and ask them to do the honor. (Chapter 5)

☐ Contact newspapers to announce your engagement. (Chapter 1)

☐ Brides: Start thinking about finalizing your dress decision.

☐ Brides: Shop for and decide on bridesmaid dresses; collect necessary measurements from attendants. (Chapter 12)

☐ Contact out-of-towners so they can start making travel plans.

☐ Decide on and meet with your officiant to discuss ceremony structure and any marriage requirements (counseling, etc.). (Chapter 7)

☐ Choose caterer, begin working on menu, send deposit and/or execute a contract. (Chapter 13)

☐ Reserve photographer and/or videographer, decide on package. (Chapter 15)

☐ Set up appointments with florists to discuss options. (Chapter 14)

☐ Book reception band or DJ, execute contract. (Chapter 16)

☐ Start planning your honeymoon. (Chapter 23)

☐ Consult with stationer or graphic artist about invitations and other stationery needs. (Chapter 9)

Six to Eight Months Before

☐ Brides: Order your gown. (Chapter 11)

☐ Reserve tent, chairs, or other equipment with rental company (unless caterer or site is taking care of it). (Chapter 10)

☐ Order your invitations and announcements. (Chapter 9)

☐ Start planning the rehearsal dinner. (Chapter 6)

☐ Book your florist. (Chapter 14)

☐ Book a baker for wedding cake. (Chapter 13)

☐ Choose ceremony music/musicians. (Chapter 16)

☐ Register for your wedding gifts. (Chapter 17)

☐ Set aside blocks of hotel rooms for out-of-town guests.

Three to Four Months Before

☐ Finalize guest list and start addressing invitations. (Chapter 9)

☐ Finalize order with florist and execute contract. (Chapter 14)

☐ Finalize menu and service details with caterer. (Chapter 13)

☐ Brides: Confirm delivery date for gown and bridesmaids' dresses, and schedule fittings. (Chapter 11, Chapter 12)

☐ Talk to people you'd like to do performances or readings as part of the ceremony. (Chapter 7)

☐ Compile packages for out-of-town guests with hotel and city information. (Chapter 5)

☐ Shop for and purchase wedding bands.

☐ Research local marriage-license requirements. (Chapter 21)

☐ Consider specific ceremony and reception decoration needs, such as a huppah, aisle runner, etc.

☐ Pick out or design a Ketubah or other marriage contract required by your religion.

☐ Grooms: Start looking to buy or rent tux or other formal attire. (Chapter 12)

☐ Coordinate the groomsmen's outfits. (Chapter 12)

☐ Make or buy favors. (Chapter 17)

☐ Schedule portrait session if you need one for a newspaper announcement.

☐ Book rehearsal-dinner site and finalize guest list.

☐ Get passports and visas if you're traveling abroad for your honeymoon. (Chapter 24)

☐ Start taking better care of yourself (eat right, exercise) so you look/feel great come wedding day.

☐ Talk to your honor attendant and best man about shower and other party plans. (Chapter 6)

Two Months Before

☐ Send out invitations.

☐ Brides: Have final wedding-dress fittings (probably several).

☐ Order or make ceremony programs. (Chapter 9)

☐ Begin working on vows, particularly if you're writing your own. (Chapter 7)

☐ Arrange wedding-day transportation for you, your wedding party, and guests (as needed). (Chapter 21)

☐ Have fun at showers and bachelor/ette parties. (Chapter 6)

Six Weeks Before

☐ Brides: Decide on and purchase all accessories (veil, shoes, lingerie, etc.) prior to final fittings.

☐ Brides: Make sure your attendants have dealt with dresses and shoes.

☐ Take the veil to your hairstylist and make sure your current 'do and veil work together.

☐ Buy gifts for the wedding party.

☐ Submit your announcement to newspapers (if you so desire).

Three to Four Weeks Before

☐ Work out wedding day timing and details—who will get the bride there, will the wedding party dress before arriving at the site, etc.

☐ Get marriage license and make appointments for blood tests (if necessary).

☐ Pick up wedding rings.

☐ Have final meeting with officiant.

☐ Finalize vows, readings, and other special ceremony details.

☐ Confirm wedding-night and honeymoon reservations. (Chapters 22, 24)

☐ Send rehearsal-dinner invitations.

☐ Start putting together the seating plan if there's a seated reception meal. (Chapter 8)

☐ Work on a list of "must-play" (and must-not play) songs for your DJ or band. (Chapter 16)

☐ Get final prewedding haircut if necessary. (Chapter 21)

☐ Do trial runs of hair and makeup and schedule wedding-day appointments. (Chapter 21)

☐ Get a head start on those thank-you notes. (Chapter 17)

One to Two Weeks Before

☐ Start calling guests who haven't R.S.V.P.'d for the wedding and rehearsal dinner. (It's okay to do this, you need a final head count!)

☐ Finalize seating chart and make placecards.

☐ Confirm date, location, time, and playlist with band/DJ and ceremony musicians.

☐ Touch base with officiant.

☐ Work out schedule and transportation for greeting guests and attendants.

☐ Confirm location, date, and time with photographer and forward a "must-take" photo list.

☐ Confirm location, date, and time with videographer.

☐ Confirm final headcount with caterer.

☐ Confirm head count, delivery time, and location with cake maker.

☐ Confirm delivery locations, times, and final arrangement count with florist.

☐ Call location manager and make sure your vendors all have access at the time they need it.

☐ Grooms: Get your final haircut.

☐ Fax transportation providers' schedule and addresses for pickups on wedding day.

☐ Call entire wedding party to make sure everyone has the date, time, and directions.

☐ Brides: Pick up the dress and veil.

☐ Brides: Practice walking in your wedding shoes.

☐ Grooms: Pick up your tux and try it on. (Don't wait till the day of to do this.)

☐ Prepare your toasts. (Chapter 8)

☐ Confirm all final payments with your vendors.

☐ Plan any additional night-before activities for friends and/or attendants.

☐ Shop and pack for honeymoon.

Day Before

☐ Cut checks, or make arrangements, for vendors' final payments.

☐ Calculate tips and give necessary cash to appointed person(s).

☐ Put final payments and tips in carefully marked envelopes and give to responsible person to distribute on wedding day.

☐ Brides: Pull together wedding gown, all accessories, and a last-minute emergency kit.

☐ Distribute wedding-day directions, schedule, and contact list to all parents, attendants, and vendors.

☐ Confirm all travel plans (including transportation to airport, etc.).

☐ Prepare announcements to be mailed on wedding day.

☐ Brides: Get manicure and pedicure and confirm big-day beauty appointments.

☐ Rehearse the ceremony.

☐ Have fun and relax at your rehearsal dinner.

There is a fully interactive to-do list on
The Knot Online at www.theknot.com.

Your Big-Day Budget

Before you make any financial commitments, decide where your dollars are going to be spent. We've created this worksheet with approximate percentage breakdowns to give you some general guidelines—but don't be restricted by it. Every couple's priorities are different, and you may decide to allot more money to the things that are important to you.

Budget Category	Estimate	Actual
Ceremony 2% of budget = $_____		
Ceremony Location Fee	$_____	$_____
Officiant fee/Donation	$_____	$_____
Ceremony Accessories (chuppah, candles, etc.)	$_____	$_____
Ceremony Sub-Total	$_____	$_____

Budget Category	Estimate	Actual

Reception 50% of budget = $_____

	Estimate	Actual
Reception Location Fee	$_____	$_____
Rentals (tent, tables, toilets, etc.)	$_____	$_____
Food/Service	$_____	$_____
Champagne/Wine	$_____	$_____
Bar/Bartenders	$_____	$_____
Cake(s)/Cutting Fee	$_____	$_____
Reception Sub-Total	$_____	$_____

Attire 11% of budget = $_____

	Estimate	Actual
The Dress	$_____	$_____
Alterations	$_____	$_____
Headpiece/Veil	$_____	$_____
Bride's Accessories (gloves, bag, jewelry, etc.)	$_____	$_____
Shoes	$_____	$_____
Lingerie	$_____	$_____
Hair & Makeup	$_____	$_____
Manicure & Pedicure	$_____	$_____
Groom's Tux/Suit	$_____	$_____
Groom's Accessories (shoes, tie, cufflinks, etc.)	$_____	$_____
Attire Sub-Total	$_____	$_____

Budget Category	Estimate	Actual

Flowers & Decorations   8% of budget = $_____

Ceremony Site Decorations	$_____	$_____
Bride's Bouquet	$_____	$_____
Bridesmaids' Bouquets	$_____	$_____
Boutonnieres	$_____	$_____
Corsages	$_____	$_____
Centerpieces	$_____	$_____
Other Reception Decorations	$_____	$_____

Flowers Sub-Total $_____ $_____

Music   7% of budget = $_____

Ceremony Musicians	$_____	$_____
Cocktail Hour Musicians	$_____	$_____
Reception Band/Disc Jockey	$_____	$_____

Music Sub-Total $_____ $_____

Budget Category	Estimate	Actual

Reportage   7% of budget = $_____

Photographer's Fee/Package	$_____	$_____
Videographer's Fee	$_____	$_____
Additional Prints/Videos	$_____	$_____
Wedding Cameras	$_____	$_____

Reportage Sub-Total $_____ $_____

Stationery   3% of budget = $_____

Invitations & Reply Cards	$_____	$_____
Announcements	$_____	$_____
Postage	$_____	$_____
Thank You Notes/Stationery	$_____	$_____
Ceremony Programs	$_____	$_____

Stationery Sub-Total $_____ $_____

Wedding Rings   2% of budget = $_____

Bride	$_____	$_____
Groom	$_____	$_____

Rings Sub-Total $_____ $_____

Budget Category	Estimate	Actual

Transportation   1% of budget = $_____

	Estimate	Actual
Limo/Car Rental	$_____	$_____
Guest Shuttle/Parking	$_____	$_____

Transportation Sub-Total $_____ $_____

Gifts   3% of budget = $_____

	Estimate	Actual
Attendant Gifts	$_____	$_____
Favors	$_____	$_____

Gifts Sub-Total $_____ $_____

SUB-TOTAL $_____ $_____

**Tips, Taxes, Overages
10% of Sub-Total** $_____ $_____

**Wedding Consultant Fee (optional)
Up tp 10% of budget** $_____ $_____

GRAND TOTAL $_____ $_____

> There is a fully interactive budgeter on
> The Knot Online at www.theknot.com.

Your Phone Book

Bridal Shop/Seamstress

Name: _____

Address: _____

_____

Contact: _____

Phone: _____

Fax: _____

Hours of Operation: _____

Amount Budgeted: _____

Estimate Provided: _____

Date of Contract: _____

Payment Method: _____

Date/Time of Final Confirmation: _____

Bridesmaids' Dress Shop/Seamstress

Name: _____

Address: _____

_____

Contact: _____

Phone: _____

Fax: _____

Hours of Operation: _____

Amount Budgeted: _____

Estimate Provided: _____

Date of Contract: _____

Payment Method: _____

Date/Time of Final Confirmation: _____

Formalwear Shop

Name: _____

Address: _____

_____

Contact: _____

Phone: _____

Fax: _____

Hours of Operation: _____

Amount Budgeted: _____

Estimate Provided: _____

Date of Contract: _____

Payment Method: _____

Date/Time of Final Confirmation: _____

Ceremony Location

Name: _____

Address: _____

_____

Contact: _____

Phone: _____

Fax: _____

Hours of Operation: _____

Amount Budgeted: _____

Estimate Provided: _____

Date of Contract: _____

Payment Method: _____

Date/Time of Final Confirmation: _____

Officiant

Name: _____

Address: _____

_____

Contact: _____

Phone: _____

Fax: _____

Hours of Operation: _____

Amount Budgeted: _____

Estimate Provided: _____

Date of Contract: _____

Payment Method: _____

Date/Time of Final Confirmation: _____

Reception Location

Name: _____

Address: _____

_____

Contact: _____

Phone: _____

Fax: _____

Hours of Operation: _____

Amount Budgeted: _____

Estimate Provided: _____

Date of Contract: _____

Payment Method: _____

Date/Time of Final Confirmation: _____

Caterer

Name: _____

Address: _____

_____

Contact: _____

Phone: _____

Fax: _____

Hours of Operation: _____

Amount Budgeted: _____

Estimate Provided: _____

Date of Contract: _____

Payment Method: _____

Date/Time of Final Confirmation: _____

Baker

Name: _____

Address: _____

_____

Contact: _____

Phone: _____

Fax: _____

Hours of Operation: _____

Amount Budgeted: _____

Estimate Provided: _____

Date of Contract: _____

Payment Method: _____

Date/Time of Final Confirmation: _____

Florist

Name: _____

Address: _____

_____

Contact: _____

Phone: _____

Fax: _____

Hours of Operation: _____

Amount Budgeted: _____

Estimate Provided: _____

Date of Contract: _____

Payment Method: _____

Date/Time of Final Confirmation: _____

Musicians (Ceremony)

Name: _____

Address: _____

_____

Contact: _____

Phone: _____

Fax: _____

Hours of Operation: _____

Amount Budgeted: _____

Estimate Provided: _____

Date of Contract: _____

Payment Method: _____

Date/Time of Final Confirmation: _____

Musicians/DJ (Reception)

Name: _____

Address: _____

_____

Contact: _____

Phone: _____

Fax: _____

Hours of Operation: _____

Amount Budgeted: _____

Estimate Provided: _____

Date of Contract: _____

Payment Method: _____

Date/Time of Final Confirmation: _____

Photographer

Name: _____

Address: _____

_____

Contact: _____

Phone: _____

Fax: _____

Hours of Operation: _____

Amount Budgeted: _____

Estimate Provided: _____

Date of Contract: _____

Payment Method: _____

Date/Time of Final Confirmation: _____

Videographer

Name: _____

Address: _____

_____

Contact: _____

Phone: _____

Fax: _____

Hours of Operation: _____

Amount Budgeted: _____

Estimate Provided: _____

Date of Contract: _____

Payment Method: _____

Date/Time of Final Confirmation: _____

Transportation

Name: _____

Address: _____

_____

Contact: _____

Phone: _____

Fax: _____

Hours of Operation: _____

Amount Budgeted: _____

Estimate Provided: _____

Date of Contract: _____

Payment Method: _____

Date/Time of Final Confirmation: _____

Your Wedding-Day Contact List

ROLE	NAME	CONTACT NUMBER	ARRIVAL TIME
Bride:	_____	_____	_____
Groom:	_____	_____	_____
Bride's Parents:	_____	_____	_____
	_____	_____	_____
	_____	_____	_____
	_____	_____	_____
Groom's Parents:	_____	_____	_____
	_____	_____	_____
	_____	_____	_____
	_____	_____	_____
Maid of Honor:	_____	_____	_____
Best Man:	_____	_____	_____

ROLE	NAME	CONTACT NUMBER	ARRIVAL TIME
Bridesmaids:	_____	_____	_____
	_____	_____	_____
	_____	_____	_____
	_____	_____	_____
	_____	_____	_____
Groomsmen:	_____	_____	_____
	_____	_____	_____
	_____	_____	_____
	_____	_____	_____
	_____	_____	_____
Ushers:	_____	_____	_____
	_____	_____	_____
	_____	_____	_____
	_____	_____	_____
	_____	_____	_____
Officiant(s):	_____	_____	_____
	_____	_____	_____
	_____	_____	_____
Photographer:	_____	_____	_____
Videographer:	_____	_____	_____
Formalwear Shop:	_____	_____	_____
Bridal Shop:	_____	_____	_____

ROLE	NAME	CONTACT NUMBER	ARRIVAL TIME
Formalwear Shop:	_____	_____	_____
Hair & Makeup:	_____	_____	_____
Reception Hall Manager:	_____	_____	_____
Rentals:	_____	_____	_____
Caterer:	_____	_____	_____
Baker:	_____	_____	_____
Car Service/Limo:	_____	_____	_____
Ceremony Location Contact:	_____	_____	_____
Ceremony Musicians:	_____	_____	_____
Reception Musicians:	_____	_____	_____

Bridesmaids' Measurements

Name: _____

Address: _____

_____

Phone Number: _____

Fax Number: _____

Bust: _____   ☐ Send style order form

Waist: _____   ☐ Call in measurements

Hips: _____   ☐ Have fitting

Height: _____   ☐ Buy shoes

Shoe Size: _____

Name: _____

Address: _____

_____

Phone Number: _____

Fax Number: _____

Bust: _____   ☐ Send style order form

Waist: _____   ☐ Call in measurements

Hips: _____   ☐ Have fitting

Height: _____   ☐ Buy shoes

Shoe Size: _____

Name: _____

Address: _____

_____

Phone Number: _____

Fax Number: _____

Bust: _____   ☐ Send style order form

Waist: _____   ☐ Call in measurements

Hips: _____   ☐ Have fitting

Height: _____   ☐ Buy shoes

Shoe Size: _____

Name: _____

Address: _____

_____

Phone Number: _____

Fax Number: _____

Bust: _____   ☐ Send style order form

Waist: _____   ☐ Call in measurements

Hips: _____   ☐ Have fitting

Height: _____   ☐ Buy shoes

Shoe Size: _____

Name: _____

Address: _____

_____

Phone Number: _____

Fax Number: _____

Bust: _____   ☐ Send style order form

Waist: _____   ☐ Call in measurements

Hips: _____   ☐ Have fitting

Height: _____   ☐ Buy shoes

Shoe Size: _____

Name: _____

Address: _____

_____

Phone Number: _____

Fax Number: _____

Bust: _____   ☐ Send style order form

Waist: _____   ☐ Call in measurements

Hips: _____   ☐ Have fitting

Height: _____   ☐ Buy shoes

Shoe Size: _____

Appendix B: Resources

Your Wedding Clothes

Bridal Gown Designers/Manufacturers

Alfred Angelo: 800–531–1125
Alfred Sung Bridal: 800–981–5496
Alvina Valenta Couture Collection: 212–354–6798
Amalia Carrara: 212–719–3058
Amsale: 800–765–0170
Ana Hernandez: Inc. 781–485–0881
Ange D'Amour: 800–288–3888
Badgley Mischka: 212–921–1585
Bianchi: 800–669–2346
Birnbaum & Bullock: 212–242–2914
Bonny Bridal: 800–528–0030
Bridal Originals: 618–345–2345
Bridals by Justine: 800–866–4696
Camelot Collection: 800–925–5954
Carmela Sutera: 212–921–4808
Carmi Couture Collection: 212–921–7658
Carolina Herrera Bridal Collection: 212–944–5757
Chris Kole: 718–786–3319
Christian Dior: 800–341–3467
Christos: 212–921–0025
Country Elegance: 818–765–1551
Cynthia C. & Co.: 212–966–2200

Diamond Bridal Collection: 212–302–0210
Emme Bridal: 281–634–9225
Eugenia Bridal: 610–866–5181
Eve of Milady: 212–736–9250
Fink Originals: 212–947–4140
Forever Yours: 800–USA–BRIDE
Galina: 212–564–1020
Ginza Collection: 800–654–7375
Golden Gate Bridal: 800–233–9919
Helen Morley Designs Ltd.: 212–594–6404
Holly Harp: 212–832–6464
Impressions: 800–BRIDAL–1
Ilissa by Demetrios: 212–967–5222
Impression Bridal: 281–634–9200
Jane Wilson-Marquis: 212–477–4408
Janell Berte: 717–291–9894
Jasmine Collection: 630–295–5880
Jeannette Russell: 412–741–7471
Jessica McClintock: 800–333–5301
Jim Hjelm Couture Collection: 800–686–7880
L'amour Bridal: 800–664–5683
Lazaro Collection: 212–764–5781

L'ezu Atelier: 213–383–8322
Lila Broude: 212–921–8081
Lili: 626–336–5048
Loralie Originals: 800–4–LORALIE
Manale Bridal Collection: 212–760–0121
Marisa: 212–944–0022
Mary's Bridals–P.C. Mary's: 281–933–9678
Max Chaoul (Paris): 011–43–25–44–02
Mika Inatome: 212–966–7777
Melissa Sweet: 404–467–4181
Mon Cheri: 212–869–0800
Monique Lhuillier: 213–838–0100
Mori Lee (a.k.a. Regency Bridal): 818–385–0930
Nancy Issler: 732–438–0099
Pallas Athena: 818–285–5796
Paloma Blanca: 416–504–4550
Pat Kerr: 901–525–LACE
Peggendott Originals: 248–559–8376

Peter Langner: 011–39–6–3200525
Priscilla of Boston: 617–242–2677
Private Label by G: 800–858–3338
Reem Bridal: 212–431–9232
Robert Legere: 212–366–1494
Scassi-Forsyth Enterprises: 804–971–3853
Signature Designs: 800–654–7375
Silvia Designs: 760–323–8808
St. Pucchi Couture: 800–932–0249
Sweetheart: 212–947–7171
Tomasina: 412–563–7788
Venus Couture: 818–285–5796
Vera Wang: 212–575–6400
Wallentin Collection: 972–721–7048
Wearkstatt: 212–941–6960
Youlin Collection: 908–754–5783
Yumi Katsura: 212–772–3760

Traditional African Wedding Wear/Accents

Cassandra Bromfield: 718–398–1050
Jonathan Adewami (Nigerian Fabrics
    and Fashions): 718–260–9416

Laurie A. Sanders: 718–217–2899
Therez Fleetwood: 212–714–8058

Veils and Headpieces

Bel Aire: 800–992–9225
Edward E. Berger Bridal Millinery: 212–594–0400
Headpieces by Toni: 618–244–4842
Homa Creations: 973–655–1239
Juliet Veils: 800–558–5438
Paris: 513–948–8888
Reem Acra: 212–431–9232

Regalia Veils: 617–723–3682
Sposabella Lace: 212–354–4729
Symphony Bridal Veils: 212–827–0941
Tia Mazza: 212–989–4349
T&G Bridal: 800–223–6061
Vera Wang: 212–575–6400
Washington Millinery Co.: 301–963–4444

Bridesmaid Dresses

Alfred Angelo: 800–531–1125
Bianchi: 800–669–2346
Bill Levkoff: 800–LEVKOFF
Champagne Formals: 212–302–9162
Christian Dior: 800–341–3467
Dessy Creations: 800–633–7791
Galina: 212–564–1020

Jessica McClintock: 800–333–5301
Jim Hjelm Occasions: 800–686–7880
Jordan: 212–921–5560
New Image: 888–4–NEW–IMAGE
Nicole Miller: 800–365–4721
Watters and Watters: 972–960–9884
Vera Wang: 212–575–6400

Women's Shoes

Dyeables: 800–431–2000
Kenneth Cole: 800–KEN–COLE
Nina: 800–233–6462
Manolo Blahnik: 212–582–3007

Peter Fox: 212–431–7426 or 310–393–9669
Saugus Shoes: 800–443–6155
Stuart Weitzman: 212–750–2555
Vanessa Noel: 212–333–7882

Bridal Bags/Purses

Carolina Herrera: 212–944–5757
Challoner: 212–274–1437

Dyeables: 800–431–2000
Violette Nozieres: 212–874–6412

Gloves

Carolina Amato: 212–532–8413

Flower Girl Dresses

Jessica McClintock: 800–333–5301
Joan Calabrese: 610–353–4892
Monique Lhuillier: 213–838–0100
Pegeen: 973–442–0799

Strasburg: 205–880–0400\
Sweetheart Gowns ("Sweetie" dresses):
    212–947–7171
Wooden Soldier: 800–375–6002

Ring Bearers' Outfits

Pegeen: 973–442–0799
Wooden Soldier: 800–375–6002

Tuxedos

Oscar de la Renta: 201–343–8180
Lord West, Pierre Cardin, Perry Ellis: 800–275–9684
Raffinati: 800–554–8212
Ralph Lauren: 800–775–7656

Men's Accessories

Brooks Brothers: 800–274–1816
C.J. Haas & Co. (cuff links): 800–603–0040
Joseph Abboud: 800–999–0600
Nicole Miller: 800–365–4721

Raffinati: 800–554–8212
Ralph Lauren: 800–775–7656
Terence Teng (vests): 212–772–1519
XMI (ties and vests): 800–745–0010

Men's Shoes

Allen-Edmonds: 800–235–2348
Bally: 800–852–2030
Brooks Brothers: 800–274–1816

Johnston & Murphy: 212–697–9375
Kenneth Cole: 800–KEN–COLE
Paul Fredrick: 800–247–1417

Cleaners

Imperial Gown: 800–WED–GOWN (nationwide cleaners)

For Your Wedding

Online Resources

The Knot, the number one wedding resource; www.theknot.com and AOL keyword: knot.

Organizations

Association of Bridal Consultants: 860–355–0464
American Rental Association: 800–334–2177
International Special Events Society: 800–688–ISES
National Limousine Association: 800–NLA–7007
Nuccio and Associates (Wedding Insurance): 800–ENGAGED (364–2433)

Personalizing

The Essential Guide to Lesbian and Gay Weddings, by Tess Ayers and Paul Brown (HarperCollins, 1994)
Jumping the Broom: The African American Wedding Planner, by Harriette Cole (Henry Holt, 1995)
Interfaith Wedding Ceremonies: Samples and Sources (Dovetail Publishing, 1996; there's also a newsletter for Christian/Jewish couples; call 800–222–0070)
The New Jewish Wedding, by Anita Diamant (Summit Books, 1986; reprinted by Fireside)
Wild Geese and Tea: An Asian-American Wedding Planner, by Shu Shu Costa (Riverhead Books, 1997)

Locations

America's Historic Places: An Illustrated Guide to Our Country's Best (Reader's Digest, 1988)

Between Earth and Sky: Legends of Native American Sacred Places, by Joseph Bruchac (Harcourt Brace, 1996)

Gene Kilgore's Ranch Vacations, by Gene Kilgore (John Muir Publications, 1996)

Haunted Hotels: A Guide to American and Canadian Inns and Their Ghosts, by Robin Mead (Rutledge Hill Press, 1995)

Nights to Imagine: Magical Places to Stay in America, by Peter Guttman (Fodors, 1996)

The Official Guide to American Historic Inns, Bed & Breakfasts and Country Inns, by Deborah Sakach (American Historic Inn, Inc., 1996)

The Outrageous Atlas: A Guide to North America's Strangest Places, by Richard A. Rogers and Laurine Rogers (Citadel Press, 1993)

Places: A Directory of Public Places for Private Events and Private Places for Public Functions (Tenth House Enterprises, updated annually; call 212–737–7536 to order)

Invitation Catalogs

The American Wedding Album: 800–428–0379

Ann's Wedding Stationery: 800–557–2667

Creations by Elaine: 800–323–2717

Dawn: 800–528–6677

Heritage Weddings: 800–892–4291

Now & Forever: 800–451–8616

The Precious Collection: 800–553–9080

For Your Honeymoon

Tourism Bureaus

Tourism Office Worldwide Directory:
   www.towd.com
Caribbean Tourism: 212–682–0435
Fiji Visitors Bureau: 310–568–1616
Hawaii Visitors Bureau: 800–353–5846

Jamaica Tourism: 800–233–4582
Las Vegas Tourism: 702–735–1616
Mexico Tourism: 800–44–MEXICO
Puerto Rico Tourism: 800–223–6530
U.S. Virgin Islands Tourism: 800–372–USVI

Tour Operators

The United States Tour Operators Association:
   800–GO–USTOA; www.ustoa.com
Backroads Travel: 800–462–2848 (for an
   adventure afloat in your own sea kayak)
Contiki Tours: 800–CONTIKI; www.contiki.com
   (groups, 18–35 years old)

Amelia Tours: 800–742–4591 (upscale
   group or independent tours)
Abercrombie & Kent: 800–323–7308
   (private guides to exotic places)

Discount Travel Brokers

STA Travel: 800–777–0112; www.sta-travel.com
Council Travel: 800–226–8624;
   www.counciltravel.com
Cheap Tickets: 800–377–1000

Mr. Cheap: 800–MRCHEAP
Quikbook: 800–789–9887
Hotel Reservations Network: 800–964–6835
Players Express Vacations: 800–458–6161

Hotels

All the Hotels on the Web: www.all-hotels.com
America's Best Bed & Breakfasts, Country Inns, and Small Hotels:
  www.virtualcities.com/ons/Oonsadex.htm

DESTINATION WEDDINGS

Caribbean and South Pacific

Sandals: 800–SANDALS
SuperClubs: 800–859–SUPER
Swept Away-Negril, Jamaica: 800–545–7937

Almond Beach Village, Barbados: 800–425–6663
Namale Resort, Fiji: 800–588–3454

Europe and Asia

Sheraton Grand Hotel, Edinburgh,
  Scotland: 800–325–3535
Adare Manor, Adare, Ireland:
  800–GO–ADARE

ITT Sheraton (five hotels thoughout China):
  800–325–3535
Hotel Imperial Vienna: 43–15–01–100
Hotel Villa Cipriani: Asola, Italy: 39–423–952–166

United States

Mission Inn, Riverside, California:
  909–784–0300
Palm Island Resort, Gulf Coast of Florida:
  941–697–2709
Caesars Pocono Resorts, Pennsylvania:
  800–233–4141
Las Vegas Wedding Chapel Listings:
  www.vegas.com/wedding/chapels.html

Las Vegas Index: www.lvindex.com
Hawaii Weddings: www.hawaiiweddings.com
Niagara Tourist Home Page:
  promo-web.com/niagara/index.htm
Disney World: www.disney.com/Disney World

Cruise Ship Weddings

A Wedding For You: 800–929–4198

American Hawaii Cruises: 800–474–9934

Miscellaneous

American Society of Travel Agents: 703–739–2782
Travel Facts: www.travelfacts.com
Best Beaches in the USA:
www.petrix.com/beaches/index.html

State Parks Online:
  www.mindspring.com/~wxmot/parks.html
ZooNet Index:
  www.mindspring.com/~zoonet/states.html

Index

Photo Credits

Cover photo: John Dolan, New York, NY; 212–462–2598.

Page 3: AP/Wide World Photos.

Pages 13 and 200: Philippe Cheng, New York, NY; 212–627–4262.

Pages 20, 73, 154, 172, 231, 252, 256, and 268: Karen Hill, New York, NY; 212–529–6926.

Page 35: William Vazquez.

Page 30: Matthew Mindlin.

Page 43: Phil Cantor Photography, New York, NY; 800–487–1065.

Page 47: David Ross, R&R Creative Photography, Newhall, CA; 818–508–6660.

Page 62: Greg Hark Photographics, Miami Beach, FL; 305–673–8929.

Page 88: Krasner/Trebitz Photography, Brooklyn, NY; 718–832–3130.

Pages 103, 135, 209, and 302: Rob Fraser, New York, NY; 212–941–0433.

Pages 107 and 204: Christopher Smith, New York, NY; 212–219–8862.

Page 123: Theo Wargo.

Page 141: Jerry Bryan Studios, Carlsbad, CA; 760–434–3318.

Page 183: Lynne Brubaker, Keswick, VA; 804–296–9376.

Page 234: Laure A. Leber, New York, NY; 212–477–7378.

Page 265: Day Photographic Studio, Indianapolis, IN; 317–464–9166.

Page 279: Bennett Studios.

Page 288: Jared Bernstein Photography, Aberdeen, NJ; 732–441–9155.

Author photo: Andrew Eccles, New York, NY; 212–941–4743.